Emile Garcke, John Manger Fells

**Factory Accounts - Their Principles and Practice**

a handbook for accountants and manufacturers with appendices on the

nomenclature of machine details

Emile Garcke, John Manger Fells

**Factory Accounts - Their Principles and Practice**

*a handbook for accountants and manufacturers with appendices on the nomenclature of machine details*

ISBN/EAN: 9783337252199

Printed in Europe, USA, Canada, Australia, Japan

Cover: Foto ©Andreas Hilbeck / pixelio.de

More available books at **www.hansebooks.com**

# FACTORY ACCOUNTS

## THEIR PRINCIPLES AND PRACTICE

A Handbook for Accountants and Manufacturers

WITH APPENDICES ON

THE NOMENCLATURE OF MACHINE DETAILS; THE INCOME TAX ACTS; THE RATING OF FACTORIES; FIRE AND BOILER INSURANCE; THE FACTORY AND WORKSHOP ACTS, ETC.

INCLUDING ALSO

*A GLOSSARY OF TERMS AND A LARGE NUMBER OF SPECIMEN RULINGS*

BY

EMILE GARCKE AND J. M. FELLS

"The counting-house of an accomplished merchant is a school of method wherein the great science may be learned of ranging particulars under generals, of bringing the different parts of a transaction together, and of showing at one view a long series of dealing and exchange."
DR. JOHNSON, *in Preface to Rolt's "Dictionary of Commerce."*

Fourth Edition, Revised and Enlarged

LONDON
CROSBY LOCKWOOD AND SON
7, STATIONERS' HALL COURT, LUDGATE HILL
1893
[*All rights reserved*]

# PREFACE TO THE SECOND EDITION.

THIS work is, we believe, the first attempt to place before English readers a systematised statement of the principles regulating Factory Accounts; and of the methods by which those principles can be put into practice and made to serve important purposes in the economy of manufacture.

It is not necessary to convince men of business of the advantages and importance of correct mercantile book-keeping; but as regards their factories and warehouses they are for the most part content to accept accounts which are not capable of scientific verification. Such accounts can only be regarded as memoranda of transactions.

Our aim has been to show not only that as great a degree of accuracy can be attained in factory book-keeping as in commercial accounts, but that the books of a manufacturing business can scarcely be said to be complete and reliable unless they are supplemented by, and to a large extent based upon, the accounts special to a factory.

The principles of Factory Accounts do not differ in the main from those general rules on which all sound book-keeping is based, and we have but applied fundamental axioms to the practice of an important and extending branch of industrial accounts; and with the view of rendering the book of special utility to Accountants we have not dealt with the principles and practice of accounts in so far as they apply merely to elementary and commercial book-keeping, as to do so would, in large measure, be a work of supererogation. Moreover, we hope that the diagrams showing the relation between Factory and Commercial books will, with the numerous specimens the book contains, render the information we have to present of service to those who, while concerned in manufacture, and therefore interested in our subject, have not occasion to inquire closely into the practice of accounts.

The various Appendices dealing with the legal, financial, and other questions connected with factory administration are submitted in the belief that they will be regarded as indicative of matters calling for the careful consideration of those engaged in industrial pursuits.

*October, 1887.*

## NOTE TO THE FOURTH EDITION.

IN preparing this edition for the press we have thought it well to refer to some matters of factory routine and registration which have not been dealt with in former editions. The Appendices have also been brought as closely as possible up to date, Appendix E now containing a summary of the provisions of the Factory Acts of 1889 and 1891, as well as the earlier Acts.

We take the opportunity of again remarking (as on the occasion of the Third edition) how gratified we have been to observe the increased amount of attention which has been given, by Accountants and others interested in the routine of manufacturing establishments, to the subject treated of in this work, since the First edition was published in 1887.

BEDFORD PARK. LONDON, W.
*August,* 1893.

# CONTENTS.

## CHAPTER I.
### INTRODUCTORY.

The Development of the Modern Factory System.—The Advantage of Combination and Specialization of Labour. —Legislation.—The History of the Factory System.— Extension of Routine and Registration.—The Need for Factory Books of Account.—Fundamental Principles of Book-keeping Applicable, but Special Methods Required.—Requirements of a Manufacturing Business. —The Need of Analysis of Expenditure—of ascertaining Profit or Loss on Individual Transactions—on Branches of Business.—Stock ascertainable without Survey.—Its Comparison with Cash.—Cost in Relation to Indirect Charges and Depreciation.—The Utility of Systematised Factory Books—and Accurate Accounts —their Moral Effect on Employés.—Inadequacy of ordinary Commercial Books—Assimilation of Factory Books with them.—Consistency of Specialization with Concentration in Accounts.—Merging of Departmental Books in General Ledger.—The Utility of Adequate Office Organization—its Economy.—The Specialization of Labour.—The Scope of this Work—its Relation to Treatises on General Book-keeping.—Specimen

Rulings.—Exterior of Books.—Principles applicable to Liquid, Mixing, and other Trades.—Diagrams showing Assimilation of Accounts. — The Differentiation of Records.—The Requisites of a Wages System.—The Purchase and Consumption of Material.—The Production of Commodities.—Definition of Prime Cost.—The Sale of Commodities.—Distinction between Stores and Stock.—Depreciation.—Surveys and Stock-taking.—A Symbolic Nomenclature.—The Factory and Workshop Acts.—The Income Tax Acts.—The Rating of Machinery.—The Law of Insurance . . . 1—13

## CHAPTER II.

### LABOUR.

Initial Step in the Organization of a Factory.—The Utility of a proper Wages System—it Minimises Error—Prevents Fraud.—"Dummy Men."—Piece-work. — Sick and other Funds.—Factory Acts.—Receipts from Employés.—Systematic Allocation of Wages.—Registration of Time.—Time Office.—Workmen's Checks.—Mess Room.—Time Book. — Absentee Book. — Overtime Book.—Analysis of Time.—Time Boards or Records. —Time Allocation Book.—Verification of Time.—Out-Works Time Records.—Check on Excessive Overtime Work.—Returns and Analysis of Overtime—Solidarity of Labour.—Premiums for Punctuality.—Fines for Unpunctuality.—Piece-work.—Forms to be used—Settlement of Balances—Non-continuous Working — Log Book—an Analysis Book—its Advantages.—Advice of Men Engaged, Dismissed, or Fined.—A Wages Rate Book.—Records of Service of Employés.—Supplemental Wages Advice.—The Wages Book—its Compilation and Analysis.—Stoppages and Deductions.— The Truck Act.—Receipts for Wages.—Amounts not

Claimed.—Payments to Deputies.—The Method of Payment.—The Allocation of Wages—Agreement with Wages Book.—Allocations of Fines and other Deductions.—Adhesion to Factory Rules.—Character Book.—Address Book.—Registers and Certificates under Factory Acts.—Appropriations of Fines.—Rent as Wages . . . . . . . . 14—42

DIAGRAM I.—THE ASSIMILATION OF WAGES AND COMMERCIAL BOOKS.

## CHAPTER III.

### STORES.

The Purchase of Material for Plant, Manufacturing, or Retailing—Initiatory Stage.—Stores Requisition Book.—The Advantage of Orders for Stores emanating from one Centre.—Stores Requisition Form.—The Sanction to Purchase.—Orders to Vendors—their Conditions.—Registration of Invoices.—Stores Received Book.—Invoice Register.—Stores Ledgers—Accounts in.—Endorsement of Invoices—their Allocation.—Agreement of Commercial and Factory Books as to Material Purchased and Periodical Survey.—The Consumption of Material—Initiatory Stage.—Instruction to Manufacture.—Estimates to precede Expenditure.—Limitation of Issue of Material.—Stores Warrants.—Stores Issued Book.—The Registration and Analysis of Stores Warrants.—Material Returned to Vendors.—Stores Rejected Book.—Credit Notes—their Registration.—Surplus Material—Advantage of Returning it to Store.—Stores Debit Note.—Shop Returns Book.—Transfers between Store and Warehouse . . . . 43—58

DIAGRAM II.—ASSIMILATION OF STORES AND COMMERCIAL BOOKS.

## CHAPTER IV.
### PRIME COST.

The Distinction between Stock and Stores—Utility of the Distinction.—Uniformity in Registration of Cost.—Authority to Manufacture.—Cost of Parts and Processes.—The Advantage of Correct and Complete Analysis of Cost.—"The Economy of Machinery and Manufactures."—"The Economics of Industry."—The Utility of a Symbolic Nomenclature.—Channels of Expenditure.—Fixed Capital.—The Localization of Maintenance Expenses—the Wages of Supervision—of Distribution — of Registration. — Factory General Charges—their Registration.—Prime Cost Ledger—how Compiled—its Agreement with the Commercial Books.—Stock Debit Note.—Stock Received Book.—Stock Ledger. — Goods in course of Manufacture.—Actual and Estimated Costs.—The Methods of Apportioning Factory General Charges.—The Utility of the Prime Cost Ledger extended to Plant and other Accounts.—Cost in Relation to Standing Charges.—Depreciation and Profit.—System in which Wages and Material constitute Prime Cost.—Method of Charging Indirect Expenses in proportion to Wages Paid—and to Wages and Materials. — Skilled and Unskilled Labour.—Depreciation in Relation to Cost.—Interest and Profit in Relation to Cost . . . . 59—74

DIAGRAM III.—THE ASSIMILATION OF PRIME COST AND COMMERCIAL BOOKS.

## CHAPTER V.
### STOCK.

Realization or Distribution of Manufactured Commodities —involves Four Classes of Transactions being brought

## CONTENTS.

into Account by corresponding but independent Processes of Book-keeping.—The Agreement of the Commercial and Factory Books.—Transfer from Factory to Warehouse.—Stock Debit Note.—The Stock Received Book.—Transfer from Warehouse to Factory—the Rejected Stock.—Transfer Notes—Transfer Books—their Agreement.—Transfer Analysis Book.—The Sale of Commodities.—Orders from Customers, how dealt with.—Orders Received Book.—Advice to Warehouseman.—Stock Requisition.—Stock Issued Book.—Warehouseman's Daily Return of Stock Issued.—Sales Analysis Book.—Stock Returned by Customers—its Registration—and Analysis.—Stock Returned Debit Note.—Stock Returned by Customers Book.—The Concentration of Books.—The Pricing of Loaned Articles—its Relation to the Profit and Loss Account.—The Agreement of the Commercial and Factory Books exemplified.—Wholesale and Retail Transactions—their Distinction—their Combination—their Registration.—The Manufacture of Complete or Subsidiary Parts—the Localization of their Cost . 75—92

DIAGRAM IV.—THE ASSIMILATION OF STOCK AND COMMERCIAL BOOKS.

## CHAPTER VI.
### FIXED CAPITAL.

Mill's Definition of Fixed Capital.—Depreciation of Buildings and Plant—varying Views.—Depreciation in Relation to Maintenance.—Factors in Determination of Depreciation Rate—Adherence to Depreciation Rate for Period of Time.—The Rough-and-ready Method.—Depreciation in Relation to Capital—to Current Expenditure—to Railway and Water Companies—to Reserve Funds—to Obsolescence—to the Life of the

Object — to the Cost of Maintenance. — Varying Methods in vogue.—The Ascertainment and Allocation of Cost of Deterioration — direct Method.— Method of Periodical Valuation—its Advantages—its Disadvantages—its Results when Fallacious—its Bearing on Capital and Revenue Accounts.—Loss on Capital and Loss on Revenue Accounts.—Mr. Buckley and the Case of the Neuchatel Asphalte Company—a Practical View of the matter.—The Revenue Account in Relation to Market Value of Fixed Assets in a going Concern.—The Establishment of Sinking and Reserve Funds.—Losses on Capital Account.—The Need of Insurance.—The Income Tax Acts in Relation to Fixed Capital.—The Life of an Object the best Basis for Depreciation Rate—the Difficulties of this Method—the Advantages.—Leases—an Amortization Table—a Hypothetical Ledger Account.—Dilapidations.—Classification of Assets.—Fixed and Loose Plant—Patterns—Tools—the Appropriation of their Cost.—The Numbering of Distinctive Objects.—The Expenditure on Plant—its Registration.—Plant Ledger.—Plant Debit Note.—The Ratio between the Life and Cost of a Machine.—Plant Journal.—The Appropriation of Residual Values.—Plant Debit Summary. —The Cost of Fuel—its Apportionment.—The Apportionment of Standing Charges in Relation to Profit and Loss—to Cost of Production.—The Valuation of Patents and Good-will . . . . . 93—114

## CHAPTER VII.

### SURVEYS.

The Utility of Stores and Stock Ledgers in Relation to Stock-taking and the General Accounts.—The Balance

CONTENTS.

Sheet independent of a Stock-taking.—Factory Accounts in Relation to Book-keeping by Single Entry.—Surveys in Relation to Commercial Ledgers.—The Utility of Verifying the Details of Inventories—the Comparative Advantages of Partial and General Surveys.—The Need of a Standard of Efficiency in Stock-takings.—Summarising Survey Results.—The Agreement of the Inventories with the Factory and Commercial Ledgers.—Surveys in Relation to Stores, Stock, and Plant.—Mechanical Divisions and Aids in Surveys.—The Essentials of a Stores and Stock System.—The Efficiency of Control over Commodities.—Departmental Transfers.—Excessive Supplies in Stores or Stock.—The Valuation of Commodities in Relation to Cost of Production and Market Prices.—Survey Prices in Relation to Establishment Expenses and Standing Charges.—The Realization of Profit.—The Valuation of Raw Material and Exceptional Commodities.—Valuation in Relation to Obsolescence.—Valuation of Old Material.—Reduction in the Valuation of Stocks . . . . . . . 115—125

## CHAPTER VIII.
### CONCLUSION.

Subsidiary Books.—Summary of Chapter.—The Registration of Plant or Machinery acquired on the Purchase Hire System.—The Accounts of Government, Railway, and similar Factories and Workshops.—Registration of Costs by Means of Cards and Symbols—its Disadvantages.—Cartage Accounts.—Horses and Vehicles.—Freight Books.—The Railway and Canal Traffic Act, 1888—Rates and Charges Confirmation Acts, 1891-2.—Railway Sidings.—Wagon and Van Books.—Lighter and Barge Books.—Craft Register.—Packing Cases—

xiv                       CONTENTS.

Method of Registering Cost of Empties.—Coal Accounts. —Gas and Water Meter Books.—Brigade and Fire Hose Books.—Casualty Book.—Patterns Accounts.—Log Book.—Accounts relating to Sick, Provident, Superannuation, and similar Funds.—Books and Forms required under Factory Acts.—Scope and Conditions of Factory and Workshop Acts.—Economic Aspects of Overtime, Piece-work, and Double Shifts in Relation to Fixed Capital. — Views of Mr. Sedley Taylor. — Relative Pecuniary Value of Task and Time Work.—Conflict of Capital and Labour.—The Opinion of the late Professor Fawcett on the Labour Question.—Views of other Authorities on the possible Development of the Factory System.—Opinion of Lord Brassey.—Joint Stock Enterprise.—Opinion of the late Professor Jevons on Industrial Partnerships.—Co-operative Production in England.—Success of Industrial Associations on the Continent.—Economic Basis of Industrial Partnerships.—Evidence afforded by Official Records.—Views of Representative Working Men on Profit Sharing.—Industrial Remuneration Conference. - Boards of Arbitration.—Influence of Proper System of Accounts   126—149

## APPENDICES.

A.—NOMENCLATURE OF MACHINE DETAILS (Paper by Mr. Oberlin Smith)   .   .   .   .   .   .   150—157

B.—THE INCOME-TAX ACTS IN THEIR BEARING ON PROFITS OF MANUFACTURE   .   .   .   .   .   158—164

C.—THE RATING OF FACTORIES CONTAINING MACHINERY
165—173

D.—NOTES ON THE LAW OF FIRE AND BOILER INSURANCE
174—185

E.—Summary of the Factory and Workshop Acts 186—225

F.—Table for Determining Amortization of Leases, &c. . . . . . . . . 226—232

GLOSSARY OF TERMS . . . . . 233—240

INDEX . . . . . . . 241—264

## TABLE OF SPECIMEN RULINGS.

|  | Specimen No. | Page |
|---|---|---|
| Time Book, No. 1 | 1 | 18 |
| „ No. 2 | 2 | 19 |
| „ No. 3 | 3 | 19 |
| Overtime Book | 4 | 19 |
| Time Record Sheet | 5 | 20 |
| Time Allocation Book | 6 | 22 |
| Out-Works Time Record Sheet | 7 | 23 |
| Overtime Return | 8 | 25 |
| Overtime Comparison Book | 9 | 25 |
| Piece-work Return | 10 | 27 |
| Piece-work Analysis Book | 11 | 29 |
| Wages Advice | 12 | 30 |
| Wages Rate Book | 13 | 32 |
| Wages Book | 14 | 34 |
| Summary of Wages | 15 | 34 |
| Unclaimed Wages Book | 16 | 36 |
| Pay Wages Note | 17 | 37 |
| Wages Remittance Form | 18 | 37 |
| Cash Sheet | 19 | 38 |
| Money Tray | 20 | 39 |
| Abstract of Wages | 21 | 40 |
| Stores Requisition | 22 | 45 |

| | Specimen No. | Page |
|---|---|---|
| Stores Requisition Book | 23 | 46 |
| Invoice Register Book | 24 | 48 |
| Stores Received Book | 25 | 48 |
| Stores Ledger | 26 | 49 |
| Invoice Endorsement | 27 | 50 |
| Instruction to Foreman of Works | 28 | 52 |
| Stores Warrant | 29 | 53 |
| Stores Issued Book | 30 | 53 |
| Stores Rejected Book | 31 | 55 |
| Stores Debit Note | 32 | 56 |
| Shop Returns Book | 33 | 57 |
| Prime Cost Ledger | 34 | 66 |
| Stock Debit Note | 35 | 67 |
| Stock Received Book | 36 | 68 |
| Stock Ledger | 37 | 69 |
| Transfer Note | 38 | 81 |
| Transfer Book | 39 | 81 |
| Orders Received Book | 40 | 83 |
| Stock Requisition and Advice to Warehouseman | 41 | 83 |
| Stock Issued Book | 42 | 84 |
| Stock Requisition | 43 | 86 |
| Stock Returned Debit Note | 44 | 86 |
| Stock Returned by Customers Book | 45 | 87 |
| Amortization Table | 46 | 108 |
| Plant Ledger | 47 | 110 |
| Plant Debit Note | 48 | 111 |
| Plant Debit Summary | 49 | 112 |
| Stock Survey Sheet | 50 | 118 |
| Cartage Advice | 51 | 132 |
| Railway Rate Book | 52 | 134 |
| Wagon and Van Statement Form | 53 | 134 |
| Wagon Journey Repairs Book | 54 | 135 |
| Time Sheet for Lighter, Barge, or Boat | 55 | 136 |
| Craft Register | 56 | 136 |
| Fuel Summary Form | 57 | 138 |

# FACTORY ACCOUNTS:

## THEIR PRINCIPLES AND PRACTICE.

### CHAPTER I.

#### INTRODUCTORY.

WITH the rapid development of the modern Factory System has arisen the need for regulations which would not have had application at a time when production was carried on with little, if any, industrial organization. The extent to which by the aid of machinery the specialisation of labour is now carried, generally involves the passing of an article through as many hands or machines as there are processes in its production, and renders a further extension of routine and registration necessary. When artisans performed in their own dwellings and with their own hands, unassisted by steam or other motive power, all the operations necessary to the production of a complete article, the need for the regulation by statute of the periods and conditions of employment was not very obvious, whilst the most simple form of accountancy sufficed to ascertain the cost of an article thus produced.

*The modern Factory System.*

The establishment of large factories, however, where numbers of persons of both sexes co-operate through the division of labour in the production of articles of consumption, has changed the industrial conditions of society.

Under these altered conditions employers find it economical to adopt methods of supervision and of registration which, *prima facie*, make production more costly. The advantages, however, of the combination of labour—of each workman confining himself to one process, and that always the one for which he is best fitted—are so great that the expenses of the necessary organization are insignificant in comparison. Experience has shown that wherever the magnitude of the operations renders it practicable, every further extension of this principle of specialisation results, in spite of the increased expense of administration, in an economic advantage.

The legislation of recent years with regard to factories and workshops, regulating the employment of children and women and their hours of labour, as well as providing for their health, education, and safety, affords but one of the many indications of the universality and complexity of the methods of organized production which now obtain. Although this change in our industrial arrangements has already been fraught with many far-reaching consequences both material and moral, it has been of comparatively recent growth. "In the course of little more than a century the industrial **The Factory** framework of the whole civilised world has **System: its** been radically reconstructed, and more **history.** changes have occurred in consequence, even more obvious and tangible changes—changes con-

## DEFINITION OF FACTORY ACCOUNTS.

spicuous upon the very face and features of the country itself—than for certainly the whole of a previous thirteen hundred years." But it is only quite recently that any endeavour has been made to trace the continuity of "the various impulses, historical and economical, that have been concerned in the evolution of this particular method of production."*

Under these circumstances it is not perhaps surprising that systems of regulating the intricate affairs pertaining to a factory have hitherto been determined entirely by empirical methods.

Although the term Factory Accounts may be familiar, and its meaning sufficiently evident to persons acquainted with manufacturing business, or experienced in any operations requiring records to be kept of materials, plant, and stock, yet it is not infrequently assumed, even by accountants, that the ordinary commercial method of book-keeping by double entry, supplemented by the special subsidiary books which every trade demands, suffices for every kind of business.† The fundamental principles applicable to accounts necessarily hold good throughout all the branches of book-keeping; but many businesses involve, in addition to the mercantile transactions familiar to every one acquainted with the routine of an office or counting-house, multifarious and often extensive operations, of which the employment of labour

*Misconception as to factory books.*

*General principles of bookkeeping and particular trades.*

---

\* "Introduction to a History of the Factory System," by R. Whately Cooke Taylor. London: Bentley. 1886.

† Thus, *The Accountant*, in reviewing an earlier edition of this work, said: "It is rather concerned with the wages and time books, stock books, and matters of a similar nature, which as a rule do not come within the scope of an accountant's duties."

INTRODUCTORY.

and payment of wages, the purchase of raw materials and their conversion into manufactured commodities, are but some of the outward manifestations; and for their proper registration special methods of book-keeping have to be devised. In the case of manufacturing firms, the operations referred to call for careful analyses of expenditure, and sometimes necessitate the storage of large quantities of various kinds of raw material, and the warehousing of goods to a considerable extent, as well as the manufacture, purchase, or erection, and gradual wearing out, of valuable plant and tools. All this implies accurate adjustments of accounts. When large sums are paid in wages, it is essential, if the business is to be economically conducted, that the time during which the workpeople are employed and the work upon which they are engaged, should be accurately and sufficiently recorded. It is equally important that the material should be systematically charged to the work on which it is used. It is only by these means that employers can know the cost in wages and material of any article of their manufacture, and be able to determine accurately and scientifically, not merely approximately and by haphazard, the actual profit they make or loss they sustain, not only on the aggregate transactions during a given period, but also upon each individual transaction. In a business, the operations of which vary widely in character, this special knowledge as to the pecuniary result of a particular piece of work is of paramount importance, for it is not only conceivable but very probable that the presence or absence of this information may determine the policy to be pursued in accepting or rejecting large

*Requirements of a manufacturing business.*

*Profit or loss on individual transactions.*

# REQUIREMENTS OF A MANUFACTURING BUSINESS.

**Profitable and unprofitable branches.** contracts. There is always a danger, when only the general result of a business is known, of departments or processes which are relatively unremunerative being unduly fostered, and of those which yield more than the average profit not being adequately attended to. Employers should not, as is too frequently the case, be entirely dependent upon the periodical profit and loss accounts for their knowledge as to the financial result of their transactions, but should at any time, and at any stage of manufacture, be able to ascertain, *pro tanto*, rapidly and reliably, the actual, and not merely the estimated, cost of production of any given article of their manufacture.

**Stock should be knowable without survey.** They should also be able to determine, without the delay consequent on a survey or inventory, the quantity of stock and of raw material on hand, or of any particular item or part thereof. It would be discreditable to any cashier if his principal could not ascertain by a glance at the books the amount of cash in hand, but found it necessary to have the money counted; and there can be no reason why the same punctilious book-keeping should not be adopted in the case of goods. It is not too much to say that for a manufacturing or trading concern to be well organized, the storekeeper or warehouseman should be able to state, by referring to his Stores or Stock Ledgers, the actual quantities of any kind of material, or stock, on hand with the same facility and precision as the accountant can ascertain from the books the balance of cash at the bankers, or the amount of securities in the safe.

These are only a few of the questions which present themselves in a cursory consideration of the nature of

6    INTRODUCTORY.

**Prime cost and depreciation.** Factory Accounts. The subject of Prime Cost admits of very varied treatment. When the indirect charges and depreciation are of a more or less fixed character, it is probably sufficient to know the cost of an article in wages and materials only, but if the indirect expenses and wear and tear of plant form a more direct element in the cost of production, it would be highly desirable to apportion such items among the various operations or departments.

**Indirect charges.** The allocation of indirect charges thus presents many interesting problems, whilst the numerous methods of "writing off," and of determining the proper incidence of items such as deterioration of plant, tools, buildings, deserve the serious attention of owners of property, and tax to no mean degree the abilities of accountants, and their power of obtaining an absolutely accurate statement of affairs.

For the above-mentioned purposes, among others, systematised factory books are essential. The advantage of such books, clearly representing the actual state of affairs, is particularly evident when a business is for **Sale of business, &c.** disposal; or is being converted from a private firm into a joint stock company; or when the whole or some part of the factory has been destroyed by fire and it is necessary to prepare a claim on insurance companies. Then it is that the figures in the commercial books require to be substantiated in detail. There is little doubt also that under a well-organized **Moral effect of proper accounts upon employes.** system of Factory Accounts, each employé feels that he is contributing to the attainment of accurate records of costs; and that it is necessary that his account of the time he spends, and the material he uses, should be adequate and precise.

## ASSIMILATION OF ACCOUNTS.

This begets general confidence in the manner in which the accounts are kept, and on occasion of strikes or reduction of wages, or resort to the sliding scale, employés have less hesitation in accepting the results shown by the books as correct and as based on fair principles.

It will be seen, even from this superficial summary, that it is not feasible to record accurately, and with **Ordinary commercial books inadequate.** requisite detail, in the ordinary commercial books, all the numerous entries necessary for the proper registration of the operations of a large manufacturing establishment. It is moreover essential that factory books should have columns for the weight or measurement of materials and the number of articles, in addition to cash columns for values; and this, which is an indispensable condition in factory books, would not serve any useful or practical purpose in commercial books, but would on the contrary mar their utility. The insufficiency of the commercial books alone to represent the transactions is conspicuously evident in the case of undertakings of the magnitude of railway, gas, and water companies.

Factory books must not, however, be considered, as is generally the case, to be merely memoranda books, which are not necessarily required to balance. They **Assimilation of all books.** should so assimilate to the books of the counting-house that the obvious advantage of having a balance-sheet made up from the General Ledger, embracing the balances of the ledgers and books kept in the stores and warehouses, is not sacrificed. No matter how far the subdivision of departments of an establishment be carried, or to whatever extent the principle of localising the book-keeping be applied, the concentration of the accounts—the merging

*Specialisation consistent with concentration.* of the departmental books in the General Ledger—should be kept constantly in view. There is not any special theoretical or practical difficulty in establishing a separate set of books for each and any of the departments, if it be not attempted to make the proper working of all dependent upon the proper working of each, or if no regard be had to the necessity of attaining the highest degree of efficiency and despatch with the minimum expense. On the other hand to devise upon sound principles, and to carry out efficiently and economically, a system of accounts which necessitates the whole of the departmental book-keeping in a large establishment being subsidiary to one centre,

*Economy of clerical labour.* is a science as well as an art. That a system is not economical which is inefficient is but a truism, and although we appreciate the importance, and indeed the necessity, of minimising clerical labour, we feel there is no occasion to lay particular stress upon this consideration, as the tendency is to dispense with services which an adequate recognition of the value of sound book-keeping would probably show to be indispensable. Book-keepers and clerks being, unlike factory workpeople, only indirectly engaged in the production of wealth, are often regarded in comparison with them as "unproductive" workers—using the expression not invidiously, but in the sense in which economists employ it. Too generally the routine of the office is limited by the number of clerks from time to time engaged, instead of the system of accounts and routine best adapted for the business being determined on, and a staff employed proportionate to the work to be done. The wisdom of initiating by

# ORDINARY COMMERCIAL BOOK-KEEPING. 9

the dismissal of one or more clerks the retrenchment which in times of depression may be called for, is not always apparent. The maintenance of a perfect organization may enable economies to be practised, in comparison with which the whole cost of the office staff is insignificant. It is well, therefore, to weigh carefully the *pro et con* before relaxing vigilance over expenditure and the salutary checks upon wastefulness and extravagance in manufacture which a good system of accounts affords. One of the disadvantages of insufficient records being kept is that book-keepers and clerks have often to spend much time in obtaining from foremen and workmen, after the event, information which should reach the counting-house in a regular and systematic manner. This is contrary to the principle that true economy is to be found in the specialization of labour, and in clerks devoting themselves to clerical and foremen and workmen to mechanical work.

**Division of work.**

The task we have set ourselves is to explain the nature of factory books and the method of keeping them, and to show the *modus operandi* whereby the subdivision and localization of the accounts may be made consistent with the system of book-keeping by double-entry obtaining in the counting-house. We do not propose to enter upon a detailed explanation of the Ledger, Journal and Cash Book, and of the subsidiary books which constitute the system of commercial accounts. The numerous excellent treatises extant on general book-keeping render this needless, and we shall assume on the part of our readers that acquaintance with the elements of the subject which is essential to a proper understanding of factory and other accounts. For this reason chiefly we

**The scope of this work.**

**Ordinary commercial books not explained.**

## INTRODUCTORY.

do not think it necessary to follow the precedent of writers on commercial book-keeping by tracing the entries of an imaginary firm through a series of model books. We do not hesitate, however, to give specimen rulings of the books and forms suggested in these pages for adoption, and for facility of reference these specimens are numbered consecutively, as indeed should be the case in actual practice. In this connection it may be well to premise that some regard should be had to the exterior of the books, an advantage being derivable from the books of each department or of each class being distinguishable by their bindings; similarly, papers of different colours should be used for the various forms suggested. As in the majority of businesses the articles dealt in are reckoned in weight we think it well to show the specimen rulings with weight columns. The principles enunciated are, however, equally applicable to the liquid and mixing trades, such as those of brewers, distillers, manufacturing chemists and others, as well as to paper and other industries in which there is a continuous production of one kind of commodity. As it is not possible to show the specimen rulings of books applicable to every trade we show only those of one class. The relation of the various books to each other will be found further elucidated by the diagrams at the conclusions of Chapters II. to V., showing the manner in which the books and forms assimilate to each other and converge into the Commercial Ledger.

*Specimen rulings.*

*Exterior of books and distinguishing features.*

*General applicability of books.*

*Diagrams.*

Whilst not presuming to suggest that the forms and books of which specimen rulings are given apply universally and are incapable of modification either by subdivision or concentration, it is believed that the principles underlying them are of general application and that the rulings will serve as useful examples.

In the next chapter we deal with the subject of Labour, defining the requisites of a proper wages system; and explaining, in as much detail as is needful, the purpose of the books and the nature of the routine which in our opinion should be adopted by manufacturers. It will then be necessary to explain the forms it is desirable to observe in connection with the purchase and consumption of materials for the purpose of manufacture, or the maintenance of plant and buildings. The question of Stores and the manner of dealing with the invoices for goods purchased will next demand our attention. In this connection we shall have occasion to explain the uses of the Stores Ledger and its relation to the subsidiary stores books and to the Commercial Ledger. Having considered the book-keeping and routine relating to the two chief classes of expenditure for the purpose of production of commodities, *i.e.* labour and material, we shall be in a position to consider the important books in which this expenditure is concentrated, analysed, and properly apportioned to the resultant objects. The books by means of which this is accomplished are the Prime Cost Books. Their object is to enable a manufacturer to ascertain the cost to him of any given operation, and thus afford him one of the principal factors in the conduct of his business. There are many systems of Prime Cost in vogue, but the writers who in dealing with book-keeping generally have touched upon the subject are not agreed upon the definition of the term Prime Cost. In some instances the confusion of ideas and language has been

*Outline of contents.*

*Definition of prime cost.*

carried so far as to render it necessary to speak of net and gross prime cost. Throughout these pages we take Prime Cost to mean, as shown in the Glossary, and as in fact the words imply, only the original or direct cost of an article. Cost of production, on the other hand, we define to be the total expenditure incurred in the production of a commodity.

The sale or distribution of manufactured commodities will next be dealt with, and at this point we think it well to draw a clear distinction between materials for manufacture and articles in the manufactured state. Until materials are converted into manufactured articles we speak of them as stores, but when so converted they are termed stock; and the book-keeping we recommend is based on this view. The accounts in the Prime Cost Ledger are debited with wages and materials spent in manufacture, and are credited with the stock produced. The importance of this distinction between stores and stock will be evident when the subject is dealt with in detail. The fifth chapter treats of the Stock Books, which, though in some respects analogous in their functions to the Stores Books, are as distinct from them as is consistent with the principle of a system by which all the books of the establishment are required to merge into the Commercial Ledger.

*Distinction between stores and stock.*

This practically completes the outline of what constitutes the absolutely essential books in a system of Factory Accounts. But there are many other matters which have too important a bearing upon the subject of this work to admit of being passed over in a treatise upon factory book-keeping. Such are the questions of depreciation of buildings, plant, tools, stores and stock, and of surveys or inventories. These matters are dealt with in subsequent chapters. In our cursory consideration of the former of these questions we refer to various methods of determining a rate of depreciation. As regards the question of surveys or stock-taking we do not presume, in view of the varying requirements of different trades, to do more than to offer some more or less obvious suggestions which have a general application.

The Appendices contain a reprint of a paper on the advantages derivable from the use of symbolic nomenclature for parts of machines, a summary of the Factory and Workshop Acts, some notes on the law of rating of factories containing machinery, and also some notes on the law of Fire Insurance and on the Income Tax Acts and other matters having reference to the subject of this work.

# CHAPTER II.

## LABOUR.

THE initial step in the organization of a factory must perforce be the adoption of a system by which each per-

*A wages system the initiative in the organi- zation of a factory.*

son employed at a rate of pay on a time scale shall receive payment for the exact time employed. Such a system should necessarily be one in which the workpeople have confidence, and in which they themselves co-operate.

In the present chapter we show how each employé's record of his or her own time may, through the instru-

*Proper wages system mini- mises error. Summary of chapter.*

mentality of the leading hand in the shop and of the time clerk, be compared, checked, and if need arise, corrected by the record kept by the timekeeper. By these means the possibility of an error either by over or under payment is reduced to a minimum, whilst fraud necessitates for its successful perpetration the complicity of the employé, the timekeeper, the leading hand of the shop in which such employé works, the time clerk, and of the clerk in the counting-house who makes up the Wages Book, and also of the cashier who pays the wages. Such collusion is almost, if not altogether, impossible.

Further, we show that, by means of a weekly return, it is impossible for any one connected with either the counting-house or the factory to enter in the books

**Creation of dummy men prevented.** wages for "dummy men." This phrase is used to designate such a system of fraud as can only exist in a large undertaking where it is possible for the foreman, the timekeeper, or the pay clerk, either singly or in conspiracy, to show a larger number of men employed than is actually the case.

By the use of the same return, fraud, through the unauthorised alteration of the rates of pay of the work-**Weekly return of alteration of rate.** people, is prevented, and the authorised rate recorded for future reference. The regulation and recording of piece-work prices, and the payment of piece-work balances to those employés who have been paid during the continuance of piece-work at time rates, is described; as are also the modes of controlling time made outside the factory and of preventing undue recourse to overtime.

It is then shown how deductions may, if required, be made from the wages of the employé, for rent, fines for non-observance of rules, &c., in respect of savings bank, **Sick and other funds.** sick, superannuation, or other funds; or of the amounts of adverse balances on piece-work, or of the deductions authorised by the Factory Acts. Attention is called to the fact that the Wages Book may be correctly and concisely compiled from these various returns, and that it, in its turn, may, if thought well, be summarised for the use of the principal into even a more condensed form.

The possibility of obtaining receipts from employés with very little trouble is dealt with, provision against **Receipts for Wages. Duties of time clerk.** the misappropriation of unclaimed wages suggested, and consideration given to the mode of payment. The work of the time clerk in reference to the systematic allocation of the wages for the Prime Cost Books, and of the timekeeper or other employé in reference to the records required by the Factory Acts is explained. The necessity of compiling a list of addresses and of obtaining information as to the character of employés, as well as some miscellaneous matters, are incidentally dealt with.

At the entrance to a factory there is almost invariably found a small building, where the time of the entry and exit of every employé is registered by a gate or time keeper. This is effected, as regards the entry, by each employé, on entering the factory, being required to pass the time office and mention the number which has been allotted to him at the commencement of his engagement, receiving from the timekeeper a metal check, or other ticket, bearing his number and taken from a board, on which the checks have previously been consecutively arranged.

<small>Time office and workmen's checks.</small>

On leaving the factory the employé should deposit this check in a box placed outside the time office. The checks will be sorted by the timekeeper, and can, in any case of doubt or dispute, be compared with the entries made by him in a book which is hereafter described. The checks having been again placed on the board, the process referred to is repeated each time the workpeople enter or leave the premises.

Should a mess-room have been provided for the use of the employés there will not be any obstacle to the carrying out of the system if the mess-room is outside the timekeeper's lodge, but should it be situated inside the works, the checks can be issued from that point after meal hours.

<small>Mess-room.</small>

The timekeeper having admitted the workpeople, proceeds to register their time. He sees by the presence or absence of checks on the board what employés are, or are not, in the factory. In a book so ruled as to show each employé's name and number, and each day of the week divided into four parts (for the time made before breakfast, after breakfast, after dinner, and overtime, or such other divisions as may be most suitable for the business), the timekeeper enters the employés present. This is in most cases done by a vertical stroke, absence being denoted by a horizontal one. In some cases the four divisions of time above referred to are shown in the form of a square, thus □; or in cases where three divisions only are required, by means of a triangle, thus △. In the square, the top stroke is supposed to represent the time before breakfast, the down stroke, right hand, that after breakfast, the base, the time after dinner, and the up-stroke left hand, any overtime that may be made. In the triangle the down stroke left hand, is presumed to represent the first division of time, the base the second, and the up-stroke, right hand, the third. In printing the book the various lines of the square or angle may be faintly printed, and when entries are made, inked over completely or partially, as required.

*Method of keeping time books.*

Absence during any or all of these divisions is of course made apparent by the omission of the stroke or strokes. Specimens Nos. 1, 2, and 3 show a Time Book so ruled.

If the employés are working in two or three shifts a separate Time Book may be used for each shift; or one book may be so ruled as to take all three returns. The time of the workpeople who are admitted into the works, or allowed to leave, at

*Double or treble shift.*

C

intervals between any of these divisions, may be shown by a red ink note of the number of minutes or hours' difference between the time at which they should have presented and did present themselves for admittance and departure, or, if the square and the triangle are adopted, by recognised shortenings of the strokes. The time at which employés are admitted into the works if they are late in arriving, will, of course, follow prescribed rules. No employé should be allowed to leave work at an irregular time unless provided with a permit signed by his foreman.

If it be deemed desirable to have a record of the employés **Absentee** who periodically ab- **Book.** sent themselves, it may be kept in an Absentee Book ruled to show the names of those away on any particular day, and to bring out prominently the names of those who are most frequently absent. The same principle may be applied in recording, by means of a Time Lost Book, the names of those who are unpunctual.

# REGISTRATION OF TIME. 19

It may also be desirable to keep a similar record as to overtime (Specimen No. 4).

### TIME BOOK.—Specimen No. 2.

| No. | Name. | Trade. | Wed. | Thurs. | Fri. | Sat. | Sun. | Mon. | Tues. | Total Hours. |
|---|---|---|---|---|---|---|---|---|---|---|
| | | | △ | ⌐ | ∧ | ∠ | △ | △ | ∠ | |

### TIME BOOK.—Specimen No. 3.

| No. | Name. | Trade. | Wed. | Thurs. | Fri. | Sat. | Sun. | Mon. | Tues. | Total Hours. |
|---|---|---|---|---|---|---|---|---|---|---|
| | | | ☐ | ⊔ | ⊏ | ⊓ | ⊐ | ⊓ | ⊔ | |

### OVERTIME BOOK.—Specimen No. 4.

| Date. | Employé's No. | Time. | | Hours worked. | Allowance: | | | Total Time. | Remarks as to work. |
|---|---|---|---|---|---|---|---|---|---|
| | | From | To | | ¼ | ½ | Double. | | |

Having thus booked the time, entry by entry, and day by day, the timekeeper at the conclusion of the week or fortnight, as the case may be, proceeds to cast across and enter in the column provided, the total time made by the employé during such period, and then forwards the book to the office.

Each employé having been provided with a time board, enters on it, in accordance with the instructions received from his foreman, a record of how his day's time is spent, giving in two or three words or in symbols, the nature of his work, the number of the order (if for plant or buildings, called the working order number, if for manufacturing any commodities, the manufacturing or stock order number), and the time spent thereon.

*Use of employé's time boards or record sheets.*

These time records are perhaps most convenient if written on a form, which can be easily gummed at one end to a board. On these forms or time slips it is well to have two divisions ruled—the one for a record of ordinary time, the other for overtime.

TIME RECORD SHEET.—SPECIMEN No. 5.

Name_____  No._____

| Day. | Nature of Work. | Order No. | Time. | | | |
|---|---|---|---|---|---|---|
| | | | Ordinary. | | Over. | |
| | | | Piece Work. | Day Work. | Piece Work. | Day Work. |
| | | | | | | |

## TIME RECORD SHEETS.

The records should be initialled by the shop foreman or leading hand, and after being so initialled copied by the time clerk into a Time Allocation Book. In a business in which the work is highly specialized, and in *Time records, when posted to Prime Cost Ledgers.* which the employé is engaged on one piece or form of work only, and on that for some considerable time, it is possible, and may be found advantageous, to use these time slips as the direct sources of entry in the Prime Cost Books * instead of the wages being analysed in the manner described later. It is essential that in either case the total entries made in the Prime Cost Books on account of wages should agree with the total wages expended.

The Time Allocation Book previously referred to is *Time Allocation Book.* cast up by the time clerk and forwarded, at the end of each payment period, to the office.

The two records of time made, viz., the Time Book (as prepared by the timekeeper), and the Time Alloca-*Verification of time return.* tion Book (as entered from the workpeople's own records, which are initialled by the leading hand), are, when sent to the office, compared, and in cases where differences arise, explanations obtained by the Wages Book clerk from the employé or the timekeeper. Should the explanation then given not be satisfactory, or should it not be received in time, it is incumbent on the clerk making up the Wages Book to see that the employé, pending the settlement of the question, is paid only for the lesser number of hours.

A suggested form for a Time Allocation Book, which may be ruled so as to take the records for a week, fort-

* See Chapter IV.

night, or month, is shown (Specimen No. 6).

Where employés are engaged outside the factory or works for any considerable period, and are unable to present themselves at the time office on commencing or finishing work, it is desirable to have an Out-works Time Record Sheet (Specimen No. 7), which the leading hand on the premises where the work is being carried on is asked to sign as a guarantee of the time being correctly recorded.

This Time Record serves as an authority to the timekeeper for the necessary entries in his book. In the margin of that book it is stated that the time was made outside the factory or works, the place and date being also shown. The time clerk will treat this Time Record Sheet as equivalent to the Time Slip or Board previously alluded to.

OUT-WORKS TIME RECORD SHEET.—SPECIMEN No. 7.

Workman's No. _____   Name _____

| Date 189 . | Day. | Where engaged. | Description of Work. | Order No. | From | | To | | Time Worked | Remarks. |
|---|---|---|---|---|---|---|---|---|---|---|
| | | | | | H. | M. | H. | M. | | |
| | | | | | | | | | | |

N.B.—In all cases where possible this sheet must be signed by the person for whom the work is being done, or his representative, and must be posted so as to reach the time clerk by _____ a.m., on _____ day.

(Reverse side.)

_____

_____ 189

To _____

_____

_____

We shall be obliged by your seeing that the other side of this Time Sheet is correctly filled up as regards the time of arriving at and leaving your premises; and, having done so, by your signing the same.

Should you desire overtime to be made please enter in the "Remarks" column that it is done at your request.

As these regulations are made to prevent mistakes and abuses, we trust they will have your kind attention.

_____

It is well to draw the special attention of the customer for whom work is being done outside the factory, to the request that he will note in the "Remarks" column any overtime made by his order, as many seem either to ignore or be ignorant of the fact, that the higher rate generally paid for overtime adds very considerably to the cost of the work.

The economic aspects of overtime in relation to fixed capital are dealt with in a subsequent chapter. For our present purpose it suffices to say that if the employer desires to keep a check upon, and to reduce to a minimum, the overtime that is worked, he may require the foreman or leading hand to send him at the end of each period of payment a return of overtime made (Specimen No. 8).

**Return of overtime.**

This return is initialled by the foreman or leading hand to show that the overtime has been sanctioned, and the clerk making up the Wages Book, to whom the return is handed, sees that no overtime other than that shown therein is allowed to pass through that book.

Instructions might be given either to the time clerk or to the Wages Book clerk, or to both, to prepare a statement showing the amount spent on overtime in excess of the amount that would have been paid had the same work been done at ordinary rates.

This return might simply show the amount paid in excess in each trade or to each individual, or it might be in a more complete form, as shown in Specimen Ruling No. 9.

In factories where, owing to the solidarity of labour, a large number of men and women are unable to commence, or fully carry out, their work unless a smaller number of men or women of a particular trade are

## RETURN OF OVERTIME.

**OVERTIME RETURN.—Specimen No. 8.**

Return of Overtime made at _____ Works, For the Week ending _____ 189 .

| Name. | Occupation. | Wednesday. | | Thursday. | | Friday. | | Saturday. | | Sunday. | | Monday. | | Tuesday. | | Total hours during week. |
|---|---|---|---|---|---|---|---|---|---|---|---|---|---|---|---|---|
| | | Order No. | Time. H. M. | Order No. | Time. H. M. | Order No. | Time. H. M. | Order No. | Time. H. M. | Order No. | Time. H. M. | Order No. | Time. H. M. | Order No. | Time. H. M. | |

Workman's No.

**OVERTIME COMPARISON BOOK.—Specimen No. 9.**

| Name. | No. | Trade. | W. No. | Day Rate. | Overtime Rate. | W. No. | Day Rate. | Overtime Rate. | W. No. | Day Rate. | Overtime Rate. | W. No. | Day Rate. | Overtime Rate. | W. No. | Day Rate. | Overtime Rate. | Total Amount. | Day Work. | Overtime Work. | Excess on Overtime. |
|---|---|---|---|---|---|---|---|---|---|---|---|---|---|---|---|---|---|---|---|---|---|

present, it is sometimes found advisable to insure the greater punctuality on the part of the smaller number by instituting a system of fines for late, and of premiums for early, attendance. Thus the man who was punctual would get his premium and wages for the time made, whilst the unpunctual man would, besides losing pay for the time he was absent, be fined. The number of times each employé is unpunctual is reported to the office by the timekeeper, and can of course be checked, from the Time Books and record slips, if thought necessary. The amount of premium or fine in each case would then be passed through the Wages Book.

Despite the former strenuous opposition of trade unions, the system of payment by results, generally known as piecework, is extending. Not only do "the ablest and strongest masters generally insist on it as necessary to enable them to carry out their plans freely and to get their men to use their best energies, and such employers naturally beat in the race those who yield to the unions,"* but the employés are beginning to recognise that the advantages of the system are not confined to the employers, and are withdrawing or modifying their opposition.

If piece-work is resorted to each employé should, when starting on it, be supplied with a Piece-work Return Form (Specimen No. 10), which should specify the nature of the work, the extent of the job, and the rate at which it is undertaken. On the completion of the work he should return this sheet, having entered thereon the number of hours spent on that particular job, for which he has been paid

**Method of recording piece-work.**

---

* "Economics of Industry." By A. and M. P. Marshall. London: Macmillan.

## REGISTRATION OF PIECEWORK.

### PIECE-WORK RETURN.—Specimen No. 10.

Week ending_____189 .

        Workman's Name_____No._____Rate

   Started on_____, 189 , at_____

                                     _____ Foreman.

| Order No. | Reg. No. | Quantity. | Description of Work. | Rate. | £ | s. | d. |
|---|---|---|---|---|---|---|---|
|  |  |  |  |  |  |  |  |
|  |  |  |  |  |  |  |  |
|  |  |  |  |  |  |  |  |

|  | Date. | Hrs. | Date. | Hrs. | Date. | Hrs. | Date. | Hrs. | Overtime Allowances. |
|---|---|---|---|---|---|---|---|---|---|
| Wednesday |  |  |  |  |  |  |  |  |  |
| Thursday |  |  |  |  |  |  |  |  |  |
| Friday |  |  |  |  |  |  |  |  |  |
| Saturday |  |  |  |  |  |  |  |  |  |
| Monday |  |  |  |  |  |  |  |  |  |
| Tuesday |  |  |  |  |  |  |  |  |  |

Last Piece-rate_____        Total time_____at_____

Last percentage on Day-work_____    Balance_____

                                      Percentage on Day-work_____

Signature of Workman_____

No. received as above                           _____

   Signature of Piece-work Clerk_____

                                                  _____ Foreman.

Balance entered in Wages Book_____ 189 .

                                         Exd._____

                                                  Time Clerk.

in ordinary course. The Return having been initialled by the viewer of the work, should be passed on to the time clerk, who will check the time entries made thereon from his Time Allocation Book, will give it monetary form, and enter the difference between the value of the output at piece-rate and the amount already paid at time-rate in his Allocation Book. Any balances favourable to the employé may of course be placed to his or her credit at the next piece-work settlement, whilst adverse balances may either then be deducted from the time pay, or from the next favourable piece-rate balance.

In some cases it will probably be found impracticable, owing to the nature or pressure of other work, to keep an employé continuously on the work which he has taken at a piece-rate. Under these circumstances the foreman or leading hand should at once notify the time clerk, in writing, that he has taken the employé off piece-work and put him on time-work. It may perhaps be found desirable for the foreman or leading hand to keep a Log Book, in which such interruptions to piece-working are noted. In a large establishment this function might be discharged by the piece-work viewer.

In any event it will be found very desirable to have a record as to interruption to piece-working to which reference may, if necessary, be made at the time of settlement.

The time clerk having duly examined and vouched the piece-work returns will forward the same to the office, where they may be re-checked, if thought desirable, in a general or detailed manner.

Considerable advantage accrues from a Piece-work Analysis or Register Book being compiled from these

THE ANALYSIS OF PIECE-WORK COSTS. 29

sheets. Such a book would, as indicated in Specimen No. 11, **Piece-work Analysis Book.** show the various rates at which work was undertaken, as also the percentage in which any kind of piece-work is favourable or unfavourable to either the employer or the employé; and it would serve as a record or check in fixing piece-work rates. From this source also could be obtained comparisons between the percentage of piece-work rates and day-work prices ruling in the various shops or departments.

Having been checked, these piece-work balances may be entered in the Wages **Return of men engaged or left.** Book (Specimen No. 14). It will also be found advantageous, and in large establishments indispensable, for a return or returns to be sent by the foreman at regular intervals, either to the clerk responsible for the Wages Book or to the principal, enumerating the names, trades, and rates of pay of employés who have been engaged since the date of the last return, and giving similar information concerning those who have resigned or been discharged. This return should also record any increases in the rates of pay, any transfers from one department to another, also the names of employés who are to be fined for neglect of duty or for any other cause, of those who are to receive premiums for some special reason, and of those who are on leave, or are absent from illness or injury, but to whom wages or allowances are to be paid.

WAGES ADVICE.—SPECIMEN No. 12.

RETURN OF MEN ENGAGED, RESIGNED, DISCHARGED, PROMOTED, TRANS-
FERRED OR FINED, AND OF ALLOWANCES AND PREMIUMS,

at _____ Works, for the Week ending _____ 189

ENGAGED.

| No. | Name. | Occupation. | Rate. | Name and Address of last Employer. |
|---|---|---|---|---|
|  |  |  |  |  |

LEFT.

| No. | Name. | Occupation. | Remarks. |
|---|---|---|---|
|  |  |  |  |

[*Specimen continued.*

## RETURN OF MEN EMPLOYED.

### WAGES ADVICE.—Specimen No. 12—(*continued*).

#### Promoted or Transferred.

| No. | Name. | Occupation. | From | To | Rate. | | Remarks. |
|---|---|---|---|---|---|---|---|
| | | | | | From | To | |
| | | | | | | | |

#### Fined.

| No. | Name. | Occupation. | Amount. | Fined for |
|---|---|---|---|---|
| | | | | |

#### Allowances and Premiums.

| No. | Name. | Occupation. | Amount. | Premium allowed for | Remarks. |
|---|---|---|---|---|---|
| | | | | | |

Entered on Pay-sheet by_____     Signature_____

These returns should be duly entered in a Wages Rate Book **Wages Rate Book.** (Specimen No. 13), from which book at any period the rate of pay entered in the Wages Book for all or any of the employés can be checked.

Unless a special book recording the length of the employé's service and of his or her varying rates of pay and other details is kept, the Wages Rate Book may be made to serve such purpose.

If a large number of employés follow the same trade, **Successive advances in rates.** or if there is a recognised scale of rises on a period of employment basis, it may be well to supplement the Wages Advice (Specimen No. 12) by a return, sent into the counting-house on the first day of each month, showing the names and numbers of those to whom it is proposed during the month to grant increased pay. This form is almost identical with the Wages Rate Book (Specimen No. 13), with the exception that before the

## THE WAGES BOOK.      33

columns showing the successive advances there should be inserted two columns, the first showing the rate of pay in force, and the second the proposed rate. The " remarks" column should be used for stating the reasons for the advance. The sole utility of this form seems to be that through its use the principal has only to settle the question of proposed increases once a month instead of once a week; and is thereby enabled to make inquiries as to the character and capacity of any employé who is recommended for an increase of pay.

It will be seen from the foregoing that the compilation of the Wages Book is not a difficult matter, and **Compilation of Wages Book.** that if ordinary care and attention are given to it a clerical mistake should not occur; whilst the number of persons through whose hands the returns pass, each acting as a check on the others, should prevent peculation and fraud.

The specimen ruling of a Wages Book (No. 14) is, we venture to think, applicable in detail to most, and in general to all, trades.

This specimen ruling shows columns for the entry of any stoppages or deductions for rent, fuel, sick and provident societies, superannuation fund, or other purposes, but it must be remembered that under the "Truck Amendment Act of 1887" no such stoppage or deduction can be made, unless there is a written agreement or request, signed by the employé, authorising such deduction or stoppage. All employés, therefore, who require such deductions to be made should be requested to sign a Stoppage Agreement Form, or Book, should the latter be the more convenient.

If it is necessary to have a permanent record of the character of an employé, as evidenced by the fines

D

## WAGES BOOK.—Specimen No. 14.

Week Ending _____ 189_ .

Columns:
- No.
- Name.
- Occupation.
- Rate.
- Time Made.
- Amount.
- Overtime (Time | Amt.)
- Piecework Credit Balances.
- Premiums or Allowances.
- Total.
- Fines.
- Piecework Debit Balances.
- Stoppages. [These columns may be used for the stoppages on account of Savings Bank, Superannuation Fund, Medical Attendance, Fuel, &c.]
- Total Deductions.
- Total to be Paid.
- Remarks.

## SUMMARY OF WAGES.—Specimen No. 15.

Week Ending _____ 189_ .

Columns:
- Trades.
- No. of Men.
- Amount.
- Overtime.
- Piece-work Credit Balances.
- Premiums and Allowances.
- Totals.
- Fines.
- Piece-work Debit Balances.
- Savings Bank, Superannuation Fund and other Deductions.
- Total Deductions.
- Total Paid.
- Remarks, including average rate of pay, &c.

imposed or the premiums granted, such information might, by means of additional columns, be inserted in the Rate Book, or special books arranged with reference to trades, as well as to individuals, might be used for this purpose.

Whether a separate banking account for wages be kept or not, the employer may find it desirable to have a summary of the Wages Book prepared (Specimen No. 15), showing the number of men and women employed in the various trades, the aggregate of their wages, their average rates of pay, &c.

*Summary of wages.*

Before passing from this branch of our subject it may be well to mention that even in large establishments what is in reality a receipt for the wages paid may be obtained from each employé by a process which entails but little trouble. The time or pay clerk (as may be considered the more expedient) would write out on a slip of paper, ruled and printed for the purpose, the date, the employé's number, and the amount receivable. These forms can be distributed by the various foremen to their subordinates prior to the pay. Each employé presenting himself at the pay-table will hand in this form to the pay clerk. These receipts can be compared with the Wages Book.

*Receipts for wages.*

If instead of a Wages Book pay sheets or bills are used, the receipts might be obtained on the original documents by distributing them in the different shops, but this would involve considerable labour as compared with the procedure first described.

In all cases where men do not present themselves at the pay-table in ordinary course the pay clerk should make an entry in a book

*Unclaimed Wages Book.*

specially provided for that purpose, showing the man's name, the date, and the amount of his pay (Specimen No. 16).

UNCLAIMED WAGES BOOK.—Specimen No. 16.

| No. | Name. | Trade. | Amount. | For Week ending | Date Paid. | Received by |
|---|---|---|---|---|---|---|
| | | | | | | |

A signature should be obtained in this book for the money of each employé, who obtains his or her wages in any way other than at the pay-table on the ordinary pay-day.

By means of this book also the principal may at once see what wages have not been claimed, and can give instructions as to the disposal of such amounts as have been so long outstanding as to render their being claimed improbable.

Where any considerable number of employés are unable, owing to their hours of work, to be at the pay-table at the appointed time, there may be two or more pays, or the employés so absent may empower one of their fellow-workers to receive wages on their behalf (Specimen No. 17).

*Payment of wages to deputy.*

In cases in which employés are engaged permanently or temporarily outside the factory, a receipt for the wages remitted them may with equal ease be obtained by means of a form ruled and printed in copyable ink (Specimen No. 18).

*Payment of wages to employés outside factory.*

## THE RECEIPTS FOR WAGES.

### PAY WAGES NOTE.—Specimen No. 17.

*Memo.* _____189 .

*To the Cashier.*

Please pay the bearer, \* \* \* \*, my wages, amounting to £          , for the week ending _____189 .

Name_____

Occupation_____

No._____

The Person receiving the amount above named is responsible for delivering the money to the person to whom it is due.

### WAGES REMITTANCE FORM.—Specimen No. 18.

_____          _____189 .

Dear Sir,

We enclose you herewith _____ amounting to £_____ in payment of wages and expenses during the _____ ending _____ 189 as per details below. Please obtain the receipts on this form and return to

Nos. of Notes_____

,, Postal Orders_____

| Name. | No. | Time. | Rate. | Wages. | Overtime. | Expenses. | Deduction on account of Superannuation Fund, &c., as per advice. | Total amount received. | Received in payment as per amount opposite my name. |
|---|---|---|---|---|---|---|---|---|---|
| | | | | | | | | | |
| | | | | | | | | | |
| | | | | | | | | | |

As regards the method of paying wages we may point out that in large establishments it is almost obligatory that, prior to drawing the amount from the bank, the totals of each page of the Wages Book should be analysed, so that such proportions of gold, silver, and copper may be obtained as will prevent the necessity for further change. This is done by means of a cash sheet (Specimen No. 19), which also serves as a check upon the addition of each page in the Wages Book, and is further useful, in localising mistakes in the process of counting out the money to be paid to each employé, by assigning to each page of the Wages Book the exact proportion of cash required to pay all the wages entered on that page. The process of distributing wages is generally by means of small tin boxes bearing the numbers by which the workpeople are known, and which of course agree with the numbers of their checks (see p. 16).

*Method of paying wages.*

CASH SHEET.—SPECIMEN No. 19.

| No. of Page. | Notes. | Sovereigns. | Half-Sovereigns. | Silver. | Copper. |
|---|---|---|---|---|---|
|  |  |  |  |  |  |
|  |  |  |  |  |  |
|  |  |  |  |  |  |

These tin boxes are placed in trays constructed to hold 100 each, and arranged in ten squares (Specimen No. 20).

*Money trays.*

## THE METHOD OF PAYING WAGES. 39

MONEY TRAY.—Specimen No. 20.

| 1 | 2 | 3 | 4 | 5 | 6 | 7 | 8 | 9 | 10 |
|---|---|---|---|---|---|---|---|---|---|
| 11 | 12 | 13 | 14 | 15 | 16 | 17 | 18 | 19 | 20 |
| 21 | 22 | 23 | 24 | 25 | 26 | 27 | 28 | 29 | 30 |
| 31 | 32 | 33 | 34 | 35 | 36 | 37 | 38 | 39 | 40 |
| 41 | 42 | 43 | 44 | 45 | 46 | 47 | 48 | 49 | 50 |
| 51 | 52 | 53 | 54 | 55 | 56 | 57 | 58 | 59 | 60 |
| 61 | 62 | 63 | 64 | 65 | 66 | 67 | 68 | 69 | 70 |
| 71 | 72 | 73 | 74 | 75 | 76 | 77 | 78 | 79 | 80 |
| 81 | 82 | 83 | 84 | 85 | 86 | 87 | 88 | 89 | 90 |
| 91 | 92 | 93 | 94 | 95 | 96 | 97 | 98 | 99 | 100 |

The employés are called to the pay-table by their numbers and in consecutive order, the cashier, or some official who has not been engaged in the process of counting the money, handing to each employé his or her particular tin against the presentation of the receipt form (explained on page 35). Where, owing to the large number of hands, the pay would otherwise take up much time, it may be found expedient to have two or more pay-tables, or there may be variation, one set of workpeople being paid first one week, second another week, and so forth; but on the whole it is advisable that the process of paying wages should be completed in as few minutes as possible.

From the Time Allocation Book (Specimen No. 6) the

time clerk should make an abstract weekly, fortnightly, or monthly as required, showing the various working or stock orders on which time has been spent. This summary or abstract should show against the various orders the cost of labour during that period in the respective departments or trades (Specimen No. 21).

<small>Wages abstract for purpose of prime cost.</small>

The totals so compiled should agree with that in the Wages Book for the same period. This abstract of wages will form the basis of the debit to the Prime Cost Ledger (see Chapter IV.) for labour expended upon the various operations carried on.

It is evident that the totals so entered on the Abstract of Wages Sheet may easily be traced back to the Time Allocation Book, and that any more detailed information that may be required can thus be easily and promptly obtained.

The diagram opposite page 42 will serve to show the relation of the various forms and books referred to in this chapter.

<small>Diagram of books and forms.</small>

## DUTIES OF TIMEKEEPERS.

**Adhesion to factory rules by employés.** It remains to be observed that when a person who has been engaged presents himself or herself for work, the timekeeper should obtain his or her signature to a book or form declaratory that the rules of the factory have been duly read and noted. The timekeeper should also obtain the name **Character book.** and address of the last employer, and fill in and forward to the counting-house a character form for transmission to the latter. This form when returned duly filled in should be pasted and duly indexed in a guard book called a Character Book. The address of every employé should be taken when engaged, **Address book.** and should be entered in an Address Book. It is very desirable that periodically the whole of the employés should be asked for their addresses, and these when obtained compared with the existing entries. In cases in which workpeople may be required on urgent or pressing work it is especially desirable to know their correct addresses, and it may therefore be necessary to impose a fine for not notifying change of address.

The timekeeper should furthermore keep Registers, in accordance with the Factory Acts, of the children, **Register of women and children.** young persons, and women employed in the factory, as well as a record of the cleansing and whitewashing, &c., of the shops as required by those Acts. He should also inform some responsible person when any children are engaged, and should see that the necessary certificates as to education are produced, and that the certifying surgeon after making the examination required by the Act duly attests the Register.

We have not dealt with the appropriation of fines

**Houses belonging to firms occupied by work-people.** imposed, or the deductions on account of superannuation, sick, or other funds, or with the occupation by employés of houses belonging to the firm, as these more correctly appertain to the books of the system of commercial accounts, with which it is not our province here to deal. In the last case, should an arrangement be made by which the work-people, in consideration of not paying rent for the houses they occupy, receive less wages than they otherwise would, then the interest on the capital invested in the buildings forms an element in the cost of production, and should be debited to the Prime Cost Ledger as a percentage upon the wages paid or in common with the indirect expenses to be referred to later. In practice, however, it is found that it is preferable to pay full wages, and to collect the amount of the rent from the work-people who occupy the houses, such amount being dealt with as revenue.

DI*

SHOWING THE RELATION OF THE BOOKS

(*The numbers, where shown,*

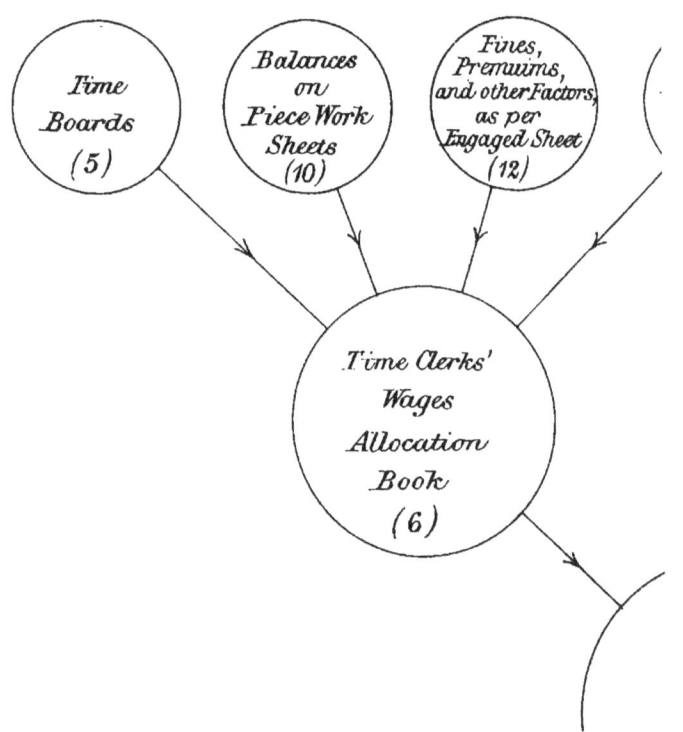

## I.

)RMS USED IN CONNECTION WITH WAGES.

*ond to the specimen rulings.)*

*rks*
*ecord*
*ts*
*w )*

Time Book.

*(1. 2. 3.)*

# CHAPTER III.

## STORES.

ONE of the first points to be considered in a review of the accounts of a manufacturing or trading concern is **Purchase of materials.** necessarily the question of the purchase of the materials or commodities which are essential to the carrying on of the business, whether the articles obtained are to be used as plant, or are for the purpose of manufacturing, or simply to be retailed. We aim, therefore, in this chapter to show the wants to be provided for in order to insure economy in the purchase and consumption of material, and to suggest those forms by which an employer may assure himself that the raw materials of his trade are being bought in the cheapest market, and economically and properly used.

The initiative in the purchase of materials must necessarily be taken by those more directly engaged with the **Initiatory stage.** details of manufacture, such as the foreman or overlooker. The storekeeper having found either that he has not any supply of the required or similar material, or that his stock is low and needs replenishing, enters a record of his requirements in a Stores Requisition Book, which can be periodically submitted to the principal, whose province it is to determine when, and in what quantity, it is desirable to purchase material.

If there are numerous branches the Requisition Book would be entered up in the counting-house, daily or weekly as the exigencies of the business require, from the forms sent in by the heads of the several departments. These requisitions may be as shown (Specimen No. 22). The Stores Requisition Book should contain columns for entering in the date of requisition, a description of the goods, the department or purpose for which they are required, and the name of the firm to whom it is proposed to give the order. Columns showing the rate at which the goods are to be supplied, the quantity in stock, the last purchasing price, and the name of last supplier, may also be provided for the guidance of the principal. When the entries in the Requisition Book have been examined and allowed, an order for the articles would be issued. The advantage of all orders for the purchase of goods emanating from one centre, instead of each department being able to supply its own individual needs, is that the principal of the business is not only able to control in a very large degree the character and amount of the consumption, but is able to contract far more favourably for the supply of the goods required than could otherwise be the case. Even if by this concentration a little delay in obtaining supplies is caused, it need not lead to inconvenience, as the requisitions can, in the majority of cases, very well be made in anticipation of the demand arising.

Should the principal determine to contract for the supply of certain goods over a period of time, it is desirable that the invitation-to-tender forms issued by him should be uniform, and should state clearly and concisely the conditions on which the goods will be purchased and paid for. This form should also state when and where the patterns or samples may be seen and the date on which tenders will be received and opened.

It is desirable also that a Stores Contract Book should be kept, that particulars of each contract should be entered therein, and the date of the various supplies, so that the position under the contract may be rapidly and easily known.

Specimen ruling No. 23 shows the heading of a Stores Requisition Book, which will probably suffice in most cases, but the other headings referred to would also be found useful.

The date and amount of the invoice can, of course, only be inserted at the conclusion of the transaction and when the goods are delivered, but their entry gives a useful record, and is valuable as a check.

STORES REQUISITION.—Specimen No. 22.

No._____   _____Department.   189 .

A supply of the undermentioned articles is required.

| Article. | Purpose. | Date of last supply. | Quantity last supplied. | By whom supplied. | Rate of last supply. | Present Stock and Remarks. |
|---|---|---|---|---|---|---|
|  |  |  |  |  |  |  |

## STORES REQUISITION BOOK.—Specimen No. 23.

| Date of requisition. | Goods required. | Wanted by | Purpose. | To be ordered from | Order. | | Invoice. | | Remarks. |
|---|---|---|---|---|---|---|---|---|---|
| | | | | | No. | Rate. | Amount. | Date. | |
| | | | | | | | | | |

**Order Form.** It having been decided to order the material requisitioned, there should be made out from such requisitions the order to the vendors. These orders should specify the conditions as to delivery, carriage, packing, on which the goods are ordered, the place and time at which they will be received, the terms of payment, and instructions as to sending advice notes, invoices, and statements of account.

It is sometimes considered that if the order forms have counterfoils, or are press-copied, and signed by a responsible person, the necessity for a Requisition Book is not very apparent. It will be found, however, in practice that while the work required to keep such a book is but slight, the facilities it affords for reference, and for noting the orders when executed, present very great advantages. It is a question of the relative value of labour, and it is often more economical for a clerk to regularly give a portion of his time to certain work than for an employer to have occasionally to give a few minutes.

Different systems obtain in different trades of dealing with the registration of invoices for goods supplied.

## REGISTRATION OF INVOICE.  47

**Registration of invoices.** Many firms stipulate for invoices in duplicate or triplicate to be distributed among, and dealt with by, the departments concerned. In almost all cases it is stipulated that an advice note of the dispatch of the goods should be sent to the officer in charge at the place to which the goods are sent. In such cases the officer in charge may be requested to send to the head office daily a Stores Received Form ruled to show the species of goods, from whom and whence they have been received, the weight, measurement, number, remarks as to condition, and having a column for the initials of the clerk at the head office who compares this advice note with the goods. The system which appears the more systematic and orderly, is that of making one invoice perform all functions. When this plan is adopted the vendor of the goods should be requested to send the invoice direct to the counting-house, notwithstanding that in pursuance of directions the goods are delivered at the works or elsewhere accompanied by a delivery note. Immediately on receipt of the invoice it should be examined with the view of ascertaining whether the general conditions of the order have been complied with, and whether the price charged is as stipulated. If found to be correct, the invoice should be numbered and sent to the storekeeper, foreman, or other person to whom the goods have been delivered, for him to certify as to the correctness or otherwise of their quantity and quality; and they can also be signed by the works manager as to quality if an additional check is thought necessary. After comparison the counterfoil or copy of the order should be so marked or ticked as to show that the invoice has been received. It may be advisable, if the number of invoices is large, to enter them on receipt

48  STORES.

in a Register Book (Specimen No. 24). The storekeeper
**Stores Re-** in turn enters the invoice in a Stores Received
**ceived Book.** Book (Specimen No. 25), and marks on it the
folio on which it has been entered in that Book.

INVOICE REGISTER BOOK.—SPECIMEN No. 24.

| No. of Invoice. | From whom received. | Nos. of Orders. | Folio in Requisition Book. | Amount of Invoice. | Date sent to Storekeeper. | Date returned by Storekeeper | Date handed to Bought Day Book clerk. |
|---|---|---|---|---|---|---|---|
| | | | | | | | |

STORES RECEIVED BOOK.—SPECIMEN No. 25.

| Date. | No. of Invoice. | Supplied by | Articles. | Dimensions. | No. | Weight. | | | Rate. | Amount. | Account to be charged. | Stores Ledger folio. |
| | | | | | | Cwts. | Qrs. | Lbs. | | | | |
|---|---|---|---|---|---|---|---|---|---|---|---|---|
| | | | | | | | | | | | | |

The entries in the Stores Received Book are in their
**Stores** turn posted in the Stores Ledger to the Dr.
**Ledger.** sides of the accounts to which they belong.
These two books bear the same relation to materials that
the Dr. side of the Cash Book and the Cash Account in
the Commercial Ledger bear to the cash.

STORES LEDGER. 49

The accounts in the Stores Ledger vary widely in different factories or works. In engineering, building, and many other trades, metals and timbers are naturally, under their various subdivisions, the chief amongst a number of other important headings. The many uses of this book will be more fully explained as we proceed with our subject, and particularly in the chapter on Surveys. It will suffice at this stage to mention that it is the duty of the clerk keeping the Stores Ledgers to see that the store of certain commodities never falls below the minimum quantity named by the principal.

References to the various records in connection with the purchase of material, and the certificates as to the quality of **Certification** the goods pur-**of Invoices.** chased and of the correctness of the quantity and rate can be
E

best shown on the invoice itself by means of india-rubber stamps typed as shown below (Specimen No. 27).

INVOICE ENDORSEMENT.—Specimen No. 27.

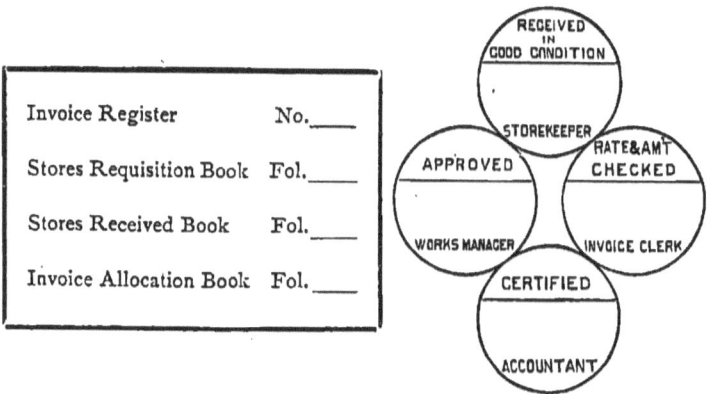

Upon being returned to the counting-house the in-
*Invoice Allo-* voices are entered in an Invoice Allocation or
*cation Book.* Bought Day-book, from which the items are posted in the aggregate in the Commercial Ledger to the debit of Stores, and in detail to the credit of the vendors of the goods. As these are counting-house books we do not show specimen rulings.

It will be obvious that by these means the debit to the General Stores Account in the Commercial Ledger, on account of material purchased, will agree with the aggregate of the special accounts posted from the Stores Received Book to the Stores Ledger.

The result of the periodical survey of the stores (or stock-taking) would under this system agree not only
*Result* with the Stores Ledger in regard to the
*of stock-* particular classes of materials, but should
*taking.* also agree collectively with the Stores

Account in the Commercial Ledger. This is a matter of paramount importance in securing accuracy in factory accounts, and in removing one of the principal elements of uncertainty in a balance-sheet.

So far we have only traced the records it is advisable to make in connection with the purchase and receipt of materials. We have now to consider the routine appertaining to the withdrawal of material from store for the manufacture of stock, or for any other purpose.

**Consumption of materials.**

The initiative in the expenditure of material should, in the case of a manufacturing concern, take the form of an instruction from the principal or manager of the business to the manager of the works to make for stock the required commodities, and authorise for that purpose the withdrawal from store, by the methods to be described, of such material as may be thought necessary. This instruction would probably take a form such as that shown (Specimen No. 28), and might be with two counterfoils, or, by means of carbonised sheets, with two duplicates.

Before any order to manufacture is given it is advisable, as tending to produce greater economy in cost of production, that the person best acquainted with its processes and details should estimate the probable cost to be incurred in wages and materials, in the production of the articles in question. This estimate should be a minimum rather than a maximum one, and the storekeeper having been furnished with particulars of it, should not without special authority issue more material for the order than is estimated. There is always a tendency for more time

**Estimate to precede manufacture.**

and material to be spent in manufacture than are absolutely necessary, and the probability is that when once a surplus quantity of material has been withdrawn from store, instead of being returned undiminished, it is in great part, if not entirely, lost in wasteful processes or in other ways; or the effectual localisation of cost may be hindered by foremen exchanging material with each other without the exchange being properly recorded.

INSTRUCTION TO FOREMAN OF WORKS.—SPECIMEN No. 28.

| Date_____ | Date_____ | Date_____ |
|---|---|---|
| Stock Order No.—— | Stock Order No.—— | Stock Order No.—— |
| To_____ | To_____ | To Mr._____ |
| Particulars of Order. | Particulars of Order. | Please make for Stock to the above number the undermentioned articles, and for that purpose employ labour, and withdraw material from Store as per accompanying estimate, No.—— |

Foreman_____

Date of completion_____

The foreman having received instructions to proceed with the manufacture, should draw upon the storekeeper for material to the estimated extent by means of a requisition, which for technical distinction may be called a Stores Warrant, and which may either have a counterfoil as shown (Specimen No. 29), or be written in

## ISSUE OF STORES.

**Stores Warrant.** duplicate by means of carbon sheets; or on a single sheet printed in copying ink, so that the form itself, as well as the entries written on it, may be copied by means of a press.

STORES WARRANT.—Specimen No. 29.

| No.—— Requested from Store, 189—— | No.—— Entered in Stores Issued Book, fol.—— Requested and received from Storekeeper, _____189__ |
|---|---|

| Article | No. of Order. | Purpose. | No. | Article | No. of Order. | Purpose. | No. | Weight. cwt. \| qrs. \| lbs | Rate. | £ s. d. |
|---------|---------------|----------|-----|---------|---------------|----------|-----|--------------------|-------|---------|
|         |               |          |     |         |               |          |     |                    |       |         |

**Stores Issued Book.** The storekeeper should enter all materials issued by him, in compliance with warrants, in the Stores Issued Book (Specimen No. 30), which in due course is posted in the Stores Ledger to the debit of the respective accounts.

STORES ISSUED BOOK.—Specimen No. 30.

| Date. | No. of Warrant. | Supplied to | Articles | Working No. or Purpose. | Dimensions. | No. | Weight. cwt. \| qrs. \| lbs. | Rate. | Amount. | Ledger Fol. | Remarks. |
|-------|-----------------|-------------|----------|-------------------------|-------------|-----|-----------------------|-------|---------|-------------|----------|
|       |                 |             |          |                         |             |     |                       |       |         |             |          |

Some little difficulty may be experienced both by the storekeeper and the clerk keeping the Prime Cost Books *Numbering* referred to in the next chapter, unless some *Stores* arrangement is made by which all warrants *Warrants.* are numbered consecutively. ·When they all emanate from one centre they may be consecutively typed in the books when printed, but when they emanate from foremen of several departments or leading hands in various shops, it will be found advantageous for the storekeeper to be provided with a numbering machine, with which to type all warrants as they reach him. The warrants from the different shops or departments may be printed on differently tinted papers.

All labour and material expended in manufacture of goods should be booked to the Number (which for con- *Stock Order* venience may be called the Stock Number, *Nos.* as distinguished from the Working Number referred to on page 20, and which is assigned to orders for expenditure other than that incurred in manufacture for stock) appearing on the order given by the principal.

The Stores Warrant when entered in the Stores Issued Book, should be forwarded to the counting-house, where *Prime Cost* it would find its way into the Prime Cost *Book.* Book, and the stores account in the Commercial Ledger. The process by which this is effected will be explained in the next chapter.

Before leaving the subject of the stores books, however, it is necessary to explain that materials returned *Stores Re-* to vendors are entered in a Stores Rejected *jected Book.* Book (Specimen No. 31), which, in its purpose, is co-extensive with the Stores Issued Book.

The entries in this book are based upon the credit

## STORES CREDIT NOTES.

### STORES REJECTED BOOK.—Specimen No. 31.

| Date. | No. of Credit Note. | Returned to | Articles. | Dimensions. | No. | Weight. | | | Rate. | Amount. | Account to be Credited. | Stores Ledger Folio. |
|---|---|---|---|---|---|---|---|---|---|---|---|---|
| | | | | | | Cwts. | Qrs. | Lbs. | | | | |

notes received from the vendors for the goods returned. The storekeeper should on returning any goods to the vendors enter the transaction in the Stores Rejected Book, leaving only the spaces for the number and date of credit note, and the rate and value of the returns blank, until he has received through the counting-house the credit note from the vendors. The office is advised of the rejection of goods either by an entry on the invoice or by means of a Stores Sent Away form.

This Stores Sent Away form may require registration in the counting-house in the same way as an invoice, and the book records will be similar. If it **Registration of credit notes.** be thought inadvisable to open a credit note register, the notes may be registered in red ink in the Invoice Register Book and the words "credit note" might be added. The credit note may bear references corresponding to those impressed on the invoices by means of an india-rubber stamp. Specimen ruling No. 27 will equally apply in this case, save in the titles of the books referred to, which would be :—

      Credit Note Register No._____

      Stores Rejected Book Fol._____

      Goods Returned Outward Book Fol._____

STORES.

It will probably be found that in many cases a reference to the Stores Requisition Book can be dispensed with on the credit note.

STORES DEBIT NOTE.—SPECIMEN No. 32.

| No.—— | | | | No.—— | | | | | | |
|---|---|---|---|---|---|---|---|---|---|---|
| Sent into Store,—— 189 . | | | | Dept.—— Entered in Shop Returns Book, fol.—— Sent to and received by Storekeeper ——, 189 . | | | | | | |
| Article. | No. of Order. | Purpose. | No. | Article. | No. of Order. | Purpose. | No. | Weight. | | Amount. |
| | | | | | | | | Cwts. | Qrs. | Lbs. | Rate. | £ s. d. |

In addition to the process of receiving, examining, and, if need be, rejecting stores supplied by vendors, **Return to store of surplus material.** and of issuing material for manufacture, the storekeeper will receive from the foremen or overlookers material which has been drawn out in excess of the quantity required, or the scrap material from some manufacturing operation. It is not unusual for material drawn out of store in excess of requirements to remain in the factory, and be used for the next similar stock order, but this procedure is open to serious objection, and the desirability of sending the **Stores Debit Note.** material back to the store with a Stores Debit Note (Specimen No. 32) cannot be too strongly urged. Not only does the direct return of

## SHOP RETURNS BOOK. 57

material to store prevent waste or improper appropriation, but it conduces to the localization of the cost of manufacture. If the surplus material is not so treated, the stock order, in respect of which it has been withdrawn, will appear at a higher cost than it should, while the work upon which such material is used without warrant will have the benefit without being charged. In either case the records of cost of production are fallacious, and loss may thus be incurred.

The Stores Debit Note having been posted by the storekeeper in a Shop Returns Book (Specimen No. 33),
**Shop Returns Book.** is forwarded to the counting-house, where it is dealt with as recording a factor in the prime cost, as will be explained in the following chapter.

SHOP RETURNS BOOK.—SPECIMEN No. 33.

| Date. | No. of Stores Debit Note. | Returned by | Articles. | Order No. or job for which Articles were withdrawn. | Dimensions. | No. | Weight. | | | Rate. | Amount. | | | Stores Ledger Folio. |
|---|---|---|---|---|---|---|---|---|---|---|---|---|---|---|
| | | | | | | | Cwts. | Qrs. | Lbs. | | £ | s. | d. | |
| | | | | | | | | | | | | | | |

The entries in the Shop Returns Book are (as shown in the Diagram II.) posted to the Dr. side of the Stores Ledger.

There is another source from which a storekeeper may receive goods, viz., from the warehouse of the firm.
**Transfers between store and warehouse.** These cases are likely to be exceptional, and can be more fully and conveniently dealt with in the subsequent chapter on Stock. At pre-

sent it suffices to say that the departmental adjustments of accounts, as between the warehouseman in charge of the manufactured commodities or stock, and the storekeeper in charge of the raw material of trade or stores, are made by means of a Transfer Book. The nature of this book will be explained later, and it is necessary to anticipate the subject at this stage only to the extent of stating that so far as the storekeeper is concerned, the items in the Transfer Book are posted in the Stores Ledger to the Dr. side of the respective accounts in the same way as other receipts of material.

The storekeeper may sometimes have sent into store, material which has been recovered from plant and buildings, or parts of machinery which is no longer serviceable. In these cases the stores accounts will be debited in the usual manner, by means of a Plant Recovered Note. These transactions in relation to the capital account of the business will be dealt with in the chapter on Fixed Capital (Chapter VI.).

In conclusion we refer to Diagram II. as giving a complete view of the books and forms mentioned in this chapter, and their connection with each other, and also to the remarks in the Introductory Chapter to the effect that the books are suggested more for the purpose of showing what the transactions are than to give stereotyped forms which shall be applicable to every case without modification. It will be manifest that, provided the principles are not lost sight of, there is every scope for further division, or greater concentration, as may be required.

Showing the Relation of the F

(*The numbers, where*

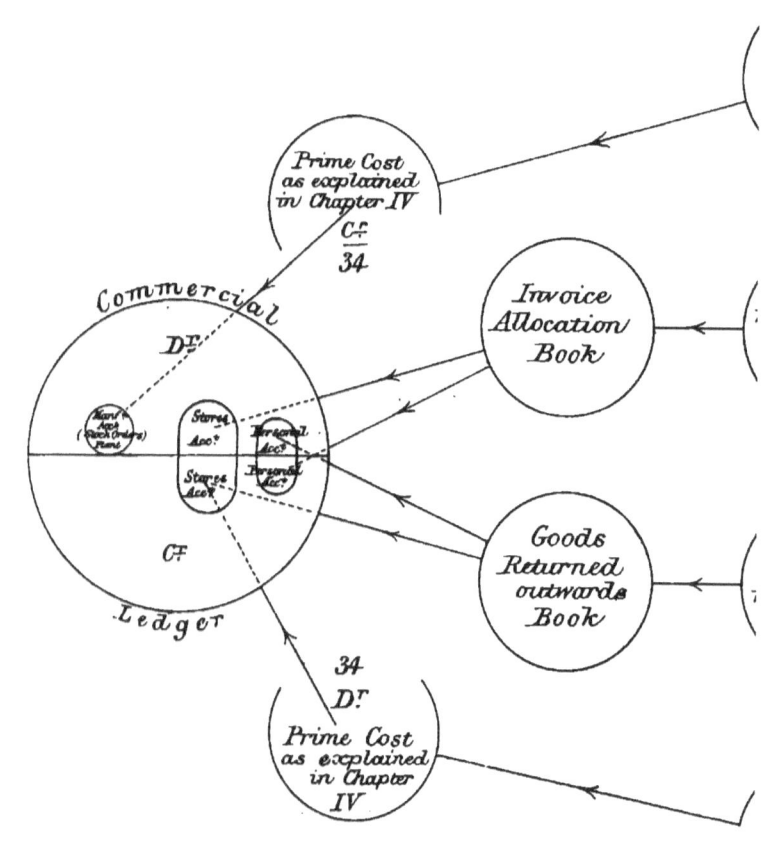

f II.

'ORMS USED IN CONNECTION WITH STORES.

*pond to the specimen rulings.)*

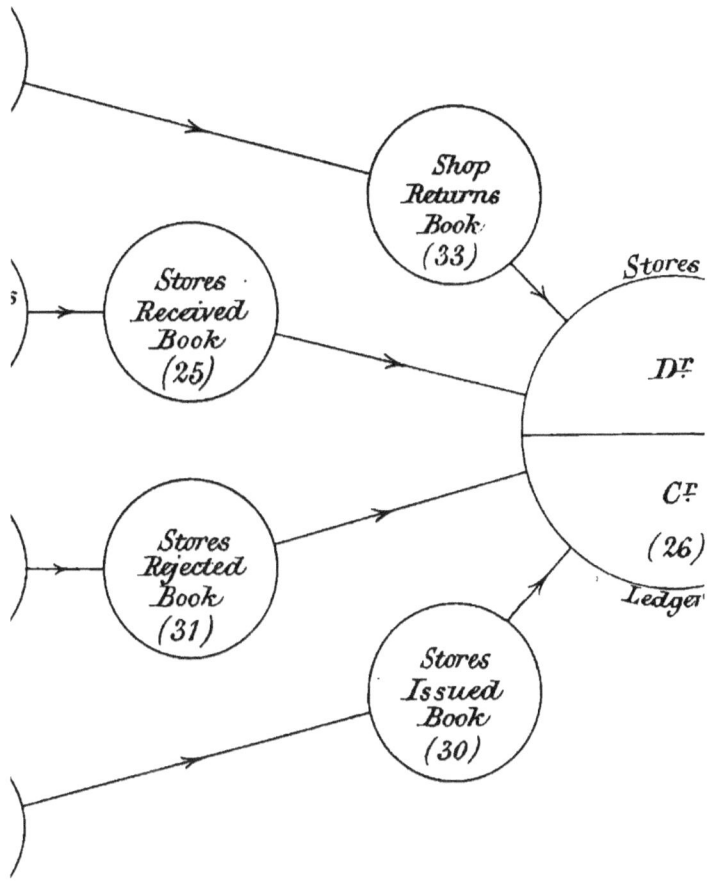

*and between Store, Warehouse, and Plant, being contingent
ients, are not shown on this diagram.*

## CHAPTER IV.

### PRIME COST.

**Recapitulation.** IN the two preceding chapters we have dealt with the routine appertaining to the payment of wages and to the receipt and issue of material. We now propose to indicate the manner in which these two so far independent factors may together with other, but subsidiary, items of expenditure be united, with the view of obtaining a record of the prime cost of production.

As in the next chapter we shall deal with the distribution of commodities, we do not here refer to the question of stock, except in so far as it has a bearing upon the question of stores and cost of production generally. We think it well at the outset, however, to explain that, so far as the manufacture of commodities is concerned, we regard it as axiomatic that all articles, whether produced in pursuance of an order received from outside or in anticipation of future demand, should be booked as if they were intended to constitute part of the standing stock in trade.

**Distinction between stock and stores.** This method of describing as stock all articles manufactured necessarily involves a clear distinction being drawn between material used in manufacture, and the manufactured article which is the product of the expenditure of labour and material, or in other words between stores and stock. The utility may not be at once apparent of passing through the Stock Books, as distinguished from the Stores Books, commodities manufactured to supply a definite order, and which are not likely to form part either of the normal, or of the exceptional, stock in hand of the business, but it will be evident that there is a distinct advantage in treating all orders to manufacture in the same way, whether they be of a special or of a standard nature. Confusion necessarily arises if part of an order for articles made in the factory is treated as if supplied from stock, and another part as if supplied from stores. We recommend therefore that all material and parts required for purposes of manufacture should be withdrawn from store and charged to their proper stock orders. If the article has in reality been manufactured in execution of a customer's order, it should be withdrawn from the warehouse, and credited to the stock accounts, by the process described. The importance of uniformity in the treatment of the orders to manufacture is particularly exemplified when the cost of any article which has not previously been made, or made only to a very limited extent, is to be taken as the basis of calculations in view of more extensive transactions. A simple illustration will make our meaning clear. If a customer orders a suite of furniture to be made, we maintain that instead of the expense of executing that order being debited to one account, the several pieces making up the suite should be made to separate stock orders. In this way, while the cost of each individual piece would be known, the cost of the suite would be ascertainable by aggregating the costs of all the pieces, whereas, if the whole of the labour and material required for the production of the complete suite had been indiscriminately charged to one account, it would be difficult to determine the cost of any one piece, should it be required to be replaced or to be manufactured more extensively. It is well to exclude all probable sources of error, and this is largely promoted by clearly recognising the distinction we have drawn between material and manufactured goods.

It having been decided to manufacture certain commodities, the instruction referred to in the preceding chapter (Specimen No. 28) will be issued. One part of the form will convey to the manager or foreman instructions to manufacture; the other is for the use of the clerk keeping the Prime Cost Ledger, and will be taken by him as an advice of what orders are in hand and as a guide to the folios to be reserved for such orders in his Ledger. The counterfoil, to which the forms can be attached upon the completion of the order, will be retained by the principal.

<small>Initiatory stage of manufacture.</small>

It is not only important to know the cost of each individual article produced, but equally so to ascertain the cost of any particular part, or of any particular process of manufacture. Localization of cost should be carried as far as possible, so that the varying rates of realizable profit on parts may be known, and the pressure to minimise cost of production be applied in the right direction. The tendency to the specialization of labour has grown, and is growing, with the extension of the factory system, and the economy thereby induced can only be rendered thoroughly effective by a complete analysis of cost. As a well-known writer on this subject has said, "One of

<small>Cost of each separate process.</small>

the first advantages which suggests itself as likely to arise from a correct analysis of the expense of the several processes of any manufacture is the indication which it would furnish of the course in which improvement should be directed. If any method could be contrived of diminishing by one-fourth the time required for fixing on the heads of pins, the expense of making them would be reduced about thirteen per cent.; whilst a reduction of one-half the time employed in spinning the coil of wire out of which the heads are cut, would scarcely make any sensible difference in the cost of manufacturing the whole article. It is therefore obvious that the attention would be much more advantageously directed to shortening the former than the latter process." *

The fact that since this passage was written the process of manufacturing pins has been shortened and cheapened in the way referred to, serves to bring into clear relief the truth of the principles enunciated by the writer.

A description of the advantages arising out of the division of labour from a politico-economical point of view does not fall within the scope of this treatise. Suffice it, therefore, to say that these advantages have been ably expounded by Mr. Babbage, and more recently by Professor Alfred Marshall and Mary Paley Marshall.†

The principles applied in these pages to recording the cost of production of any article are equally applicable

---

\* "On the Economy of Machinery and Manufactures," by Charles Babbage. 4th edition. London: John Murray.

† "The Economics of Industry," by Alfred Marshall and Mary Paley Marshall. London: Macmillan & Co.

to recording the cost of any or all of the parts of that article. Either subsidiary stock orders numbered consecutively may be passed, or the stock orders for parts may be denoted by the number of the original stock order and a letter of the alphabet. Upon the completion of all the component parts, the accounts in the Prime Cost Ledger of the various stock orders could be grouped, so as to constitute in the aggregate the cost of the complete article.

For the purpose of booking, with the minimum amount of labour, the expenditure upon small parts, a nomenclature enabling every detail to be accurately and concisely defined by a symbol is exceedingly desirable. It would, on account of the labour involved, be an obstacle to the consummation of the object in view if the size, purpose, and relative position of every separate piece had to be expressed in ordinary language. It affords us much satisfaction, therefore, to be able to reproduce, through the courtesy of the author, a paper by Mr. Oberlin Smith,* in which is suggested a symbolic nomenclature of the kind required, if the system of taking out prime cost is to be applied to small parts.

*Nomenclature of parts.*

As all labour and material are not directly spent in the manufacture of articles, but are partly devoted to the maintenance, repair, or renewal of buildings and plant, and to other objects, it becomes necessary to record the expenditure upon the subsidiary purposes, and to provide for its distribution over the various manufacturing operations or orders.

*Expenditure other than for manufacturing purposes.*

Whilst the cost of setting tools and machinery to per-

\* See Appendix A.

form certain operations may be charged directly to the stock order on which the expenditure is incurred, labour or material spent in the erection of additional, or the maintenance, repair, and renewal of existing machinery, cannot directly be apportioned to any particular stock order, as the cost of the use of machinery in every case is mainly dependent on the life of the machine. The considerations which should determine the amount to be debited to any stock order on this account will be most conveniently referred to in the chapter on Fixed Capital in connection with the question of the charges to be made for the use of machinery. Another direction of expenditure lies in the maintenance, repair, and renewal, extension, or erection of workshops, warehouses, stores, and other buildings. All such expenditure may be recorded under general or various sub-headings in the Prime Cost Ledger, or preferably in separate Plant and Buildings Ledgers. The utility of these separate ledgers will be more apparent after a perusal of the chapter already referred to. The recurring items in the maintenance of machinery and buildings may, so as to insure the maximum amount of localization of cost, receive a distinctive series of numbers, and thus the cost for each floor, or wing of a building, may be ascertained. For expenditure on such recurring items, the manager of the works may receive standing instructions; but expenditure on special items of maintenance, or of additions to fixed capital should be estimated for, and authorised in the same way as the execution of Stock Orders (pages 51-2). When in order to proceed with a certain stock order, it is necessary to make special tools to enable the work to be done, it will be convenient to charge all time and

*Localization of maintenance expenses.*

material spent on their production to a tool order bearing the same number as the stock order number to which the goods are to be made. The cost of these will be recorded in the same way as the cost of other tools, but the number to which they are made serves to identify them, and as they have been made specially, and may or may not be again required, their cost must be considered in the determination of the selling price of the articles, the manufacture of which necessitated their production.

Other channels of expenditure, such as the wages of foremen, gatemen, timekeepers, and others who are engaged in supervision, or in the distribution of stores, in keeping time records, or in any similar work, may be recorded either under a special heading for General Charges in the Prime Cost Ledger, or in a Factory General Charges Book. As will be explained in a subsequent paragraph, these expenses may at any period be summarised, for the purpose of distributing their incidence, and a ratio established between them and the total amount of the wages expended on the various orders during the same period.

*Factory general charges.*

We are now able to consider the functions of the book in which the prime cost of any manufactured article is aggregated and recorded, with a view of obtaining the cost of production. This book is the Prime Cost Ledger, in which are summarised the allocation of wages spent on manufacture, alluded to in Chapter II., and the various warrants for stores used in manufacture, alluded to in Chapter III. In addition to these two channels of expenditure it will be observed

*Prime cost ledger.*

that the Prime Cost Ledger (Specimen No. 34), provides a column for sundry disbursements which are allocated to the respective working or stock orders, from the Petty Cash Book or its equivalent, or from any similar source. The items of sundry disbursements thus charged are of course debited to manufacturing account in the Commercial Ledger, a process which is facilitated by means of inserting in the Petty Cash Book a column showing the accounts to which the items in question are chargeable.

These records having been made, the clerk keeping the Prime Cost Ledger will periodically draw out the total of his debits for the given period, under the various heads for the several items of wages, materials, and miscellaneous disbursements. He will see that in the case of wages the total agrees with the amount of the wages account in the Commercial Ledger, which also coincides with the totals of the Wages Book for the corresponding period.  He will also see that in the case of materials his totals agree with the credits to the stores account in the Commercial Ledger for stores issued, cognizance being taken of the credits in the Prime Cost Book; the corresponding debits to stores represent the materials drawn out to a given number but not consumed on that job, and therefore returned to store, as explained later.  As regards petty cash, the totals should agree with the debit through the commercial books to sundry disbursements on manufacturing account.

Before explaining the credit side of the Prime Cost Ledger it will be well to give a specimen of the form **Stock debit note.** called a Stock Debit Note (Specimen No. 35), which is made out concurrently with the sending of commodities into stock.

STOCK DEBIT NOTE.—Specimen No. 35.

| No._____ Sent into warehouse____189 | | | | | No._____ Sent to and received by warehouseman _____189 Stock Received Book folio_____ | | | | | | | |
|---|---|---|---|---|---|---|---|---|---|---|---|---|
| Article. | No. of Order. | No. or Weight. | | | Article. | No. of Order. | No. | Weight. | | | Rate. | Amount. |
| | | No. | Cwts. | Qrs. | Lbs. | | | | Cwts. | Qrs. | Lbs. | | £  s.  d. |

Sent into warehouse by_____    Received into warehouse by_____

This form, which may have a counterfoil, or be copied by means of carbon sheets, emanates from the leading hand in the shop. The monetary column is filled in by the prime cost clerk from such data as he has in his Ledger, and the contents of the note are entered by him on the credit side of that book. The warehouseman or other person in charge of the manufactured goods will, in his turn, make the necessary entry **Stock re-** in the Stock Received Book (Specimen No. **ceived book.** 36), which bears the same relation to stock that the Stores Received Book, explained in Chapter III., bears to stores.

STOCK RECEIVED BOOK.—SPECIMEN No. 36.

| Date. | No. of Stock Debit Note. | No. of Order. | Article. | Dimensions. | No. | Weight. | | | Rate. | £ s. d. | Stock Ledger folio. |
|---|---|---|---|---|---|---|---|---|---|---|---|
| | | | | | | Cwts. | Qrs. | Lbs. | | | |
| | | | | | | | | | | | |

**Stock** The entries in the Stock Received Book **ledger.** are posted in the Stock Ledger (Specimen No. 37).

Besides the Stock Debit Note there are posted to the credit side of the Prime Cost Ledger the credit notes (referred to in Chapter III.) for surplus or scrap raw material returned to the store.

**Balancing** By abstracting the credit side of the Prime **prime cost** Cost Ledger periodically, it will be seen that **ledger.** it agrees with the amounts passed through the commercial books to the debit of stock account (and credit of stock orders account) for stock sent into warehouse, and with the debit to the stores account (also credited to stock orders account) for surplus or scrap material returned from the workshops. The amounts standing to the debit of uncompleted stock orders in the Prime Cost Ledgers will represent the cost price value, *pro tanto*, of the goods in course of manufacture, and will agree with the balance on manufacturing account in the Commercial Ledger.

It is evident that (in the event of any of the articles made to a Stock Order being appropriated before completion of all) unless **Balances on stock orders.** the pricing of the Stock Debit Notes for articles sent into the warehouse is deferred until the whole of the order is completed, which would involve needless inconvenience, some element of error may enter into the calculations made by the prime cost clerk as to the cost at which the commodities are being manufactured. This contingency will only arise where it is found inexpedient to proceed concurrently with the manufacture of all the articles comprised under the Stock Order No. to which labour and material are being booked. That is to say, while all materials required for the manufacture of a given number of articles may have been withdrawn from store, it may be found necessary to complete and consign to the warehouse a smaller number of the articles first, instead of proceeding, *pari passu*, with the manufacture of all. But this difficulty is more apparent than real, inasmuch as any debit or credit balances which, upon completion of an order, may be found to exist, can be adjusted by the commodities last produced to that order being taken into stock, at prices slightly reduced or increased to the extent of the difference; or the balance may, if preferred—and must necessarily if all the articles comprised in the Stock Order are disposed of—be at once carried to the debit or credit of trading account, or the sales account of any particular branch.

Having shown that all the direct channels of expenditure can be summarised in the Prime Cost Ledger, it **Allocation of factory general charges.** remains for us to show how the incidence of the shop expenses capable of direct apportionment, and the cost of factory superintendence, may, by means of a Prime Cost Journal, be fairly distributed over the various manufacturing operations.

In some establishments the direct expenditure in wages and materials only is considered to constitute the cost; and no attempt is made to allocate to the various working or stock orders any portion of the indirect expenses. Under this system the difference between the sum of the wages and materials expended on the articles and their selling price constitutes the gross profit, which is carried in the aggregate to the credit of profit and loss, the indirect factory expenses already referred to, together with the establishment expenses and depreciation, being particularised on the debit side of that account. This method has certainly simplicity in its favour, but a more efficient check upon the indirect expenses would be obtained by establishing a relation between them and the direct expenses. This may be done by distributing all the indirect expenses, such as wages of foremen, rent of factory, fuel, lighting, heating, and cleaning, &c. (but not the salaries of clerks, office rent, stationery and other establishment charges to be referred to later), over the various jobs, as a percentage, either upon the wages expended upon the jobs respectively, or upon the cost of both wages and materials. If, for example, the aggregate wages expended in manufacture during the year amount to £10,000, and the materials consumed to £6,000, while the indirect factory expenses amount to £800, then if the latter are to be distributed in proportion to the wages paid, the cost of each job would be increased by 8 per cent. of the labour expended upon it; or if the indirect expenses are to be distributed in proportion to the first cost in wages and materials, each job would be increased 5 per cent. of the amount of its prime cost. In the majority of undertakings it will prove a sounder method to charge the indirect expenses as a percentage upon the *direct wages* only, and not upon the material, for the prices of some raw materials fluctuate so very widely that the other method described would render the cost comparisons of one year with another to some extent misleading.

In referring to the allocation of factory expenses in proportion to the labour expended upon the articles manufactured, we have taken the *amount* of wages paid as one of the factors in the equation, but it is quite conceivable that the wages paid respectively for skilled and for unskilled labour may vary so largely as to make such an equation fallacious in particular cases, though quite correct in the aggregate; and that a relation based upon the *time* during which the labour is employed, instead of upon the *amount* of the wages paid, would be more accurate. For instance, unskilled labour of a given amount is employed during a much longer period than skilled labour of the same cost, and it does not appear quite reasonable that it should bear only the same proportionate charge for superintendence, lighting, fuel, and such other expenses, the amount of which is greater or less according to the time the workmen are employed. When dealing with the question of the depreciation of plant, we shall have occasion to describe in some detail a method of distributing the incidence of a charge over a variety of objects upon the time basis, and that method can, if it be adopted for the purpose for which it is primarily devised, also be made applicable to the case under consideration.

The item of Depreciation may, for the purpose of taking out the cost, simply be included in the category of the indirect expenses of the factory, and be distributed over the various enterprises in the same way as those expenses may be allocated; or it may be dealt with separately and more correctly

## ALLOCATION OF INDIRECT EXPENSES.

in the manner already alluded to and hereafter to be fully described. The establishment expenses and interest on capital should not, however, in any case form part of the cost of production. There is no advantage in distributing these items over the various transactions or articles produced. They do not vary proportionately with the volume of business. A large increase in the value of orders received would not necessitate a like augmentation of the office staff, nor would a sudden and serious falling off in trade enable a firm to effect an immediate or proportionate reduction of general expenditure. The establishment charges are, in the aggregate, more or less constant, while the manufacturing costs fluctuate with the cost of labour and the price of material. To distribute the charges over the articles manufactured would, therefore, have the effect of disproportionately reducing the cost of production with every increase, and the reverse with every diminution, of business. Such a result is greatly to be deprecated, as tending neither to economy of management nor to accuracy in estimating for contracts. The principals of a business can always judge what percentage of gross profit upon cost is necessary to cover fixed establishment charges and interest on capital.

Owing to the diversity of methods of dealing with the matters under review, it has not been thought advisable to complicate the Prime Cost Ledger (Specimen No. 34), by the addition of one or more columns to meet the requirements of any particular mode of allocating the indirect expenses, especially as no difficulty will be experienced in adapting the book to suit any system of taking out the cost that may be decided upon, provided the methods described in the previous chapters of booking the cost of labour and material be adhered to. In most cases, however, it will suffice simply to enter the percentages of indirect factory expenses and depreciation at the end of each account in the Prime Cost Ledger. The latter, when embracing any items of indirect expenses, should strictly be termed the Cost Ledger; but to avoid unnecessary complexity, we have adhered to the term Prime Cost Ledger, even when the book so referred to registers cost of production and not merely prime cost.

# DIAGRAM III.

### Showing the Relation of the Books and Forms used in connection with Prime Cost.

*(The numbers, where shown, correspond to the specimen rulings.)*

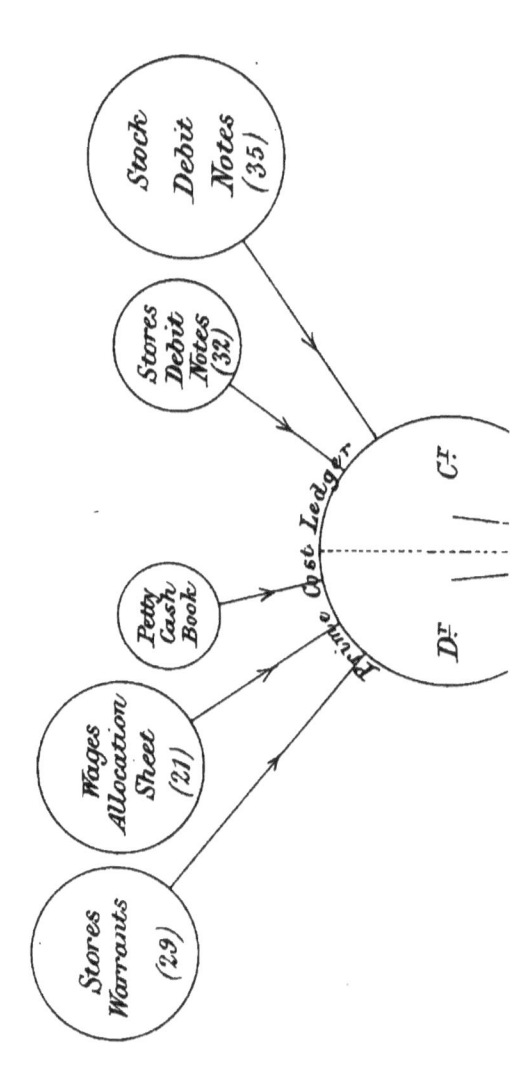

Commercial Ledger

Dr. Stock Orders, Plant Accts, Buildings, etc.

Cr. Stores Acct, Wages Acct, Petty Cash acct, etc.

[Between pp. 74 and 75.

## CHAPTER V.

### STOCK.

WE are now prepared to consider the final stage of the book-keeping appertaining to the production and disposal of commodities. In the preceding chapters we have endeavoured to show as comprehensively as the limits of this treatise admit, the manner in which the multifarious transactions relating to the purchase and expenditure of labour and material are recorded in the factory books, and how those books assimilate to the commercial accounts of a manufacturing business.

*Résumé.*

In the second chapter we have dealt with the employment of labour and the payment of wages; in the third, with the purchase and consumption of materials or stores, and in the fourth, with the prime cost of the manufactured article called stock.

In this chapter we propose to trace the records which should be made in connection with the realization or distribution of the manufactured commodities. This branch of our subject embraces, so far as book-keeping is concerned, four distinct classes of transactions:—

*Manufactured commodities. Four classes of transactions.*

1st. The transfer of the finished article from the factory as stock into the warehouse.

2nd. The return of articles from the warehouse to the factory for the various reasons which will be mentioned.

3rd. The sale or distribution of stock or manufactured articles.

4th. The return to the warehouse of stock issued, or of stock which was originally sold, but has been rejected or returned by the purchaser.

All these transactions have to be traced into both the stock books and the commercial books, and in the case of the sale of stock, and in that of the return or rejection of the stock issued or sold (the third and fourth classes respectively), the book-keeping is complicated by the fact that each transaction has to be brought into the Commercial Ledger at two different prices. That is to say, when an article is sold it is taken out of stock at the price at which it stands in the Stock Ledger, and, in the case of an absolute sale, it is invoiced to the customer at a higher price. As a consequence, a sale will appear in the Commercial Ledger to the debit of a customer, and to the credit of trading account, at the invoice price; whilst by a corresponding but independent process of book-keeping, the same transaction will appear at a lower or the cost price to the credit of stock account, and to the debit of trading account. The converse will be the case when stock is taken back from a customer and sent into the warehouse, the price at which it is credited to a customer's account not generally being the same as that at which it is debited to stock. In this way the stock account in the Ledger always shows the aggregate cost value of the stock-in-trade; the personal accounts, the amount received, or to be received, by the

*Two prices for same article.*

*Stock Books.*

firm in respect of the goods sold; while the trading account (which is debited with the items representing the value of goods issued from stock, and credited with the sales debited to personal accounts) will bring out the difference between the cost price and the selling price, which will be carried to profit and loss account, as the gross profit or loss. This process is effected by entering the sales in two separate books corresponding to each other, the one dealing with the invoice prices, the other with the cost prices, and likewise by entering the stock returned to warehouse in two books which perform similar functions for the cancelled sales.

The two books in the first of these cases would be respectively the customary Day Book, containing records of the invoices rendered, and the Sales Analysis Book, containing records of the stock requisition forms (Specimen No. 43) for stock issued. In the case of the return of stock the two books would be respectively the Sales Cancelled Book, containing records of the credit notes sent to customers, and the Stock Returned by Customers Analysis Book, containing records of the Stock Returned Debit Notes (Specimen No. 44). The advantage of carrying out the suggestions made in the introductory chapter as to distinguishing books by their bindings will be manifest in the case of these four books. The Stock Issued Book and the Stock Returned Book are kept by the warehouseman, whilst the corresponding books, viz., the Sales Analysis Book, and the Sales Cancelled Analysis Book, are kept in the counting-house.

In giving titles to some of these books we do so primarily with the desire to indicate their functions, and, *Titles of books.* as already stated, the forms suggested must be taken to mark the transactions which it

# STOCK.

is necessary to register rather than the outlines of the records.

The four counting-house books are posted to the Ledger; the Day Book individually to the debit of personal accounts, and collectively, by means of the Journal, to the credit of trading account; the Sales or Stock Issued Analysis Book to the credit of stock account and to the debit of trading account; the Sales Cancelled Book, the converse of the Day Book, individually to the credit of personal accounts, and collectively to the debit of trading account; and the Sales Cancelled or Stock Returned Analysis Book, being the converse of the Sales Analysis Book, to the debit of stock account and to the credit of trading account. (See Diagram IV.)

*Posting of stock accounts in Commercial Ledger.*

We can now proceed to a detailed examination of the book-keeping relating to this branch of our subject.

The first class of transactions is, as before stated, the transfer of the finished article from the factory to the warehouse. The form by means of which this transfer is effected has already been referred to as the Stock Debit Note (Specimen No. 35).

*First class of transactions: Factory to warehouse.*

This debit note is entered by the warehouseman in the Stock Received Book (Specimen No. 36), and posted to the debit of the Stock Ledger.

*Stock Received Book.*

Upon reaching the counting-house the Stock Debit Note is entered to the credit of the Prime Cost Ledger, as explained in the preceding chapter, and the total debits to stock, in respect of articles finished, are journalised month by month to the debit of stock account in the Commercial Ledger.

*Stock Debit Note.*

With regard to the return of articles from the ware-

## TRANSFERS BETWEEN STORE AND WAREHOUSE. 79

house to the factory, which constitutes the second class of entries, it may be remarked that although the articles made for stock may all have been manufactured under the personal supervision of those who will more or less be connected with their sale, and questions as to the rejection of goods are not likely to be nearly as numerous as if the articles had been made by an outside contractor, still the question of the return to the factory of finished articles, either on account of bad workmanship or alteration of design, may arise and must be provided for in the book-keeping. In all such cases it will be desirable to send into the store, at the time the finished article is refused as stock, a Transfer Note (warehouse debit to store).

*Second class of transactions: Warehouse to factory.*

*Rejected stock.*

In Specimen No. 38 this Transfer Note is shown with a counterfoil; but a duplicate, by means of carbonised paper, can also be used.

The articles rejected as stock having been sent into store, it will remain to be determined what alterations, if any, are to be made. Should further labour or material be required to be expended, a new stock order will be issued, and the recording of the expenditure will follow the routine laid down for the manufacture of commodities.

The adjustments as between warehouse and store are best recorded by the warehouseman and storekeeper entering the transfer notes in a Transfer Book. The warehouseman will, of course, enter on the credit side of his Transfer Book the credits to his stock for the finished articles forwarded by him to the store. On the debit side of his Transfer Book he will enter the debit notes received by him from

*Transfer Books and Notes.*

the storekeeper for articles transferred from store to warehouse. The latter class of entries arise out of transactions of a retail character, which in the case of a manufacturing concern may be taken to be exceptional, but as the existence of such a combination is possible, the concluding part of this chapter will be devoted to its consideration.

<small>Retail transactions.</small>

With regard to the Transfer Books, the entries made by the storekeeper will, naturally, be the reverse of those made by the warehouseman, and the store will be credited with all articles forwarded to, and debited with all articles received from, the warehouse. The two Transfer Books will therefore always balance. It will be necessary to post the items in the Transfer Books to the Stores and Stock Ledgers respectively, so as to bring out the correct balances, not only as between these Factory Ledgers in the aggregate, but also as between the individual Stores and Stock Ledger accounts.

The specimen ruling of the Store Transfer Book (No. 39) will, with necessary alteration of headings, apply equally to the Warehouse Transfer Book of which it is the counterpart.

Whilst we think it necessary to state in full detail the principles to be remembered in dealing with these transfers, it must in any individual case be left to the accountant to determine whether the circumstances of any particular business admit of the functions of the two Transfer Books being adequately performed by one book.

The transfer notes between store and warehouse, and *vice versa*, can, if the nature and extent of the transactions warrant it, when forwarded to the countinghouse, be entered in a Transfer Analysis Book, and the

TRANSFERS BETWEEN STORES AND WAREHOUSE. 81

TRANSFER NOTE (WAREHOUSE TO STORE).—SPECIMEN NO. 38.

Returned from Stock to Stores, _____ 189__ No. _____

| Article. | Why transferred | Original Order No. | No. | Weight. | | | Rate. | Amount. | Folio. |
|---|---|---|---|---|---|---|---|---|---|
| | | | | Cwts. | Qrs. | Lbs. | | | |

_____ Warehouseman. _____ Storekeeper.

STORE TRANSFER BOOK.—SPECIMEN NO. 39.

DR. For the undermentioned goods transferred from stock. By the undermentioned goods returned to stock. CR.

Returned by _____ Received by _____

| Date. | Transfer Note No. | Article. | Supplied by | Why returned. | No. | Weight. | | | Rate. | Amount. | Folio. |
|---|---|---|---|---|---|---|---|---|---|---|---|
| | | | | | | Cwts. | Qrs. | Lbs. | | | |

G

82                    STOCK.

Journal entry for the commercial books be based on the amounts so arrived at; or, if the transactions are few they can be recorded from the Transfer Notes into the Journal direct.

The book-keeping in relation to the sale of commodities may be said to be initiated by the receipt of an **Sale of commodities.** order, and as regards the factory, will hold good whether received direct from a customer or through an agent. The questions of discount or commission which present themselves in the latter case are transactions which it is necessary to deal with in the commercial books only. The principal of the firm, if he accepts the order, will probably initial it by way of authorising its execution. Should the stock of the commodities ordered be exhausted, or should the articles require to be specially manufactured, an order to manufacture the given or a larger number of similar articles for stock, should, as already explained, be passed concurrently with the acceptance of the order.

The customer's order having been accepted may be **Orders Received Book.** registered in an Orders Received Book (Specimen No. 40). The order may then be passed on for execution to the warehouseman, who should have received a standing instruction to return all orders to the counting-house when completed. If it be thought unadvisable to pass the original order (which may contain references to the terms of payment, commission, or discount, &c.) to the warehouseman, he may **Advice to warehouseman.** be provided with a copy or with extracts from the Orders Received Book, or a special form of advice may be sent to him.

## STOCK ISSUES.

### ORDERS RECEIVED BOOK.—Specimen No. 40.

| Date of Order. | Order No. | Customer's Order No. | Ordered by | Nature of Order. | Delivery Requested by | Date Supplied. | Date Invoiced. | Remarks. Enter in this column route by which goods are to be sent, also marks for cases, and any special instruction. |
|---|---|---|---|---|---|---|---|---|
|   |   |   |   |   |   |   |   |   |

The advice may take the form shown in Specimen No. 41.

### Specimen No. 41.

Stock Requisition and Advice to Warehouseman———189——No.——

Please forward the undermentioned Articles to——— at———    Customer's Order No. or Reference———
per——— Marking Cases ———    Stock Requisition Book, fol.———
                                Sales Analysis Book, fol.———

| Article, with Full Description. | No. | Weight. | | | Rate. | Amount. | Remarks. |
|---|---|---|---|---|---|---|---|
|   |   | Tons. | Cwts. | Qrs. | Lbs. |   |   |
|   |   |   |   |   |   |   |   |
| Ready for dispatch———189 ———Warehouseman. Approved——— |   |   |   |   |   |   |   |

The form could also be made to serve the warehouseman as a Stock Requisition, and it would, in that case, **Stock Issued Book.** be entered in the Stock Issued Book. In cases in which the goods are ready for shipment, and further instructions have to be given concerning them, the form would be sent to the counting-house, and if the dispatch of the goods be approved, the requisition could be returned to the warehouseman with the information inserted thereon. It is necessary to follow this routine if, as is sometimes the case, it is not possible for the customer to give complete instructions as to forwarding when placing the order, or if special arrangements as to payment before, or on, delivery have to be made.

STOCK ISSUED BOOK.—SPECIMEN No. 42.

| Date. | Sale Order No. | Article. | No. | Weight. | | | Rate. | Amount. | Ledger Fol. |
|---|---|---|---|---|---|---|---|---|---|
| | | | | Cwts. | Qrs. | Lbs. | | | |
| | | | | | | | | | |

Should the original order be sent to the warehouseman the stock may be drawn from the warehouse, according to the conditions of the business, either by posting the order direct to a Stock Issued Book (Specimen No. 42), or by means of a Requisition Form (Specimen No. 43).

*Stock Requisitions.*

The requisition would likewise require posting in the Stock Issued Book. But in this case that book would require, for purposes of reference, an additional column for the No. of the Stock Requisition. The Stock Issued Book will of course in turn be posted to the credit side of the Stock Ledger.

Where there is a great variety in the articles sold, or multiplicity of transactions, it may be desirable that the

## SALES ANALYSES.

**Daily return of stock issued.** counting-house should be kept regularly informed of the stock issued each day. This can be done either by alternate Stock Issued Books being kept, so that the previous day's record of stock issued may be always at the counting-house and the current day's record in the warehouse; or the warehouseman may send in every morning a Stock Sent Away Form, showing all stock that has been issued during the previous day, giving in each case the Order No., so that the clerk invoicing may immediately turn to the Orders Received Book and see the stipulations and conditions on which the order was accepted.

It is also desirable that the amount of the stock requisitions should, in the counting-house, be entered and **Stock Issued or Sales Analysis Book.** analysed in a Stock Issued or Sales Analysis Book. This book (of which we do not give a specimen ruling, as it pertains to the office) should be so ruled that the various items entered from the Stock Requisitions might be analysed under the various branches of the business. The aggregate of the totals of such branches would necessarily agree for any given period with the totals of the stock requisitions for the same period, and necessarily also with the totals of the warehouseman's Stock Issued Book.

The fourth class of transactions referred to at the outset **Fourth class of transactions: Stock back to warehouse.** of this chapter involve the procedure to be adopted in the factory with regard to stock which is rejected or returned, after having been sent out for inspection or approval, on loan, hire, or exhibition.

**Stock Returned Debit Note.** The warehouseman on receipt of such goods will make out a Stock Returned Debit Note (Specimen No. 44).

## STOCK REQUISITION FORM.—Specimen No. 43.

| Article. | Sale Order No. | No. | Weight (Cwts. Qrs. Lbs.) | Article. | No. of Sale Order. | No. | Weight (Cwts. Qrs. Lbs.) | Rate. | Amount. | Stock Issued Book Fol. |
|---|---|---|---|---|---|---|---|---|---|---|
| | | | | | | | | | | |

No.——   No.——   Entered in Stock Issued Book, Fol.——
Requested from Warehouse ——— 189 .   Requested and Received from Warehouse ——— 189 .

Requested by ———   Received by ———

## STOCK RETURNED DEBIT NOTE.—Specimen No. 44.

| Article. | Sale Order No. | No. | Weight (Cwts. Qrs. Lbs.) | Rate. | Amount. | Article. | Sale Order No. | No. | Weight (Cwts. Qrs. Lbs.) | Rate. | Amount. | Fol. |
|---|---|---|---|---|---|---|---|---|---|---|---|---|
| | | | | | | | | | | | | |

No.——   No.——
Stock returned to Warehouse ——— 189 .   Stock returned to Warehouse ——— 189 .

Returned by ———   Received by ———

# CONCENTRATION OF BOOKS.

**Stock Returned by Customers Book.** These Stock Debit Notes will be duly entered in a Stock Returned by Customers Book (Specimen No. 45), which will be posted to the debit side of the Stock Ledger.

STOCK RETURNED BY CUSTOMERS BOOK.—SPECIMEN No. 45.

| Stock Debit Note. | Article. | Sale Order No. | No. | Weight. | | | Rate. | Amount. | Stock Ledger Fol. |
|---|---|---|---|---|---|---|---|---|---|
| | | | | Cwts. | Qrs. | Lbs. | | | |
| | | | | | | | | | |

**Stock Returned Analysis Book.** The Stock Returned Debit Notes are in the counting-house entered and analysed in a Stock Returned by Customers Analysis Book, which is the converse of the Sales Analysis Book already referred to. As an instance of the possibility of concentrating the books, whilst adhering to the principle laid down, it is well to mention that in an establishment where there is little variety in the articles sold, or where the sales are not numerous, the stock requisition might form the basis on which goods are invoiced from the counting-house. In such cases the Sales, or Day Book (debit to customers), should be provided with a column in which could be entered against the respective invoices the stock price of the article as shown on the requisitions. It would thus be possible to obtain by the mere process of addition the total amount of the invoices rendered, and the value at stock prices of the articles so invoiced, thus obviating the need for a Stock Issued (or Sales) Analysis Book.

**Concentration of Books.**

## STOCK.

Equally the Stock Returned Debit Note for goods returned by customers might be treated as the basis for the credit note to the customer, and the Sales Cancelled Book (credit to customers) might be so ruled as to show the invoicing, as well as the cost rates of the stock invoiced and returned, thus obviating the need for a Stock Returned Analysis Book. This concentration of books does not prevent an analysis being made of the invoices or credit notes, nor of the corresponding stock requisition or stock debit notes, under departmental or other heads.

In the case of articles sent out for inspection or on loan, it is very desirable that whilst a *pro forma* invoice, **Goods on loan.** at the normal selling price, should accompany them, the articles should, until an order is received or a definite sale effected, be dealt with in the Sales or Day Book at their stock prices as the invoicing rates. We cannot too strongly insist on the great disadvantage of treating loaned goods in any other way. The system of showing book profit on these transactions is most fallacious, and so misleading that fortunately it cannot be resorted to extensively, or for any length of time, without causing serious embarrassment. It is evident that the stock loaned is not likely to be a constant quantity or of fixed value, and that if treated in precisely the same way as goods sold the profit and loss account for any period is unduly increased at the expense of other periods.

It will be manifest that the entries in the Stock Ledgers consist of debits for stock received from the **Recapitulation.** factory and for stock returned from customers, and of credits for stock sold to customers and stock transferred to store; and that the balances under the various headings will show the number and the value of the various articles on hand, and the aggregate of such balances the total value of the stock, which should of course agree with the total value shown by the Commercial Ledger, and with the results of the surveys.

It will be obvious also that, as regards the counting-house, the various items in the Day Book and the Sales Cancelled Book being posted respectively to the debit and credit of the various purchasers, the sum of such items will in the case of the Day Book give the total credit to trading account for invoices rendered, and in the case of the Sales Cancelled Book the debit to trading account for stock returned by customers.

The total of the Sales Analysis Book gives the amount which through the Journal is debited to trading account and credited to stock, and the total of the Stock Returned by Customers Analysis Book gives the amount which through the Journal is debited to stock and credited to trading account.

When these entries have been made the trading account will show with absolute exactness the gross profit realised, and the balance of the stock account (after journalising the debits to stores and credits to stock on account of transfers) will be the value of the stock ready for sale. The relation of these various transactions one to another will be made manifest by Diagram IV.

In an earlier part of this chapter we alluded to the possible combination of a manufacturer not only distributing the commodities he manufactured, but also, in exceptional cases, acting as a retailer of goods produced by others.

**Further notes on retail transactions.**

It must not be overlooked that there is a fundamental distinction in these transactions. If a manufacturer acts to any extent as a retailer, it will be well to draw a clear line of demarcation between his two branches of business. In the retail branch, which is an ordinary buying and selling, and not a manufacturing, business, the book-

**Retail warehouse.** keeping is such as properly pertains to the counting-house. In an extensive business where this combination obtains, it may be desirable to establish a separate retail warehouse as distinguished from the warehouse which is the repository of the manufactured stock.

If, however, the retail transactions are exceptional, and their volume does not warrant in practice any absolute division from the manufacturing portion of the business, the articles which are bought merely for reselling, and on which neither time nor material are expended in the factory, can be dealt with either as stores or, as we think preferably, as stock.

If they are dealt with as stores, the procedure followed is that described in Chapter III. for the receipt and

**Store method.** withdrawal of material, save that the stores warrants for articles withdrawn for sale, when they reach the counting-house, should be entered in a Stores Sold Analysis Book, the items in that book being posted to the debit of a stores sold, retail trading, or other similar account in the Commercial Ledger, the credit to that account being the total of the invoices rendered to customers for goods retailed, and the balance representing the gross profit or loss on that branch of the business.

If articles for retailing be treated as stock, the invoices from the vendors can be passed to the warehouseman,

**Stock method.** the procedure being similar to that for invoices for stores purchased, and which is

## MANUFACTURE OF PARTS.

fully described in Chapter III. In this case the invoices would, in the counting-house, be debited to stock account; and the withdrawal of the articles from the warehouse would entail a credit to the same account, and a debit to a retail trading account; this latter account being credited with the value of the invoices rendered to customers. So far as the factory is concerned, the invoice for goods purchased would pass through the Stock Received Book (Specimen No. 36) into the Stock Ledger, and the Stock Requisition (Specimen No. 43) would pass into the same ledger through the Stock Issued Book (Specimen No. 42).

An equally effective and probably more simple method would be to pass all such exceptional items from store into stock by means of the Transfer Book (Specimen No. 39). By these means all invoices for goods purchased would pass through the commercial books to the debit of one account, namely, that of stores, and conversely all invoices for goods sold would pass through the same books to the credit of the trading account, the debit to this account arising at the stock value of the goods.

We have already referred to the desirability of localising the cost of articles, and shown that the cost of parts of articles can be ascertained by following the routine described, but in concluding this chapter it will be well to refer briefly to those cases in which parts complete in themselves but subsidiary to the manufacture of other articles, are produced in greater quantity than is required for the manufacture of the articles of which they form part. This increased production may be due to certain parts being of a more permanent type than others and added to stock with less risk of obsolescence, to their greater production at one time cheapening the cost, to their being parts which may be required for renewals or repairs, to there being a dearth of work in any particular branch of the factory, or to other special causes.

Whatever be the reason for their production, all expenditure on them should be recorded as in the case of a manufacturing or stock order, and the routine described* should be followed. As the parts made in excess of the number required for the manufacture of the finished article will all have been charged to stock by means of the Stock Debit Note, those intended for sale will remain in the warehouse and be duly recorded in the Stock Books, while those parts intended for future use in manufacture will require to be transferred to the store by means of the Transfer Books, and will be drawn out of store by means of Stores Warrants like all other material required for manufacture.

\* Chapter III., p. 52.

DIAGI

SHOWING THE RELATION OF THE BOOKS A?

(*The numbers, where shown, co*

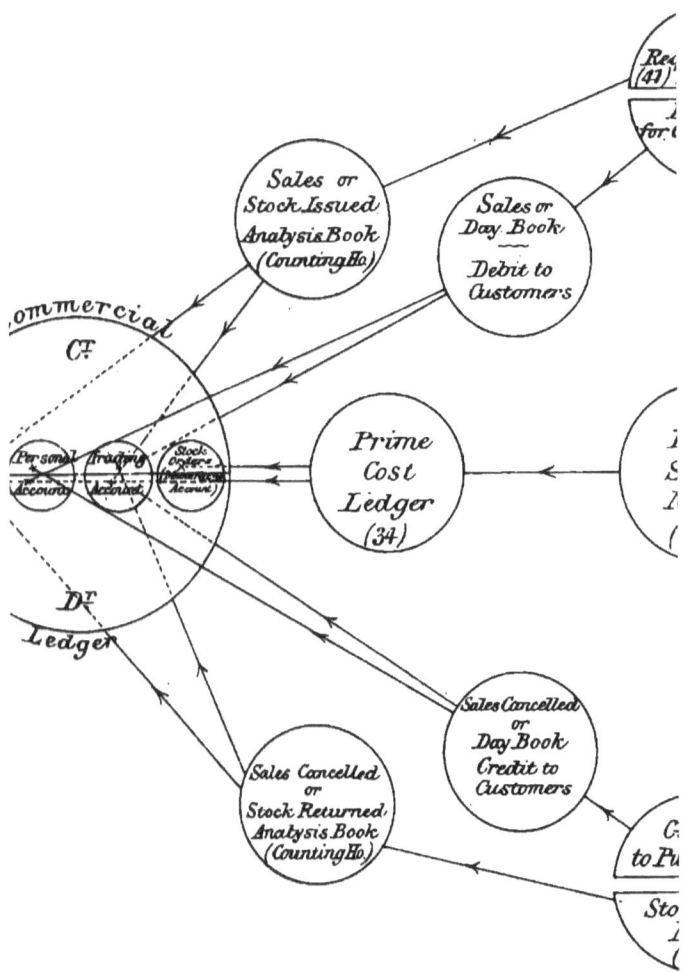

*The Transfers between Warehouse, Plant, and Si
and purely departmental adj*

IV.

FORMS USED IN CONNECTION WITH STOCK.

pond to the specimen rulings.)

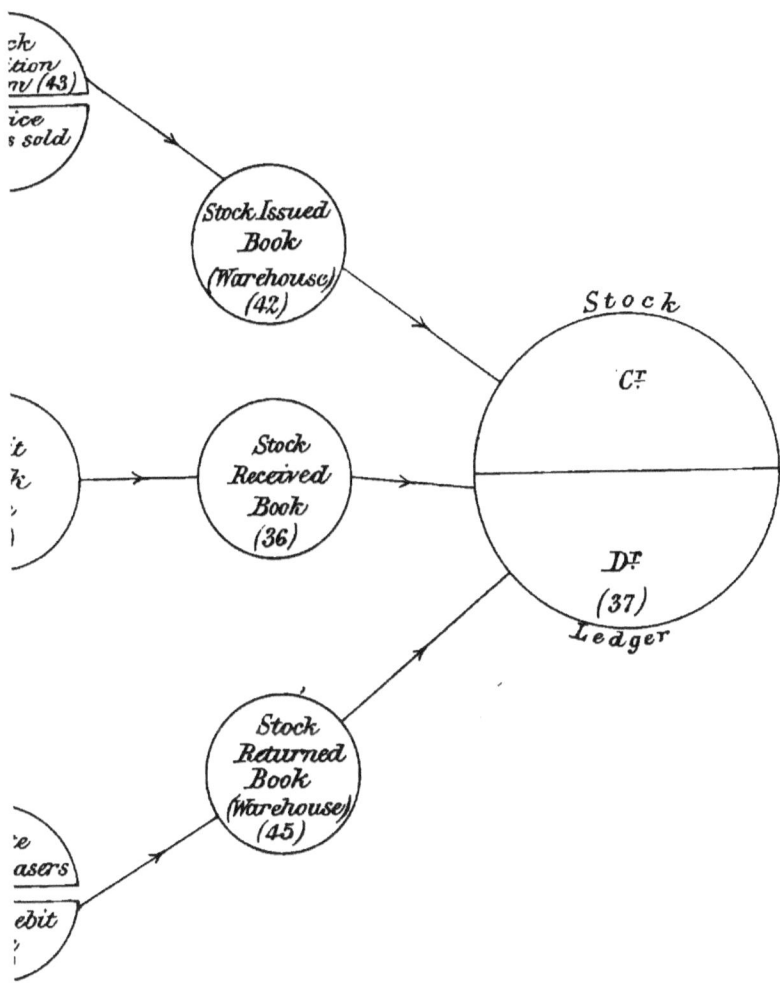

, and between Store, Warehouse, and Plant, being contingent
ments, are not shown on this diagram.

## CHAPTER VI.

### FIXED CAPITAL.

**Definition of fixed capital.** IN this chapter we purpose dealing with the accounts pertaining to instruments of production of a more or less permanent character. These, as Mill pointed out, "produce their effect, not by being parted with, but by being kept; and the efficacy of which is not exhausted by a single use. To this class belong buildings, machinery, and all or most things known by the name of implements or tools. The durability of some of these is considerable, and their function as productive instruments is prolonged through many repetitions of the productive operation. . . . . Of fixed capitals, some kinds require to be occasionally or periodically renewed. Such are all implements and buildings; they require, at intervals, partial renewal by means of repairs, and are at last entirely worn out, and cannot be of any further service as buildings and implements, but fall back into the class of materials. In other cases, the capital does not, unless as a consequence of some unusual accident, require renewal; but there is always some outlay needed, either regularly or at least occasionally, to keep it up."\*

\* "Principles of Political Economy." J. S. Mill. Book I., chap. vi., par. 1. Longmans. London.

Inasmuch as the profit or loss of an undertaking for any period is not simply the difference between the **Depreciation.** receipts and expenditure during that period, nor the current value of plant always the amount which has been paid for or expended upon it, the question of the depreciation of factories and of plant must be regarded as a factor of paramount importance in the determination of the lucrativeness or otherwise of a business, and in the valuation of properties. Many different views prevail as to the best way of **Variety of views on the** dealing with these questions, and owing to **subject.** trades and processes of manufacture varying widely it is impossible to lay down invariable rules. Questions as to the particular practice to be followed in any individual case must, to a large extent, be left to the judgment of those most intimately acquainted with **Exhaustive** the conditions of the business. A cursory **examination of subject** examination of the fundamental principles **impossible.** to be observed, and a review of the chief methods in vogue, in regard to "writing off," will not be out of place in a work dealing with Factory Accounts.

The question of maintenance is very closely associated with that of depreciation, and there are four fac-**Four factors** tors which enter into the determination of **in the determination of** any rule for arriving at the deterioration **depreciation.** which has taken place: 1st. The cost of an object, be it a building, machine, or other asset. This may be either the cost price or, in the case of the transfer of an established business, the estimated value of the object. 2nd. Its estimated tenure of life, regard being had to its functions and the conditions under which they are performed. 3rd. The extent and value of the renovation or restoration received by it from time to

## VARYING VIEWS ON DEPRECIATION.

time. 4th. Its residual value, either as scrap or as an implement which, though possibly applicable to other uses, is no longer fit for its original purpose.

Whatever rule is determined upon, it is important that it should be consistently adhered to for a term of years in order to avoid the accounts of particular years being treated abnormally, which, in the case of joint-stock companies, whose shares are constantly changing hands, would lead to much injustice being done to individual proprietors.

*Rule adopted should be adhered to.*

In many manufacturing businesses the rough-and-ready method is adopted of charging to capital, in addition to the original cost, the cost of all renewals, alterations, and extensions of buildings and machinery; and of debiting profit and loss account in respect of depreciation with a percentage of the total amount in the Ledger under those heads. In some cases even the current repairs are charged to capital, in which case a proportionately larger percentage should be written off annually for depreciation.

*The rough-and-ready method.*

*Repairs charged to Capital.*

In some undertakings no cognizance is taken of depreciation in the accounts. In the case of most railways, for instance, the deterioration of the plant is taken to be adequately and fairly provided for by the current expenditure upon repairs and renewals which is debited to revenue account. This practice is defended on the ground that by the very nature of railway property the repairs and renewals must be at least equivalent to the depreciation, and that an effectual check against any starving in maintenance is furnished by the certificates which the heads of the spending departments periodically give as to the con-

*Depreciation and current expenditure.*

dition of the permanent way, plant, tools, buildings and rolling stocks. Such a system may possibly prove unobjectionable when, an undertaking having been in operation for a number of years, a relation has been established between the expenditure and the deterioration; but there is always a danger that during its earlier years, when expenditure for repairs, renewals, and extensions is not so imperatively called for as after some years of working, the profit and loss account is not adequately debited with depreciation; and even if this be done, there is nevertheless the risk of the accounts of particular years being prejudiced. It is doubtful, also, whether the desire to maintain dividends and to show an average expenditure per mile does not lead, in the case of railway companies, to only such work being done during the half-year as will approximately cost the average amount. In the case of water companies likewise, the item of depreciation forms no part of the accounts. But water companies are allowed by Act of Parliament to place to a reserve fund surplus profits to the extent of one-tenth of the capital, and as renewals are paid for out of profits, it follows that any abnormal charges in respect of deterioration are indirectly met out of this reserve fund; consequently during the first years of working, when renewals and repairs are insignificant, and no reserve fund has been formed, there is a tendency to relieve revenue account of its fair proportion of wear and tear. In general, it may be stated that unless considerable additions and extensions are constantly made, the system of charging to revenue all repairs and renewals, instead of depreciation, will not in the long run prove satisfactory. Unless adequate provision is made a time

*Case of water companies.*

must arrive when, owing to some of the machines and tools having become wholly obsolete, or the lease of buildings having expired, an amount will have to be debited to Profit and Loss which should in strictness have been borne by previous years. In this way some years are made to appear unduly lucrative at the expense of others, instead of the depreciation being charged equally over the number of years constituting the life of the object, in direct proportion, if possible, to the actual deterioration incurred in each period. This is always at least approximately possible. In certain cases only can maintenance be said to balance depreciation. " In any particular building, machine, or appurtenance, decay or wear of some sort must take place in the course of time, and repairs, in order to compensate fully for the decline in value, must take the form of renewal. This being the case, the absolute replacement of some portion of the plant every year may thus maintain an average aggregate value. In only two kinds or classes of plant, however, can such an exact balancing of loss by repairs and renewals be ventured on; one, where the plant wears out so quickly as to need replacement at short intervals, affording constant proof, by the mere continuance of working, that not only the earning power of the factory is maintained, but also the capital value; and in a second class, that of undertakings so large and permanent as to afford a wide average of deterioration and renewal over the whole plant."* It is worthy of note, that even in the

*Distribution of depreciation over life of object.*

*Only in certain cases that maintenance balances depreciation.*

\* "The Depreciation of Factories, and their Valuation." Matheson. Spon: London.

two cases referred to Mr. Matheson speaks with some hesitancy, and alludes to such a mode of procedure as a venture. There is always the risk of plant gradually becoming obsolete, even though kept in good repair.

In some instances the amount charged to revenue account for depreciation is a fixed sum, or an arbitrary percentage on the book value. In others it varies according to the business effected, or to the balance remaining to profit and loss account, or is regulated by the desire of the firm or its managers, either on the one hand to show a large profit, or on the other to add to the stability of the concern. In comparatively few establishments, however, is the endeavour made to systematically approximate the amount charged to revenue for depreciation to the actual deterioration which has taken place, and still more rarely is it attempted, when the actual depreciation has been ascertained, to allocate it to the various departments in which it has been incurred, or better still, to the various operations which have been carried on.

*Other methods in vogue.*

*Only rarely that actual deterioration is charged.*

The direct way of determining the depreciation or appreciation of the assets of an undertaking would *prima facie* appear to be by means of a re-valuation of all the properties at periodical times. In the case of trades in which the wear and tear of plant is proportionate to the work done this course would have the advantage of charging fairly the deterioration due respectively to a period of brisk trade and to a time of depression, by manifesting in the former period a greater degree of wear and tear due to a larger volume of business, or to time contracts compelling a resort to overtime ; while in periods of

*Periodical valuation the direct method.*

depression a smaller amount would obviously be chargeable for depreciation, much of the machinery and plant having probably stood idle. But this method would in the majority of trades lead to such enormous fluctuations in the profit and loss account, especially if the periodical valuation was based upon the market price of the properties, and not simply upon their value as integral portions of a " going concern," that, except in a few trades, it would be impracticable. This would especially be the case when raw material, subject to market fluctuations, formed a large proportion of the plant and stock-in-trade. Such a method would often be a fruitful source of confusion and error. In short, to write off only such portion of the cost of the plant as represents the apparent deterioration that has taken place would be fallacious. Although machinery or plant may show no signs of diminished value or loss of earning power, yet its term of life and its value in the market must be lessened by lapse of time. A periodical survey of all buildings, plant, &c., is, however, very important, and would serve, if no other purpose, as a very valuable check upon the system of calculating depreciation that may be adopted.

*Disadvantages of this method.*

*To write off only manifest deterioration fallacious.*

Moreover, a periodical valuation of the assets, as the basis of a depreciation rate, raises considerations of very great significance, such as the question of the interdependence of the revenue and capital accounts, and the question of how far a loss or profit on capital account, *i.e.* a diminution or increase in the realizable value of any of the assets, should affect the profit and loss account. These are points of considerable interest, and deserve to be dis-

*Profit and loss on capital.*

cussed to a greater extent than the limits of this work will permit. The following observations by a leading authority on the law relating to joint-stock companies are, however, very apposite :—

"Capital may be lost in either one of two ways, which may be distinguished as loss on capital account, and loss on revenue account. If a ship-owning company's capital be represented by ten ships with which it trades, and one is totally lost and is uninsured, such a loss would be what is here called a loss on capital account. But if the same company begins the year with the ten ships, value say £100,000, and ends the year with the same ten ships, and the result of the trading, after allowing for depreciation of the ships, is a loss of £1,000, this would be what is here called a loss on revenue account.

*Opinion of Mr. Buckley.*

"Where a loss on revenue account has been sustained, there is of course no profit until that loss has been made good either by set-off of previous undivided profits still in hand, or by profits subsequently earned. But until the case of Neuchatel Asphalte Company the question was open whether a company under the Companies' Acts, which has lost part of its capital by loss on capital account, can continue to pay dividends until the lost capital has been made good.

"The case of Neuchatel Asphalte Company has now shown the true principle to be, that capital account and revenue account are distinct accounts, and that for the purpose of determining profits you must disregard accretions to or diminution of capital. Suppose I buy £100 Consols at 97, and at the expiration of a year they have fallen to 94, is my income £3 or nothing? If nothing, then if at the expiration of the year they had risen to par, my income would by parity of reasoning have been £6, not £3. Is the result affected by the question whether at the end of the year I am or am not about to sell my Consols? Suppose a tramway company lays its line when materials and labour are both dear, both subsequently fall, and the same line could be laid for half the money, and as an asset (independent of deterioration from wear) would cost for construction only half what it did cost. Is the company to make this good to capital before it pays further dividend? If so, then if the cost of materials and labour had risen after the line was laid might not the company have divided as dividend this accretion to capital? Upon such a principle dividends would vary enormously, and sometimes inversely to the actual profit of the concern.

"If revenue account be treated as a distinct account, these difficulties disappear, and subject to the difficulty which must be encountered of discriminating between revenue charges and capital charges, a safe and intelligible principle is arrived at. The creditors of the company are entitled to have the capital account fairly and properly kept; but, they are not entitled to have losses of capital on capital account made good out of revenue. It is no doubt true, that before arriving at revenue at all there are payments which must be made good to capital, on account of capital wasted or lost in earning the revenue. For instance, in the common case of leaseholds, which are a wasting property, the whole of the rental will not properly be income; in the case of colliery properties, the difference between the price at which the coal is sold, and the cost of working and raising it, will not all be income, for there must also be a deduction made in favour of capital representing the diminished value of the mine by reason of its containing so many less tons of coal; in the case of a tramway company, you will not have arrived at net profit before you have set apart a sum to make good deterioration. But when all proper allowances have thus been made in favour of capital, the balance is revenue applicable for payment of dividend."*

We take it that the practical view must be that, if at a given period the realisable value of all properties, after liquidating all liabilities, is in excess of the amount of subscribed capital, such surplus, whether the gain has been made on capital account or revenue account, constitutes profit; while the amount by which realisable assets fall short of the liabilities including the subscribed capital must be considered as loss. So long as a business is a going concern, it would probably be inadvisable for the revenue account to serve the purpose of an index of the fluctuations in the market value of the constant or fixed assets essential to the carrying on of the business, for in such a case the revenue account would oscillate perhaps from a large profit one year to large loss in the next, although the nature, volume, or lucrativeness of the current business may have remained without abnormal change. With a view, however, to providing against an eventual loss in the realisation of an asset the value of which tends to decrease, it would probably be judicious to establish a sinking fund by debiting the revenue account annually with a fixed percentage to cover all

*The practical view of the matter.*

*Profit and loss account.*

*Sinking fund.*

* "The Law and Practice under the Companies Acts." H. Burton Buckley, M.A., Q.C. London: Stevens and Haynes.

contingencies. This would also apply to plant which is not worn out before it is replaced by improved machines.

**Reserve fund.** Similarly, if the asset is improving in value we do not recommend that the increment should be placed to the credit of profit and loss account, but that it be debited to the account of that asset and credited to a reserve fund opened to provide for any future diminution in its market value. If a sinking fund has been established, the amount might be placed to its credit.

Although it does not seem practicable to lay down a universal rule that a loss on capital must be made good before further dividends, if earned on profit and loss account, can be distributed, there are cases in which it is obviously necessary that this set-off should be made. In the case already referred to of the Snipping Company with ten ships, one of which is uninsured and is lost, inasmuch as the profit and loss account has not,—from what must be assumed to be motives considered as economical,—been charged with the cost of insurance, and the risk of loss has been undertaken, that account must therefore bear the loss when it is incurred. Thus the account named would bear the total loss of one ship and the depreciation of the remaining nine.

**Insurance against losses.** Indeed, a loss which might have been provided against by insurance, or one which underwriters will not insure, except at a premium so high that the firm prefers incurring the risk to paying the cost of insurance, seems always a fair charge to profit and loss account if it has not been provided for by the creation of a reserve fund. The question of whether or not the properties of a firm are insured against fire has always to be considered in estimating the liabilities of a concern, and the few notes in the Appendix on the law relating to Fire Insurance will probably not be considered out of place in view of the importance of the subject in relation to the accounts of a factory. It will be observed that there are many points connected with effecting an insurance, the non-observance of which may invalidate the policy, and that a firm may, by omitting to carefully examine the conditions of their fire policies, find when part of their buildings or stock has been destroyed by fire, that they are not entitled to indemnification by the insurers.

The Income Tax Acts also have an important bearing upon the depreciation and valuation of assets, and no method of dealing with large assets of fluctuating value should be decided on without due regard being had to the provisions of these Acts. Under these Acts everything in the nature of property, which produces, or is capable of producing, or itself consists in, an annual income or revenue, is subject to income tax. It is not, however, in all cases necessary that a profit shall in any one year actually be made out of property, in order that its owner may become liable to the duty in that year. Under Schedule D duties are charged in respect of any trade, manufacture, adventure, or concern in the nature of trade not contained in any other schedule of the Act, and the duty is (save in a few exceptional cases) computed on a sum not less than the full amount of the balance of the profits or gains upon a fair and just average of three years.

<small>Income Tax Acts.</small>

Any increase in the value of an asset, if credited to profit and loss account, would be subject to assessment, but it by no means follows that the converse holds good, and that losses will be allowed. For this reason a firm

## DEPRECIATION ON THE LIFE BASIS.

may suffer appreciable loss, to the extent of the duty paid, by their profit and loss account reflecting the variations in the value of their assets. A firm may for one or more years, as a result of a general rise in prices, have realised large surpluses on their properties, and although they may have paid full duties in respect of such gains, it is not certain that in the event of a reaction of prices, and their losing as much as they had gained or more, such loss would be allowed to form a factor in the determination of the average profit. It is hard to say what is an allowable deduction from profit, inasmuch as the statutes for the most part define the term negatively by enumerating the deductions which are not allowed. In Appendix B will be found a synopsis of those sections of the Income Tax Acts which have a bearing upon the matters here discussed.

The ideally best way of arriving at a depreciation rate is to take the *life* of a building or machine as the basis of the rate, modified by the other three before-mentioned factors, viz. original cost plus interest, renovation, and residual value. This method, however, is attended with some difficulties in the case of properties whose tenure, unlike that of leases, is not well defined; and also in the case of a newly established business, to which the experience of other establishments has but little application. Should the nature of any particular business be such that the life of the appurtenances can be estimated with tolerable accuracy, this plan will be found to be the most scientific in its operation; for although the life of an asset may vary with the surrounding conditions, in the same way as the life of a horse depends, *cæteris paribus,*

*The life of an object the best basis.*

*Difficulties of this method.*

*Advantages of this method.*

upon the character of the work it performs, yet, if once the life of an asset has been determined—and a manager of a business which has been established a year or two should be able to frame at least an approximate estimate of the durability of the various implements he employs—there will be no difficulty in allocating the depreciation to the various processes. If, for example, **Example of** it is settled by experience that the life of a **the method.** horse employed in drawing a tramcar is three years, and that the number of journeys performed per diem is ten, then $\frac{1}{365 \times 10 \times 3}$ of the cost price, less the residual value of the horse (the cost of maintenance being charged to running expenses), will be the charge per journey for depreciation, and the same rule applies if, instead of horses, steam engines are employed, or if the rolling stock and plant are dealt with.

Leases for a definite number of years, or in perpetuity (leases renewable from time to time at the option of the **Leases afford** lessee may be regarded as leases in perpe- **good** tuity) afford a very appropriate illustration of **illustration.** the rule of basing the depreciation rate upon the life of the object. In Appendix F is reproduced a **Amortiza-** table recommended by Mr. Pixley,* which **tion table.** will be found useful in calculating the amount to be set aside annually in order to amortize a lease, and the table is also applicable to other properties, the life of which has been determined. Inasmuch as the table takes cognizance, and correctly so, of interest at the various rates shown, the Ledger account of the asset in question should be debited each year with interest at a given rate and credited with the corresponding

* "Auditors: their Duties and Responsibilities." By F. W. Pixley. 3rd edition. London: Effingham Wilson.

amortization rate shown in the table, until, at the expiration of the tenure of the lease or other object, the whole of the amount at which it stood in the books has been exhausted. The hypothetical Ledger account **Example.** (Specimen No. 46) of a five years' lease from the time of its purchase to its expiration will serve to elucidate the table referred to. The purchase price of the lease is taken at £4,500, and interest is calculated at 5 per cent. per annum, which is of course debited to the lease account, and credited to profit and loss account, a correspondingly larger amount being debited to that account in respect of amortization.

The amount which is debited each year to profit and loss account by way of amortization, is arrived at by dividing the amount of the purchase price, £4,500, by 4·329, the latter being the number in the 5 per cent. column of the table on the line corresponding to five years, that being the number of years over which the amortization is to extend, and crediting the account each year with the amount so written off.

The question of the liabilities of lessees for dilapidation and waste of premises calls for some consideration **Dilapidations.** in reference to the matters here referred to. If, under the conditions of the lease, dilapidations require to be made good upon its expiration, provision for the necessary outlays should periodically be made, preferably through a sinking fund. A convenient summary in tabulated form of the law relating to dilapidations will be found in Mr. Fletcher's book on the subject.*

In many businesses it may be found advisable, for the purpose of estimating depreciation, to divide the objects

* "Dilapidations." Banister Fletcher. London: Batsford.

108  FIXED CAPITAL.

LEDGER ACCOUNT, SHOWING THE AMORTIZATION OF A FIVE YEARS' LEASE.

(See page 107.)

SPECIMEN NO. 46.

| DATE. | DR. | £ | s. | d. | DATE. | CR. | £ | s. | d. |
|---|---|---|---|---|---|---|---|---|---|
| Of purchase | To Cash, Purchase price | 4500 | ,, | ,, | | | | | |
| End of 1st Year | To Interest at 5 % | 225 | ,, | ,, | End of 1st Year | By Profit and Loss Depreciation | 1039 | 10 | ,, |
| | | 4725 | ,, | ,, | | By Balance | 3685 | 10 | ,, |
| | | | | | | | 4725 | ,, | ,, |
| End of 2nd Year | To Balance | 3685 | 10 | ,, | End of 2nd Year | By Profit and Loss | 1039 | 10 | ,, |
| | ,, Interest at 5 % | 184 | 5 | 6 | | ,, Balance | 2830 | 5 | 6 |
| | | 3869 | 15 | 6 | | | 3869 | 15 | 6 |
| End of 3rd Year | To Balance | 2830 | 5 | 6 | End of 3rd Year | By Profit and Loss | 1039 | 10 | ,, |
| | ,, Interest at 5 % | 141 | 10 | 3 | | ,, Balance | 1932 | 5 | 9 |
| | | 2971 | 15 | 9 | | | 2971 | 15 | 9 |
| End of 4th Year | To Balance | 1932 | 5 | 9 | End of 4th Year | By Profit and Loss | 1039 | 10 | ,, |
| | ,, Interest at 5 % | 96 | 12 | 3 | | ,, Balance | 989 | 8 | ,, |
| | | 2028 | 18 | ,, | | | 2028 | 18 | ,, |
| End of 5th Year | To Balance | 989 | 8 | ,, | End of 5th Year | By Profit and Loss | 1038 | 17 | 4 |
| | ,, Interest at 5 % | 49 | 9 | 4 | | | | | |
| | | £1038 | 17 | 4 | | | £1038 | 17 | 4 |

# CLASSIFICATION OF ASSETS.

into classes, for although the general result of the business operations during a given time may be normal, yet by dealing separately with the depreciation of each class of appurtenances it may be found that some of the departments show abnormal results. A general rate of depreciation may lead principals to neglect what may, comparatively, be more profitable operations; or to push a department of the business which, if it bore its full proportion of depreciation, would yield less than the average rate of profit.

*Classification of assets.*

This separation of departments is the more desirable as the same method of allocation will obviously not apply to *loose* plant and tools and to plant and tools which are fixed.

*Fixed plant and loose plant.*

Although it is theoretically possible to frame a scheme which would enable the cost of the loose plant and tools to be allocated to the various working orders, it would generally in practice be found not worth while to carry it out. The cost of these tools is comparatively small, even in a large establishment, and under ordinary circumstances the depreciation of loose plant, tools, and patterns on any one working order so slight, that it simply suffices to book all these implements out to a loose tools and plant account. In many cases it is usual at the end of the year to allocate this account to profit and loss, and in others, to value at that period, and to write off to profit and loss account through a shop expenses or similar account 25 to 35 per cent. of the total of the book value of the loose tools and plant in use. It is evident, however, that if desired, some percentage ratio could be established between this loose tools and plant account and the amount spent on wages, and thereby the cost be allocated to any given working number; or the loose plant and tools might be re-valued annually, the difference in value being carried to profit and loss, and the cost of their repair during the year charged direct to profit and loss account. In either of these cases the amount charged to profit and loss could be allocated in common with the indirect factory expenses as a percentage upon wages as previously explained.*

The same methods are applicable to the patterns account, save that it may be desirable to place a heavier depreciation rate on patterns, as a provision against their becoming obsolete.

With fixed plant and machinery the case is different. **Plant Ledger.** Each distinctive object should be numbered, and the original value of the same entered in a Machinery or Plant Ledger (Specimen No. 47).

All material issued for, or time spent on, any machine

* Chapter IV.

## EXPENDITURE ON PLANT.

**Expenditure on Plant.** or implement belonging to this category should be duly recorded in the same way as the materials and wages consumed in the manufacture of stock are booked (see Chapters II., III., IV.). The expenditure on Plant may be carried direct to the Plant Ledger, in which case the total amount of wages, material, and sundry disbursements, in the Commercial Ledger would, for any given period, agree with the totals under similar heads debited to the Plant Ledger and the Prime Cost Ledger combined, or the expenditure may appear in the Prime Cost Ledger to the debit of the respective Plant Working Nos. Instead, however, of the latter accounts in the Prime Cost Ledger being credited by a transfer to stock, as in the case of a Stock Order, they would be credited by a transfer to plant—a Plant Debit Note (Specimen No. 48) being the

PLANT DEBIT NOTE.—SPECIMEN No. 48.

Machines at Work in _____ Shop on _____ 189 .

| No. of Machine. | Employed on Order No. | Time Working between. | To be filled in by Time Clerk or Machine Checker. | | |
|---|---|---|---|---|---|
| | | | Time Working. | Rate to be Charged. | Amount. |
| | | | | | |

medium. In either case the cost of, or expenditure upon, plant is carried to the debit of the Plant Ledger, and the process by which the amount written off in respect of depreciation is credited to the Plant Ledger, and debited to the Working Orders, which are to bear a proportion of the depreciation, is as follows. The time clerk or an assistant, or in a large establishment a machine checker, should obtain each day from the foreman of the shop an account of the time during which **Plant** each machine was working, and to what **return.** order number the work was done. At the end of each week, or other convenient period, a Plant Return (Specimen No. 49), should be compiled and sent to the counting-house.

PLANT DEBIT SUMMARY.—SPECIMEN No. 49.

Return of Machinery at Work and Charges to be made for ——— ending ——— 189 .

| No. of Machine. | Order No. | Order No. | Order No. | Order No. | Order No. | Order No. | Total for each Machine. |
|---|---|---|---|---|---|---|---|
| | | | | | | | |
| Total for each Order | | | | | | | |

The life of a machine, or, in other words, the number of working hours a machine will last, being known, **Original** the principal or some other competent person **cost and** **life of** would establish a ratio per hour between the **object.** original cost of the implement (modified by maintenance and residual value) and such working hours or life of the implement. On this basis a voucher would be prepared in the counting-house for passing through the Prime Cost Ledger the debits to the various working orders, and the credits to machinery accounts under the various numbers of the machines; or, in place **Plant** of these vouchers, it may be found conve- **Journal** nient to enter all the details through a Plant

Journal. The machine being worn out, it should be sent into Stores with a Plant Recovered Note showing **Residual Value.** its estimated realizable value, at which amount it becomes a credit to capital. Any credit or debit balance that remains on the book value of the machine may, as thought desirable, either be carried to profit and loss account or to a reserve fund, should one have been opened to provide against loss on plant. Should it be found that the machine is likely to have a longer life, or to give more working hours than was expected, the rate per hour may of course be diminished, so that future working orders may not be debited at a higher rate than is necessary, and equilibrium on the debit and credit sides of the Plant Ledger be produced.

This system of charging depreciation on the basis of the life of a machine and its cost would equally **Cost of fuel.** apply to the apportionment of the cost of engines and boilers and of the fuel used in them. The total number of hours the machinery is running will, the life and cost of the engines and boilers having been ascertained, enable working orders to be charged with their proportion of cost. Similarly, the aggregate number of hours the machinery is in use being known, the division of the fuel account for that period by this number will give the cost of fuel per hour for each working order.

When depreciation is thus allocated to the various processes in the carrying out of which the plant has **Effect on profit and loss account.** been deteriorated, it will not, of course, appear as a separate item in the profit and loss account, but will diminish the gross profit by increasing the cost of production of the articles manufactured, instead of showing larger gross profit

I

only to be reduced by a general charge for depreciation, as is the case when a lump sum is charged to profit and loss account in respect of such depreciation.

The explanation of the prime cost system given in Chapter IV. was not complicated by a reference to the subject of depreciation, which, at that stage, would have been inconvenient; but no difficulty will be found in assimilating this method of charging depreciation with that of recording cost as described in that chapter, and thus ascertaining cost of production.

*Prime cost and depreciation.*

It should be mentioned that there are items in the books of a private firm or joint-stock company to which no general rule of writing off is applicable. Such are the cost of good-will, patents, trade marks, copyright designs, &c.; for although, as in the case of patents, the life of the asset is clearly defined, the incidental advantages derived from the possession, for a term of years, of a valuable monopoly do not necessarily cease upon the expiration of the term of the patent. On the contrary, the value of the good-will may increase although the term of the patent is expiring. Assets such as those should be considered as having a combination value, differing altogether from their value *per se*. The obvious rule, therefore, is that in the balance-sheet such assets should appear at their cost value, and need not be written down unless their realizable value as integral parts of a going concern falls below their cost value. Any estimated increment may be accounted for by the creation of a special fund, as explained on p. 102, but until such estimated increased value is realized it should not be considered as an element of profit.

*Depreciation of good-will, patents, &c.*

## CHAPTER VII.

### SURVEYS.

THE most evident utility of the Stores and Stock Ledgers, kept in the manner described in the preceding chapters, is that by their means the storekeeper, warehouseman, and others concerned, are able to ascertain what is the quantity of any particular commodity on hand at any given time, without the delay and expense involved in the process generally known as "taking stock." The ability to obtain this information in an accurate and speedy manner has a very wide and important bearing upon the general accounts of the firm. Unless it is at command it is impossible, in undertakings of any magnitude, to determine, even approximately, what the result of the business is until a survey has been made. It is claimed for the system of accounts we have explained in these pages, that one of its chief advantages lies in the fact that it obviates the necessity of taking stock simply for the purpose of drawing up a balance-sheet. The economic value of this advantage to principals whose business is liable to many vicissitudes, can scarcely be overrated, for it removes one of the most powerful obstacles to the frequent closing of

*Utility of Store and Stock Ledgers.*

*Stock-taking for Balance-sheet.*

the books and ascertainment of the results of the business. There is no doubt that save for a survey being a very troublesome and expensive matter, balance-sheets would be made up much more frequently than is usually the case, and that proprietors would be kept more fully *au courant* with the tendency of their business that can be the case when the books are closed only at long intervals of time. Under the methods of book-keeping here advocated, a survey, indeed, would simply serve the purpose of substantiating the results deduced from the books of account, and it is this feature which, perhaps more than any other, distinguishes a proper system of Factory Accounts from the methods generally adopted. Factory books, when kept, are often for the most part of the nature of memoranda, being simply methods of book-keeping by single entry, and lacking both in coherence and continuity, inasmuch as they are merely disconnected entries, which can be verified and assimilated only by means of the periodical surveys.

*Many Factory Accounts mere memoranda.*

Unless Stores and Stock Ledgers are kept in some such way as described, it is imperative that the survey of all articles, if it is to answer any useful purpose, should be made at one time, for, in the absence of factory books, the only comparison of which the result of the survey admits is with the totals of the stores and stock accounts of the Commercial Ledger; but even this comparison can only be one of book values and not of quantities or measurements, and an effective verification of the details of the survey is altogether out of the question. If the survey is simultaneous it is necessary either to suspend for the time the issue and receipt of materials, or to make

*Survey and Commercial Ledger.*

subsequent additions and subtractions in respect of materials received or issued during the period of stock-taking. Disorganization generally reigns during this period, and to such an extent is this the case that it is often found necessary and convenient to suspend business while the process is going on. While pointing out the inconveniences attending periodical and simultaneous surveys of all properties, we do not wish to detract from their importance upon occasions of general audit, or change of partnership, or at any other periods when the verification of the balances of the Stores and Stock Ledgers may be required.

*Surveys and disorganization.*

The existence of the Stock and Stores Ledgers enables surveys to be taken by degrees, and at times when the state of business is such as to minimise the disorganization and attendant loss of profit. There is reason to believe that storekeepers and warehousemen would be more vigilant if they knew that, instead of a periodical survey, an inventory of any of their stores or stock might be called for at any time and without warning, and that they would be required to explain any differences between the Survey and the Ledger accounts. A further advantage of the Stores and Stock Ledgers is, that by their means any excess or deficiency of commodities shown by the surveys can be localised and easily traced.

*Surveys by degrees.*

It is to be regretted that there does not seem to be in practice any absolute standard of efficiency in regard to stock-taking, and that the term is often applied to a superficial review of the articles, and to an estimate of what is, or, worse still, to a guess at what should be, the value. In an efficient survey

*Standard of efficiency.*

every record should be based on "handling," and nothing should be estimated or taken for granted, while the pricing of the articles should be based on the principles which will be hereafter referred to.

The results of the survey should be epitomised on survey sheets, of which Specimen No. 50 shows a ruling that will be applicable to most trades. These sheets should be so arranged as to admit of comparison with the corresponding accounts in the Ledgers.

STOCK SURVEY SHEET.—SPECIMEN No. 50.

Stock of_____at_____on_____

| Description. | Supplied by | No. | Weight. | | | Rate. | Value. | Remarks. |
|---|---|---|---|---|---|---|---|---|
| | | | Cwts. | Qrs. | Lb. | | | |
| | | | | | | | | |

If the system suggested in these pages be adopted, the result of the surveys would show an agreement between the number and weights or measurements of the articles according to the inventories and those standing as balances in the Ledger, and also between the aggregate money value of the articles and the balances of the respective accounts in the Commercial Ledger. According to this system the surveys would theoretically be divided between three

*Agreement of survey results.*

## SURVEY DIVISIONS.

main departments. The storekeeper would be respon-
**Stores.** sible for the store of raw and old material and
such articles, other than manufactured commodities and
plant, as may for the time be in his charge. The next
division would be that of the warehouseman, who would
have the custody of the stock of manufactured goods;
**Stock.** and the third division would only exist where
the system of registration of plant described in the
chapter on Fixed Capital was adopted, and would comprise all fixed and loose plant and tools. As has already
**Plant.** been pointed out, however, there is no objection in principle to the two departments of Stores and
Stock being amalgamated, so far as the situation and
custody of the same are concerned, provided the important distinction in the book-keeping explained in
previous chapters is preserved. When this is done there
will be no necessity to draw for the purpose of surveys
any fundamental distinction between these two departments beyond such mechanical divisions as may in
particular cases suggest themselves with the view of
facilitating the preparation of the inventory. If that
method is properly carried out, it will be found to be
purely a matter of convenience in any business what
divisions are made in the arrangement and disposition
of the various articles. In the same way as the books,
when properly kept, will bring out the correct quantity
and value of the plant wherever the machines and tools
constituting the plant may be located, so they will also
show the value of the stores and stock, no matter where
these may be distributed. It is quite evident, however,
that the quantity of stores and stocks on hand may be
of such a magnitude as to render the division of responsibility a matter of absolute necessity. It will then

probably be found advisable, in addition to carrying out the three main divisions before suggested, to give distinctive names, numbers, or letters to the different subdivisions of the stores and warehouses, and to identify those distinguishing signs with the headings of the corresponding accounts in the Ledgers. Each floor, room, or section could be under the charge of one man, who should be responsible for the accuracy of the records of the articles in that place, and who should have a place for everything, and have everything in its place. He would save himself much trouble, and avoid confusion, by placing on all large articles, and on the lockers or partitions containing the smaller ones, labels describing the articles, and giving in the case of raw materials the name of the supplier, and in the case of manufactured articles the number of the stock or manufacturing order, the date of receipt, and, if thought advisable, the price of the article marked either in cyphers or in plain figures. The utility of indicating the price is not confined to surveys, but enables the issuer of material or stock to immediately mark on the Stores Warrant or Stock Requisition the price of the article he has issued without referring to the Ledger. The *conditio sine quâ non* of the satisfactory working of a stores or stock system is that articles should not be issued without the issuer receiving a formal requisition for them from some authorised person. The articles he has in charge should be to the storekeeper or warehouseman what cash is to a cashier. No one expects a cashier to part with money save as against a cheque or receipt, and no one, not even excepting the principal, should expect a warehouseman or storekeeper to part with goods save

*Mechanical divisions and aids.*

*Essential of stores and stock system.*

as against a written requisition or receipt. Should either the storekeeper or warehouseman feel that he has not a sufficient control over articles in his charge, owing to their not being in the magazine or warehouse, or for any other reason, the articles may be chained, padlocked, sealed, or otherwise distinguished in such a manner as to show that they are still either " stores " or " stock." In this connection it may be well to point out that in establishments where large numbers of workpeople and others pass through the gate, the watchman or gate-keeper should have instructions not to allow any raw material or manufactured goods to be taken outside the factory without the necessary permit from the storekeeper or warehouseman.

Although the distinction between Stores and Stock is fundamental, and is not likely to be lost sight of by the reader, it is well to point out the desirability of the storekeeper having a general knowledge of what kind and quantity of stock is in the warehouse, and of the warehouseman being equally well informed of what material is in store. When parts of an article are both used in manufacture and sold, there will be a supply both in the warehouse and in the store, and any sudden or abnormal demand on either of the departments can be met by the one department transferring its surplus to the other, in order to meet the emergency. An idle or excessive supply is not wanted in either branch, and although the articles common to both are not likely to be numerous, the rise or growth of such excess could be easily checked by the warehouseman being supplied at intervals with a schedule of the articles in store, which could, if necessity arose, be transferred to him as stock, and by the storekeeper being provided with

**Excess Supply.**

similar information as to the stock. It is evident also that an equally efficacious check could be applied in the counting-house, where both the stock and store of any article would be known, and whence no order to manufacture would proceed until it was shown that the number on hand was not sufficient to meet the demand.

The principles which determine the question of how materials and manufactured articles are to be priced at a survey admit of much discussion, but we cannot here do more than indicate the general axioms which should be observed in a valuation of Stores and Stock. It is obviously unsound to base a valuation one year upon the cost of production of an article, and another year upon its estimated or even ascertained market value; but, nevertheless, it is to be feared that this is not unfrequently done. The course adopted by most of the best manufacturing firms is to value the stores at the net cost or invoicing price to them, and the manufactured articles on hand at their cost of production, without any addition for profit, or for standing charges as distinguished from factory charges. The practice of including in the valuation of Stock a percentage for establishment expenses or standing charges is one which cannot be too strongly condemned, if on no other ground than that a business which is really the reverse of profitable might, by the simple device of manufacturing and accumulating a large stock, be made to appear for a time as at any rate self-supporting. That is to say, a business might be made to appear flourishing, while as a matter of fact it was becoming less solvent, by reason of its cash and other available assets being converted into manufactured stock which may never be realizable, and

*Survey Prices.*

*Price should not include establishment charges.*

## VALUATION OF MANUFACTURED ARTICLES. 123

by the standing charges (if these are included), which in the absence of *bona-fide* business transactions would represent losses, being made to figure in the balance-sheet as good assets in the shape of stock on hand.

**Profits are latent.** The right principle undoubtedly is that in a manufacturing business a profit should not ✓ be considered to have been made until a sale has been effected, or until a contract for the delivery at a future date of goods already manufactured is entered into. But in the case of the production of raw materials and in those exceptional cases in which the stock of manufactured articles could be put upon the market and realized at their normal price, a modification of this principle would seem to be necessary; for in that case the product is generally saleable at an ascertained market price (or, at any rate, at an approximation to it), and it does not seem incorrect to say that the profit which that price leaves has been earned on the production of the commodity and not on its sale. Nevertheless, even in this case, it would probably in the long run prove to be more judicious to price the commodity in the books at its cost, and only to credit profit and loss account with the profit when sales have been effected. In the majority of cases manufactured stock has to be kept till a demand for it arises and orders are received, and in the meantime it may deteriorate or the price may fall, and the system of valuing at cost has the additional advantage, when stocks are held for any length of time, of obviating the necessity for periodical alterations of the valuation and consequent adjustment of the profit and loss account owing to fluctuations in the market price of the commodities. A valuation based upon cost of production (not including in the term, standing charges and interest on capital) would hold good for a long period of time; so long, in fact, as the article was preserved in its pristine condition, unless improved processes or other causes should so reduce the cost of similar articles, as to render a corresponding reduction of the valuation of the old stock necessary in order to establish the proper relation between it and the new price that would probably rule in the market. Any deterioration which the goods on hand may undergo should, of course, be periodically written off, and when stocks become entirely obsolete they should be reduced to their scrap value. But inordinate reduction in the value of assets is not always a proceeding deserving unqualified approval. It is quite conceivable that by taking undue advantage of facilities and opportunities which may exist at particular periods for writing down the value of assets, the firm or company may be placed in the position during subsequent years of making book gains which would not be realised but for the previous artificial reduction in values. In this way the accounts of the business are apt to prove misleading, and it is well that this effect of excessive reductions in value should not be overlooked. Indeed, its dangers appear to have been recognised by the Legislature, for, under the Companies' Act, 1877, reduction of paid-up capital is limited to the amount which, according to the affidavits of responsible officials, has been lost, or is unrepresented by available assets. The old material on hand should be taken in a stores survey at the market value of such old material, or at the price at which similar old material was last disposed of, unless such price be higher than the market price, in which case the lower value should be taken. It is desirable that in

# DEPRECIATION OF STORES AND STOCK.

both the Stores and Commercial Ledger old material should be kept in an account distinct from new material. The amount by which stock is to be written down in respect of ascertained depreciation may be debited to profit and loss or subsidiary trading account, and credited to the Stock account in the Commercial Ledger through the Journal. The warehouseman would pass a stock requisition through the Stock Issued Book to the credit of his Ledger accounts in the same way as if the amount represented withdrawal of stock; and the same procedure applies in the case of reduction in the value of stores.

*[margin note: Loss on Stores and Stock.]*

# CHAPTER VIII.

### CONCLUSION.

**Subsidiary Factory books.** It remains to refer to some subsidiary books in use in factories and warehouses, and also to some matters which, although they have an important bearing on Factory Accounts, do not properly fall under any of the preceding chapters. We have studiously avoided special reference to these ancillary books and matters, so as not to detract from the main issues of our subject; and we do not now refer to them with a view of attempting to exhaust the catalogue of account-books for which a practical use may be found in a factory. Such an attempt would be altogether futile by reason of the conditions and requirements of individual businesses varying too widely to warrant anything more than a general statement being made of the fundamental principles underlying the economy and routine of a factory—principles to which all details, to be of service, must conform.

**Summary of Chapter.** In this chapter we shall first describe the method of book-keeping to be adopted in the case of plant or machinery acquired on terms of deferred payments, and mention a few considerations bearing on the subject of the accounts of Government and municipal factories, and on those of the workshops

## SUMMARY OF CHAPTER.

of railway and similar undertakings where expenditure and production are of the nature of auxiliary operations and have not for their primary object the raising of revenue. We shall then deal with a few of the books employed to record transactions with regard to such matters as cartage, van, waggon, and craft traffic, packing, and fuel. In conclusion we shall pass under review some of the economic aspects of the systems of piece-work or payment by results, and of overtime; and in this connection state the views of some of the leading authorities upon labour questions as to the possible development of the modern factory system in the direction of the general adoption, or at least recognition, of the principles underlying industrial partnerships and co-operative production.

Inasmuch as the practice of purchasing plant on what is known as the purchase hire system is becoming more general,—there being in some circumstances an economy in the acquisition of new plant, machinery, waggons, &c., on terms of deferred payments,—it will be necessary to consider the entries which should be made in recording such transactions. It has been suggested that a simple and safe method of dealing with the book-keeping pertaining to this system is to ascertain what will be the "ultimate" value of the object when the various instalments have been paid, and to divide this "ultimate" value by the number of the instalments, and credit the product to capital each time an instalment is paid, the remainder of the instalments being debited to profit and loss account. For example, it is suggested that in the case of a waggon purchased for £60, payable in twenty

*Purchase Hire System.*

instalments, the ultimate value being £40, that as each instalment is paid £2 should be charged to capital and £1 to profit and loss account. The method suggested is undoubtedly a simple one, and in many cases it is probably as correct as the circumstances require. In the illustration given we presume, though it is not stated, that the "ultimate value" of the object—after the payment of all the instalments—covers an amount for depreciation during the time it has been in use; but in any case we think it would be well that the amount charged under the various heads should be more fully specified. The difference between the cost value to the purchaser of an object acquired upon terms of deferred payments and its "ultimate," *i.e.*, ordinary value, is the product of two factors, viz., interest on the deferred payments, and the natural or normal depreciation in the value of the object during the period of hire. We submit that these factors are so essentially different that they should be separately recorded. The one bears a close relation to, and has to be considered in conjunction with, the capital account of the business, and the rate of interest borne by that account; the other is a trade expense which is regulated by the volume of business, and the corresponding wear and tear of the object and its tendency to obsolescence. An article having been acquired on the purchase hire system, should be debited to plant or other appropriate account at its value as if purchased for prompt cash, and the difference between that value and the aggregate amount payable under the purchase hire agreement should be taken to an interest on deferred payments account, the whole of the liability being carried to the credit of a personal account with the vendor of the article.

As the instalments are paid, cash account would be credited, and the personal account with the vendor would be debited, with the amounts of the instalments. The amount debited to plant or other account would be written down in accordance with the principles of book-keeping applicable to fixed capital, and already discussed, whilst the amount standing to the debit of interest on deferred payments account would be distributed over the period of hire. This is on the assumption that all the instalments are paid and the purchase of the article ultimately completed, but should this not be the case and the article be returned after an interval of hire, the personal account with the vendor would be closed by being debited with the balance standing to his credit, which would *pro tanto* be credited to the plant account and the interest on deferred payments account. Any remaining balances on these latter accounts, representing as they would the loss on the non-completion of the purchase, would be passed to profit and loss. A further advantage of the method we recommend is that it enables the article purchased on this system to be treated from the outset as if it were actually the property of the intending purchaser, and this, it will be recognised, is the only sound view to take of the transaction. If the purchase should not be completed, the accounts will show exactly what sacrifice is involved; and they would moreover at any stage of the period of hiring show the position of the transaction.

**Factories not working for profit.** There is necessarily greater simplicity in recording expenditure in those cases where production is not for profit, and articles are made or repaired only for the sole and incidental use and benefit of the concern, as, for instance, in arsenals, dockyards, and other national and municipal workshops, railway, gas, tram, and water companies, than in a factory working for profit in competition with other producers. The principles of the Factory Accounts explained in this volume are in all such cases applicable. It may, in passing, be mentioned that an ingenious and elaborate system of recording the expenditure in Government workshops by means of cards, on which the entries are made by symbols, has been described by Captain Metcalfe,* and has much to recommend it, but it does not very well admit of the assimilation of accounts with a view of drawing up periodical statements showing the profit and loss on all the operations and the actual financial position of the concern. This is, in fact, admitted by the author himself, when he says, "I have vainly tried to find some simple current method of reconciling the cost sheet with the cash accounts, since this would establish the aggregate truth of the cost sheet before the highest court of audit known to military accountability. I am convinced not only that this is impossible, unless either the papers are very much complicated, or unless substantial truth is neglected for the sake of striking a balance; but I also believe that the same result is indirectly attainable by other means already described." The defect referred to seems to us inherent in any system of recording expenditure on, and by means of, cards passing through a number of hands and performing a variety of services both in the factory and in the counting-house.

*Use of cards instead of books.*

\* "The Cost of Manufactures." Captain Henry Metcalfe. New York. Wiley. 1885.

## CARTAGE BOOKS.

The requirements of a Government arsenal, however, are not those of factories working for profit, which have to be conducted on lines enabling the proprietors in the face of keen competition with other manufacturers, to supply the demands of the public at a profit to themselves.

In almost every manufacturing business the item of cartage is a more or less serious factor. If the cartage **Cartage books.** be for the conveyance of raw material from different parts of the factory the charge is one on manufacturing account, and should be allocated to the various orders. If it be for the delivery of goods sold to customers an attempt is sometimes made to recoup the cost by debiting the customer with a charge for carriage; in other cases the expense, in view of the vexation and trouble which any other course generally produces, is borne absolutely by the firm and regarded as a charge against the profits of the business. In any event the item is one admitting, by a proper system of registration, of large economies. If cartage be done by an outside contractor, the necessary records for checking his accounts should be kept by the employé (generally the warehouseman or storekeeper), by whose orders the work is done. The contractor would receive an advice (Specimen No. 51), which should be attached to the account when rendered.

If it be thought necessary, a further check may be obtained by instructing the gatekeeper to record the times at which carters enter and leave the factory, any delay in loading or unloading being noted. If the **Horses and vehicles.** horses and vehicles are the property of the firm the purchase price of the horses should be debited to a horse account, and that of the vehicles to a vehicle account, and each account should periodically be debited with interest on the amount of the capital sum. The carters should send in weekly a return of the work done by them, and this should be summarised in a Cartage Book. A cartage account should be opened, to which should be debited the wages of the carters, stablemen, the cost of forage, stable expenses, &c., and at regular intervals an amount for depreciation from the horse account and the van account. The cartage account will of course be credited with the journeys performed at such rates as will equal the amount charged to it. It is only through keeping some such account that the employer can ascertain accurately whether it pays him better to purchase and keep horses and carts than to employ a contractor.

SPECIMEN No. 51.

Cartage advice,_____189 .

To Mr._____

Please supply me with the undermentioned.

| No. of Horses. | Description of Vehicle. | Time Required. | Time Arrived. | Time Returned. | Time on Job. | Order to be charged. |
|---|---|---|---|---|---|---|
|  |  |  |  |  |  |  |
|  |  |  |  |  |  |  |
|  |  |  |  |  |  |  |
|  |  |  |  |  |  |  |

Ordered by_____    Signature of Carman_____

In view of the need that often arises of giving quota-
**Freight book.** tions for goods inclusive of free delivery, and of checking the rates charged by the railway companies, it is very desirable to record the quotations obtained, or rates paid for freightage. Under the various Railway (Rates and Charges) Order Confirmation Acts passed in 1891 and 1892, consequent upon the Railway and Canal Traffic Act of 1888, the maximum tolls and charges for various classes of traffic over the various railways have been prescribed. Having regard to the varying conditions of the traffic, it is very desirable to compare the actual rates charged with the maximum authorised, and this can best be done by means of a book ruled as shown (Specimen No. 52).

An exceedingly useful manual, assimilating, comparing, and explaining the Confirmation Acts, together with the scale of maximum rates and charges worked out to 600 miles, has been compiled by Mr. M. B. Cotsworth, and published by Messrs. Bemrose.

In the case of firms enjoying the advantages of a railway siding a special book should be kept on the
**Railway sidings.** same principle as that applied to the Cartage Book just described. If a yearly rental is paid for sidings and trucks, this rental and any incidental items should be debited to an account to which is credited any receipts from this source. If the trucks are owned by the firm, then their purchase price, together with interest, should be debited to a trucks account, which should be credited each year with an amount for depreciation, the amount so credited being charged to an account which would in turn be credited with any amount received for the hire of trucks.

A Wagon and Van Book should also be kept, showing

## CONCLUSION.

SPECIMEN No. 52.

PARTICULARS OF RAILWAY RATES, for _____, from _____

| To. | Route. | Rate. | Mileage. | | Details of Division of Rate. | | | | | Remarks. |
|---|---|---|---|---|---|---|---|---|---|---|
| | | | Over Railway receiving Consignment | Over Other Systems. | Total. | Charge for Haulage. | | | Terminal Charges. | |
| | | | | | | Rate for Conveyance. | | Haulage Rate. | | |
| | | | | | | Over Railway receiving Consignment | Over Other Systems. | Total Rate for Conveyance. | Allowance for Provision of Trucks. | Amount. | Details of Services, &c. | |

SPECIMEN No. 53.

STATEMENT OF TRIPS MADE BY, AND EARNINGS OF WAGONS AND VANS DURING THE MONTHS OF _____

| | Number of Wagons and Vans working. | Number of Trips made. | Average Number of Trips per Wagon and Van. | Total under repairs. | Number repaired on Railway. | Earnings. | | | Average earnings per Wagon and Van. | Tonnage carried. | Average earnings per Ton. | Demurrage charged. | | | Remarks. |
|---|---|---|---|---|---|---|---|---|---|---|---|---|---|---|---|
| | | | | | | £ | s. | d. | | Tons. | | £ | s. | d. | |
| Month of 189 | | | | | | | | | | | | | | | |
| Wagons ... ... | | | | | | | | | | | | | | | |
| Vans ... ... | | | | | | | | | | | | | | | |

## WAGON BOOKS.

under the number of the wagon or van, the date it was dispatched, destination, load, date of return, and number of days' demurrage incurred, if any. The book should be so ruled as to permit of the earnings of the wagons and vans being ascertained, and the results tabulated monthly in a form convenient for comparison, as shown in Specimen No. 53.

When wagons or vans belonging to manufacturers or merchants have to be repaired on the railway company's sidings by a wagon-repairing company or by the railway company's workpeople, it is advisable to keep a record of such repair in a Wagon Journey Repairs Book (Specimen No. 54).

SPECIMEN NO. 54.

WAGONS REPAIRED BY ―――――

| No. | Dates. | | Station or siding. | Materials sent. | Nature of Repairs. | Carriage on Materials. | Charges. |
|---|---|---|---|---|---|---|---|
| | Advised. | Repaired. | | | | | |
| | | | | | | | |

It may also be serviceable to allude briefly to the desirability, where steam lighters or barges are used, of recording the work done by each lighter or barge, so that full advantage may be taken of any possible economies in cost of transit.

The captain or hand in charge of each craft should be given a Time Sheet (Specimen No. 55).

## CONCLUSION.

SPECIMEN No. 55.

TIME SHEET FOR { LIGHTER. BARGE. BOAT.

| Name of Craft. | Date and Time of leaving Works. | Loaded with | Quantity. | Destination. | Date and Time of Arrival at Destination. | Date and Time Discharged. | Date and Time started Return Journey. | Date and Time of arrival at Works. |
|---|---|---|---|---|---|---|---|---|
|  |  |  |  |  |  |  |  |  |

The Time Sheet may be so ruled on the back as to permit of the recording thereon of any back freights, return cargos, towage, or other services performed, and will, when the journey is finished, form the voucher on which payment will be made by the cashier of the amount due to the crew.

This Time Sheet should be recorded in a Craft Register (Specimen No. 56).

SPECIMEN No. 56.

THE ——————. CAPTAIN ——————.

| Date Loaded. | Where Loaded. | Destination. | Time Sheet No. | Date Arrived. | Time Occupied on journey. | Particulars of Discharge. | Date of Return. | Time Idle. | Material Carried. | Particulars of Payment. |
|---|---|---|---|---|---|---|---|---|---|---|
|  |  |  |  |  |  |  |  |  |  |  |

# FUEL ACCOUNTS.

In dealing with the question of transit of goods, it will be well to point out that cases and sheets for the packing or covering of goods should be considered **Packing accounts.** as stock, and should be registered. The cases and sheets should be made to a Stock Order No., and credited to stock in the same way as any other articles. Thus a cases or sheets account respectively would be debited with the cost of each case or sheet sent out, and credited with all charges made to customers under these heads. If any allowance be made for the return of a case it should be put into stock at a figure not exceeding the amount so allowed, and the process would be repeated until it was no longer of value as a packing case but merely as old material.

It is further desirable that the warehouseman should keep an "empties" or "cases" book, showing the cases sent out and those received back, in order to keep an effectual check upon, and prevent the loss or too rapid multiplication of packing-cases.

There are many other subsidiary books of a similar character the need for which will arise in every factory, **Coal Book.** but a detailed description cannot be attempted. Such are the Coal Books, for recording the contracts for coal and deliveries made, as well as the consumption of coal, when this is systematically charged to each working number, as explained in Chapter VI. If this procedure be adopted, the Coal Book may contain on the debit side the quantity of coal received, which would of course agree with the totals of the bills for coal supplied, and on the credit side an account compiled from the statement (already referred to) showing how the coal has been used, the difference representing the balance of coal on hand. The Coal Book and accounts may usefully be summarised monthly (Specimen No. 57), to show the various elements in the price at which it was bought. There are also Gas and Water Meter Reading Books, which show the readings of the various gas and water meters at regular periods, and the consumption during such periods, whilst by the aid of subsidiary meters the consumption in different parts of the factory is obtained and the cost localised. There are also the Brigade or Fire Hose Book, in which is recorded the periodical examination of the hose and apparatus for the extinction of fire; the Casualty Book, containing records of accidents which happen in the factory; the Pattern Book, containing particulars of patterns received and issued; the Delivery Books for obtaining carrier's receipts for goods, and a variety of other books too numerous to be enumerated.

*Gas and Water Books.*

*Precaution against fire.*

*Patterns.*

SPECIMEN No. 57.
SUMMARY OF QUANTITY AND COST OF FUEL RECEIVED
DURING THE MONTH OF _____ 189

| Date of Purchase. | Colliery or Merchant. | Quality. | Quantity. T. C. | Bought Price. | Discount. | Pit Price. | Wagon Hire. | Boat Hire. | Rates and Tolls. | Net Amount. | Remarks. |
|---|---|---|---|---|---|---|---|---|---|---|---|
| | | | | | | | | | | | |

A reference to books relating to sick, provident,

## SICK AND PROVIDENT FUNDS.

**Provident and other funds.** superannuation, and similar funds might be looked for in this chapter, but inasmuch as these are generally conducted by a committee of those interested, a description of the books required does not fall within the limits of this volume. For the convenience of the employés, their subscriptions to these funds may, as described in Chapter II., be deducted from the amounts due to them as wages, but at this point the connection of the funds with the factory books generally ends. The disposal of the amounts deducted from the wages of employés on account of fines rests, of course, with the principal. If, as is generally the case, they form a contribution to the sick fund, the necessary entries are made in the commercial books.

**Books required by Factory Acts.** The books which have to be kept under the Factory and Workshop Acts call for special mention. As will be seen from the Summary of the Acts contained in Appendix E, it is the duty of occupiers of factories and workshops to cause divers prescribed books and forms to be used. We do not, however, consider it necessary to describe them in detail, as their purpose will be sufficiently evident upon a reference to the Summary of the Statutes, and all registers, books, forms, certificates, &c., prescribed by the Secretary of State in pursuance of the Acts can be purchased ready for use.* The "very long, important, and complicated statute known as the Factory and Workshop Act, 1878," consolidates and replaces about sixteen previous statutes, and forms, with the Acts of 1883, 1889, and 1891, a complete code of factory regulations. They deal with the sanitary conditions of factories and

---

* They are published (by authority of Her Majesty's Stationery Office) by Messrs. Shaw & Sons, Fetter Lane, London.

workshops, and with the safety of the workpeople, fix the hours of work and of meals, prescribe holidays, provide for the education of children employed in factories, require certificates of fitness for employment to be obtained, and contain regulations as to the investigation of the cause of accidents. The Acts also contain conditions as to overtime, night work, domestic employment, &c., and special provisions for particular classes of factories and workshops.

There are some considerations with regard to the economic aspects of overtime, piece-work, and kindred *Economic* subjects which could not well be referred to *considera-* in that portion of the work dealing with the *tions.* book-keeping relating to those subjects, but which have too important a bearing upon our subject-matter to be passed over; as, for instance, the relation to fixed capital of the questions of payment for labour according to ordinary time, overtime, and piece.

To pay overtime rate for labour which could be more efficiently performed at the normal rate is obviously not *As to* economical on the part of an employer, who, *overtime.* indeed, seldom resorts to it save in cases of emergency and of time contracts.

The interest on fixed capital and the provision against depreciation are factors in the cost of production which *As to fixed* have a constant tendency to increase, and *capital and* these indeed are to a very large extent inde-*double* *shifts.* pendent of the number of hours employés are at work. Full advantage of the economies arising from the use of machinery is not likely to accrue until the principle of working double or treble shifts is more extensively adopted than at present. By the employment of two or three sets of men, each working eight hours a day, considerable benefit would accrue to the community. The objections commonly urged against the system are such as can be, and have been, surmounted; and experience shows that the aversion with which it is regarded by workmen is as transitory as has been their dislike to the system of payment by results, known as piece-work, which is becoming more and more general in trades in which individual workmen are able to work independently of each other, and where the piece-work rates can be fairly calculated and the work properly registered. An extensive and successful piece-work system is not indeed practicable where the solidarity of labour is so great that each workman cannot do his work independently and without the assistance of others, but where there is much division of labour piece-work is generally possible, although the parts made under that system may require the combination of several workpeople to complete or to adapt them to their final purposes.

As to piece-work.

Obvious as are the economic advantages resulting from the adoption of piece-work, it is probable that the quality of the work performed under it is either stereotyped or lowered, and that the greatest advantage can only be obtained by interesting the worker in the quality as well as the quantity of his work. It has been well pointed out that " two equally capable and energetic men, one of whom is working on his own account and the other performing at fixed wages services which have for their object the enrichment of an employer, notoriously present two very different standards of activity. The former is full of enterprise and alacrity ; the latter is wont to be slack and unaspiring and disinclined to make any effort bodily or mental not included in the average standard of performance recognised by his fellows. Where piece-work prevails, the above remark ceases to be applicable as far as mere quantity of production is concerned; but the contrast remains as great as ever in respect of the alertness of eye and brain to avoid waste of materials and injury to plant and tools, to suggest reforms in current technical procedure, to improve quality, and, generally speaking, to attain an enhanced commercial result by other methods than piling up a maximum of such work as will only just pass the scrutiny of the examiner appointed to check it. In short, full exertion of bodily and mental powers is obtainable only from men whose own interests are fully engaged in the result of the work to be performed." *

Some of the trades unions, however, have for one of their objects the limitation of the principle of piece-work, and if possible its absolute prevention. They urge that employers generally base the calculations for the piece-work rates upon the standard established by the quickest and strongest workmen, and that by these means the weaker men have, in order to earn the wages necessary for bare subsistence, to exert themselves to an undesirable extent; and that the rate of wages paid for piece-work is usually reduced by the employers almost in direct proportion to the efforts of the workmen. The fact that payment by the piece offers inducement to work being done with rapidity, to the sacrifice of finish, probably accounts for the large amount of work which might be done on the piece-work

*Trades union views.*

* "Profit-sharing between Capital and Labour." Sedley Taylor, M.A. Kegan Paul, Trench & Co., London. 1884.

method, being still paid for by the day, skilled labour, rather than rapidity of output, being required.*

With regard to the question of the relative pecuniary value of task work as against time work, each and every case must be decided on its own merits; and where the system is adopted tentatively the book referred to on page 29 is especially valuable, as showing whether labour by time or by piece is the more economical.

The regrettable difference of view between capitalists and workmen as to these matters prevents the attain-

**Conflict of capital and labour.**

ment of the highest degree of efficiency in production, and is therefore to the prejudice of all interests, but it is not possible " to expect any marked improvement in the general economic condition of the country, as long as the production of wealth involves a keen conflict of opposing pecuniary interests. The forces which ten men can exert may be completely neutralised if they are so arranged to contend against, instead of assisting, each other. Similarly, the efficiency of capital and labour must be most seriously impaired, when, instead of representing two agents assisting each other to secure a common object, they spend a considerable portion of their strength in an internecine contest. All experience shows that there can be no hope of introducing more harmonious relations, unless employers and employed are both made to feel that they have an immediate and direct interest in the success of the work in which they are engaged." †

\* For a full and fair statement of the advantages of the method of piece-work, and of the objections to it, we refer to " Methods of Industrial Remuneration," by David F. Schloss. Williams & Norgate, London, 1892.

† "Pauperism." Henry Fawcett, M.P. Macmillan & Co., London.

144   CONCLUSION.

The recognition of this fact by all who have studied
**Views of** the labour question in this country renders it
**authorities** incumbent on employers and accountants
**on labour**
**questions.** connected with industrial undertakings to
consider carefully the possible tendency of the modern
factory system, and it is therefore necessary in a book
dealing with Factory Accounts to discuss, however
briefly, the views of authorities—theorists and practical
men—upon this subject; especially as whatever the
next stage in the evolution of industrial organizations
may be, there can be little doubt that the tendency
must be more and more to greater detail and accuracy
in the preparation of accounts which form the basis of
apportionment, as between partners, or as between rival
and contending interests. The feeling of conjoint or
mutual interests referred to by Professor Fawcett can
only be developed by the employé feeling that he is a
participator in due share of the benefits arising from
greater exertion, economy and efficiency on his part;
and by the employer recognising that in the exercise of
those faculties the employés have the power of aug-
menting old, and creating new, sources of profit. As
has been well pointed out by Lord Brassey—" A more
**Lord** complete identity of interest between capital
**Brassey.** and labour is earnestly to be desired. In so
far as that consummation is to be accomplished by the
workmen themselves—and they must be active instruments in their own advancement—our hopes for the
future rest on co-operative industry. Their efforts must
commence with the simplest forms of industrial organization—those which require the least amount of capital,
and are most free from the fluctuations so painfully felt
in international commerce. In industries which cannot

be organized so readily on the co-operative plan, the extended operations of the joint-stock companies will secure the publication of profits, and afford opportunities to the workmen for participation, as holders of shares, in the profits of capital." *

An extension of the principle of joint-stock enterprise, which at present affords the most available opportunities for the investment of small sums, Joint-stock enterprise. might serve to operate in the direction desired if only the working classes could avail themselves of its advantages; but in this respect there is little encouragement to be gleaned from the past, although the laws which have been in force for some years afford facility for the co-operation of labour with capital. Great expectations have been founded upon the facilities possessed in some cases by working men to become part proprietors in the businesses in which they are engaged, but industrial co-operative associations on a large scale have yet to be established.

It was the opinion of the late Professor Jevons that, " there can be no doubt that the soundest possible solution of the labour question will eventually be found in such a modification of the terms of partnership as shall bind the interests of the employer and workman more closely together. Under such a system the weekly wages would be regarded merely as subsistence money, or advances which the employer would make to enable the labourer and his family to await the completion of the interval between manufacture and sale. The balance of the value produced would be paid at the end of the year or half-year in the form of a dividend or bonus, consisting in a share of all surplus

* Report of the Industrial Remuneration Conference. Cassell & Co., London.

profits realised beyond the necessary charges of interest, wages of superintendence, cost of depreciation and capital, reserve to meet bad debts, and all other expenses of production for which the employer can fairly claim compensation. Under the name of Industrial Partnership such an arrangement has been experimentally tried in England, and has been subject to a good deal of adverse discussion." *

This adverse criticism is to a large extent due to the failure of the tentative trials of the system of co-operative production in several cases, but the conditions under which the tests were made were unfavourable, and the circumstances in each case were not such as permit of any general or definite rule being deduced from the result.

*Co-operative production in England.*

Notwithstanding these unsuccessful attempts in England to establish industrial partnerships it must not be assumed that this country is unable to show any signs of encouragement to the advocates of this principle, and on reference to the tabulated returns of the Co-operative Productive Societies it will be seen that examples of the successful working of the system are not confined to other countries. It is, however, on the Continent that the principle of industrial partnerships has made the greatest strides, and in France, according to Mr. Sedley Taylor, "the principle of participation, organized under a great variety of different forms adapted to differing industrial conditions, has been applied with success to almost every class of undertaking, productive, distributive, or purely administrative."

*Industrial partnerships on the Continent.*

---

\* "The State in Relation to Labour," chap. x., p. 142. By W. Stanley Jevons, LL.D., F.R.S. London, Macmillan, 1882.

The system "consists in assigning to the employed, over and above their wages paid at the ordinary market rate, a part of the net profits realized by the concern for which they work," and the material successes achieved are stated to have been little short of marvellous.

The economic basis upon which the principle rests is best stated in the words of Mr. Taylor himself. "The *Their economic basis.* fund on which the participation draws is the surplus profits realised in consequence of the enhanced efficiency of the work done under its stimulating influence. Such extra profit is, therefore, obtainable whenever workmen have it in their power to increase the quantity, improve the quality, or diminish the cost price of their staple of production by more effective exertion, by increased economy in the use of tools and materials, or by a reduction in the costs of superintendence. In other words, the surplus profit realisable will depend on the influence which manual labour is capable of exerting upon production. Evidently, therefore, this influence will be greatest in branches of industry where the skill of the labourer plays the leading part, where the outlay on tools and materials bears a small ratio to the cost of production, and where individual superintendence is difficult and expensive. It will, on the contrary, be least effective in industries where mechanism is the principal agency, where interest on capital fixed in machinery is the chief element of cost price, and where the workmen assembled in large factories can be easily and effectively superintended." \*

\* "Profit Sharing." Sedley Taylor, M.A. Kegan Paul, Trench & Co., London.

The methods by which the share belonging to the employés under a system of industrial partnership is determined vary with different trades, but in the Blue Book on the subject they are fully described. The three main divisions are—1, Where the workmen's share of profits is distributed in the form of an annual cash bonus; 2, where that share is invested for the benefit of the employés; 3, where part is annually distributed among the workpeople and part invested for their benefit.

It is the absence of mutual confidence between employers and employed which is the greatest obstacle to **Obstacle to their extension.** the success of industrial partnerships, and so far is this the case in this country that a working man, speaking at the Industrial Remuneration Conference, described profit-sharing " as nothing less than a delusive bait on the part of capitalists to goad the workers on to greater intensity of toil." That this accentuated feeling is not general to any extent is proved by the public utterances on the subject of **Views of representative working men.** representative working men, and by the remarks of other speakers at that conference. The most widely-spread objection on the part of the employés is, that they have no certainty as to an employer's profit, no means of ascertaining its extent without an investigation of the accounts, and even in many cases when information has been required for boards of conciliation and arbitration, and where the result would have been communicated by the investigator to an umpire only, such an investigation has been refused.

But this difficulty could of course be overcome by an inspection of the books being confidentially made by a

**Influence of proper method of accounts.** sworn accountant, provided always that, as pointed out in a previous chapter, the groundwork of the system of accounts is such that each employé feels he is contributing to the attainment of accurate records of cost, and has general confidence in the manner in which the accounts are kept.

The other objections to the adoption of the principle of industrial partnerships, sometimes advanced by heads of firms and founded upon a "dread of the extra trouble of management and account-keeping thereby entailed,"* afford further exemplification of the need of systematic and accurate methods of dealing with Factory Accounts; and of the fact that their principles are so little comprehended as to be considered inapplicable under any new set of conditions. Our contention is that these principles have a scientific basis, rendering them applicable to any condition of industrial organization; that to demonstrate their economic results is peculiarly the province of the accountant, and to the attainment of that end a clear and complete system of Factory Accounts is essential.

* "Reports of Her Majesty's Representatives Abroad on the System of Cooperation in Foreign Countries." Blue Book, Commercial, No. 20. 1886. Hansard.

# APPENDIX A.

## NOMENCLATURE OF MACHINE DETAILS.

BY OBERLIN SMITH, PRESIDENT OF THE FERRACUTE MACHINE
COMPANY, BRIDGETON, N.J.

*A Paper read before the American Society of Mechanical Engineers, and reprinted by the kind permission of the Author.*

THAT the nomenclature of machinery, and of the tools and apparatus with which it is constructed is, in this country, in a state of considerable confusion scarcely needs demonstrating. If we look from an international point of view, and include the other English-speaking countries,—Great Britain and her colonies—the confusion becomes worse confounded. A reform is destined, in due time, to come, doubtless to be promoted in great degree by such societies as ours. This reform movement cannot be begun too soon, and should aim at giving brief and suggestive names to all objects dealt with,—each object to have but one name, and each name to belong to but one object. A simple method of beginning such a reform would be a common agreement among all our engineering schools to use each technical word in but one sense, and with no synonyms. A lesser field of reform, and one which lies more particularly within the jurisdiction of individual manufacturers, is the comparative designation of a number of sizes or kinds of the same machine. There is now no common understanding whether a series of sizes shall be numbered or lettered from the largest down, or from the smallest up. The latter is undoubtedly the most natural and suggestive method, but usually becomes confused by want of careful forethought (when starting a series) in providing " gaps " for the insertion of future sizes. If a numerical series has been already started, and become commercially established, the only systematic way to insert new sizes

## THE REQUISITES OF A SYMBOLIC NOMENCLATURE. 151

(either at the beginning or through the middle of the series) is to use fractional numbers. This, though awkward in sound and appearance, seems to be the only means of suggesting the comparative size of the article by its name. The use of arbitrary higher numbers between the others is, of course, worse than no numbers at all. The use of a series of letters does not supply this fractional loophole of escape, the euphony of A-and-a-half, K-and-three-quarters, &c., being somewhat doubtful. Another method in much favour is the use of "fancy" names, such as "Diminutive Giant," "Eureka," "Firefly," &c. These are far preferable to confused numbers, as they are not intended to convey any ideas between manufacturer and customer, and admirably succeed in their purpose. All this is a very difficult subject to deal with, and one in regard to which we can scarcely hope for any exact system. We can but point out to manufacturers two general principles to be followed: 1st, of leaving abundant *gaps*—that is, let a regular series run 10, 20, 30, 40, &c., instead of 1, 2, 3, 4, &c.; and 2nd, of using the smaller numbers for the smaller objects. The second is similar in idea to the well-known Philadelphia house-numbering system, which has worked so admirably in practice, and which has been copied by numerous other cities.

The two foregoing paragraphs are intended respectively as but casual allusions to the technical and commercial nomenclature of machinery in general. The subject is too elaborate to be treated at length in this paper, the main purpose of which is to set forth the results of the writer's experience in establishing a system of names and symbols for all the component parts, commonly called "details" of machines, or, in fact, of any manufactured articles.

That some such system is necessary, no engineer who has attempted to manufacture machinery by the modern system of duplicate (or approximately duplicate) parts, will, for a moment, question. The necessity for a specific name for each piece, which name is not, never has been, and never will be, used for any different piece of the same or any other machine, is evident, simply for purposes of identification. This identification is required mechanically at almost every stage of production. The name, or a symbol representing it, should be marked upon the drawings, the patterns, and the special tools pertaining to each piece, and, when convenient, upon the piece itself. Commercially, it is required on time cards and in indexes and pattern lists and cost books as pertaining to production. Pertaining to sales these names or symbols must appear in illustrated price lists, and in orders by and charges

## 152 NOMENCLATURE OF MACHINE DETAILS.

to customers. This, our modern method of repairs, by selling duplicate parts, renders imperatively necessary.

The requisites for a good system of names and symbols are: 1st, *isolation* of each from all others that did, do, or may exist in the same establishment. 2nd, *suggestiveness* of what machine, what part of it, and if possible, the use of said part—conforming, of course, to established conventional names, as far as practicable. 3rd, *brevity*, combined with simplicity. Of the importance of isolation to prevent mistakes and confusion; of suggestiveness to aid the memory; of brevity to save time and trouble, it is hardly necessary to speak.

Regarding the systems now in use in our best shops, this paper will not attempt detailed information. It is understood that the names are more or less scientifically arranged; depending, of course, upon the amount of study and the quality of the brains that have been expended upon them. In cases where symbols are used, supplementary to the names, they usually consist of letters or numbers, or (oftener) a combination of both. Many of them (both names and symbols) fail in symmetry and suggestiveness, because little attention has been paid to the names of the machines themselves, as regards the serial consecutiveness hinted at in paragraph 2nd. The quality of brevity often suffers, severely, because the name and symbol must, in most cases, each have the machine name prefixed, to secure their perfect isolation. The latter quality is rarely dispensed with, simply because the manufacturer's pocket would be too directly touched by the expensive resulting mistakes. A perusal of some machinery catalogues which give detailed lists of parts is very harassing to a systematic mind. They are apt to derive one part name from another, prefixing the latter as an adjective each time, until some such pleasant title as "lower-left-hand-cutting-blade-set-screw-lock-nut" is evolved. If there are symbols provided, they consist of some unknown combinations of letters part way down the list, and then change to arbitrary numbers, or perhaps to nothing at all. It will often be noticed also that no particular order appears to be followed in numerical arrangement, similar parts being scattered at random through the list.

The scheme to be described further on has been evolved gradually from the experience gained in managing a growing machine business. This scheme is far from perfect, and is probably inferior to others which have not been made public; but it seems to answer the purpose aimed at, viz., a comprehensive and elastic system which will accommodate itself to an unlimited

## THE USE OF LETTERS AND NUMBERS. 153

growth and any variation in quantity or kind of goods manufactured. This, the methods we first tried would not do, being too limited in their scope.

It should be here explained that the word "we," as just used, refers to the above-mentioned machine works, with which the writer has long been connected; and the scheme in question will be spoken of as "our symbol system." To further define terms: "machine name" and "machine symbol" refer respectively to the name and symbol of the whole machine—or other article of manufacture; for it will be noticed that the system is applicable to almost any products, except those of a textile or chemical nature. "Piece name" and "piece symbol," in like manner, refer to the separate pieces of which the whole is composed. The terms "detail," "part," and "piece," have so far been used synonymously. It is doubtful which is really the best to establish as a standard, but we have adopted "piece" as best expressing the idea of one piece of material, reduced to the last condition of subdivision. In our practice, exceptions are made to this requirement of homogeneousness in such cases as chains, ropes, belts, &c.,—also material glued or welded together—in short, anything which may (like a man) be called *one piece*, because it is not intended ever to be taken apart. The character for equality ($=$) will be used to show connection between a name and its symbol. A brief glance at the history of our system shows that at first we (like many others) hit upon the plausible idea of using numbers for machine symbols and letters for piece symbols. The numbers were somewhat "gapped," but not to such an extent as we now should practise. Examples: If four sizes of pumps were symbolled 1, 2, 3 and 4, their barrels might $=$ 1-A, 2-A, &c., and their handles $=$ 1-B, 2-B, &c. If the next product made was a series of lathe dogs, they would probably be symbolled 11, 12, 13, &c. Their frames would $=$ 11-A, 12-A, &c., and their screws, 11-B, &c. This all worked beautifully until the products became so complicated as to contain more than 26 pieces! After tampering a little with the Greek alphabet (which seemed calculated to scare our new workmen), and trying to use a mixture of small and capital letters (which looked too near alike), we fell back upon the clumsy device of repeating the alphabet, with letters doubled or tripled.

When we finally abandoned the above plan, several methods were carefully studied. The next most obvious was to use letters for machines and numbers for pieces. This allowed any quantity of the latter, but limited the machine to 26, even with no gaps provided. A certain modification of this method is, perhaps, more in use than any other system. In it letters are used for different sizes or styles of a certain kind of machine, and used over again for some other kind, *ad infinitum*. This answers the purpose, because there are not likely to be more than 26 varieties of one machine. It has, however, the fatal objection of requiring the whole machine name prefixed to each symbol, in all cases where the symbol stands alone, and does not happen to be written with the others of the set in tabular form. As the general name of a machine usually consists of at least two words, a complete piece symbol becomes too long for convenience in labelling. Examples: Force pump, K—26; Lathe dog, H—2.

Another system consists in using numbers for the machines and numbers for the pieces. This gives isolation and brevity, but no suggestiveness. A serious objection to it is the danger of blurring the numbers together, or of transposition in writing or reading them; also in the fact that either number cannot be used alone, as it can in the case of letters and numbers.

A similar system to the above consists in the use of letters for both symbols. It has the same disadvantages, and the additional one of a limitation in the quantity of letters at disposal.

Our system, as finally decided upon, is as follows: Machine names and piece names are determined by the designer, in general according with the principles already pointed out, being, of course, made as brief and suggestive as possible, with no two machine names alike, and no two piece names alike in the same machine. In this nomenclature no positive laws can be followed but those of common sense and good English. A *machine symbol* consists of a group of *three* arbitrary *letters*—capitals. A *piece symbol* consists of an arbitrary *number* and follows the machine symbol, connected by a hyphen; thus FPA-2 might symbolise the force-pump handle before alluded to—smallest size. The machine symbol may be used alone when required, as FPA.

As thus described, these symbols fully possess the qualities of isolation and brevity. To make them also suggestive, some attention must be paid to what letters to use. In practice, we aim to make the first two letters the initials of the general name of the machine, and the last letter one of an alphabetical series which will represent the sizes of the machine. An example of this is shown in the symbol for the smallest-sized force pump FPA. If there is any chance of a future smaller or intermediate size, gaps should be left in the alphabetical order. This "initial" method cannot always be strictly followed, because of such duplicates as

FPA for force pump and foot press. The remedy would be to change one initial for one beginning some synonymous adjective, that is, foot presses might be symbolised TPA, assuming that it stands for treadle press. Usually the least important machine should be thus changed. From this it will be seen that, in defining the theory of this scheme, the words "arbitrary letters" were purposely used. The idea is to make the system thoroughly comprehensive. There might be such a number of machines having identical initials that the letters would be almost arbitrary. In practice, the designer can usually succeed in making the symbols sufficiently suggestive.

In considering how many letters to use in a symbol, considerations of brevity advised two, suggestiveness three or four. Two letters did not allow of enough permutations, nor indicate well enough the kind and size of machine. Three seemed amply sufficient in the first respect, as it provided over 17,000 symbols. If, for any reason, in the future four letters should seem desirable, the addition of another would not materially change the system. If three letters hyphened to a number of one, two, or three digits should seem bulky, remember that this symbol can stand by itself anywhere and express positively the identity of the piece. Its comparative brevity is shown by comparing the second and third columns of the following table (*A*). In the different lines an idea is given of the application of the system to a variety of products not usually made in any one shop.

TABLE A.

| 1st. Full name of machine and piece. | 2nd. Our Symbol for it. | 3rd. Symbolic name as often used. | 4th. Characters in Col. 2. | 5th. Characters in Col. 3. | 6th. Excess of Col. 5 over 4. |
|---|---|---|---|---|---|
| 6" × 4' Engine lathe, spindle head | ELA—4 | Engine Lathe, A—4 | 4 | 13 | 9 |
| No. 4 Power Press, frame | PPD—1 | Power Press, D—1 | 4 | 12 | 8 |
| 7" × 14" Steam Engine, crank shaft | SEG—51 | Steam Engine, G—51 | 5 | 14 | 9 |
| Buckeye Mowing Machine, left axle nut | MMD—81 | Mowing Machine, D—81 | 5 | 16 | 11 |
| No. 3 Glass Clock, main spring | GCC—105 | Glass Mantel Clock, C—105 | 6 | 20 | 14 |
| One-hole Mouse Trap, choker wire | MTA—3 | Wooden Mouse Trap, A—3 | 4 | 17 | 13 |

## NOMENCLATURE OF MACHINE DETAILS.

### TABLE B.

**F P L**     No. 3 Foot Press.     Weight.

| Piece No. | Same as | Piece name. | Material. | Quantity. | Rough weight. | Finished weight. | Aggregate finished, weight. |
|---|---|---|---|---|---|---|---|
| 1 | ......... | Frame | Cast Iron | 1 | 220 | 200 | 200 |
| 2 | ......... | Gib | ,, | 1 | 10 | 9 | 9 |
| 3 | ......... | Side Bar | ,, | 1 | 45 | 40 | 40 |
| 4 | ......... | Front Leg | ,, | 2 | 30 | 30 | 60 |
| 5 | ......... | Back Leg | ,, | 1 | 40 | 40 | 40 |
| 6 | ......... | Treadle | ,, | 1 | 17 | 15 | 15 |
| 7 | ......... | Lever | ,, | 1 | 85 | 80 | 80 |
| 8 | FPH-8 | Lever Weight | ,, | 4 | 5 | 5 | 20 |
| 9 | ......... | Pitman | ,, | 1 | 12 | 10 | 10 |
| 10 | FPH-10 | Clamp Sleeve | ,, | 2 | 3 | $2\frac{1}{4}$ | $4\frac{1}{2}$ |
| 21 | ......... | Lever Pin | Steel | 1 | $2\frac{1}{2}$ | 2 | 2 |
| 26 | FPJ-26 | Treadle and Pitman Bolt | Iron | 3 | $\frac{3}{4}$ | $\frac{1}{2}$ | $1\frac{1}{2}$ |

Table B is a specimen of part of a page of our "Symbol Book," in which are recorded any machines which have arrived at such a state of perfection and saleability as to be marked "Standard" on our drawings.

This table almost explains itself. The piece numbers in 1st column do not have the letters prefixed, because the latter stand at the top of the column. "Same as" means that the piece is identical with a piece belonging to some other machine, and can be manufactured with it. If it is common to several machines in a set, the smallest of the set in which it occurs is given. The "quantity" column tells the number of pieces of a kind required. The last "weight" column, added upward, shows total weight of machine. The piece numbers are "gapped" after each kind of material, and also at the ends of "groups," as described further on. This is to allow for future changes and additional pieces; also that other nearly similar machines having more pieces may in general have the same piece numbers.

The order in which the pieces are numerically arranged cannot follow positive rules in all cases. In our list of instructions (too long to be here quoted) we direct a classification by *materials*. In each class we group pieces of the same general character, in regard to the prevailing work to be done upon them, and in natural "machine shop" order; *i.e.*, first planing, then drilling or boring, then turning. We also aim to place the heaviest and

## OPERATIONS IDENTIFIED BY SYMBOLS. 157

most important pieces first. Between each group we "gap" the numbers.

Regarding position in naming pieces, we assume a front to the machine (where the operator is most likely to be placed), and define direction tersely as "forward," "back," "right," "left," "down," "up." The adjectives of position prefixed to piece names are, of course, derived from these words, as "upper," "lower," &c. A perpendicular row of similar pieces, say five, would be rated upper, second, third, fourth, and lower. A number of different-sized pieces of similar name may, in like manner, be prefixed smallest, second, third, &c.

Before closing, a brief reference to certain (two) supplementary symbols may not be out of place. One is a small letter after a piece symbol (as FPL-21-a), signifying that the piece is obsolete, the standard FPL-21 having been altered.* After a second alteration, the last obsolete piece would be suffixed "b," and so on. Thus duplicate pieces of old-style machines can be identified and supplied to customers. The other symbol referred to is to indicate the number of the operation in the construction of a piece, and is written thus: FPL-21-1st, FPL-21-2nd, &c. Its use is of great value on detail drawings, time cards, and cost cards. It enables any operation (no matter how trivial) on any piece of any machine to be identified by a symbol alone. An *operation* we define as any work which is done by *one person at one time*, before passing the piece along and commencing upon another.

* In a letter to the authors, Mr. Oberlin Smith writes: "I have not yet changed the system in my own practice, and do not see anything which I think it desirable to change except the first *supplementary* symbol mentioned in the first part of the last paragraph. The principle there mentioned is not strictly logical, as it gives the same symbol to a piece in present use which in a previous year was given to a somewhat different one now obsolete. This matter I intend to modify somewhat, but have not yet had time to do so."

# APPENDIX B.

## THE INCOME-TAX ACTS

IN THEIR BEARING UPON THE PROFITS OF MANUFACTURE.

THE Income Tax is, as is well known, assessed by boards of local commissioners in conjunction with Government officials, known as "Surveyors of Taxes," according to the provisions of a series of Acts of Parliament. In case of overcharge the most convenient course is to communicate or obtain an interview with the Surveyor of Taxes as early as possible, but as the language of the Acts is very precise, there is little discretion left to those who administer them. We have therefore thought it convenient to reproduce here the exact words of the more important provisions. The chief Acts are—5 and 6 Vict. c. 35, 16 and 17 Vict. c. 34, 32 and 33 Vict. c. 67, and 43 and 44 Vict. c. 19, but there are many others.

By the Act of 5 and 6 Vict. cap. 35 (1842) the several properties, profits, and gains in respect of which duties shall be assessed and charged are classified under five schedules, known respectively as A, B, C, D, and E.

Schedule A, commonly called the Landlord's or Property Tax, prescribes the rules as to the assessment of income from lands, tenements, and hereditaments. It is levied on the occupier, but is by him recoverable from the landlord.

Schedule B prescribes the rules as to the assessment of income in respect of occupation of land, or of house property if occupied as part of a farm.

Schedule C deals with incomes arising from annuities and dividends payable out of any public revenues.

Schedule D we describe in greater detail after Schedule E, which deals with incomes derived from all public offices and employments of profit.

## SCHEDULE D.

The schedule with which we are here chiefly concerned is Schedule D, under which duties shall be charged for and in respect of the annual profits or gains arising or accruing to any person residing in the United Kingdom from any kind of property whatever, whether situate in the United Kingdom or elsewhere, or from any profession, trade, employment, or vocation, whether the same shall be respectively carried on in the United Kingdom or elsewhere. And for and in respect of the annual profits or gains arising or accruing to any person whatever, whether a subject of her Majesty or not, although not resident within the United Kingdom, from any property whatever in the United Kingdom, or any profession, trade, employment, or vocation exercised within the United Kingdom, and to be charged for every twenty shillings of the annual amount of such profits and gains. In ascertaining the profits of any person chargeable under Schedule D, it shall be lawful to estimate the value of all doubtful debts due or owing to such person; and in the case of the bankruptcy or insolvency of the debtor, the amount of the dividend which may reasonably be expected to be received on any such debt shall be deemed to be the value thereof, and the duty chargeable under the said schedule shall be assessed and charged upon the estimated value of all such doubtful debts accordingly (16 and 17 Vict. cap. 34, sec. 50).

The Rules under which the said duties shall be assessed and charged are contained in the Act of 5 and 6 Vict. cap. 35, and so far as they concern profits of manufacture, are :—

*Full Profits on average of last Three Years.*

(*a.*) The duty to be charged shall be computed on a sum not less than the full amount of the balance and profits or gains of any trade, manufacture, adventure, or concern upon a fair and just average of three years, ending on such day of the year immediately preceding the year of assessment on which the accounts of the said trade, &c., shall have been usually made up, or on the fifth day of April preceding the year of assessment, and shall be assessed, charged, and paid without other deduction than is hereinafter mentioned as allowed : Provided always, that in cases where the trade, &c., shall have been set up and commenced within the said period of three years, the computation shall be made for one year on the average of the balance of the profits and gains from the period of first setting up the same : Provided also, that in cases where the trade, &c., shall have been set up and commenced within the year of assessment, the computation shall be made according to the best knowledge and belief of the person to be assessed (5 and 6 Vict. cap. 35, sec. 100).

*On all Persons, Companies, and Occupations.*

(*b.*) The said duty shall extend to every person, body politic or corporate, fraternity, fellowship, company, or society, and to every art, mystery, adventure, or concern carried on by them respectively, in Great Britain or elsewhere.

*Deductions allowed from Gross Profits.*

(*c.*) In estimating the balance of profits and gains chargeable under Schedule D, or for the purpose of assessing the duty thereon, no sum shall be set against or deducted from, or allowed to be set against, or deducted from, such profits or gains on account of any sum expended for repairs of premises occupied for the purpose of such trade, &c., nor for any sum expended for the supply or repairs or alterations of any implements, utensils, or articles employed for the purpose of such trade, &c., beyond the sum usually expended for such purposes according to an average of three years preceding the year in which such assessment shall be made ; nor on account of loss not connected with or arising out of such trade, &c.; nor on account of any capital withdrawn therefrom ; nor for any sum employed or intended to be employed as capital in such trade, &c. ; nor for any capital employed in improvement of premises occupied for the purposes of such trade, &c. ; nor on account or under pretence of any interest which might have been made on such sums if laid out at interest ; nor for any debts, except bad debts proved to be such to the satisfaction of the Commissioners respectively ; nor for any average loss beyond the actual amount of loss after adjustment ; nor for any sum recoverable under an insurance or contract of indemnity.

## DEPRECIATION.

### *Interest to be included.*

(*d.*) No deduction shall be made on account of any annual interest, or any annuity or other annual payment, payable out of such profits or gains.

### *None but Trade Deductions allowed.*

(*e.*) No sum shall be set against or deducted from, or allowed to be set against or deducted from, such profits or gains for any disbursements or expenses whatever, not being money wholly and exclusively laid out or expended for the purposes of such trade, &c.

It follows from these stringent provisions that the common practice of deducting from the gross profits of a concern, an equivalent for the current interest on the capital employed, or an allowance for the remuneration of the working partners, or any annual payment to the representatives of deceased partners, is totally inadmissible for the purpose of Income Tax assessment. Questions will also often arise as to improvements made out of profits, enlargement of premises, purchase of improved machinery, or extra advertising for future advantage. Expenditure under these heads will be liable to be considered as capital outlay, not allowed to be deducted, especially if it is entered and shown separately from the ordinary current outgoings of the business.

### *Depreciation.*

An improvement in the management of the tax as to deductions for depreciation of plant and machinery was introduced in 1878. The provision is as follows:—

That the Commissioners shall, in assessing the profits or gains of any trade, &c., chargeable under Schedule D, or the profits of any concern chargeable by reference to the rules of that schedule, allow such deduction as they may think just and reasonable, as representing the diminished value, by reason of wear and tear during the year, of any machinery or plant used for the purposes of the concern and belonging to the person or company by whom the concern is carried on; and for the purpose of this provision, where machinery or plant is let to the person or company by whom the concern is carried on upon such terms that the person or company is bound to maintain the machinery or plant and deliver over the same in good condition at the end of the term of the lease, such machinery or plant shall be deemed to belong to such person or company. Where any machinery or plant is let upon such terms that the burden of maintaining and restoring the same falls upon the lessor he shall be entitled, on claim made to the Commissioners, to have repaid to him such a portion of the sum which may have been assessed and charged in respect of the machinery or plant, and deducted by the lessee on payment of the rent, as shall represent the income tax upon such an amount as the Commissioners may think just and reasonable as representing the diminished value by reason of wear and tear of such machinery or plant during the year: Provided that no such claim shall be allowed unless it shall be made within twelve calendar months after the expiration of the year of assessment (41 Vict. cap. 15, sec. 12).

We have already drawn attention (Chapter VI.) to the need of correctly ascertaining the amount to be charged for depreciation. In practice some difficulty may be experienced in inducing the local commissioners to permit a sufficient deduction under this head in addition to allowing for repairs actually effected. They rightly attach much weight to the allowance which the proprietors of the concern actually make as among themselves, and it is obvious that careful attention to correct book-keeping on this point, before the question is raised, will greatly facilitate a settlement. On this ground alone, the accounts should show clearly what is the amount written off for depreciation, not only in the aggregate but in detail. The manner in which this may be done is fully described in the chapter on "Fixed Capital."

*Return of Income Tax.*

There is another important provision which is not, especially in the case of small manufacturers, sufficiently utilised because it is not sufficiently well known. It is not exaggeration to say that thousands of pounds could be annually reclaimed from the Government under the 133rd section of the Act of 1842, and the 6th section of the Act of 1865. Thus, if a manufacturer has made £10,000 a year for the last three years, he will be assessed and will have to pay on £10,000 this year. If, however, at the end of this year he has only made £5,000 profit, he will be entitled to recover back the tax, already paid, on £1,666, as well as to have his assessment for next year fixed at £8,333. Too often ignorance of the law leads him to be content with the latter gain only. If his profits still remain at £5,000, he can then again get back the tax on £1,666, and have his future assessment fixed at £6,666, and so on.

These sections provide that if within or at the end of the year current at the time of making any assessment, or at the end of any year when such assessment ought to have been made, any person charged to the duties contained in Schedule D, whether he shall have computed his profits or gains on the amount thereof in the preceding or current year, or on an average of years, shall find, and shall prove to the satisfaction of the Commissioners by whom the assessment was made, that his profits or gains during such year for which the computation was made fell short of the sum so computed in respect of the same source of profit on which the computation was made, it shall be lawful for the said Commissioners to cause the assessment made for such current year to be amended in respect of such source of profit as the case shall require (5 & 6 Vict. cap. 35, sec. 133); no such reduction, however, shall be made unless the profits of the said year of assessment are proved to be less than the profits for one year on the average of the last three years, including the said year of assessment; nor shall any such relief extend to any greater amount than the difference between the sum on which the assessment has been made and such average profits for one year as aforesaid (28 Vict. cap. 30, sec. 6).

### Exceptions to the Three Years' Average.

The owners of quarries, mines, ironworks, gasworks, salt springs or works, alum mines or works, water works, streams of water, canals, inland navigation, docks, drains and levels, fishings, rights of markets and fairs, tolls, bridges, ferries, and other concerns of a like nature are assessed on their annual value or profit.

*As regards liquidations and alterations in partnerships, it is provided:—*

In case any person charged under Schedule D shall cease to exercise the profession, or to carry on the trade, on the profits of which he is assessed, or shall die or become bankrupt, or shall from any other specific cause be deprived of, or lose, the profits or gains on which the computation of duty was made, it shall be lawful for such person, or his executors or administrators, to make application within three calendar months after the end of each year to the Commissioners, and the Commissioners shall cause the assessment to be amended and give relief. Provided that where any person shall have succeeded to the trade or business, no such abatement shall be made, unless it shall be proved that the profits and gains of such trade have fallen short for some specific cause since such change or succession took place, or by reason thereof, but such person succeeding to the same shall be liable to the payment of the full duties thereon without any new assessment (5 & 6 Vict. cap. 35, sec. 134).

# APPENDIX C.

## THE RATING OF FACTORIES CONTAINING MACHINERY.

As, in the words of the preamble of a Bill introduced into the House of Commons in 1885, "Questions have from time to time arisen as to how far machinery and plant is to be taken into consideration in estimating the rateable value of the premises in which the business is carried on," it may be useful to give a brief outline of the present position of this subject. *(marginal note: Questions as to rateability.)*

The assessments originate with local surveyors and assessment committees, and in practice the greatest diversity prevails in computing them. When there are a few small factories in a district the value of the machinery is often ignored in framing the assessment, which is in such cases based on the estimated or actual net rental value, as with a shop or dwelling-house. In districts in which industry is localised the assessing authorities often take the capacity of production as the guide to the assessment, and base their computations on the spindle, horse-power, or other common factor in the trade,* whilst in many instances the assessors have adopted rules originally intended for very different kinds of property, or formulated entirely *(marginal notes: The assessing authorities. Varying modes of assessment.)*

---

* Such an assessment does not take cognizance of the wear and tear of machinery and its tendency to obsolescence, and thus bears unduly and unfairly against those factories which have been longer established than their rivals, and are already burdened with older type machinery. In a pamphlet on the "Incidence of Local Taxation," Mr. Hedley states that in 1883 the Hunslet Union Assessment Committee decided to disregard the law laid down by the High Court (in the Bishopswearmouth case) and resolved to exclude

## 166 RATING OF FACTORIES CONTAINING MACHINERY.

new modes of valuation. This want of uniformity as between district and district, handicaps certain trades in the one as compared with similar trades in the other district, whilst inequality or uncertainty of allotment is unfair as between individuals trading in the same district, for "it must always be remembered that the real end and object for the assessment of property is not to determine as a mere speculative question the rent at which it might let from year to year, but to bring the particular property down to a common basis, so that the burden of the poor-rates may be equally borne by the occupiers within the parish. This being

**Assessment should be on common basis.**

so, it does not seem unreasonable, when any difficulty arises in ascertaining how a particular property or class of property is assessed, that reference should be made to the rules that prevail in the valuation of ordinary classes of property in the parish. Special properties may require special rules, but where there is no such necessity the occupier of property has a right to have applied to his occupation the principles which determine the rateability of other property." *

That machinery *per se* is not rateable is generally admitted; indeed, any other conclusion would be inconsistent with the Act by

**Chattels not rateable.**

which personal property was declared not to be rateable. The question is as to how far in factories or works the machinery is to be taken into account as enhancing the rateable value of the hereditaments. The law on this point, if law there can be said to be, is to be found in the judges' decisions in

**Legal decisions.**

cases of appeals against assessments, and these decisions have so widely differed that the author of the legal text-book already referred to admits that it is impossible to reconcile them, whilst many factory occupiers believe that certainty and equality in assessment are only to be obtained by legislative definition of what machinery is to be considered in the assessment.

machinery from the assessment of the works, and to rate all engines at a uniform rate of £4 per horse-power. And he adds, "To rate all engines on a uniform rate of £4 per horse-power, irrespective of whether they are common engines with egg-end boilers and a few feet of shafting, or high-class engines with tubular boilers, super-heaters, and many yards of shafting, is clearly as unfair and unequal as it would be to rate all agricultural lands in the Union at a uniform rate of £2 per acre, irrespective of whether the land is worth £1 or £5 per acre."

* "A Practical Treatise on the Law of Rating," by Edward James Castle, Barrister-at-Law. Stevens, London.

The cases referred to extend over the last hundred years, but only four of these need now be taken as landmarks of the subject.

**The Phœnix Gas Company case.** In 1866 the assessment of the Phœnix Gas Company was appealed against, but it was held that the steam-engines, boilers, gasholders, retorts, and purifiers at the works and the mains in the public streets added to the permanent value of the freehold, and as such were rightly considered in the assessment.

**The Halstead silk factory case.** In the following year, however, in the case of a silk factory at Halstead it was held that looms and other machines merely screwed to the floor came under the category of movable fixtures, and were not to be considered in the assessment.\* 

**The Laing case.** In 1877-8, however, the late Lord Chief Justice Cockburn, in the case of "Laing and the Overseers of Bishopswearmouth," expressed some doubt as to the decision in the Halstead case, and with reference to the case then before the Court, said: "This strikes me as being a case the principle involved in which is of very considerable importance, in which I should hope there would be a final and binding authority upon the subject, and in which we may have to consider the effect of these cases (the cases quoted in the argument), which perhaps may prove to be somewhat in conflict with one another." 

**An important decision.** In this instance it was held that the lathes and machines for planing, drilling, punching, and riveting were properly included in the assessment, as such machinery, though some of it might be capable of being removed without injury to itself or the freehold, was "essentially necessary to the shipbuilding business to which the appellants' premises are devoted, and must be taken to be intended to remain permanently attached to them so long as these premises are applied to that present purpose."

This decision has been the subject of considerable discussion

---

\* Trade fixtures generally (using the term as inclusive of both removable and permanent fixtures) are said to be both theoretically and legally rateable, but the practice of exempting removable fixtures has become almost universal. "The law is that they are part of the premises, and pass under a mortgage, and a tenant is allowed to remove them during his term, not in the same way as he may his carpets, but only because the Courts were induced to relax the strictness of the old rules of law in order that the commercial interests of the country might be enhanced by the encouragement given to tenants to employ their capital in making improvements for carrying on trade, from the certainty of having the benefit of the expenditure secured to them at the end of their term."—"A Practical Treatise on the Law of Rating." Castle. Stevens, London.

## 168 RATING OF FACTORIES CONTAINING MACHINERY.

in the press and at meetings of the various Chambers of Commerce. It has been accepted as conclusive of the law by one well-known writer on the subject,* and by another it has been cogently contended that the facts of the case were not clearly or correctly presented to the Court.†

In view of these varying decisions or interpretations of the law, and the uncertainty and want of uniformity in assessments, the **A Rating Bill.** "Bill to amend the Law relating to the Rating of Machinery" was introduced into the House of Commons in 1885. It was proposed to enact that " in estimating for the purpose of assessment to the poor rate, county rate, borough **Definition of machinery to be rated.** rate, or any other rate leviable upon property rateable to the relief of the poor, the rateable value of any tenement or premises occupied for any trade or manufacturing purposes, the annual value of the machinery in this section specified upon such tenement or premises shall be taken into consideration, that is to say:—

"1st. Fixed motive powers, such as the water wheels and steam engines, and the steam boilers, donkey engines, and other fixed appurtenances of the said motive powers;

"2nd. Fixed power machinery, such as the shafts, wheels, drums, and their fixed appurtenances which transmit the action of the motive powers to the other machinery fixed and loose.

**Exemption of other machinery and plant from rating.**
"3rd. Pipes for steam, gas, and water.
"4th. Save as in the last section provided, no machinery or plant, whether attached to the tenement or premises or not, shall be taken into consideration in estimating such rateable value."

This Bill was not, however, proceeded with, it being thought that, if the subject was dealt with at all, it could best be done in a Local Government Bill. A decision has, however, been given in the Court of Appeal‡ which practically confirms, even if it does not extend, that given in the case of " Laing v. the Overseers of Bishopswearmouth."

This decision has been given in a case stated for the opinion of

* "Local Taxation and the Rating of Machinery."—Thomas Fenwick Hedley. Knight & Co., London.
† "Remarks on the Assessment of Rateable Value on Hereditaments containing Machinery."—Joseph Potts, Jun. Spon, London.
‡ The Queen v. The Tyne Boiler Works Company, Limited. Court of Appeal, December 1st, 1886.

## TYNE BOILER WORKS CASE.  169

the Court by the Northumberland Quarter Sessions, who held
that the Tyne Boiler Works Company had been
rightly assessed to the relief of the poor, the rateable
value of their premises being arrived at by ascertaining the gross estimated rental which a tenant from
year to year might reasonably be expected to be
willing to give for the use of them (inclusive of the
machinery and plant), and by making the statutory deductions
from such rental. The premises were occupied under a lease
from the Corporation of Newcastle-upon-Tyne, and they were
described as being rendered suitable for boiler making by their
proximity to the Tyne and as containing machinery for boiler-
making, part of such machinery being affixed to the soil, but
part, such as a hydraulic riveting machine, two hand-power
travelling cranes, and shear legs with engine and boiler, was not
attached either to the soil or the building but rested by their
own weight. There was a boiler set on a brick seating outside
the main building, and the main engine was fixed by iron screw
bolts to masonry foundations, in which a well was constructed for
the fly-wheel, and other machinery was affixed by bolts or brackets
to the walls, or to a foundation of stone or cement. As to the
machinery that was not affixed to the soil or building, the hydraulic
riveting machine rested upon cement or stone foundations, the
travelling cranes ran along the whole length of the main building
on rails laid on balks of timber resting upon brackets, and the
shear legs were placed on the edge of a timber jetty on the river.
The main shafting ran along the entire length of the main building,
and all the machines were worked by belts from the main shafting.
All the machines and plant belonged to the Company, and were
arranged and adapted for use upon the premises for the manufacturing and setting up of boilers, but there was no intention of
permanently annexing them to the soil or premises. Each of
the machines was separate, and was from time to time removed
for repairs or otherwise without injury to themselves or structural
damage to the premises, the object of the attachment described
being to steady the machines when working.

The Divisional Court having confirmed the order of the Northumberland Quarter Sessions, the Company appealed, with the
result that the judgment of the Queen's Bench Division was
affirmed. The Master of the Rolls, in giving judgment, reviewed
the various prior decisions on the subject, and stated that the rule
might be laid down thus :—Things which were on the premises to

*The most recent decision:*
*The Tyne Boiler Works case.*

**A rule of rating.** be rated, which were there for the purpose of making and which made the premises fit as premises for the particular purpose for which they were used, ought to be taken into consideration as enhancing the rateable value of those premises. Anything that would come under this category would pass by demise as between landlord and tenant, and would as such be rightly considered in the assessment.*

In 1889 the Chard (Somersetshire) Assessment Committee in assessing lace factories took into consideration the lace-making machinery on the premises. The assessment was appealed against, and the amount thereof was considerably reduced at the Somersetshire Quarter Sessions; the Assessment Committee was ordered to pay the costs. Against the reduced assessment appeals were carried to the Queen's Bench Division and the Court of Appeal, and in these appeals the original question as to the rating of machinery *per se* appears to have become ignored, for the Chard Assessment Committee after a decision in their favour in the Court of Appeal suggested a compromise by which, each party paying their own costs, the sum in dispute should be equally divided. The manufacturers accepted the compromise offered, as they were advised that the reduced assessment would represent the rateable value, quite apart from the question of rating machinery.

In similar circumstances the Gloucester and Sunderland Assessment Committees have, without there being an appeal to the Queen's Bench Division or Court of Appeal, acted on the lines of compromise carried out by the Chard Committee.

Throughout the judgments in the Bishopswearmouth and Tyne **The decision** boiler cases there seems to run an assumption that **criticised.** a hypothetical tenant might give a higher rent for premises by reason of his having the opportunity of taking the

---

* The case is thus noted in the *Law Times* of December 4th, 1886 :—" Poor Rate—Rating of Premises used for a particular purpose—Chattels on the Premises—Boiler Works—Machinery and Plant. In assessing premises to the poor rate, the question whether chattels on the premises are affixed to the soil or not is not an absolute test in determining whether or not they are to be taken into account as enhancing the value of the premises. But things which are on the premises to be rated, and which are there for the purpose of making them, and which do make them, fit as premises for the purpose for which they are used, ought to be taken into account for rating purposes. Therefore the machinery and plant of a boiler works which (whether affixed to the soil or not) is essentially necessary to the carrying on of the business to which the premises are devoted, and which is intended to remain upon the premises so long as they are used for the same purpose, ought to be taken into account as enhancing the value of the premises."

machinery contained therein. This is probably true as regards motive power and the machinery common to most trades, which is generally attached permanently to the premises, and these, on account of being so furnished, let at higher rentals. But specially designed machinery can only increase the probable rental, and therefore the assessment, if the premises are let to an incoming tenant carrying on the same trade as the outgoing tenant, and in that case part of the increased rental would be due to the opportunity of entering furnished premises, and part to the opportunity of acquiring by purchase from the outgoing tenant some of the machinery which he might otherwise remove.*

The decisions referred to will probably so intensify the confusion in the minds of the various rating authorities with regard to what is and what is not to be considered as assessable, as to lead to useful controversy with regard to what should and what should not be assessable, and eventually to legislative enactment on the subject.

Owing to the exertions of the National Society for the Exemption of Machinery from Rating, a Bill has been introduced into Parliament this year (1893), by which it is proposed to provide "that in estimating for the purpose of any valuation list, or poor or other local rate, the gross estimated rental or rateable value of any hereditament occupied for any trade, business, or manufacturing purposes, any increased value arising from machines, tools, or appliances which are not fixed or are only so fixed that they can be removed from their place without necessitating the removal of any part of the said hereditament shall be excluded.

" Provided that the gross annual value of any such hereditament shall be estimated at not less than the sum at which it might reasonably be expected to let for the purpose for which it is used on a tenancy from year to year void of the machines, tools, and appliances which it might reasonably be expected would be supplied by the tenant, if the tenant paid all the usual tenants' rates and taxes and tithe rentcharge (if any), and if the landlord undertook to bear the cost of the repairs and insurance and the other expenses (if any) necessary to maintain the said hereditament in a state to command such rent.

"Provided also that the terms machines, tools, and appliances

---

* " Trade fixtures attached to the soil are to be taken as landlord's property, subject only to the special privilege granted to the tenant who has put them up of removing them during his tenure."—" A Practical Treatise on the Law of Rating, by Edward James Castle, Barrister-at-Law.

172 RATING OF FACTORIES CONTAINING MACHINERY.

for the purposes of this Act shall not apply to any machinery, machine, or plant used in or on the hereditament for producing or transmitting first motive power, or for heating or lighting the said hereditament.

"Nothing in this Act contained shall apply to the rating of waterworks or gasworks."

Pending some settlement of the question it may be serviceable to enumerate some of the points to be considered before agreeing to or dissenting from assessments.

The basis of assessment on factories rented from year to year is naturally the actual net rental value. Questions only arise where **Checks on** the occupier's interest is that of a freeholder or a **assessments.** lessee for a term of years, and where machinery has been erected by the occupier *quâ* occupier. In either case the basis of assessment would be the gross estimated rental which in a particular district, under ordinary circumstances, a tenant from year to year might reasonably be expected to give for the use of the premises inclusive of the machinery and plant, with a deduction on account of maintenance, repairs, fire insurance, and any charges which in a term of years would have to be met before profit could be reckoned.* In the case of factories occupied by the owner it should be remembered that the assessment is made on him as an occupier, and that he should discriminate between his dual interests. Whilst calculations on the basis of the capital sunk in the building and on his plant, and the interest thereon, are aids in checking the estimated rental that would be receivable, they cannot be considered as final, or as yielding results which could be taken as the basis of assessment, owing to numerous accidental circumstances, such as the increase or decrease in the value of ground rents, and of variation of cost in the construction of new, or structural alteration in old, factories.

The same basis of assessment is often applied to the rating of workshops, using that term as distinctive of places where produc- **The basis of** tion is not made for profit, but where production or **assessment** repairs are effected for the sole use and benefit of **on work-** the occupiers. In this category fall the shops of **shops.** railway, gas, tram, water, and similar undertakings, as also arsenals, dockyards, and other national and municipal workshops.

* This deduction should, in our opinion, include a provision for obsolescence. All machinery is of a changeable nature, and provision has constantly to be made for its going out of fashion.

Aid in checking that portion of the assessment which may be said to be on account of machinery is derivable from a Machinery Ledger, if such be kept (see Chapter VI.). The value of the machinery that would pass with the freehold would be ascertainable from it, and the interest on that amount might approximately be taken as the gross annual value, the net annual value being arrived at by subtracting one-fourth or one-fifth of the gross for repairs or renewals. This rule would be equally applicable to factories working for profit, and to workshops carried on as parts of other undertakings.

# APPENDIX D.

## SOME NOTES ON THE LAW RELATING TO FIRE INSURANCE.*

### THE PROPOSAL AND THE POLICY.

IT is of the greatest importance that the form of proposal should be correctly filled in, and the questions answered, in an accurate and straightforward manner, without equivocation or ambiguity; as a misrepresentation or a concealment of a material fact, whether intentional or not, may invalidate a policy. The fact that the property proposed to be insured has been inspected by a representative of the insurance office does not relieve the assured from the responsibility of bringing under the notice of the office any circumstances which affect the degree of the risk. Good faith is always assumed to be the basis of insurance. It is open to the proposer to make a special contract with the insurers upon such conditions as may be agreed.

*Good faith the basis of insurance.*

The representations contained in the proposal or policy must be *substantially* true; but all specific conditions and statements are termed warranties, and must be absolutely and *literally* true; and this applies to descriptions of the property insured, if expressly contained or referred to in the policy.

*Representations.*
*Warranties.*

---

* The object of these notes is to indicate to factory occupiers the liabilities which, from an accountant's point of view, it is desirable to provide for by insurance or otherwise. In its legal aspects the subject of insurance against losses by fire has been dealt with in "The Law of Fire Insurance," by Charles John Bunyon, M.A. (London: C. and E. Layton. Third edition. 1885), to whom we are largely indebted for the subject matter of these notes.

## THE PROPOSAL AND THE POLICY. 175

Immediately the policy of insurance is received by the insured he should carefully examine it, and if the property is not **Correction** correctly described or the policy contains any other **of policy.** error, it should, without loss of time, be returned to the office for correction. If the required alteration is not inconsistent with the conditions of the policy it can be made by endorsement, but if the alteration is intended to vary the contract a new policy should be applied for.

In view of the fact that in the case of large insurances the risk is generally divided between several offices, and that consequently several policies are issued to the insured, it is **Common** recognised as a great convenience that the leading **form of** **policy.** offices now practically adopt a common form of policy.

The liability of the insurers continues for the term specified in the policy, but when the policy is renewable the assured is allowed **Renewal of** fifteen days' grace, and if a fire occur during this **policy.** interval he will be fully protected; but in that event he should immediately pay the premium. It is not customary to grant days of grace in the case of policies for short definite periods, and a policy of insurance is not, except by special agreement, determinable before the expiration of the specified term. The offices generally reserve to themselves the right to decline to renew a policy; and if they exercise this right and notify the assured of the fact, or if they give notice that they will not renew the policy except at a higher premium, and the assured declines to agree to this, the policy will expire absolutely on the date specified, the days of grace not being allowed.

The risks of fire insurance are classed as ordinary, hazardous, extra hazardous, and special, but the published rates and classifi- **Classifica-** cations afford very imperfect means of ascertaining **tion of risks.** the premiums payable in any individual case. The rates of premiums vary from 1s. 6d. per cent. for ordinary dwelling-houses to £5 5s. per cent. and more for dangerous stores and premises, and for the special risks of some factories. An understanding on this point is, therefore, invariably arrived at before an insurance is effected.

Most of the leading offices belong to what is known as the Tariff Association, a combination which has for its object the **Tariff sys-** fixing of minimum rates for certain particularly **tem.** hazardous risks. This, no doubt, accounts in a large measure for the existence of co-operation on the part of manufacturers and others for purposes of mutual insurance; and also for the fact that insurances to a considerable amount are effected with American and Continental fire offices; but it is not at all certain that the public are prejudiced by the operation of the tariff system, which has the effect of encouraging the persons engaged in the hazardous trades in question to take extra precautions against fire, with the results of diminishing the exceptional losses and of ultimately bringing the rates of premiums down to the normal level of other trades.

When large insurances have to be effected by a firm it may be advisable to place the business in the hands of an insurance broker, who may be able to secure much better terms for his client than the latter could obtain by negotiating with the offices direct. It must be remembered, however, that an insurance broker occupies, in a measure, a dual position, and that while in some matters he may act for the office, in others he may represent the assured. Even if he is the agent of an insurance company, the latter is not bound to undertake a risk which he has accepted. If the company decline a proposal made through a broker and notify their decision to him, they will not be liable if a fire takes place before he has been able to communicate the refusal to his client. The responsibility of the insurance office cannot be said to commence until they have, by the issue of a receipt, accepted the premium or a deposit; and a broker is personally responsible if having agreed to effect an insurance he neglects to do so and a fire takes place. When the insurance is provisional only, and subject to the office making an inspection of the property, it is usual to grant the office twenty-eight days for this purpose, within which period it has the option to decline the risk ; but should a fire occur during the interval, and the office has not declined, it would be liable.

*Position of agent.*

### The Nature of the Contract and of the Risk.

Except in the case of a valued policy, and subject to the special conditions of average (referred to later) a policy of insurance against fire is a contract to indemnify the assured to the extent of his loss not exceeding the amount of the insurance, and this, together with the expense of extinguishing the fire, is the measure of the liability of the insurers. If therefore the assured receives from the office the

*Insurance a contract of indemnity.*

# THE NATURE OF THE CONTRACT AND THE RISK. 177

full value of the property destroyed he will have to give the office the benefit of the salvage, and of any rights tending to reduce the loss, which he possesses. If, for instance, the **Subrogation.** person whose property is destroyed by fire is able to recover the loss from a party other than the insurer, the latter, if he had satisfied the claim, would be able to sue in the name of the assured the person actually responsible for the loss. A person whose property has been negligently set on fire by his neighbour will, if he is insured, be able to recover from either the latter or the fire office. If he recovers under his policy the office would be entitled to proceed in the name of the assured against the person who caused the conflagration. This raises a very serious point for manufacturers and others to consider, for, although their own property may be fully protected, they may by negligently causing the destruction of their neighbour's property incur serious loss without protection. "The right of the office rests upon the doctrine of subrogation, by which if a man has two distinct remedies against different parties for one and the same claim, one of such parties paying the whole amount, is entitled to recover it from the other party if primarily liable, in the name of the person originally injured."*

The indemnity is personal to the assured and cannot, "except by way of mortgage," be assigned without the consent of the **Policy not** insurers endorsed upon the policy. It is essential **assignable.** that the assurer should have an interest in the property both when effecting the insurance and at the time of the fire. The conditions of some policies are exceedingly stringent in this respect, and provide for the insurance being cancelled in the event of any modification in the insurable interest. It sometimes happens that the conditions are so framed as to render the policy void upon the demise of the assured; or upon the admission of a new partner.

When a sale of buildings or of other properties, which are insured, is intended, and it is decided to transfer the insurance, **Transfer of** an understanding should be come to with the office. **properties.** Immediately a contract for sale is concluded the purchaser becomes in equity the beneficial owner, and is the sufferer in the event of the property not being insured and a fire taking place. The vendor of the property is not bound to tell the purchaser whether or not the property is insured; and even if there is a policy in favour of the vendor existing at the time of

\* "The Law of Fire Insurance," p. 125.

the fire, the purchaser is not, in the absence of a specific agreement, entitled to any benefit under it. But he can call upon the insurers to expend the insurance money in reinstatement. In the case of leaseholds, it should be stated that in the event of the property being destroyed by fire subsequently to the date of the contract, the purchaser may be bound under the conditions of the lease to rebuild. It is advisable in the interest of the purchaser that these risks should be provided against in the contract for sale, or that immediately it is signed he should insure the property.

When the policy becomes void, or when the interest of the insured in the property ceases from any cause before the expiration of the term of the insurance, the insurers are not bound to return the proportionate part of the premium in respect of the unexpired portion of the term. Most fire policies, however, provide for the transfer of the insurance upon the removal of the objects insured, and it is usual for the offices to transfer their indemnity from one property to another, provided their risk is not increased; and they will take into consideration the unexpired proportion of the premium in fixing a new rate.

**Premiums not returnable.**

Fire insurances are based either on a valued policy, or are specific, or are subject to the conditions of average. Valued policies are those in which the office and the insured agree to assign to the property insured a definite value, which in case of fire shall be the amount to be reimbursed to the insured quite irrespective of the actual loss sustained by him. Such policies are unsatisfactory and very rare; and the onus of proving that the property has been valued rests with the insured. Specific insurances are those in which the insurers are liable for the actual loss, not exceeding the amount for which the property is insured. The third category of fire insurance, embracing the conditions of average, calls for most careful consideration by the assured. The effect of these conditions is to make the insured his own underwriter to the extent by which his property is under insured; and in the event of fire he would be able to recover from the offices only such proportion of the loss as the sum insured by them bears to the total value of the property. Thus, if a manufacturer effected an insurance, under the average conditions, upon his stock worth £60,000, and subsequently increased the goods on hand by £20,000 and a fire occurred destroying £40,000 worth of stock,

**Valued policies.**

**Specific insurances.**

**Conditions of average.**

he would be able to recover only £30,000, that being the proportion of the loss which the amount of the insurance (£60,000) bears to the total value of the stock (£80,000) at the time of the fire. The insured, in this case, being in the position of an underwriter for one-fourth of the risk, would be entitled to participate to that extent in the salvage. The average conditions are necessarily inoperative if the value of the property does not exceed the amount covered by the policy.

"The subject of alterations after the date of the policy in the structure or use of the buildings, either as regards the trades carried on or the goods deposited in them, has been of all others the most fruitful of disputes between the assurers and the assured. In the decided cases the question has generally turned upon the construction of the conditions, and the fire offices, tutored by experience, certainly endeavour to guard themselves in every possible manner against unanticipated hazards. In spite, however, of the ingenuity of their advisers, cases must occasionally arise to which no condition is applicable, and the question remains for solution how far an alteration not in terms expressly forbidden affects the contract. The true solution would appear to be found by ascertaining whether by the alteration the description is rendered inapplicable, or whether any express representation as to the future use of the premises has been violated, and whether there is any condition in the policy applicable to the case."*

*Alterations in the risk.*

It is important before making any alteration in, or addition to, the property insured, to ascertain whether the description amounts to a warranty, as in that case the policy would be invalidated by a violation of the description; and when the policy expressly disallows any alteration or addition, even a temporary modification would vitiate the policy. Repairs, however, are quite permissible, although they may while being carried out increase the risk of fire.

"A question arises when the assured, having effected an insurance upon the stock-in-trade or machinery, undertakes after the date of the policy an additional or different trade or business, not a part of, or incidental to, the first. This is often specially provided for by a condition; when it is not so, two questions may arise. First, whether the alteration has caused any increase of risk; secondly, whether the new stock is covered by the insurance. Assuming that there has been no unauthorised increase of risk to

* "The Law of Fire Insurance," pp. 86, 87.

void the policy, if a claim is made for a loss upon property forming part of the new or additional stock, the question must turn upon the wording of the policy, and whether, applying the ordinary rules of construction, it can be fairly inferred that the property destroyed was within the terms of the contract."*

There can be no doubt that a manufacturer whose trade is described in the policy would not be able to claim indemnification under that policy for loss of stock of another trade which he had taken over since the insurance upon his original stock was effected. When the insurance is upon goods of an ordinary character, the addition of goods which are regarded as hazardous would invalidate the policy.

It is well that in every case of alteration or addition the policy should be carefully examined, with the object of ascertaining whether the risk has been increased beyond that contemplated by the insurers, and whenever there is any doubt the insurance office should be communicated with. It is better in most cases that the owner should pay a higher rate of premium than incur the risk of being his own insurer. The omission to communicate a material fact to the insurers would entitle them to cancel the policy; but they may waive this right by endorsement of the policy, or even by accepting the renewal premium after they have had notice of a violation by the insured of the conditions of the policy.

Liability does not attach to the insurers unless the loss is proximately caused by fire. The mere heat of a stove, if it causes **Fire must be proximate cause of damage.** damage to property, will not, in the absence of combustion of substances other than the fuel in the stove, be sufficient to support a claim against the insurers; nor will the insurers "be responsible for any loss on goods or utensils damaged or destroyed whilst undergoing any process in which the application of fire heat is necessary."

With regard to loss by explosion many intricate questions present themselves, and the provisions on this point inserted in policies vary widely; but of course the risk can be **Explosives.** indisputably defined by special conditions. The production, storage, and distribution of petroleum, gunpowder, and other explosives is now regulated by special Acts of Parliament.

Ordinary oil and coal gas, for purposes of lighting and heating, **Oil and gas.** are allowed by all policies, but gas must not be made on the premises; and some offices expressly recognise liability for losses caused by gas explosions.

* "The Law of Fire Insurance," p. 95.

## THE ADJUSTMENT OF THE LOSS.

As one of the alterations of which the offices require notice may be mentioned the adoption of electric lighting. The electric light is deemed to be a special risk unless it has been installed in accordance with the rules of the Phœnix Fire Office, or of those drawn up by the Society of Telegraph Engineers and Electricians.

**Electricity.**

The offices are not, it would appear, unwilling to insert in their policies the condition that losses by lightning will be made good, but in the absence of such provision disputes may arise.

### THE ADJUSTMENT OF THE LOSS.

The insured should, in the event of a fire, give immediate notice to the offices, and prepare to furnish them with such proof of the loss as may be required by the policies. Sometimes it is stipulated that particulars of the damage shall be furnished by a given date to entitle the insurer to recover, and it is important that this condition should be strictly complied with. The nature of the evidence of loss required to be produced varies with circumstances, in some cases even a statutory declaration being required, but the best proofs obtainable are generally the account books, invoices, &c. If the accounts are properly kept the adjustment of the loss is very materially facilitated.

**Proof of loss.**

**Value of proper accounts.**

The account books and business papers are not usually insurable, but their loss, and the consequent inability on the part of the insurer to produce satisfactory evidence of the loss, is frequently regarded, by those who have to assess the damages, as a cause for suspicion.

The claim made upon the insurers should be well founded, and be such as can be evidenced by the books, for although the insured may be justified in making a claim in excess of the amount admitted by the insurers, still a large and unsubstantiated claim may by a jury be regarded as an indication of *mala fides*, and it is generally provided in the policy that any attempt on the part of the insured to defraud the insurers shall avoid the insurance.

**Right of insurers to enter premises.**

The insurers, it appears, have the right to enter the premises where a fire has occurred, and to remain in possession for a reasonable time for the purpose of enabling them to assess the damage; and by the Metropolitan Fire Brigade Act of 1865, as well as by numerous other Local Acts, power is given to the officers of the brigade to take such measures as they may deem expedient for the protection of life and property, and to break into, or pull down, any premises for the purpose of putting an end to a fire; and any damage that may thereby be caused is covered by the insurance against fire. **Consequen-** The insured is bound to do everything in his power **tial losses.** at the time of the fire to lessen the loss to the insurers. The costs of extinguishing a fire, as a rule, fall on the insurers, and there are other consequential losses which are generally borne by them, but it is always advisable that they should be specifically mentioned in the policy. Such are, for instance, the expenses attending the removal of properties, which fall primarily on the salvage; and the loss arising from theft at the time of the fire. But avoidable losses or expenses will not be made good, and goods destroyed by fire during removal are not covered.

The insurance being an indemnity, only the actual loss at the time of the fire will be reimbursed; and the insured cannot claim **Co-insurers.** compensation in excess of his actual loss. If he is insured in several offices he is bound to declare the fact when a fire occurs, and the loss is then distributed rateably among the several offices. The insured is not entitled to compensation for such consequential damages as loss of future profits, interest, or rent, unless specifically covered by the policy.

It is quite permissible to insure the rent payable during rein-**Rent.** statement, but the offices usually limit this to an amount representing one year's rent. This is a point of some importance to a tenant, inasmuch as his tenancy is not affected by a fire, and until such tenancy has expired he is bound to pay rent, although the premises may be burnt down. But this may be provided for by an express agreement in the lease that in the event of the premises being destroyed or damaged by fire, rent shall cease until they are reinstated.

With regard to the valuation of the properties destroyed, this is usually based upon their state of repair and condition at the **Valuation of** time the fire broke out, and the insured cannot claim **properties.** to be supplied with new properties in place of those destroyed, if these, although they were before the fire still applicable to their original uses, have undergone considerable wear and tear. In the case of stocks on hand the cost of production, not including any percentage for profit, is generally the basis upon

## VALUATION OF PROPERTIES.

which indemnification is made; but even this measure of compensation may be unobtainable if the properties have depreciated considerably as a result of obsolescence or of having been superseded by improved articles. With marketable merchandise, however, the indemnification is made on a different basis. In that case " the price current on the day of the fire will fix the amount of the liability of the insurers. The cost to the assured has nothing to do with the matter. .... If the goods have risen in value the payment of the cost price would be no indemnity, while if the insured were to receive the cost price of goods which had fallen in value, or which having been on hand for a considerable period had become depreciated, the same objection would arise, and in the event of a fall in the produce market such a rule might be a serious temptation to arson."* There would be an exception, however, in the case of merchandise whose value had either improved or deteriorated after the date of sale but before the time of delivery, during which interval the goods had been destroyed by fire. These points are usually specially provided for in the policy.

It has already been stated that if the insured has been fully indemnified, and the policy contains no conditions of average, the salvage will belong to the insurers, but if the insured is inadequately covered, then the value of the salvage to the extent of his deficiency will be his property.

**Salvage.**

An invariable provision in fire policies is that the insurers shall have the option of reinstating instead of paying the estimated amount of the loss incurred by the insured, but, except occasionally in the cases of buildings and machinery, this option is seldom exercised by the insurance offices.

**Reinstatement.**

As a matter of practice the course generally pursued with regard to settlement of claims is to put up the damaged goods for sale by auction, the proceeds, after deducting the expenses, being handed to the insured, and the office making up the difference between the net proceeds of the salvage and the amount insured.

**Auctions.**

Insurers are not liable for loss owing to the assortment being broken, and they cannot be required, on the ground that companion articles are damaged, to sell by auction articles in good condition.

When the insurance is in favour of several persons any one of

* "The Law of Fire Insurance," p. 151.

## 184 ON THE LAW RELATING TO FIRE INSURANCE.

them can receive the insurance money after adjustment and give **Insurance in** discharge; but if the policy has been mortgaged, **joint names.** and the office have notice of the fact, they will require the mortgagee to join in the receipt, and under the Building Act the mortgagee or other person interested can call upon the insurers to expend the insurance money in reinstatement.

### BOILER INSURANCE.

Losses due to the explosion of boilers or collapse of flues are not covered by ordinary fire policies. Such losses can, however, be provided against by insurance with the companies carrying on this branch of insurance business. These companies generally undertake also the repairs, alterations, and maintenance of boilers, the inspection of steam boilers and engines, and the supply of steam power.

The insurers are guaranteed :—1. The responsible inspection of the boilers by an officer of the Insurance Company, with a written report of the result, at periodical intervals, or whenever necessary. 2. Indemnity to the assured up to the amount of the insurance, against all damage, not only to the boiler, but to the surrounding property, which may result, otherwise than by fire, from the explosion of the boiler or the collapse of the flues, provided that the explosion or collapse is not consequent on the over-loading of the safety-valves, or by the wilful act of the insured; and against injury to persons consequent upon the explosion, provided such injury is not covered by any other policy of insurance.

These Insurance Companies are also generally prepared to undertake, by a special contract, all repairs of boilers necessitated by wear and tear, as well as the periodical inspection and indication of engines.

Insurance can further be made on boilers with internal furnaces, if in good condition and adapted to the pressure required. In such cases the insurance covers all damage to the boiler itself, its mountings and the adjacent property, up to the full amount insured *in cases of actual explosion*, but does not cover any damage to, or injury of, the internal flues in cases of collapse.

Periodical inspection, with a written report, giving information and containing advice, but without insurance, is also undertaken by the same companies.

It will be seen from these notes how important is the bearing such questions of insurance against losses have upon the accounts **Importance of subject to accountants.** of a manufacturer, and how necessary it is for accountants to give due consideration to these and kindred subjects in order that losses which, if sustained, would cause serious embarrassment, if not insolvency, may be adequately provided against. It is very desirable, having regard to this point of view, that all insurance policies should be entered in an Insurance Register, which should be so ruled as to admit of a complete record of all the salient features of the policies; the extent of, and the premiums on, the insurances; and of the grouping of the various offices with which the policies are effected.

# APPENDIX E.

## SUMMARY OF THE PROVISIONS OF THE FACTORY AND WORKSHOP ACTS, 1878, 1883, 1889, & 1891, AFFECTING EMPLOYERS OF LABOUR AND OCCUPIERS OF FACTORIES.

THE Act which came into force on the 1st January, 1879 (41 Vic.,
**Arrange-** chap. 16), has for its object the consolidation and
**ment of Act.** amendment of the law relating to Factories and Workshops.

It is divided into four parts, viz. :—
1. The general law relating to Factories and Workshops, including provisions as to Sanitation, Safety, Employment, and Meal Hours, Holidays, Education of Children, Certificates of Fitness for Employment, and Accidents.
2. Special provisions relating to particular classes of Factories, &c.
3. Administration, Penalties, and Legal Proceedings, including provisions as to Inspection, Certifying Surgeons, Fines, &c.
4. Definitions, Savings, Application to Scotland and Ireland, and Repeal.

There are also six Schedules, containing special provisions, lists of Factories and Workshops, Acts Repealed, &c., &c.

The general provisions of the Act of 1883 are summarised with the provisions of the Act of 1878. The special provisions as to whitelead factories, bakehouses, are summarised after the general provisions of the Acts.

The Act of 1891 (54 & 55 Vic., chap. 75) is divided into seven parts, relating to :—
1. Sanitary Provisions.
2. Safety.

# SANITATION.

3. Special Rules and Requirements.
4. Period of Employment.
5. Holidays.
6. Conditions of Employment.
7. Miscellaneous.

There are also two Schedules, the first containing Rules as to Arbitration between Occupiers of Factories or Workshops on the one hand, and the Chief Inspector on behalf of the Secretary of State on the other; the second containing a list of Enactments Repealed.

The additions to, or variations made by the Act of 1891 in the provisions of the Act of 1878 are shown in square brackets.

The Cotton Cloth Factories Act of 1889 (52 & 53 Vic., chap. 62), dealing with a special class of factory solely, is summarised at the end of this Appendix.

## I. WITH REGARD TO SANITATION.

**Ventilation.** The Act provides that every factory * shall be kept in a cleanly state and free from effluvia; it shall be ventilated and not overcrowded (Sec. 3); the inspector, who may take with him into a factory [and into workshops conducted on the system of not employing any child, young person, or woman therein, and into laundries (Sec. 2, i. 1891)], **Duty of Inspector, and powers after.** a medical officer of health or other officer of sanitary authority, shall give notice to sanitary authority of defect (Sec. 4).

**Power of Secretary of State as to sanitary provisions in workshops.** [The Secretary of State if satisfied that the provisions of the law relating to public health as to effluvia arising from any drain, privy or other nuisance, or with respect to cleanliness, ventilation, overcrowding, or lime-washing are not observed, he may, by order, authorise and direct an inspector or inspectors under the principal Act to take, during such period as may be mentioned in the order, such steps as appear necessary or proper for enforcing the said provisions (Sec. 1, i. 1891).]

**Power of Inspector after notice to sanitary authority.** [Where notice of such defect is given by the inspector and proceedings are not taken within a reasonable time for punishing or remedying the defect, the inspector may take the like proceedings for punishing or remedying the same as the sanitary

* The expression "factory" means textile factory and non-texile factory, or either (Sec. 93).

188 SUMMARY OF THE FACTORY AND WORKSHOP ACTS.

authority might have taken, and shall be entitled to recover from the sanitary authority all such expenses in the proceedings as he may incur and are not recovered from any other person, and have not been incurred in any unsuccessful proceedings (Sec. 2, ii. 1891).]

Every factory not painted with oil or varnished once, at least, within seven years shall be limewashed once, at least, within every **Painting** fourteen months, and if so painted or varnished, shall **and lime-** be washed with hot water and soap once, at least, **washing.** within every fourteen months; but where it appears to a Secretary of State that in any factory these regulations are not **Special** required, or are inapplicable, he may grant a special **exception.** exception (Sec. 33). There are special provisions to **Bakehouses.** secure cleanliness of bakehouses (Sec. 34 and 35), and in a factory, &c., where grinding, glazing, or **Fan to be** polishing is carried on an inspector may direct a fan, **provided.** &c., to be provided (Sec. 36).

A child, young person, or woman shall not be employed in **Protection** wet spinning unless means be adopted for protect- **against** ing the workers from being wetted, and where hot **wetting.** water is used for preventing the escape of steam into the room (Sec. 37).

**As to work-** [It is provided that every workshop and every work- **shops.** place within the meaning of the Public Health Act, 1875, shall be kept free from effluvia arising from any drain, water-closet, earth-closet, privy, urinal, or other nuisance, and unless so kept shall be deemed to be a nuisance liable to be dealt with summarily under the law relating to public health (Sec. 4, 1891).]

II. WITH REGARD TO SAFETY AND ACCIDENTS.

The Act provides that every hoist or teagle, certain flywheels, [all dangerous parts of machinery,] and every part of a steam- **Machinery** engine and water-wheel, shall be securely fenced, that **to be fenced.** every wheel-race and every part of the mill gearing *

---

* The expression "mill gearing" comprehends every shaft, whether upright, oblique, or horizontal, and every wheel-drum or pulley by which the motion of the first moving power is communicated to any machine appertaining to a manufacturing process. [The expression "machinery" includes any driving strap or band, and the expression "process" includes the use of any locomotive (Sec. 37, 1891).]

shall be secured, and that all fencing shall be maintained in efficient state (Sec. 5).

Where an inspector considers that in a factory any part of the machinery moved by steam or other mechanical power to which the provisions of the Act, with respect to fencing, do not apply, is not securely fenced, or where an inspector considers that a vat, **Arbitration** pan, or other structure is dangerous to any *child* or **as to fencing.** *young person*, he shall serve on the occupier a notice requiring him to fence the machinery, vat, &c.; but the occupier may within seven days serve a requisition to refer the matter to arbitration, and thereupon the matter shall be referred to arbitration (Secs. 6 and 7). Likewise, where an inspector **Faulty** **fixing of** observes in a factory that any grindstone worked by **grindstone.** steam, &c., is faulty, or is fixed in faulty manner, he shall, subject to the same provisions as to arbitration, serve on the occupier a notice requiring him to replace and properly fix such faulty grindstone (Sec. 8).

A child shall not be allowed to clean any machinery in a factory while the same is in motion, nor shall a young person or woman **Cleaning** be allowed to clean mill-gearing in a factory while **machinery** the same is in motion, nor shall a child, young person **in motion.** or woman be allowed to work between the fixed and traversing part of any self-acting machine while the machine is in motion (Sec. 9).

**Special rules** [Where the Secretary of State certifies that in his **and require-** opinion any machinery or process or particular de- **ments as to** scription of manual labour used in a factory or work- **dangerous** **and un-** shop (other than a domestic workshop) is dangerous **healthy inci-** or injurious to health * or dangerous to life or limb, **dents of em-** or that the provision for the admission of fresh air is **ployment.** not sufficient, or that the quantity of dust generated or inhaled is dangerous or injurious to health, the chief inspector may serve on the occupier a notice in writing, proposing such special rules or requiring the adoption of such measures as appear to the chief inspector to be reasonably practicable and to meet the necessities of the case.

[Unless within twenty-one days after receipt of the notice the occupier serves on the chief inspector a notice in writing that he

[* By Notice in the *London Gazette* the Home Secretary has certified that, in his opinion, the processes carried on in the manufacture of earthenware, the manufacture of explosives in which di-nitro-benzole is used, chemical works, and quarries, are dangerous or injurious to health.]

## 190 SUMMARY OF THE FACTORY AND WORKSHOP ACTS.

objects to the rules or requirement, the rules shall be established, or, as the case may be, the requirement shall be observed.

[If the notice of objection suggests any modification, the Secretary of State shall consider the suggestion and may assent thereto with or without any further modification which may be agreed on between the Secretary of State and the occupier, and thereupon the rules shall be established, or, as the case may be, the requirement shall be observed, subject to such modification.

[If the Secretary of State does not assent to any objection or modification suggested by the occupier, the matter in difference shall be referred to arbitration under this Act, and the date of the receipt of the notice of objection by the Secretary of State shall be deemed to be the date of the reference, and the rules shall be established, or the requisition shall have effect, as settled by an award on arbitration.

[Any notice under this section may be served by post.

[With respect to arbitrations under this Act the provisions in the First Schedule to this Act shall have effect.

No person shall be precluded by any agreement from doing, or be liable under any agreement to any penalty or forfeiture for doing, such acts as may be necessary in order to comply with the provisions of this section (Sec. 8, i.-vii. 1891).]

When there occurs in a factory or a workshop any accident which either causes to a person employed in the factory, &c., loss of life or bodily injury, caused by machinery moved by power, or vat, or pan [and is of such a nature as to prevent the person injured from returning to his work and doing five hours' work on any day during the next three days after the occurrence of the accident (Sec. 22, 1891), written notice of the accident shall forthwith be sent to the inspector and the certifying surgeon.

**Notices to be given of accidents.**

[The notice required where the person killed or injured is not moved to his own residence must state both his residence and the place to which he has been removed (Sec. 22, ii. 1891).

[Where a death has occurred by accident, the coroner shall forthwith advise the district inspector of the time and place of the holding of the inquest, and any relative of the person whose death may have been caused by the accident, and any inspector, and the occupier of the factory or workshop in which the accident occurred, and any person appointed by the order in writing of the majority of the workpeople employed in the factory or workshop shall be at liberty to attend and examine any witness, either in person, or by his counsel, solicitor, or agent, subject nevertheless to the order of the coroner (Sec. 22, iii. 1891).

**As to Scotland.** [A public inquiry in open court is to be held by the sheriff, upon the petition of any party interested, and the sheriff must advise the district inspector as to the inquiry. The law as to the liberty of the inspector, the occupier of the factory, or a representative of the workpeople employed in the factory to examine any witness, &c., is the same as in England (Sec. 33, v. 1891).]

If any such accident occurs to a person employed in a factory or workshop where the occupier is not the actual employer, the latter shall immediately report the same to the occupier. But an accident of which notice is required by Sec. 63 of Explosives Act, **Investigation by surgeon.** 1875, to be sent to a government inspector, need not be reported to the certifying surgeon (Sec. 31). A certifying surgeon shall, with the least possible delay after receiving notice, proceed to the factory or workshop, and make a full investigation of the accident, and within twenty-four hours report to the inspector. For the purpose of such investigation, the certifying surgeon shall have the same powers as an inspector (Sec. 32). If any person is killed or suffers any bodily **Penalties for negligence.** injury in consequence of the occupier of a factory having neglected to fence any machinery, or in consequence of the occupier of a factory or workshop having neglected to fence any vat, &c., he shall be liable to a fine not exceeding £100, the whole or part of which may be applied for the benefit of the injured person, or otherwise, as a Secretary of State determines (Sec. 82).

**Provision against fire.** [Every factory of which the construction is commenced after the first day of January one thousand eight hundred and ninety-two, and in which more than forty persons are employed, shall be furnished with a certificate from the sanitary authority of the district in which the factory is situate that the factory is provided on the storeys above the ground floor with such means of escape in case of fire for the persons employed therein as can reasonably be required under the circumstances of each case. A factory not so furnished shall be considered not to be kept in conformity with the principal Act, and it shall be the duty of the sanitary authority to examine every such factory, and on being satisfied that the factory is so provided to give such a certificate as aforesaid.

[With respect to all factories to which the foregoing provisions do not apply, and in which more than forty persons are employed, it shall be the duty of the sanitary authority of every district, as soon as may be after the passing of this Act, and afterwards from time to time, to ascertain whether all the factories within their district are provided with the means of escape as aforesaid, and, in the case of any factory which is not so provided, to serve on the owner of the factory a notice in writing specifying the measures necessary, and requiring him to carry out the same before a specified date, and thereupon the owner shall, notwithstanding any agreement with the occupier, have power to take such steps as are necessary for complying with the requirements, and, unless such requirements are complied with, the owner shall be liable to a fine not exceeding one pound for every day that such non-compliance continues. In case of a difference of opinion between the owner of the factory and the sanitary authority, the difference shall, on the application of either party, be referred to arbitration. The parties to the arbitration shall be the sanitary authority on the one hand and the owner on the other, and the award on the arbitration shall be binding on the parties thereto. If the owner alleges that the occupier of the factory ought to bear or contribute to the expenses of complying with the requirement, he may apply to the county court having jurisdiction where the factory is situate, and thereupon the county court, after hearing the occupier, may make such order as appears to the court just and equitable (Sec. 7, i. and ii. 1891).]

III. WITH REGARD TO EMPLOYMENT AND MEAL HOURS OF CHILDREN, YOUNG PERSONS, AND WOMEN.*

The Act provides : The occupier of a factory or workshop shall specify, in a notice affixed in the factory, &c., the period of **Notices to** employment, the times allowed for meals, and **be affixed.** whether the children are employed on the system of morning and afternoon sets or of alternate days. The periods of employment, &c., shall be deemed to be those specified in such notice; and all the children in the factory, &c., shall be employed on either of these systems, according as is specified in

* Unless the context otherwise requires, child means a person under the age of fourteen years; young person means a person of the age of fourteen years and under the age of eighteen years; woman means a woman of eighteen years of age and upwards.

such notice. But the occupier may from time to time, within the limits allowed by the Act, alter such notice, provided that a change shall not be made until after the occupier has served on an inspector, and affixed in the factory or workshop, notice of his intention to make such change, and shall not be made oftener than once a quarter, unless for special cause allowed in writing by an inspector (Sec. 19).

*With respect to the Employment of Young Persons and Women in a Textile Factory,\** it is provided: The period of employment **Hours of** shall either begin at 6 A.M. and end at 6 P.M., or **employ-** begin at 7 A.M. and end at 7 P.M., except on Saturday, **ment.** when the period of employment shall begin either at 6 A.M. or at 7 A.M. Where the period of employment on Saturday begins at 6 A.M., that period shall end at 1 P.M. as regards employment in any manufacturing process, and at 1.30 P.M. as regards employment for any other purposes, if not less than one hour is allowed for meals; and at 12.30 and 1 P.M. respectively, if less than one hour is allowed for meals. Where the period of employment on Saturday begins at 7 A.M., that period shall end at 1.30 P.M. as regards any manufacturing process, and at 2 P.M. as regards employment for any other purposes. There shall be allowed for meals during the said period on every day except Saturday not less than two hours, of which one hour at least shall be before 3 P.M., and on Saturday not less than half an hour. A young person or woman shall not be employed continuously for more than four hours and a half without at least half an hour's interval for a meal (Sec. 11).

*With respect to the Employment of Children in a Textile Factory,* the Act provides: Children shall not be employed except on the **Morning** system either of morning and afternoon sets or of **and after-** alternate days only. The period of employment for **noon sets.** a child in a morning set shall, except on Saturday, begin at the same hour as if the child were a young person and end at 1 P.M., or at the beginning of dinner time if that time begins

\* The expression "textile factory" means any premises wherein or within the close or curtilage of which steam, &c., is used to move or work machinery employed in preparing, manufacturing, or finishing, or in any process incident to the manufacture of cotton, wool, hair, silk, flax, hemp, jute, tow, chinagrass, cocoa-nut fibre, or other like material either separately or mixed together, or mixed with any other material or any fabric made thereof. Provided that print works, bleaching and dyeing works, lace warehouses, paper mills, flax scutch mills, rope works, and hat works shall not be deemed to be textile factories (Sec. 93).

before 1 o'clock. In an afternoon set the period shall, except on Saturday, begin at 1 P.M., or at any later hour at which the dinner time terminates, and end at the same hour as if the child were a young person. On Saturday the period shall begin and end at the same hour as if the child were a young person. A child shall not be employed in two successive periods of seven days in a morning set, nor in two successive periods of seven days in an afternoon set, and shall not be employed on two successive Saturdays, nor on Saturday in any week, if on any other day in same week his period, &c., has exceeded 5½ hours. When a child **Alternate** is employed on alternate day system the period, &c., **day system.** and the time allowed for meals shall be the same as if the child were a young person, but the child shall not be employed on two successive days, and shall not be employed on the same day of the week in two successive weeks. A child shall not on either system be employed continuously for any longer period than he could be if he were a young person without an interval of at least half an hour for a meal (Sec. 12).

By the Act of 1883 it is declared that, notwithstanding anything in Section 12 of the Act of 1878, the period of employment for a child in an afternoon set in a factory or workshop where the dinner-time does not begin before two o'clock in the afternoon may begin at noon, provided that in such cases the period of employment in the morning set shall end at noon.

*Exceptions.*—If the period of employment for young persons and women in textile factories used solely for the making of elastic web, ribbon, or trimming begins at 7 A.M., and the whole time between that hour and 8 o'clock is allowed for meals, a child, young person, or woman shall not, between 1st November and 31st March next following, be prevented being employed continuously without an interval of at least half an hour for a meal for the same period as if the factory were a non-textile factory. Where it is proved to the satisfaction of a Secretary of State that in any other class of textile factories the persons employed require it, he may extend this exception (Sec. 48). The regulations with respect to the employment of young persons in textile factories shall not prevent the employment in the part of a textile factory in which a machine for the manufacture of lace is moved by steam, &c., of any male young person above the age of sixteen years between 4 A.M. and 10 P.M., if he is employed in accordance with the following conditions, viz. (*a*) where such young person is employed on any day before the beginning or after the end of the ordinary period of employment, he shall be allowed for meals between 4 A.M. and 10 P.M., not less than nine hours; (*b*) where such young person is employed on any day before the beginning of the ordinary period of employment he shall not be employed on the same day after the end of that period; and (*c*) where such young person is employed on any day after the end of the ordinary period of employment, he shall not be employed next morning before the beginning of the ordinary period of employment. For the purpose of this exception the ordinary period of employment means the period for young persons under the age of sixteen years or women in the factory; or if none are employed, means such period as can under the Act be fixed for the employment of such young persons and women, and notice of such period shall be affixed (Sec. 44).

*With respect to the Employment of Young Persons and Women in a Non-textile Factory\* and of Young Persons in a Workshop*, the **Hours of employment.** Act provides: The period of employment, except on Saturday, shall (unless specially excepted) either begin at 6 A.M. and end at 6 P.M., or begin at 7 A.M. and end at 7 P.M. The period of employment on Saturday shall (unless specially excepted) begin at 6 A.M., or at 7 A.M., and end at 2 P.M. There shall be allowed for meals during the said period on every day except Saturday not less than one hour and a half, of which one hour at least shall be before 3 P.M., and on Saturday not less than half an hour. A young person or a woman in a non-textile factory, and a young person in a workshop, shall not be employed continuously for more than five hours without an interval of at least half an hour for a meal (Sec. 13).

\* The expression "non-textile factory" means (1) any of the following places, viz., print works, bleaching and dyeing works, earthenware works, lucifer match works, percussion-cap works, cartridge works, paper-staining works, fustian-cutting works, blast furnaces, copper mills, iron mills, foundries, metal and india-rubber works, paper mills, glass works, tobacco factories, letterpress printing works, bookbinding works, flax scutch mills; (2) any of the following premises or places wherein or within the close or curtilage or precincts of which steam, &c., power is used in aid of the manufacturing process carried on, viz., hat works, rope works, bakehouses, lace warehouses, ship-building yards, quarries, pit banks; (3) any premises wherein or within the close, &c., of which any manual labour is exercised by way of trade or for purposes of gain in or incidental to any of the following purposes, viz., the making of any article or part of any article, the altering, repairing, ornamenting, or finishing of any article, the adapting for sale of any article, and wherein or within the close, &c., of which steam, &c., power is used in aid of the manufacturing process carried on (Sec. 93).

**Period of employment on Saturday.** [The period of employment on Saturday for a young person or woman in a non-textile factory or workshop may be from 6 A.M. to 4 P.M., with an interval of not less than two hours for meals—if the period of employment of such young person or woman has not exceeded eight hours of any day in the same week, and notice of such non-employment has been affixed and served on the inspector (Sec. 15, 1891).]

*With respect to the Employment of Children in a Non-textile Factory or a Workshop* the Act provides: Children shall not be **Morning and afternoon sets.** employed except either on the system of morning and afternoon sets, or (in a factory or workshop in which not less than two hours are allowed for meals on every day except Saturday) on the system of alternate days **Alternate day system.** only. The period for a child in a morning set on every day, including Saturday, shall begin at 6 or 7 A.M., and end at 1 P.M., or at the beginning of dinner time, if that time begins before 1 o'clock. The period for a child in an afternoon set on every day, including Saturday, shall begin at 1 P.M., or at any hour later than 12.30 P.M., at which the dinner time terminates, and end on Saturday at 2 P.M., and on any other day at 6 or 7 P.M., according as the period for children in the morning set began at 6 or 7 A.M. A child shall not be employed in two successive periods of seven days in a morning set, nor in two successive periods of seven days in an afternoon set, and shall not be employed on Saturday in any week in the same set in which he has been employed on any other day of the same week. When a child is employed on the alternate day system the period shall, except on Saturday, either begin at 6 A.M. and end at 6 P.M., or begin at 7 A.M. and end at 7 P.M.; the period of employment for such child shall on Saturday begin at 6 or 7 A.M. and end at 2 P.M.; there shall be allowed to such child for meals during the said period not less on any day, except Saturday, than two hours, and on Saturday not less than half an hour; the child shall not be employed on two successive days, and shall not be employed on the same day of the week in two successive weeks. A child shall not on either system be employed continuously for more than five hours without an interval of at least half an hour for a meal (Sec. 14).

By the Act of 1883 it is declared that, notwithstanding anything in Section 14 of the Act of 1878, the period of employment for a child in an afternoon set in a factory or workshop where the dinner-time does not begin before two o'clock in the afternoon may begin at noon, provided that in such cases the period of employment in the morning set shall end at noon.

*With respect to the Employment of Women in Workshops* the Act provides: In a workshop which is conducted on the system of employing children and young persons, or either of them, a woman shall not be employed except during the same period, and subject to the same restrictions, as if she were a young person. In a workshop which is conducted on the system of not employing children or young persons [the period of employment for a woman shall, except on Saturday, be a specified period of twelve hours taken between 6 A.M. and 10 P.M.; and shall on Saturday be a specified period of eight hours between 6 A.M. and 4 P.M.; there shall be allowed to a woman for meals and absence, not less, except on Saturday, than one hour and a half, and on Saturday not less than half an hour (Sec. 13, *a*, *b*, 1891).] The occupier must give the inspector notice of his intention to conduct his workshop on system of not employing children or young persons (Sec. 15).

**Childbirth.** [An occupier of a factory or workshop shall not knowingly allow a woman to be employed therein within four weeks after she has given birth to a child (Sec. 17, 1891).]

Section 16 contains provisions *with respect to the Period of Employment and Meal Times of Children, &c., employed in Domestic Workshops.* [A child under the age of eleven years shall not be employed in a factory or workshop (Sec. 18, 1891).] A child, young person, or woman shall not (unless specially excepted) be employed on Sunday (Sec. 21).

**Children under 11.**

**Sunday work.**

Unless specially excepted, the following regulations shall be observed in a factory and workshop:—

All children, young persons, and women shall have the times allowed for meals at the same hour of the day. A child, &c., shall not during meal times be employed in factory, &c., or remain in rooms in which manufacturing process is carried on (Sec. 17).

**Meal times.**

The provisions which require that all children, &c., shall have the meal times at the same hour shall not apply in the cases of children, young persons, and women employed in the following factories:—Blast furnaces, iron mills, paper mills, glass works, and letterpress printing works, nor in

**Exceptions.**

the cases of male young persons employed in that part of any printworks or bleaching and dyeing works in which the process of dyeing or open-air bleaching is carried on. And the provisions which require that a child, &c., shall not during the meal time be employed in a factory, &c., or be allowed to remain in any room in which manufacturing process, &c., is carried on, shall not apply in the case of children, &c., in the following factories:— Iron mills, paper mills, glass works (save otherwise provided), and letterpress printing works, nor in the case of a male young person in part of any print-works or bleaching or dyeing works in which the process of dyeing or open-air bleaching is carried on, to the extent that the said provisions shall not prevent him during the meal time from being employed or being allowed to remain in any room in which any manufacturing process is carried on, and shall not prevent during the times allowed for meals to such male young persons, any other young person, or any child or woman, from being employed in the factory or allowed to remain in any room in which any manufacturing process is **Extension of** carried on. Where it is proved to the satisfaction of **exceptions.** a Secretary of State that in any factories or workshops it is necessary to extend thereto these exceptions, he may extend the same (Sec. 52).

**Prohibitions** A child or young person shall not be employed in **to employ-** a part of a factory or workshop in which there is **ment.** carried on the process of silvering of mirrors by mercurial process, or the process of whitelead making. A child or female young person shall not be employed in the part of a factory in which the process of melting or annealing glass is carried on. A girl under the age of sixteen years shall not be employed in the making or finishing of bricks or tiles, not being ornamental tiles, or the making or finishing of salt. A child shall not be employed in a part of a factory or workshop in which there is carried on any dry grinding in the metal trade or the dipping of lucifer matches. A child under the age of eleven shall not be employed **Notice of** in any grinding in the metal trades other than dry **prohibitions.** grinding, or in fustian cutting. Notice of these prohibitions shall be affixed in the factory, &c., to which they apply (Sec. 38).

A child, young person, or woman shall not be allowed to take a meal, or to remain during the time allowed for meals, in the **Meal times.** parts of factories or workshops following: viz. in the case of glass works, in any part in which the materials

## PERIODS OF EMPLOYMENT.

are mixed; in the case of glass works where flint glass is made in any part in which the work of grinding, cutting, or polishing is carried on; in the case of lucifer match works, in any part in which any manufacturing process or handicraft (except wood cutting) is carried on; in the case of earthenware [or china] works, in any part known or used as dippers' houses, dippers' drying-room, or china scouring-room. Notice of this prohibition shall be affixed in the factory, &c., to which it applies. Where it appears to a Secretary of State that in any class of factories, &c., or parts thereof not named, the taking of meals therein is injurious, he may extend this prohibition; and if the prohibition is proved to be no longer necessary, he may rescind the order of extension (Sec. 39).

*Notice to be affixed.*

*Extension of prohibition.*

In any factory or workshop in which any of the following processes or handicrafts are carried on, viz. lithographic printing, Turkey red dyeing, the making of any article of wearing apparel, making of furniture hangings, artificial flower making, bonbon making, valentine making, fancy box making, envelope making, almanac making, playing card making, machine ruling, biscuit making, firewood cutting, job dyeing, aerated water making, bookbinding, letterpress printing, or a part of a factory or workshop which is a warehouse not used for any manufacturing process, &c., and in which persons are solely employed in polishing, cleaning, wrapping, or packing up goods, the period of employment for young persons and women, if so specified in prescribed notice, may, except on Saturday, begin at 8 A.M. and end at 8 P.M., and on Saturday may begin at 8 A.M. and end at 4 P.M., or where it begins at 7 A.M. may end at 3 P.M.; and the period of employment for a child in a morning set may begin at the same hour, and in the afternoon set may end at the same hour. Where it is proved to the satisfaction of a Secretary of State that the customs, &c., of any class of non-textile factories, &c., require it he may extend this exception (Sec. 42).

*Exceptions.*

Where it is proved to the satisfaction of a Secretary of State that the customs, &c., of any class of non-textile factories or workshops require it, he may grant a special exception that the period of employment for young persons and women, if so specified in prescribed notice, may, on any day, except Saturday, begin at 9 A.M. and end at 9 P.M., and in such case the period of employment for a child in a morning set shall begin at 9 A.M., and in the afternoon set shall end at 8 P.M.

*Extension of exceptions.*

## 200 SUMMARY OF THE FACTORY AND WORKSHOP ACTS.

(Sec. 43). Where it is proved to the satisfaction of a Secretary of State that the customs, &c., of any non-textile factories or workshops require some other day in the week to be substituted for Saturday as regards the hour at which the period of employment for children, young persons, and women is to end on Saturday, he may grant a special exception authorising the occupier of such factory, &c., to substitute, by a notice affixed in the prescribed way, some other day for Saturday, and in such case the Act shall apply in like manner as if the substituted day were Saturday and Saturday were an ordinary workday (Sec. 46). In the process of Turkey red dyeing, the employment of young persons and women on Saturday until 4.30 P.M. is permitted, but the additional number of hours so worked shall be computed as part of the week's limit of work, which shall in no case be exceeded (Sec. 47).

In print works and bleaching and dyeing works the period of employment for a child, &c., and the times allowed for meals shall be the same as if the works were a textile factory, save that nothing in the section shall prevent the continuous employment of a child, &c., in the works without an interval of half an hour **Jewish** for a meal for the period allowed in a non-textile **occupiers.** factory (Sec. 40). Where the occupier of a factory or workshop is a person of the Jewish religion, the regulations as to employment shall not prevent him from employing young persons and women on Saturday from after sunset till after 9 P.M., if he keeps his factory, &c., closed on Saturday till sunset, and if he keeps his factory closed on Saturday both before and after sunset, he may, subject to certain limitations, employ young persons, &c., one hour on every other day of the week, in addition to the hours allowed by the Act (Sec. 50).

**Factories,** The provisions which relate to cleanliness, &c., to **&c., not em-** meal times, to affixing notice, to allowance of holi-**ploying** days to children, &c., or to the sending notice of **children, &c.** accidents, shall not apply to domestic workshops. Where the occupier of a workshop has served on an inspector such notice of his intention to conduct his workshop on that system, the workshop shall be deemed to be conducted on the said system until the occupier changes it, and no change shall be made until the occupier has served a notice on the inspector. Such change shall not be made oftener than once a quarter, unless for special cause allowed by an inspector (Sec. 61).

The regulations with respect to the employment of women shall

**Flax scutch mills.** not apply to flax scutch mills which are conducted on the system of not employing either children or young persons, in accordance with the preceding section, and are worked intermittently (Sec. 62).

**Extension of exceptions.** Where it appears to a Secretary of State that the adoption of special means for the cleanliness, &c., of a factory or workshop is required in pursuance of any exception under this Act, either for a longer period than is otherwise allowed, or at night, he may direct that the adoption of such means shall be a condition of such employment, and he may rescind the order (Sec. 63).

**Notice of exception to be affixed.** An occupier of a factory or workshop, not less than seven days before he avails himself of any special exception under the Act, shall serve on an inspector, and (unless specially excepted) affix notice of his intention so to avail himself, and whilst he avails himself of the exception, shall keep the notice affixed. An occupier of a factory or workshop shall enter in the prescribed register and report to an inspector the prescribed particulars respecting the employment of a child, &c., in pursuance of an exception (Sec. 66) [such report to be sent to the inspector not later than eight o'clock in the evening on which the child, young person, or woman is employed. In default of these regulations the occupier is liable, on summary conviction, to a fine not exceeding £5 (Sec. 14, i. and ii. 1891).]

*With respect to Overtime* the Act provides : The regulation of the Act with respect to employment of young persons and women shall not prevent the employment of young persons and women during a period beginning at 6 A.M. and ending at 8 P.M., or beginning at 7 A.M. and ending at 9 P.M., or beginning at 8 A.M. and ending at 10 P.M., in factories and workshops where the

**Material which is liable to be spoiled.** material which is the subject of manufacturing process or handicraft is liable to be spoiled by weather (viz., flax scutch mills, a factory, &c., in which is carried on the making or finishing of bricks or tiles not being ornamental tiles, the part of rope works in which is carried on the open air process, the part of bleaching and dyeing works in which is carried on open air bleaching or Turkey red dyeing, a factory in which is carried on glue making), and where press of work arises at certain recurring seasons of the year (viz., letterpress printing works, bookbinding works, and a factory, &c., in which is carried on the manufacturing process or handicraft of lithographic printing, machine ruling, firewood cutting, bonbon and Christmas present making, almanac making, valentine making, envelope making, aerated water making, playing card making), **Sudden press** and where the business is liable to sudden press of **of orders.** orders arising from unforeseen events (viz., a factory, &c., in which is carried on the manufacturing process or handicraft of the making-up of any article of wearing apparel, the making-up of furniture hangings, artificial flower making, fancy box making, biscuit making, job dyeing, and a part of a factory, &c., which is a warehouse not used for any manufacturing process or handicraft, and in which persons are solely employed in polishing, cleaning, wrapping or packing up goods). Provided that the **Domestic** exception shall not apply to domestic workshops, or **workshops.** to a workshop which is conducted on the system of not employing any child or young person, and provided that there shall be allowed to every young person or woman, for meals, not less than two hours, of which half an hour shall be after five P.M., and that any young person or woman shall not be so employed on the whole for more than five days in any one week nor for more than forty-eight days in any year. Where it is proved to the **Extension of** satisfaction of a Secretary of State that in any non- **exception.** textile factories or workshops it is necessary, by reason of the material which is the subject of the manufacturing process or handicraft therein being liable to be spoiled by the weather, or by reason of press of work arising at certain recurring seasons of the year, or by reason of the liability of the business to a sudden press of orders arising, to employ young persons and women, and that such employment will not injure their health, he may extend this exception (Sec. 53).

By Section 13 of the Act of 1883 Section 53 of the Act of 1878 was declared to only authorise overtime employment of young persons or women to take place in any factory or workshop on forty-eight days in twelve months, and in reckoning such period of forty-eight days, every day on which any young person or woman has been employed overtime is to be taken into account.

If in any of the following factories or workshops, viz. bleaching and dyeing works, print works, iron mills in which male young **Hours of** persons are not employed during any part of the **work when** night, foundries in which male young persons are **uncom-** not employed during any part of the night, and paper **pleted.** mills in which young persons are not employed during any part of the night—the process in which a child, young person, or woman is employed, is in an incomplete state at the end of the period of employment, the provisions of the Act shall not prevent such child, &c., from being employed for a further period not exceeding thirty minutes, provided that such further periods when added to the total number of hours of the periods of employment of such child, &c., in that week do not raise that total above the number otherwise allowed under the Act. Where it is proved to the satisfaction of a Secretary of State that in any non-textile factories or workshops the time for completion of a process cannot be accurately fixed, and that the extension of this exception can be made without injury to health, he may extend this exception (Sec. 54).

**Dyeing and bleaching.** Nothing in the Act shall prevent the employment of young persons and women for the purpose only of preventing any damage in the process of Turkey red dyeing or in the process of open-air bleaching (Sec. 55).

**Exceptions to hours of work.** The regulations of the Act shall not prevent the employment of women during a period beginning at 6 A.M. and ending at 8 P.M.; or beginning at 7 A.M. and ending at 9 P.M., in a factory or workshop in which any part of the following processes is carried on, viz., the process of making preserves from fruit, the process of preserving or curing fish, or the process of making condensed milk, provided such women are employed in accordance with the following conditions: There shall be allowed to every such woman for meals during the period of employment not less than two hours, of which half an hour shall be after 5 P.M.; and any such woman shall not be so employed on the whole for more than five days in any one week nor for more than ninety-six days in any one year.

**Saving for persons in process of cleaning fruit.** [Nothing in the principal Act shall apply to the process of cleaning and preparing fruit so far as is necessary to prevent the spoiling of the fruit on its arrival at a factory or workshop during the months of June, July, August and September (Sec. 32, 1891).]

**Extension of these exceptions.** Where it is proved to the satisfaction of a Secretary of State that in any non-textile factories or workshops it is necessary to employ women in manner authorised by this exception and that their health will not be injured thereby, he may extend this exception (Sec. 56). By Section 13 of the Act of 1883 Section 56 of the Act of 1878 was declared to only authorise overtime employment of women to take place in any factory or workshop on ninety-six days in twelve months, and in reckoning such period of ninety-six days every day on which any woman has been employed overtime is to be taken into account. Where it appears to a Secretary of State that factories driven by water power **Factories** are liable to be stopped by drought or flood, he may **liable to be** grant a special exception, permitting the employment **stopped by** of young persons and women during a period of **drought or** employment from 6 A.M. until 7 P.M., but no person **flood.** shall be deprived of the prescribed meal hours, nor be so employed on Saturday, and that as regards factories liable to be stopped by drought such special exception shall not extend to more than ninety-six days in any period of twelve months, and as regards factories liable to be stopped by floods such special exception shall not extend to more than forty-eight days in any period of twelve months. This overtime shall not extend in any case beyond the time already lost during the previous twelve months (Sec. 57).

**Employment** *With respect to Night Work*, the Act provides:— **of children,** The employment of male young persons during the **&c., at night.** night is permitted in the following factories and workshops, viz., blast furnaces, iron mills, letterpress printing works, and paper mills, provided the period of employment shall not exceed twelve consecutive hours and shall begin and end at the hours specified in the prescribed notice; the provisions with respect to the allowance of time for meals to young persons during the period of employment shall be observed with the necessary modifications as to the hour at which the times allowed for meals are fixed; a male young person employed during any part of the night shall not be employed during any part of the twelve hours preceding or succeeding the period of employment; a male young person shall not be employed on more than six nights, or in the case of blast furnaces or paper mills seven nights in any two weeks.

The provisions with respect to the period of employment on **Saturdays** Saturday, and with respect to the allowance of eight **and holi-** half holidays in every year or of whole holidays in **days.** lieu of them, shall not apply to a male young person employed in day and night turns in pursuance of this exception. Where it is proved to the satisfaction of a Secretary of State that **Extension of** in any non-textile factories or workshops it is neces- **exception.** sary, by reason of the nature of the business, &c., to employ male young persons of sixteen years of age and upwards, at night, and that such employment will not injure their health, he may extend this exception to such factories, &c. (Sec. 58). In a factory or workshop in which the process of printing newspapers is carried on, on not more than two nights in the week, nothing in the Act shall prevent the employment of a male young person of sixteen years of age and upwards, at night, during not more than two nights in a week as if he were no longer a young person (Sec. 59). In glass works nothing in this Act shall prevent any male young person from working according to the accustomed hours of the works, provided the total number of hours of the periods of employment shall not exceed sixty in any one week, and the periods of employment for any such young person shall not exceed fourteen hours in four separate turns per week, or twelve hours in five separate turns per week, or ten hours in six separate turns per week, or any less number of hours in the accustomed number of separate turns per week, so that such number of turns do not exceed nine, and such young person shall not work in any turn without an interval of time not less than one full turn, and there shall be allowed to such young person during each turn the like times for meals as are required by the Act to be allowed in any other non-textile factory or workshop (Sec. 60).

### IV. WITH REGARD TO HOLIDAYS.

**Certain holidays to be allowed.** The Act provides: The occupier of a factory or of a workshop shall (unless specially excepted) allow to every child, young person, and woman the following holidays, that is to say, Christmas Day, either Good Friday, or, if specified in prescribed notice, the next following Bank Holiday, and in addition eight half holidays in every year; but a whole holiday may be allowed in lieu of any two such half holidays. At least half of the said half holidays or whole holidays shall be allowed between the 15th of March and the 1st of October in every year. Cessation from work shall not be deemed to be a half or whole holiday unless a notice has been affixed [during the first week in January, and a copy thereof has on the same day been forwarded to the inspector of the district: Provided that any such notice may be changed by a subsequent notice affixed and sent in like manner not less than fourteen days before the holiday or half holiday to which it applies (Sec. 16, 1891).] A half holiday shall comprise at least one half the period of employment on some day other than Sunday (Sec. 22).

**Ireland.** [In Ireland, in lieu of any two half holidays there shall be allowed as a holiday, to every child, young person, and woman employed in a factory or workshop the whole of the 17th day of March, when that day does not fall on a Sunday, or at the option of the occupier of the factory, either Good Friday (unless that day is otherwise fixed as a holiday) or Easter Tuesday (Sec. 34, 1891).] If all the children, young persons, and women in a factory or workshop are of Jewish religion, the occupier may give them any two Bank Holidays (under the Act of 1875) in lieu of Christmas Day and Good Friday, but in that case such factory or workshop shall not be open for traffic on Christmas Day or Good Friday (Sec. 50, iii.). Where it is proved to the satisfaction of a Secretary of State that the customs, &c., of any non-textile factories or workshops require it, he may grant to such factories, &c., a special exception authorising the occupier to allow all or any of the half or whole holidays in lieu of them, on different days to any of the children, young persons, and women employed in his factory, &c., or to any sets of such children, &c., and not on the same days (Sec. 49). [In Scotland in lieu of Christmas Day, and either Good Friday or the next public holiday there shall be allowed as a holiday to every child, young person, and woman employed in a factory or workshop within a burgh or police burgh, the two days in each year set apart by the Church of Scotland for the observance of the sacramental fast in the parish in which the factory or workshop is situate. In such burghs or police burghs where the fast days have been abolished or discontinued, two whole days in each year must be allowed separated by an interval of not less than three months, as shall be fixed by the magistrates or police commissioners in such burghs or police burghs, the said authorities as the case may be, are required to fix, and from time to time, if it shall seem expedient to them to do so, to alter such holidays, and give public notice thereof fourteen days before the date at any time fixed (Sec. 33, iv. 1891).] Section 51 provides for the employment of Jews by Jews on Sunday.

V. WITH REGARD TO THE EDUCATION OF CHILDREN AND CERTIFICATES OF FITNESS FOR EMPLOYMENT.

The Act provides: The parent of a child employed in a factory or in a workshop shall cause that child to attend some recog-

## CERTIFICATES OF FITNESS.

nised efficient school.* The child, when employed in a morning **Attendance** or afternoon set shall in every week, during any part **at school.** of which he is so employed, be caused to attend on each work-day for at least one attendance; and when employed on the alternate day system, shall on each work-day preceding each day of employment in the factory or workshop be caused to attend for at least two attendances. An attendance shall be between 8 A.M. and 6 P.M. Provided that a child shall not be required to attend school on Saturday, or on any **Saturdays.** holiday or half holiday, and that the non-attendance of the child shall be excused on every day on which he is certified by the teacher of the school to have been prevented from attending by sickness or other unavoidable cause, &c. **Sickness.** Where there is not within a distance of two miles a **If school is** recognised efficient school, the child may attend **two miles** another school, temporarily approved by the in-**distant.** spector. A child who has not in any week attended school for all the required attendances shall not be employed in the following week until he has attended school for the deficient number of attendances. The Education Department shall publish lists of recognised efficient schools (Sec. 23). The occupier of **Certificate of** a factory or workshop in which a child is employed **attendance.** shall periodically obtain from the teacher of the school attended by the child a prescribed certificate respecting the attendance of such child. The occupier shall keep every such certificate for two months, and shall produce the same to an **Payment of** inspector when required (Sec. 24). The school **school fees.** managers may apply in writing to the occupier of the factory, &c., to pay weekly a sum not exceeding 3d. nor one-twelfth of the wages of the child, which the occupier shall be liable to pay so long as he employs the child, and while the child attends the school, and he may deduct the sum from the wages of the **Certificate of** child (Sec. 25). When a child of the age of thirteen **efficiency.** years has obtained a certificate of proficiency in reading, writing, and arithmetic, or standard of attendance, that child shall be deemed to be a young person for the purpose of the Act (Sec. 26).

In a factory a child or a young person under the age of sixteen shall not be employed for more than a specified number of days,

* For definitions of the terms "Certified efficient school" and "Recognised efficient school," see Secs. 95, 105.

## 208 SUMMARY OF THE FACTORY AND WORKSHOP ACTS.

**Certificate of fitness.** unless the occupier of the factory has obtained a prescribed certificate of the fitness of such child, &c., for employment. A certificate of fitness shall be granted by the certifying surgeon, and shall be to the effect that he is satisfied that the person named in the certificate is of the age specified, and is not incapacitated for working daily for the time allowed by law in the factory (Sec. 27). An occupier of a workshop is authorised to obtain, if he thinks fit, from certifying surgeons certificates of the fitness of children and of young persons under sixteen years of age in like manner as if the workshop were a factory (Sec. 28). Where an inspector is of opinion that a child or a young person under sixteen years of age is incapacitated for working daily for the time allowed by law in a factory or workshop, he may serve written notice on the occupier, requiring that the employment of such child, &c., be discontinued, and the occupier shall then cease to employ such child, &c., unless the **Certificates of fitness may be annulled.** certifying surgeon has, after the service of the notice, certified that such child, &c., is not so incapacitated (Sec. 29). In certain events, an inspector may by notice annul the surgeon's certificate, and thereupon the certificate shall be of no avail for the purposes of the Act. When a child becomes a young person a fresh certificate of fitness **Production of certificates.** must be obtained. The occupier shall, when required, produce to an inspector at the factory or workshop in which a child or young person is employed the certificate of fitness of such child, &c. (Sec. 30).

Where it appears to a Secretary of State that it is expedient he may extend to workshops the prohibition of the employment of **Prohibition to employment without certificate.** children, &c., under sixteen years of age without a certificate of fitness, and thereupon the provisions with respect to certificates of fitness shall apply to such workshops as if they were factories. If the prohibition is proved to the satisfaction of the Secretary of State to be no longer necessary in any workshops to which it has been extended, he may rescind the order of extension (Sec. 41).

Where there is no certifying surgeon resident within three miles of a factory or workshop, the poor-law medical officer shall be the **Certifying surgeon.** certifying surgeon for such factory, &c. (Sec. 71). A surgeon who is the occupier of a factory or workshop, or is interested therein, shall not be a certifying surgeon for that factory, &c. (Sec. 72). A certificate of fitness shall not be granted except upon personal examination of the person named therein.

## CERTIFICATES OF FITNESS.

A certifying surgeon shall not examine a child or young person for the purpose of a certificate of fitness, or sign any such certificate, elsewhere than at the factory or workshop where such child, &c., is, or is about to be, employed, unless the number of children, &c., employed is less than five, or unless allowed by an inspector. If a certifying surgeon refuses to grant for any person examined a certificate, he shall when required give his reasons in writing (Sec. 73). The occupier may agree with the certifying **Fees for examination.** surgeon as to the amount of fees to be paid in respect of examinations and grant of certificates. In the absence of any agreement the fees shall be: 2s. 6d. for each visit, and 6d. for each person after the first five examined at that visit, when the examination is at a factory or workshop not exceeding one mile from the surgeon's residence. When the factory, &c., is more than one mile from the surgeon's residence, the above fees and an additional 6d. for each complete half-mile over and above the mile. When the examination is at the residence of the surgeon, or at a place appointed by the surgeon, 6d. for each person examined. The fees shall be paid upon completion of examination, or upon the signing of the certificates, or as directed by inspector. The occupier may deduct the fee, or any part of it, but not exceeding 3d., from the wages of the person for whom the certificate was granted. A Secretary of State may alter the fees (Sec. 74).

**Report of certifying surgeon.** [Every certifying surgeon shall in each year make at the prescribed time a report to the Secretary of State as to the persons inspected during the year, and the result of the inspection (Sec. 19, 1891).

[When the age of any child or young person under the age of sixteen years is required to be ascertained or proved for the purposes of this Act, or for any purpose connected with **Certificate of birth in case of children and young persons under 16.** the elementary education or employment in labour of such child, &c., any person shall, on presenting a written requisition containing the particulars which may be from time to time prescribed by the Local Government Board, and on payment of a fee of 6d., be entitled to obtain a certified copy under the hand of a registrar or superintendent registrar of the entry in the register, of the birth of that child or young person. The form of requisition shall on request be supplied without charge by every superintendent registrar and registrar of births, deaths, and marriages (Sec. 20, 1891; Sec. 35, 1891; Sec. 104, 1878).]

## VI. WITH REGARD TO THE IMPOSITION OF FINES.

The Act provides: If a factory or workshop is not kept in conformity with the Act the occupier shall be liable to a fine not exceeding £10. But the Court in addition to, or instead of inflicting, such fine, may order means to be adopted for the purpose of bringing the factory or workshop into conformity with **Employ-** the Act (Sec. 81). Where a child, young person, or **ment of** woman is employed in a factory or workshop, con-**children.** trary to the provisions of this Act, the occupier of the factory, &c., shall be liable to a fine not exceeding £3, or, if the offence was committed during the night, £5, for each child, &c., so employed; and where a child, &c., is so employed in a factory, &c., within the meaning of Sec. 16, the occupier shall be liable to a fine not exceeding £1, or if the offence was committed during the night, £2, for each child, &c., so employed (Sec. 83).

[The fine imposed in case of a second or subsequent con-**Minimum** viction for the same offence within two years of the **penalties in** last conviction for that offence, shall be not less than **certain** £1 for each offence (Sec. 28, 1891).] A child, &c., **cases.** who is not allowed times for meals and absence from work, as required by the Act, or during any part of the times allowed for meals, &c., is employed in the factory or workshop, &c., shall be deemed to be employed contrary to the provisions of the Act (Sec. 83). If a child or young person is employed in a factory or workshop contrary to the provisions of the Act, the **Liability of** parent shall be liable to a fine not exceeding £1 **parent.** for each offence, unless it appears to the Court that such offence was committed without the consent, &c., of the parent; and if the parent neglects to cause such child to attend school in accordance with the Act, he shall be liable to a fine not exceeding £1 for each offence (Sec. 84). Sec. 85 deals with the fines and penalties to which every person shall be liable who **Forgery of** commits a forgery of any certificate for the purposes **certificates,** of this Act, who personates any person named in a **&c.** certificate, or who wilfully connives at any such offences, and who wilfully makes a false entry in any register, &c., **Offence com-** or who wilfully makes a false declaration. Where an **mitted by** offence for which the occupier of a factory or work-**occupier's** shop is liable to a fine has in fact been committed **agent.** by some agent, &c., such agent, &c., shall be liable to the same fine as if he were the occupier (Sec. 86). Where the

## FINES AND PENALTIES.

occupier of a factory or workshop is charged with an offence against this Act, he shall be entitled to have any other person whom he charges as the actual offender brought before the Court at the time appointed for hearing the charge; and if the occupier of the factory or workshop proves to the satisfaction of the Court that he had used due diligence to enforce the Act, and that the other person had committed the offence without his knowledge, &c., the other person shall be summarily convicted of such offence and the occupier shall be exempt from any fine. When it is made to appear, to the satisfaction of an inspector at the time of discovering the offence, that the occupier of the factory or workshop had used all due diligence to enforce the Act, then the inspector shall proceed against the person whom he believes to be the actual offender, without first proceeding against the occupier (Sec. 87). A person shall not be liable in respect of a repetition of the same kind of offence from day to day to any larger amount of fines than the highest fine fixed by the Act for the offence, except where the repetition of the offence occurs after an information has been laid for the previous offence, or where the offence is one of employing two or more children, &c., contrary to the provisions of the Act (Sec. 88). The occupier of a factory or workshop shall be liable to a fine of £5 if the holidays required by Sec. 22 are not fixed pursuant thereto (Sec. 22). The provisions with regard to legal proceedings under the Act are contained in Secs. 89—92.

*Where occupier is charged with offence of other person.*

*Cumulative fines.*

[If the owner of a factory constructed before January 1st, 1892, after having been served with a notice by the sanitary authority specifying the measures necessary to provide the factory with means of escape from fire, fails to comply with the requirements before a specified date, he is liable to a fine not exceeding £1 for every day that such non-compliance continues (Sec. 7, 1891).

*Fines for non-compliance with regulations as to provision against fire.*

[If any person who is bound to observe the special rules established for any factory or workshop acts in contravention of or fails to comply with such rules, he is liable on a summary conviction to a fine not exceeding £2, and the occupier of the factory or workshop is also liable to a fine of not exceeding £10, unless he proves he has taken all reasonable means to prevent the contravention or non-compliance (Sec. 9, 1891).

*Penalty for contravention of special rules and requirements.*

**For non-compliance with regulations as to employment overtime.**
[If the occupier of a factory or workshop fails to make an entry or report respecting the employment overtime of any child, young person or woman, he is liable on summary conviction to a fine not exceeding £5 (Sec. 14, ii. 1891).

**Fine for omission to supply operatives with particulars as to payment by piece.**
[If the occupier of a factory or workshop fails to supply any person employed therein who is paid by the piece, with sufficient particulars as to rate of wages, he is liable to a fine not exceeding £10, and in case of a subsequent conviction within two years of the last, a fine of not less than £1 is imposed.

**Liability of operative or any other person on disclosing particulars of payment for a fraudulent purpose.**
[If an operative disclose such particulars with a fraudulent object, or for purpose of gain, whether they be furnished directly to him or to a fellow workman, he is liable to a fine of not exceeding £10 for each offence, and if any person solicit or procure an employé to disclose such particulars with a like object he is also liable to a fine for each offence of not exceeding £10 (Sec. 24, 1891).

**Limitation of time for summary proceedings.**
[In summary proceedings for offences and fines under the principal Act, an information may be laid within three months after the date at which the offence comes to the knowledge of a factory inspector, or in case of an inquest being held in relation to the offence, then within two months after the conclusion of the inquest, so, however that it shall not be laid after the expiration of six months from the commission of the offence (Sec. 29, 1891).

**Fine for not keeping list of outworkers.**
[Any occupier or contractor engaged in certain trades not keeping proper list of outworkers shall be liable to a fine not exceeding £2.] *

VII. WITH RESPECT TO THE POWERS OF INSPECTORS AND SANITARY AUTHORITY.

The Act provides that an inspector shall have power to do all or any of the following things:—(1) To enter and examine at reasonable times, by day and night, a factory or workshop when he has reasonable cause to believe that any person is employed therein, and to enter by day any place which he has reasonable cause to believe to be a factory or workshop. (2) To take with

* For list of trades and other details *vide* "Miscellaneous Regulations."

him a constable into a factory in which he has reasonable cause to apprehend any serious obstruction. (3) To require the production of registers, certificates, &c., and examine and copy the same. (4) To make such examination and inquiry as may be necessary to ascertain whether the enactments relating to public health and the enactments of this Act are complied with so far as respects the factory or workshop and the persons employed. (5) To enter any school in which he has reasonable cause to believe that children employed in a factory or workshop are being educated. (6) To examine as he thinks fit every person he finds in a factory or workshop or school, and to require such person to be so examined with respect to matters under the Act, and to sign a declaration of the truth of the matter respecting which he is so examined. (7) To exercise such other powers as may be necessary for carrying the Act into effect. The occupier of every factory and workshop shall furnish the means required by an inspector as necessary for an entry, &c., or the exercise of his powers under the Act. Every person who wilfully delays an inspector in the exercise of his power, or who fails to comply with a requisition of an inspector, or to produce any document, &c., or who conceals or prevents a child from appearing before an inspector, shall be liable to a fine not exceeding £5, and the occupier of factory or workshop shall be liable to a fine not exceeding £5, or where the offence is committed at night, £20. For such offence committed in domestic workshop the occupier shall be liable to a fine not exceeding £1, or if at night £5 (Sec. 68). [The fine imposed under this section in case of a second or subsequent conviction for the same offence within two years of the last conviction for that offence, shall be not less than £1 for each offence (Sec. 28, 1891).] Every inspector shall be furnished with the prescribed certificate of his appointment; and on applying for admission to a factory or workshop shall, if required, produce the same to the occupier (Sec. 70).

**Power of Inspector in case of default.** [An inspector may take proceedings for punishing or remedying any default in compliance with the law relating to public health as might be taken by the sanitary authority of the district in which the workshops or laundries are situate, and is entitled to recover from that sanitary authority all expenses incurred in such proceedings which are not recovered from any other person, and have not been incurred in any unsuccessful proceeding (Sec. 1, ii. 1891).

## 214 SUMMARY OF THE FACTORY AND WORKSHOP ACTS.

**Power of sanitary authority.** [In their duty with respect to workshops, a sanitary authority and their officers shall, without prejudice to their other powers, have all such powers of entry, inspection, taking legal proceedings or otherwise, as an inspector under the principal Act.

[It is provided that if any child, young person, or woman is employed in a workshop, and the medical officer of the sanitary authority becomes aware thereof, he shall forthwith give written notice to the factory inspector of the district (Sec. 3, 1891).

[Where on the certificate of a medical officer of health or inspector of nuisances it appears to any sanitary authority that the limewashing, &c., of any workshop, or part thereof, is necessary for the health of the persons employed therein, the sanitary authority shall give notice of the same to the occupier or owner to purify, cleanse, &c., as the case may require. If the occupier or owner fails to comply therewith he is liable to a fine not exceeding 10s. per day during such non-compliance, and the sanitary authority may, if they think fit, cause the necessary cleansing, &c., to be done, and may recover in a summary manner the expenses incurred by them from the person in default (Sec. 4, ii. and iii. 1891).

**Recovery of expenses incurred by sanitary authority under sec. 7, 1891, with regard to provision against fire.** [All expenses incurred by sanitary authority in the execution of this section, are to be defrayed (*a*) in the case of an authority of an urban district, as part of their expenses of the general execution of the Public Health Act, 1875; and (*b*) in the case of an authority of a rural district, as special expenses incurred in the execution of the Public Health Act, 1875; and such expenses shall be charged to the contributory place in which the factory is situate.

[In the application of this section to the administrative county of London, the London County Council shall take the place of the sanitary authority, and their expenses shall be defrayed as part of their expenses in the management of the Metropolitan Building Act, 1855, and the Acts amending the same (Sec. 7, iii. and iv. 1891).]

VIII. WITH REGARD TO MISCELLANEOUS REGULATIONS.

The Act provides : Every person shall, within one month after he begins to occupy a factory, [or workshop, conducted on the system of not employing any child, young person, or woman

## REGISTER OF CHILDREN.

**Notice to inspector before starting factory.** therein (Sec. 26, 1891,) serve on an inspector a notice containing the name, situation, and address of the factory; the nature of the work; the nature and amount of the moving power therein; and the name of the firm under which the business of the factory is to be carried on; and in default shall be liable to a fine not exceeding £5 (Sec. 75). [And when an inspector receives such notice he shall forthwith forward the notice to the sanitary authority of the district (Sec. 26, 1891).]

Where an inspector by notice names a clock open to public view for the purpose of regulating the period of employment in a factory or workshop, the period of employment and **Public clock.** meal times for children, &c., in that factory, &c., shall be regulated by that clock, which shall be specified in the notice affixed in the factory, &c. (Sec. 76).

The occupier of every factory and workshop (in which a child or young person under the age of sixteen years is prohibited from **Register of children.** being employed without a certificate of fitness) shall keep in the prescribed form, and with the prescribed particulars, registers of the children, &c., employed, and of their employment, and of other matters under the Act. The occupier of a factory, &c., shall send to an inspector such extracts from any register as the inspector requires. Where, by reason of the number of children, &c., employed in a factory, &c., to which this section does not apply, it seems expedient to a Secretary of State so to do, he may order the occupier of that factory, &c., to keep a register under this section, and while such order is in force this section shall apply to that factory or workshop. In the event of a contravention of this section in a factory, &c., the occupier shall be liable to a fine not exceeding 40s. (Sec. 77).

There shall be affixed at the entrance of a factory and a workshop, and in such other parts thereof as an inspector directs, and **Notices, &c., to be affixed.** be constantly kept so affixed in the prescribed form, and in such position as to be easily read by the persons employed—(1) the prescribed abstract of the Act; (2) a notice of the name and address of the prescribed inspector; (3) a notice of the name and address of the certifying surgeon; (4) a notice of the clock (if any) by which the period of employment and meal times are regulated; and (5) every notice, &c., required by the Act to be affixed. In the event of a contravention of this section in a factory or workshop the occupier shall be liable to a fine not exceeding 40s. (Sec. 78).

## 216 SUMMARY OF THE FACTORY AND WORKSHOP ACTS.

**Service of notices, &c.**
Sec. 79 deals with the notices, requisitions, &c., under the Act, and with the manner in which same are to be served.

Any Act in force relating to weights and measures shall extend to weights, measures, scales, steelyards, &c., used in a factory or workshop, and every inspector of, or other person authorised to examine, weights and measures, shall inspect, stamp, mark, search for, and examine the said weights, &c., and for that purpose shall have the same powers and duties as he has in relation to weights, &c., used in the sale of goods (Sec. 80).

**Weights and measures.**

**Where hirer of machine is not occupier.**
Where in a factory the owner or hirer of a machine, &c., moved by steam, &c., in or about which machine, &c., children, young persons, or women are employed, is some person other than the occupier of a factory, and such children, &c., are in the employment and pay of the owner or hirer of such machine, &c., in any such case such owner or hirer shall, so far as respects any offence which may be committed, be deemed to be the occupier of the factory (Sec. 99).

**Presence in factory or workshop.**
If a person is found in a factory or workshop such person shall, for the purposes of the Act, be deemed to be employed therein, except at meal times or while all the machinery is stopped, or for the sole purpose of bringing food to the persons employed in the factory or workshop between the hours of four and five in the afternoon, provided that yards, playgrounds, and places open to the public view, schoolrooms, waiting-rooms and other rooms belonging to the factory in which no machinery is used or manufacturing process carried on, shall not be deemed to be part of the factory or workshop (Sec. 92).

**Bakehouses.** Special regulations as to bakehouses are laid down in Sections 34, 35, 45, 61, and 93.

**Particulars to be supplied in case of payment by piece.**
[Every person who is engaged as a weaver in the cotton, worsted, or woollen, or linen or jute trade, or as a winder, weaver, or reeler in the cotton trade, and is paid by the piece, in or in connection with any factory or workshop, shall have supplied to him with his work sufficient particulars to enable him to ascertain the rate of wages at which he is entitled to be paid for the work, and the occupier of the factory or workshop shall supply him with such particulars accordingly.

[If the occupier of the factory or workshop fails to supply such particulars then, unless he proves that he has given the best

## SPECIAL RULES.

information in his power, he shall be liable for each offence to a fine not exceeding £10, and in the case of a second or subsequent conviction for the same offence within two years from the last conviction for that offence not less than £1.

[Provided always, that in the event of anyone who is engaged as an operative in any factory or workshop receiving such particulars, and subsequently disclosing the same with a fraudulent object or for the purpose of gain, whether they be furnished directly to him or to a fellow workman, he shall be liable for each offence to a fine not exceeding £10.

[Provided also, that anyone who shall solicit or procure a person so engaged in any factory to disclose such particulars with the object or purpose aforesaid, or shall pay or reward such person, or shall cause such person to be paid or rewarded, for so disclosing such particulars, shall be guilty of an offence, and shall be liable for each offence to a fine not exceeding £10 (Sec. 24, 1891).]

**List of outworkers.** [Every occupier of a factory or workshop shall, if so required, on an order of the Secretary of State, keep in a prescribed form, and with the prescribed particulars, lists showing the names of all persons directly employed by him, either as workman or as contractor, in the business of the factory or workshop, outside the factory or workshop, and the places where they are employed; and every such list shall be open to inspection by an inspector under the principal Act or by any officer of a sanitary authority. In the event of contravention of this section the occupier or contractor is liable to a fine not exceeding 40s. By an order gazetted Nov. 4th, 1892, and which came into force on Nov. 20th, 1892, this provision is made to apply to—

    The Manufacture of Articles of Wearing Apparel.
    The Manufacture of Electro Plate.
    Cabinet and Furniture Making, and Upholstery Work.
    The Manufacture of Files.

The order referred to also gives the form in which the lists are to be kept.]

### AMENDMENT AND PUBLICATION OF SPECIAL RULES.

[After special rules are established in any factory or workshop the Secretary of State may from time to time propose to the occupier of the factory or workshop any amendment of the rules, or any new rules; and the provisions with respect to the original rules shall apply to all such amendments and new rules in like manner, as nearly as may be as they apply to the original rules. The occupier may from time to time propose in writing to the chief inspector, with the approval of the Secretary of State, any amendment of the rules or any new rules, and the provisions of this Act with respect to a suggestion of an occupier for modifying the special rules proposed by a chief inspector, shall apply to all such amendments and new rules in like manner, as nearly as may be, as they apply to such a suggestion (Sec. 10, 1891).

[Printed copies of all special rules for the time being in force under this Act shall be kept posted up in legible characters in conspicuous places in the factory or workshop where they may be conveniently read by the persons employed. A printed copy of all such rules shall be given by the occupier to any person affected thereby on his or her application.

[If the occupier of the factory or workshop fails to comply with any provision of this section, he is liable on summary conviction to a fine not exceeding £10. Every person who pulls down, injures, or defaces any special rules when posted up in pursuance of this Act, or any notice posted up in pursuance of the special rules, he is liable on summary conviction to a fine not exceeding £5 (Sec. 11, 1891).

[An inspector, when required, shall certify a copy which is shown to his satisfaction to be a true copy of any special rules for the time being established under this Act for any factory or workshop, and a copy so certified is evidence (but not to the exclusion of other proof) of those special rules, and of the fact that they are duly established under this Act (Sec. 12, 1892).]

As to Arbitration.

[1. The parties to the arbitration are the occupiers of the factory or workshop on the one hand and the chief inspector, on behalf of the Secretary of State.

[2. Each of the parties may, within fourteen days after the date of the reference, appoint an arbitrator.

[3. No person shall act as arbitrator or umpire under this Act who is employed, manages, or is interested in, the factory or workshop to which the arbitration relates.

[4. The appointment of arbitrator shall be in writing, and notice of appointment shall be sent to the other party to the arbitration, and shall not be revoked without the consent of that party.

[5. The death or removal of, or other change in, any of the parties to the arbitration shall not affect the proceedings under this schedule.

[6. If within the said fourteen days either of the parties fails to appoint an arbitrator, the arbitrator appointed by the other party may proceed to hear and determine the matter in difference, and in that case the award of the single arbitrator shall be final.

[7. If before an award has been made any arbitrator dies or becomes incapable to act, or for seven days refuses or neglects to act, the party by whom that arbitrator was appointed may appoint some other person to act in his place ; if he fails to do so within seven days after notice in writing from the other party for that purpose, the remaining arbitrator may proceed to hear and determine the matter in difference, and in that case the award of the single arbitrator shall be final.

[8. In either of the foregoing cases where an arbitrator is empowered to act singly, on one of the parties failing to appoint, the party so failing may, before the single arbitrator has actually proceeded in the arbitration, appoint an arbitrator, who shall then act as if no failure had occurred.

[9. If the arbitrators fail to make their award within twenty-one days after the day on which the last of them was appointed, or within such extended time (if any) as may have been appointed for that purpose by both arbitrators under their hands, the matter in difference shall be determined by the umpire appointed as hereinafter mentioned.

[10. The arbitrators, before they enter on the matter referred to them, shall appoint by writing under their hands an umpire to decide on points on which they may differ.

[11. If the umpire dies or becomes incapable of acting before he has made his award, or refuses to make his award within a reasonable time after the matter has been brought within his cognizance, the persons or person who appointed such umpire shall forthwith appoint another umpire in his place.

[12. If the arbitrators refuse or fail, or for seven days after the request of either party neglect to appoint an umpire, then on the application of either party an umpire may be appointed by the chairman of the quarter sessions within the jurisdiction of which the factory or workshop is situate.

[13. The decision of every umpire on the matters referred to him shall be final.

[14. If a single arbitrator fails to make his award within twenty-one days after the day on which he was appointed, the party who appointed him may appoint another arbitrator to act in his place.

[15. Arrangements shall, whenever practicable, be made for the matters in difference being heard at the same time before the arbitrators and the umpire.

[16. The arbitrators and the umpire, or any of them, may examine the parties and their witnesses on oath, and may also consult any counsel, engineer, or scientific person whom they may think it expedient to consult.

[17. The payment, if any, to be made to any arbitrator or umpire for his services shall be fixed by the Secretary of State and with the costs of the arbitration and award shall be paid by the parties, or one of them, according as the award may direct. Such costs may be taxed by a master of the Supreme Court, or, in Scotland, by the auditor of the Court of Session, and the taxing officer shall, on the written application of either of the parties, ascertain and certify the proper amount thereof. The amount, if any, payable by the Secretary of State shall be paid as part of the expenses of inspectors under the principal Act. The amount, if any, payable by the occupier of the factory or workshop may in the event of non-payment be recovered in the same manner as fines under the principal Act (Sec. 7 and 8, 1891).]

THE FACTORY AND WORKSHOP ACT, 1883 (46 & 47 Vic., chap. 53),

Was passed to amend the law relating to certain factories and workshops.

*With regard to White Lead Factories*, it provides: It shall not be lawful to carry on a white lead factory unless such factory is **Certificate** certified by an inspector to be in conformity with the **of con-** Act (Sec. 2). This shall not be done unless certain **formity to** conditions—as to ventilation of stacks and stoves, as **be obtained.** to providing means for washing and bathing, as to providing proper room for meals, as to providing overall suits, &c., for certain of the employés, and as to supplying acidulated drinks—are complied with (Sec. 3). These conditions may be altered, revoked, or added to by a Secretary of State (Sec. 3).

## WHITE LEAD FACTORIES.

Within reasonable time a white lead factory shall be inspected, and if found to be in compliance with the Act a certificate to that effect shall be made (Sec. 4). If subsequently it appears to an inspector that the factory is not kept in conformity with the Act, he shall specify to the occupier in what respect default is made, and if default is not remedied, the Secretary of State may withdraw certificate (Sec. 5). The occupier of a white lead factory which is carried on without a certificate shall for every day be liable to a fine not exceeding £2 (Sec. 6).

There shall be established in every white lead factory special rules for the guidance of the persons employed, to prevent injury to health in the course of their employment. Such rules shall be observed as if they were enacted in the Act. If any person who is bound to observe such rules acts in contravention of or fails to comply with the same, he shall be liable to a fine not exceeding £2, and the occupier shall also be liable to a fine not exceeding £5 (Sec. 7). The occupier shall frame and transmit to the chief inspector such special rules within three months after the opening of a white lead factory. The proposed special rules shall, during not less than two weeks before such rules are transmitted to the chief inspector, be posted up for the information of persons employed in the factory, and a certificate that such rules have been posted up shall be sent to the chief inspector with the rules signed by the persons sending the same. The Secretary of State may approve such rules either with or without alteration, and on his approval being signified, the special rules as approved shall be established. But no such alteration shall be made without notice to the occupier, to enable him to state his objections (Sec. 8). After special rules are established the occupier may from time to time propose in writing to the chief inspector any amendment of such rules. A Secretary of State may at any time propose to the occupier any new special rules, and such new rules shall, as settled after consideration of the objections, if any, of the occupier, be established (Sec. 9). If the occupier makes any false statement with respect to the posting up of the special rules, he shall be liable to a fine not exceeding £20, and if special rules are not transmitted within the specified time to the chief inspector for the approval of a Secretary of State, such Secretary may establish for that factory such special rules as he may see fit (Sec. 10). Printed copies of all special rules for the time being in force shall be kept posted up in legible characters in conspicuous places in the factory. A printed copy of such

*Special rules to be framed.*

rules shall on application be given to any persons affected thereby. If the occupier fails to comply with any provision of this section he shall be liable to a fine not exceeding £10 (Sec. 11). Every person who injures special rules when posted up shall be liable to a fine not exceeding £5 (Sec. 12).

### BAKEHOUSES.

**Sanitation.** The special regulations laid down as to bakehouses in Sec. 34, 35, 45, 61, and 93 of the Act of 1878, and those in Sec. 15, 16, and 17 of the Act of 1883, enact that in places with a population of more than five thousand people, bakehouses shall be limewashed once in every six months, or be painted with three coats of oil paint every seven years, and be washed with hot water and soap every six months (Sec. 34, 1878), and that no new bakehouse shall be occupied unless the following regulations are complied with:—(1.) No water-closet, earth-closet, privy, or ashpit shall be within or communicate directly with the bakehouse. (2.) Any cistern for supplying water to the bakehouse shall be separate from any cistern for supplying water to water-closet. (3.) No drain or pipe for carrying off fœcal or sewage matter shall have an opening within the bakehouse (Sec. 15, 1883). The regulations as to limewashing, &c., apply to all bakehouses (Sec. 61, 1878). A place on the same level with the bakehouse, and forming part of the same building, shall not be used as a sleeping-place, unless effectually separated from the bakehouse by a partition extending from the floor to the ceiling; and unless there be an external glazed window of at least nine superficial feet in area, of which at least four and a half superficial feet are made to open for ventilation (Sec. 35, 1878). Sec. 93 **Employ-** (1878) provides for the application of the Act to **ment.** bakehouses, if men only be employed. Sec. 45 (1878) provides for the employment of male young persons in bakehouses between 5 A.M. and 9 P.M. Sec. 15, 16 and 17 (1883) prescribe the penalties for non-compliance with the Acts, and provide for the enforcement of the law as to retail bakehouses by the local authorities.

[The expression retail bakehouse shall not include any place which is a factory within the meaning of the principal Act (Sec. 36, 1891).]

## Cotton Cloth Factories.

Special provisions are contained in the Cotton Cloth Factories Act (52 and 53 Vic., chap. 62), which came into force on March 1st, 1890.

**Interpretation.** Cotton Cloth Factory means any room, shed, or workshop, or any part thereof, in which the weaving of cotton cloth is carried on (Sec. 4).

Expression referring to artificial raising of temperature or production of humidity shall include the raising of temperature or production of humidity by any artificial means whatsoever except by gas when used for lighting purposes only (Sec. 4).

**Temperature and humidity of the atmosphere.** The amount of moisture in the atmosphere of a cotton cloth factory shall not at any time be in excess of such amount as is represented by the number of grains of moisture per cubic foot of air shown in schedule A of the Act, but such table may be repealed or varied by a Secretary of State provided notice of such repeal or variation is laid before Parliament for forty days and objection is not taken thereto (Sec. 5 and 6). A copy of this table shall be kept hanging in a frame, and properly glazed near to the thermometers in the factory (Sec. 7). It is provided that in a cotton cloth factory, the temperature shall not at any one time be artificially raised above 70 degrees, except in so far as may be necessary to the process of giving humidity to the atmosphere (Sec. 5 and 6).

**Thermometers to be employed.** There shall be provided, maintained, and kept in correct working order in every cotton cloth factory two sets of standardised wet and dry bulb thermometers. One set shall be fixed in the centre, and one at the side of the factory, or in such other position as may be directed and sanctioned by an inspector of factories, so as to be plainly visible to the operative (Sec. 7).

**Reading of thermometers.** Every day that any operatives are employed in a factory the occupier, manager, or person for the time being in charge of the factory, shall read the thermometers twice daily, between ten and eleven o'clock in the forenoon and between three and four in the afternoon, and shall record the readings each time on a form prescribed in schedule B of the Act. The forms shall be kept hung up near the thermometers, and after being duly filled up, shall be forwarded at the end of each month to the inspector of the district. A copy shall be kept at the factory for reference (Sec. 7).

The forms shall be *prima-facie* evidence as to humidity (Sec. 2 and 7, 5).

**Notice of artificial production of humidity to be given.** Occupiers of factories in which humidity is artificially produced shall give notice in the case of factories in which humidity is thus produced at the commencement of the Act within one week after the commencement of the Act, and in other cases at or before the time at which the artificial production is commenced (Sec. 8).

**Notice of cessation.** If there is cessation in the production of humidity by artificial means, and the occupier gives notice in writing of the cessation, the provisions of this Act shall not apply to such factory (Sec. 11).

**Ventilation.** Arrangements shall be made and maintained to the satisfaction of the inspector of the district for admitting every hour during which work is carried on not less than 600 cubic feet of fresh air for each person employed therein, and the arrangements for this ventilation shall be kept in operation subject as far as possible to the control of the persons employed therein (Sec. 9).

**Provisions for preventing inhalation of dust.** Where it appears to an inspector that dust is generated and inhaled to an injurious extent, and that such inhalation could be prevented by the use of mechanical or other means, he may serve on the occupier a notice requiring him to adopt such means as the inspector requires to prevent the inhalation. Within seven days

**Arbitration.** after receipt of such notice the occupier may serve on the inspector a requisition to refer the matter to arbitration. The arbitration may be by two skilled arbitrators, one appointed by the occupier and the other by the inspector, or the arbitrators may select an umpire. The decision shall be given twenty-one days after the last arbitrator, or twenty-one days after the umpire, is chosen, or within such further time as the occupier and inspector by writing allow. If the decision be not so given the matter shall be referred to the arbitration of an umpire to be appointed by the judge of the county court within the jurisdiction of which the factory is situate.

If the arbitrators or their umpire decide it is unnecessary or

## COTTON CLOTH FACTORIES.

impossible to prevent the inhalation of such dust, or that the means required by the inspector are not reasonable, the occupier shall not be compelled to carry out the notice, which shall be cancelled, and the expense of arbitration shall be paid as the expenses of the inspectors under the Act.

**Expenses of arbitration.**

If the occupier does not serve notice of arbitration he shall carry out the notice of the inspector.

If the arbitrator or umpire decide that the notice, or any modification thereof, shall be carried out, the expense of the arbitration shall be paid by the occupier, and shall be recoverable from him by the inspector in the county court.

Non-compliance by the occupier with the provisions as to inhalation of dust shall be deemed to be a contravention of the Act (Sec. 12).

**Visits of Inspectors.** Every factory shall be visited by an inspector of factories at least once in every three months. The inspector shall report in a prescribed form to the chief inspector of factories as to his examination into the temperature, humidity of the atmosphere, ventilation and quantity of fresh air in the factory (Sec. 10).

**Penalties.** The inspector shall give notice in writing to the occupier of any acts or omissions constituting contravention of, or non-compliance with, the provisions of the Act, and if such acts and omissions are continued, not remedied, or repeated within twelve months after notice has been given the occupier shall be liable on summary conviction for the first offence to a penalty of not less than £5 nor more than £10, and for every subsequent offence to a penalty of not less than £10 nor more than £20 (Sec. 13).

It may be mentioned that a former Chief Inspector of Factories and Workshops has published some exceedingly valuable Hints on the Administration of the Factory and Workshops Act, 1878,\* and that he has reprinted the Act with notes and references to decided cases.

\* "Hints on the Administration of the Factory and Workshops Act, 1878." By Alexander Redgrave, C.B. Shaw and Sons, London.

# APPENDIX F.
## TABLE FOR DETERMINING AMORTIZATION OF LEASES, &c.
*(For examples, see page 232).*

| Years. | Years Pur. 3 per Cent. | | Years Pur. 4 per Cent. | | Years Pur. 5 per Cent. | | Years Pur. 6 per Cent. | Years. |
|---|---|---|---|---|---|---|---|---|
| $\tfrac{1}{2}$ | ·489 | $\tfrac{1}{2}$ | ·485 | $\tfrac{1}{2}$ | ·482 | $\tfrac{1}{2}$ | ·479 | $\tfrac{1}{2}$ | $\tfrac{1}{2}$ |
| 1 | ·971 | 1 | ·962 | 1 | ·952 | 1 | ·943 | 1 | 1 |
| $1\tfrac{1}{2}$ | 1·446 | $1\tfrac{1}{2}$ | 1·428 | $1\tfrac{1}{2}$ | 1·411 | $1\tfrac{1}{3}$ | 1·395 | $1\tfrac{1}{2}$ | $1\tfrac{1}{2}$ |
| 2 | 1·913 | 2 | 1·886 | 2 | 1·859 | $1\tfrac{3}{4}$ | 1·833 | $1\tfrac{3}{4}$ | 2 |
| $2\tfrac{1}{2}$ | 2·374 | $2\tfrac{1}{4}$ | 2·335 | $2\tfrac{1}{4}$ | 2·297 | $2\tfrac{1}{4}$ | 2·259 | $2\tfrac{1}{4}$ | $2\tfrac{1}{2}$ |
| 3 | 2·829 | $2\tfrac{3}{4}$ | 2·775 | $2\tfrac{3}{4}$ | 2·723 | $2\tfrac{3}{4}$ | 2·673 | $2\tfrac{3}{4}$ | 3 |
| $3\tfrac{1}{2}$ | 3·276 | $3\tfrac{1}{4}$ | 3·207 | $3\tfrac{1}{4}$ | 3·140 | $3\tfrac{1}{4}$ | 3·075 | 3 | $3\tfrac{1}{2}$ |
| 4 | 3·717 | $3\tfrac{3}{4}$ | 3·630 | $3\tfrac{3}{4}$ | 3·546 | $3\tfrac{3}{4}$ | 3·465 | $3\tfrac{1}{2}$ | 4 |
| $4\tfrac{1}{2}$ | 4·152 | $4\tfrac{1}{4}$ | 4·045 | 4 | 3·942 | 4 | 3·844 | $3\tfrac{3}{4}$ | $4\tfrac{1}{2}$ |
| 5 | 4·580 | $4\tfrac{1}{2}$ | 4·452 | $4\tfrac{1}{2}$ | 4·329 | $4\tfrac{1}{4}$ | 4·212 | $4\tfrac{1}{4}$ | 5 |
| $5\tfrac{1}{2}$ | 5·002 | 5 | 4·851 | $4\tfrac{3}{4}$ | 4·707 | $4\tfrac{3}{4}$ | 4·570 | $4\tfrac{1}{2}$ | $5\tfrac{1}{2}$ |
| 6 | 5·417 | $5\tfrac{1}{2}$ | 5·242 | $5\tfrac{1}{4}$ | 5·076 | 5 | 4·917 | 5 | 6 |
| $6\tfrac{1}{2}$ | 5·827 | $5\tfrac{3}{4}$ | 5·626 | $5\tfrac{1}{2}$ | 5·435 | $5\tfrac{1}{3}$ | 5·255 | $5\tfrac{1}{4}$ | $6\tfrac{1}{2}$ |
| 7 | 6·230 | $6\tfrac{1}{4}$ | 6·002 | 6 | 5·786 | $5\tfrac{3}{4}$ | 5·582 | $5\tfrac{1}{2}$ | 7 |
| $7\tfrac{1}{2}$ | 6·628 | $6\tfrac{1}{2}$ | 6·371 | $6\tfrac{1}{4}$ | 6·129 | $6\tfrac{1}{4}$ | 5·901 | 6 | $7\tfrac{1}{2}$ |
| 8 | 7·020 | 7 | 6·733 | $6\tfrac{3}{4}$ | 6·463 | $6\tfrac{1}{2}$ | 6·210 | $6\tfrac{1}{4}$ | 8 |
| $8\tfrac{1}{2}$ | 7·406 | $7\tfrac{1}{2}$ | 7·087 | 7 | 6·789 | $6\tfrac{3}{4}$ | 6·510 | $6\tfrac{1}{2}$ | $8\tfrac{1}{2}$ |
| 9 | 7·786 | $7\tfrac{3}{4}$ | 7·435 | $7\tfrac{1}{2}$ | 7·108 | 7 | 6·802 | $6\tfrac{3}{4}$ | 9 |
| $9\tfrac{1}{2}$ | 8·161 | $8\tfrac{1}{4}$ | 7·776 | $7\tfrac{3}{4}$ | 7·419 | $7\tfrac{1}{2}$ | 7·085 | 7 | $9\tfrac{1}{2}$ |
| 10 | 8·530 | $8\tfrac{1}{2}$ | 8·111 | 8 | 7·722 | $7\tfrac{3}{4}$ | 7·360 | $7\tfrac{1}{4}$ | 10 |
| $10\tfrac{1}{2}$ | 8·894 | 9 | 8·439 | $8\tfrac{1}{2}$ | 8·018 | 8 | 7·627 | $7\tfrac{3}{4}$ | $10\tfrac{1}{2}$ |
| 11 | 9·253 | $9\tfrac{1}{4}$ | 8·760 | $8\tfrac{1}{2}$ | 8·306 | $8\tfrac{1}{4}$ | 7·887 | 8 | 11 |
| $11\tfrac{1}{2}$ | 9·606 | $9\tfrac{1}{2}$ | 9·076 | 9 | 8·588 | $8\tfrac{1}{2}$ | 8·139 | $8\tfrac{1}{4}$ | $11\tfrac{1}{2}$ |
| 12 | 9·954 | 10 | 9·385 | $9\tfrac{1}{2}$ | 8·863 | $8\tfrac{3}{4}$ | 8·384 | $8\tfrac{1}{2}$ | 12 |
| $12\tfrac{1}{2}$ | 10·297 | $10\tfrac{1}{4}$ | 9·688 | $9\tfrac{1}{4}$ | 9·132 | $9\tfrac{1}{4}$ | 8·622 | $8\tfrac{1}{2}$ | $12\tfrac{1}{2}$ |
| 13 | 10·635 | $10\tfrac{3}{4}$ | 9·986 | 10 | 9·394 | $9\tfrac{1}{2}$ | 8·853 | $8\tfrac{3}{4}$ | 13 |
| $13\tfrac{1}{2}$ | 10·968 | 11 | 10·277 | $10\tfrac{1}{4}$ | 9·649 | $9\tfrac{1}{4}$ | 9·077 | 9 | $13\tfrac{1}{2}$ |
| 14 | 11·296 | $11\tfrac{1}{4}$ | 10·563 | $10\tfrac{1}{2}$ | 9·899 | 10 | 9·295 | $9\tfrac{1}{4}$ | 14 |
| $14\tfrac{1}{2}$ | 11·619 | $11\tfrac{1}{2}$ | 10·843 | $10\tfrac{3}{4}$ | 10·142 | $10\tfrac{1}{4}$ | 9·507 | $9\tfrac{1}{2}$ | $14\tfrac{1}{2}$ |
| 15 | 11·938 | 12 | 11·118 | 11 | 10·380 | $10\tfrac{1}{2}$ | 9·712 | $9\tfrac{3}{4}$ | 15 |
| $15\tfrac{1}{2}$ | 12·252 | $12\tfrac{1}{4}$ | 11·388 | $11\tfrac{1}{2}$ | 10·612 | $10\tfrac{1}{2}$ | 9·912 | 10 | $15\tfrac{1}{2}$ |
| 16 | 12·561 | $12\tfrac{1}{2}$ | 11·652 | $11\tfrac{3}{4}$ | 10·838 | $10\tfrac{3}{4}$ | 10·106 | 10 | 16 |
| $16\tfrac{1}{2}$ | 12·866 | $12\tfrac{3}{4}$ | 11·911 | 12 | 11·059 | 11 | 10·294 | $10\tfrac{1}{4}$ | $16\tfrac{1}{2}$ |
| 17 | 13·166 | $13\tfrac{1}{4}$ | 12·166 | $12\tfrac{1}{4}$ | 11·274 | $11\tfrac{1}{4}$ | 10·477 | $10\tfrac{1}{2}$ | 17 |
| $17\tfrac{1}{2}$ | 13·462 | $13\tfrac{1}{2}$ | 12·415 | $12\tfrac{1}{2}$ | 11·484 | $11\tfrac{1}{2}$ | 10·655 | $10\tfrac{3}{4}$ | $17\tfrac{1}{2}$ |
| 18 | 13·754 | $13\tfrac{3}{4}$ | 12·659 | $12\tfrac{3}{4}$ | 11·690 | $11\tfrac{3}{4}$ | 10·828 | $10\tfrac{3}{4}$ | 18 |
| $18\tfrac{1}{2}$ | 14·041 | 14 | 12·899 | 13 | 11·890 | 12 | 10·995 | 11 | $18\tfrac{1}{2}$ |
| 19 | 14·324 | $14\tfrac{1}{4}$ | 13·134 | $13\tfrac{1}{4}$ | 12·085 | 12 | 11·158 | $11\tfrac{1}{4}$ | 19 |
| $19\tfrac{1}{2}$ | 14·603 | $14\tfrac{1}{2}$ | 13·364 | $13\tfrac{1}{4}$ | 12·276 | $12\tfrac{1}{4}$ | 11·316 | $11\tfrac{1}{4}$ | $19\tfrac{1}{2}$ |
| 20 | 14·877 | 15 | 13·590 | $13\tfrac{1}{2}$ | 12·462 | $12\tfrac{1}{2}$ | 11·470 | $11\tfrac{1}{2}$ | 20 |

## TABLE FOR DETERMINING THE AMORTIZATION OF LEASES, &c.

(*For examples, see page 232.*)

| Years. | Years Pur. 7 per Cent. | | Years Pur. 8 per Cent. | | Years Pur. 9 per Cent. | | Years Pur. 10 per Cent. | | Years. |
|---|---|---|---|---|---|---|---|---|---|
| ½ | ·475 | ½ | ·472 | ½ | ·469 | ½ | ·465 | ½ | ½ |
| 1 | ·935 | 1 | ·926 | 1 | ·917 | 1 | ·909 | 1 | 1 |
| 1½ | 1·379 | 1½ | 1·363 | 1¼ | 1·347 | 1¼ | 1·332 | 1¼ | 1½ |
| 2 | 1·808 | 1¾ | 1·783 | 1¾ | 1·759 | 1¾ | 1·736 | 1¾ | 2 |
| 2½ | 2·223 | 2¼ | 2·188 | 2¼ | 2·154 | 2¼ | 2·120 | 2 | 2½ |
| 3 | 2·624 | 2½ | 2·577 | 2½ | 2·531 | 2½ | 2·487 | 2½ | 3 |
| 3½ | 3·012 | 3 | 2·952 | 3 | 2·893 | 3 | 2·836 | 2¾ | 3½ |
| 4 | 3·387 | 3½ | 3·312 | 3¼ | 3·240 | 3¼ | 3·170 | 3¼ | 4 |
| 4½ | 3·750 | 3¾ | 3·659 | 3¾ | 3·572 | 3½ | 3·488 | 3½ | 4½ |
| 5 | 4·100 | 4 | 3·993 | 4 | 3·890 | 4 | 3·791 | 3¾ | 5 |
| 5½ | 4·439 | 4½ | 4·314 | 4¼ | 4·194 | 4¼ | 4·080 | 4 | 5½ |
| 6 | 4·767 | 4¾ | 4·623 | 4½ | 4·486 | 4½ | 4·355 | 4¼ | 6 |
| 6½ | 5·083 | 5 | 4·920 | 5 | 4·765 | 4¾ | 4·618 | 4½ | 6½ |
| 7 | 5·389 | 5½ | 5·206 | 5¼ | 5·033 | 5 | 4·868 | 4¾ | 7 |
| 7½ | 5·685 | 5¾ | 5·482 | 5½ | 5·289 | 5¼ | 5·107 | 5 | 7½ |
| 8 | 5·971 | 6 | 5·747 | 5¾ | 5·535 | 5½ | 5·335 | 5¼ | 8 |
| 8½ | 6·248 | 6¼ | 6·002 | 6 | 5·770 | 5¾ | 5·552 | 5½ | 8½ |
| 9 | 6·515 | 6½ | 6·247 | 6¼ | 5·995 | 6 | 5·759 | 5¾ | 9 |
| 9½ | 6·774 | 6¾ | 6·483 | 6½ | 6·211 | 6¼ | 5·956 | 6 | 9½ |
| 10 | 7·024 | 7 | 6·710 | 6¾ | 6·418 | 6½ | 6·145 | 6¼ | 10 |
| 10½ | 7·265 | 7¼ | 6·929 | 7 | 6·616 | 6½ | 6·324 | 6¼ | 10½ |
| 11 | 7·499 | 7½ | 7·139 | 7¼ | 6·805 | 6¾ | 6·495 | 6½ | 11 |
| 11½ | 7·724 | 7¾ | 7·341 | 7¼ | 6·987 | 7 | 6·658 | 6¾ | 11½ |
| 12 | 7·943 | 8 | 7·536 | 7½ | 7·161 | 7¼ | 6·814 | 6¾ | 12 |
| 12½ | 8·154 | 8¼ | 7·723 | 7¾ | 7·327 | 7¼ | 6·962 | 7 | 12½ |
| 13 | 8·358 | 8¼ | 7·904 | 8 | 7·487 | 7½ | 7·103 | 7 | 13 |
| 13½ | 8·555 | 8½ | 8·077 | 8 | 7·640 | 7½ | 7·238 | 7¼ | 13½ |
| 14 | 8·745 | 8¾ | 8·244 | 8¼ | 7·786 | 7¾ | 7·367 | 7¼ | 14 |
| 14½ | 8·930 | 9 | 8·405 | 8½ | 7·926 | 8 | 7·489 | 7½ | 14½ |
| 15 | 9·108 | 9 | 8·559 | 8½ | 8·061 | 8 | 7·606 | 7½ | 15 |
| 15½ | 9·280 | 9¼ | 8·708 | 8¾ | 8·189 | 8¼ | 7·717 | 7¾ | 15½ |
| 16 | 9·447 | 9½ | 8·851 | 8¾ | 8·313 | 8¼ | 7·824 | 7¾ | 16 |
| 16½ | 9·608 | 9½ | 8·989 | 9 | 8·431 | 8½ | 7·925 | 8 | 16½ |
| 17 | 9·763 | 9¾ | 9·122 | 9 | 8·544 | 8½ | 8·022 | 8 | 17 |
| 17½ | 9·914 | 10 | 9·249 | 9¼ | 8·652 | 8¼ | 8·114 | 8 | 17½ |
| 18 | 10·059 | 10 | 9·372 | 9¼ | 8·756 | 8¾ | 8·201 | 8¼ | 18 |
| 18½ | 10·200 | 10¼ | 9·490 | 9½ | 8·855 | 8¾ | 8·285 | 8¼ | 18½ |
| 19 | 10·336 | 10¼ | 9·604 | 9½ | 8·950 | 9 | 8·365 | 8¼ | 19 |
| 19½ | 10·467 | 10½ | 9·713 | 9¾ | 9·041 | 9 | 8·441 | 8½ | 19½ |
| 20 | 10·594 | 10½ | 9·818 | 9¾ | 9·129 | 9¼ | 8·514 | 8½ | 20 |

## 228 DETERMINING AMORTIZATION OF LEASES, ETC.

### TABLE FOR DETERMINING THE AMORTIZATION OF LEASES, &c.
*Continued.*

| Years. | Years Pur. 3 per Cent. | | Years Pur. 4 per Cent. | | Years Pur. 5 per Cent. | | Years Pur. 6 per Cent. | | Years. |
|---|---|---|---|---|---|---|---|---|---|
| $20\frac{1}{2}$ | 15·148 | $15\frac{1}{4}$ | 13·812 | $13\frac{3}{4}$ | 12·644 | $12\frac{3}{4}$ | 11·619 | $11\frac{1}{2}$ | $20\frac{1}{2}$ |
| 21 | 15·415 | $15\frac{1}{2}$ | 14·029 | 14 | 12·821 | $12\frac{3}{4}$ | 11·764 | $11\frac{3}{4}$ | 21 |
| $21\frac{1}{2}$ | 15·678 | $15\frac{3}{4}$ | 14·242 | $14\frac{1}{4}$ | 12·994 | 13 | 11·905 | 12 | $21\frac{1}{2}$ |
| 22 | 15·937 | 16 | 14·451 | $14\frac{1}{2}$ | 13·163 | $13\frac{1}{4}$ | 12·042 | 12 | 22 |
| $22\frac{1}{2}$ | 16·192 | $16\frac{1}{4}$ | 14·656 | $14\frac{3}{4}$ | 13·328 | $13\frac{1}{4}$ | 12·174 | $12\frac{1}{4}$ | $22\frac{1}{2}$ |
| 23 | 16·444 | $16\frac{1}{2}$ | 14·857 | $14\frac{3}{4}$ | 13·489 | $13\frac{1}{2}$ | 12·303 | $12\frac{1}{4}$ | 23 |
| $23\frac{1}{2}$ | 16·691 | $16\frac{3}{4}$ | 15·054 | 15 | 13·645 | $13\frac{3}{4}$ | 12·429 | $12\frac{1}{2}$ | $23\frac{1}{2}$ |
| 24 | 16·936 | 17 | 15·247 | $15\frac{1}{4}$ | 13·799 | $13\frac{3}{4}$ | 12·550 | $12\frac{1}{2}$ | 24 |
| $24\frac{1}{2}$ | 17·176 | $17\frac{1}{4}$ | 15·436 | $15\frac{1}{2}$ | 13·948 | 14 | 12·669 | $12\frac{3}{4}$ | $24\frac{1}{2}$ |
| 25 | 17·413 | $17\frac{1}{2}$ | 15·622 | $15\frac{1}{2}$ | 14·094 | 14 | 12·783 | $12\frac{3}{4}$ | 25 |
| $25\frac{1}{2}$ | 17·647 | $17\frac{3}{4}$ | 15·804 | $15\frac{3}{4}$ | 14·236 | $14\frac{1}{4}$ | 12·895 | 13 | $25\frac{1}{2}$ |
| 26 | 17·877 | 18 | 15·983 | 16 | 14·375 | $14\frac{1}{4}$ | 13·003 | 13 | 26 |
| $26\frac{1}{2}$ | 18·104 | 18 | 16·158 | $16\frac{1}{4}$ | 14·511 | $14\frac{1}{4}$ | 13·108 | 13 | $26\frac{1}{2}$ |
| 27 | 18·327 | $18\frac{1}{4}$ | 16·330 | $16\frac{1}{4}$ | 14·643 | $14\frac{1}{2}$ | 13·211 | $13\frac{1}{4}$ | 27 |
| $27\frac{1}{2}$ | 18·547 | $18\frac{1}{2}$ | 16·498 | $16\frac{1}{2}$ | 14·772 | $14\frac{1}{2}$ | 13·310 | $13\frac{1}{4}$ | $27\frac{1}{2}$ |
| 28 | 18·764 | $18\frac{3}{4}$ | 16·663 | $16\frac{3}{4}$ | 14·898 | 15 | 13·406 | $13\frac{1}{2}$ | 28 |
| $28\frac{1}{2}$ | 18·978 | 19 | 16·825 | $16\frac{3}{4}$ | 15·021 | 15 | 13·500 | $13\frac{1}{2}$ | $28\frac{1}{2}$ |
| 29 | 19·188 | $19\frac{1}{4}$ | 16·984 | 17 | 15·141 | $15\frac{1}{4}$ | 13·591 | $13\frac{1}{2}$ | 29 |
| $29\frac{1}{2}$ | 19·396 | $19\frac{1}{4}$ | 17·139 | $17\frac{1}{4}$ | 15·258 | $15\frac{1}{4}$ | 13·679 | $13\frac{3}{4}$ | $29\frac{1}{2}$ |
| 30 | 19·600 | $19\frac{1}{2}$ | 17·292 | $17\frac{1}{4}$ | 15·372 | $15\frac{1}{4}$ | 13·765 | $13\frac{3}{4}$ | 30 |
| $30\frac{1}{2}$ | 19·802 | $19\frac{3}{4}$ | 17·442 | $17\frac{1}{2}$ | 15·484 | $15\frac{1}{2}$ | 13·848 | $13\frac{3}{4}$ | $30\frac{1}{2}$ |
| 31 | 20·000 | 20 | 17·588 | $17\frac{1}{2}$ | 15·593 | $15\frac{1}{2}$ | 13·929 | 14 | 31 |
| $31\frac{1}{2}$ | 20·196 | $20\frac{1}{4}$ | 17·732 | $17\frac{3}{4}$ | 15·699 | $15\frac{3}{4}$ | 14·003 | 14 | $31\frac{1}{2}$ |
| 32 | 20·389 | $20\frac{1}{2}$ | 17·874 | $17\frac{3}{4}$ | 15·803 | $15\frac{3}{4}$ | 14·084 | 14 | 32 |
| $32\frac{1}{2}$ | 20·579 | $20\frac{1}{2}$ | 18·012 | 18 | 15·904 | 16 | 14·158 | $14\frac{1}{4}$ | $32\frac{1}{2}$ |
| 33 | 20·766 | $20\frac{3}{4}$ | 18·148 | $18\frac{1}{4}$ | 16·003 | 16 | 14·230 | $14\frac{1}{4}$ | 33 |
| $33\frac{1}{2}$ | 20·950 | 21 | 18·281 | $18\frac{1}{4}$ | 16·099 | 16 | 14·300 | $14\frac{1}{4}$ | $33\frac{1}{2}$ |
| 34 | 21·132 | $21\frac{1}{4}$ | 18·411 | $18\frac{1}{2}$ | 16·193 | $16\frac{1}{4}$ | 14·368 | $14\frac{1}{4}$ | 34 |
| $34\frac{1}{2}$ | 21·311 | $21\frac{1}{4}$ | 18·539 | $18\frac{1}{2}$ | 16·285 | $16\frac{1}{4}$ | 14·434 | $14\frac{1}{2}$ | $34\frac{1}{2}$ |
| 35 | 21·487 | $21\frac{1}{2}$ | 18·665 | $18\frac{3}{4}$ | 16·374 | $16\frac{1}{4}$ | 14·498 | $14\frac{1}{2}$ | 35 |
| $35\frac{1}{2}$ | 21·661 | $21\frac{3}{4}$ | 18·788 | $18\frac{3}{4}$ | 16·462 | $16\frac{1}{2}$ | 14·561 | $14\frac{1}{2}$ | $35\frac{1}{2}$ |
| 36 | 21·832 | $21\frac{3}{4}$ | 18·908 | 19 | 16·547 | $16\frac{1}{2}$ | 14·621 | $14\frac{3}{4}$ | 36 |
| $36\frac{1}{2}$ | 22·001 | 22 | 19·027 | 19 | 16·630 | $16\frac{1}{2}$ | 14·680 | $14\frac{3}{4}$ | $36\frac{1}{2}$ |
| 37 | 22·167 | $22\frac{1}{4}$ | 19·143 | $19\frac{1}{4}$ | 16·711 | $16\frac{1}{2}$ | 14·737 | $14\frac{3}{4}$ | 37 |
| $37\frac{1}{2}$ | 22·331 | $22\frac{1}{4}$ | 19·256 | $19\frac{1}{4}$ | 16·791 | $16\frac{3}{4}$ | 14·792 | $14\frac{3}{4}$ | $37\frac{1}{2}$ |
| 38 | 22·492 | $22\frac{1}{2}$ | 19·368 | $19\frac{1}{2}$ | 16·868 | $16\frac{3}{4}$ | 14·846 | $14\frac{3}{4}$ | 38 |
| $38\frac{1}{2}$ | 22·652 | $22\frac{1}{2}$ | 19·477 | $19\frac{1}{2}$ | 16·943 | 17 | 14·898 | 15 | $38\frac{1}{2}$ |
| 39 | 22·808 | $22\frac{3}{4}$ | 19·584 | $19\frac{1}{2}$ | 17·017 | 17 | 14·949 | 15 | 39 |
| $39\frac{1}{2}$ | 22·963 | 23 | 19·690 | $19\frac{3}{4}$ | 17·089 | 17 | 14·998 | 15 | $39\frac{1}{2}$ |
| 40 | 23·115 | 23 | 19·793 | $19\frac{3}{4}$ | 17·159 | $17\frac{1}{4}$ | 15·046 | 15 | 40 |

## TABLE FOR DETERMINING THE AMORTIZATION OF LEASES, &c.

*Continued.*

| Years. | Years Pur. 7 per Cent. | | Years Pur. 8 per Cent. | | Years Pur. 9 per Cent. | | Years Pur. 10 per Cent. | | Years. |
|---|---|---|---|---|---|---|---|---|---|
| 20½ | 10·717 | 10¾ | 9·919 | 10 | 9·212 | 9¼ | 8·583 | 8½ | 20½ |
| 21 | 10·836 | 10¾ | 10·017 | 10 | 9·292 | 9¼ | 8·649 | 8¾ | 21 |
| 21½ | 10·950 | 11 | 10·111 | 10 | 9·369 | 9¼ | 8·712 | 8¾ | 21½ |
| 22 | 11·061 | 11 | 10·201 | 10¼ | 9·442 | 9½ | 8·772 | 8¾ | 22 |
| 22½ | 11·168 | 11¼ | 10·288 | 10¼ | 9·513 | 9½ | 8·829 | 8¾ | 22½ |
| 23 | 11·272 | 11¼ | 10·371 | 10¼ | 9·580 | 9½ | 8·883 | 9 | 23 |
| 23½ | 11·372 | 11¼ | 10·451 | 10½ | 9·645 | 9¾ | 8·935 | 9 | 23½ |
| 24 | 11·469 | 11½ | 10·529 | 10½ | 9·707 | 9¾ | 8·985 | 9 | 24 |
| 24½ | 11·563 | 11½ | 10·603 | 10½ | 9·766 | 9¾ | 9·032 | 9 | 24½ |
| 25 | 11·654 | 11¾ | 10·675 | 10¾ | 9·823 | 9¾ | 9·077 | 9 | 25 |
| 25½ | 11·741 | 11¾ | 10·744 | 10¾ | 9·877 | 10 | 9·120 | 9 | 25½ |
| 26 | 11·826 | 11¾ | 10·810 | 10¾ | 9·929 | 10 | 9·161 | 9¼ | 26 |
| 26½ | 11·908 | 12 | 10·874 | 10¾ | 9·979 | 10 | 9·200 | 9¼ | 26½ |
| 27 | 11·987 | 12 | 10·935 | 11 | 10·027 | 10 | 9·237 | 9¼ | 27 |
| 27½ | 12·063 | 12 | 10·994 | 11 | 10·072 | 10 | 9·273 | 9¼ | 27½ |
| 28 | 12·137 | 12¼ | 11·051 | 11 | 10·116 | 10 | 9·307 | 9¼ | 28 |
| 28½ | 12·209 | 12¼ | 11·106 | 11 | 10·158 | 10¼ | 9·339 | 9¼ | 28½ |
| 29 | 12·278 | 12¼ | 11·158 | 11¼ | 10·198 | 10¼ | 9·370 | 9½ | 29 |
| 29½ | 12·344 | 12¼ | 11·209 | 11¼ | 10·237 | 10¼ | 9·399 | 9½ | 29½ |
| 30 | 12·409 | 12½ | 11·258 | 11¼ | 10·274 | 10¼ | 9·427 | 9½ | 30 |
| 30½ | 12·471 | 12½ | 11·305 | 11¼ | 10·309 | 10¼ | 9·454 | 9½ | 30½ |
| 31 | 12·532 | 12½ | 11·350 | 11¼ | 10·343 | 10¼ | 9·479 | 9½ | 31 |
| 31½ | 12·590 | 12½ | 11·393 | 11½ | 10·375 | 10¼ | 9·503 | 9½ | 31½ |
| 32 | 12·647 | 12¾ | 11·435 | 11½ | 10·406 | 10½ | 9·526 | 9½ | 32 |
| 32½ | 12·701 | 12¾ | 11·475 | 11½ | 10·436 | 10½ | 9·548 | 9½ | 32½ |
| 33 | 12·754 | 12¾ | 11·514 | 11½ | 10·464 | 10½ | 9·569 | 9½ | 33 |
| 33½ | 12·805 | 12¾ | 11·551 | 11½ | 10·492 | 10½ | 9·589 | 9½ | 33½ |
| 34 | 12·854 | 12¾ | 11·587 | 11½ | 10·518 | 10½ | 9·609 | 9½ | 34 |
| 34½ | 12·902 | 13 | 11·621 | 11½ | 10 543 | 1c½ | 9·627 | 9¾ | 34½ |
| 35 | 12·948 | 13 | 11·655 | 11¾ | 10·567 | 10½ | 9·644 | 9¾ | 35 |
| 35½ | 12·992 | 13 | 11·686 | 11¾ | 10·590 | 10½ | 9·661 | 9¾ | 35½ |
| 36 | 13·035 | 13 | 11·717 | 11¾ | 10·612 | 10½ | 9·677 | 9¾ | 36 |
| 36½ | 13·077 | 13 | 11·747 | 11¾ | 10·633 | 10¾ | 9·692 | 9¾ | 36½ |
| 37 | 13·117 | 13 | 11·775 | 11¾ | 10·653 | 10¾ | 9·706 | 9¾ | 37 |
| 37½ | 13·156 | 13¼ | 11·803 | 11¾ | 10·672 | 10¾ | 9·720 | 9¾ | 37½ |
| 38 | 13·193 | 13¼ | 11·829 | 11¾ | 10·691 | 10¾ | 9·733 | 9¾ | 38 |
| 38½ | 13·230 | 13¼ | 11·854 | 11¾ | 10·709 | 10¾ | 9·745 | 9¾ | 38½ |
| 39 | 13·265 | 13¼ | 11·879 | 12 | 10·726 | 10¾ | 9·757 | 9¾ | 39 |
| 39½ | 13·299 | 13¼ | 11·902 | 12 | 10·742 | 10¾ | 9·768 | 9¾ | 39½ |
| 40 | 13·332 | 13¼ | 11·925 | 12 | 10·757 | 10¾ | 9·779 | 9¾ | 40 |

TABLE FOR DETERMINING THE AMORTIZATION OF LEASES, &c.
*Continued.*

| Years. | Years Pur. 3 per Cent. | | Years Pur. 4 per Cent. | | Years Pur. 5 per Cent. | | Years Pur. 6 per Cent. | | Years. |
|---|---|---|---|---|---|---|---|---|---|
| 40½ | 23·265 | 23¼ | 19·894 | 20 | 17·228 | 17¼ | 15·093 | 15 | 40½ |
| 41 | 23·412 | 23½ | 19·993 | 20 | 17·294 | 17¼ | 15·138 | 15¼ | 41 |
| 41½ | 23·558 | 23½ | 20·090 | 20 | 17·360 | 17¼ | 15·182 | 15¼ | 41½ |
| 42 | 23·701 | 23¾ | 20·186 | 20¼ | 17·423 | 17½ | 15·225 | 15¼ | 42 |
| 42½ | 23·843 | 23¾ | 20·279 | 20¼ | 17·485 | 17½ | 15·266 | 15¼ | 42½ |
| 43 | 23·982 | 24 | 20·371 | 20¼ | 17·546 | 17½ | 15·306 | 15¼ | 43 |
| 43½ | 24·119 | 24 | 20·461 | 20½ | 17·605 | 17½ | 15·345 | 15¼ | 43½ |
| 44 | 24·254 | 24¼ | 20·549 | 20½ | 17·663 | 17¾ | 15·383 | 15½ | 44 |
| 44½ | 24·387 | 24½ | 20·635 | 20¾ | 17·719 | 17¾ | 15·420 | 15½ | 44½ |
| 45 | 24·519 | 24½ | 20·720 | 20¾ | 17·774 | 17¾ | 15·456 | 15½ | 45 |
| 45½ | 24·648 | 24¾ | 20·803 | 20¾ | 17·828 | 17¾ | 15·491 | 15½ | 45½ |
| 46 | 24·775 | 24¾ | 20·885 | 21 | 17·880 | 18 | 15·524 | 15½ | 46 |
| 46½ | 24·901 | 25 | 20·965 | 21 | 17·931 | 18 | 15·557 | 15½ | 46½ |
| 47 | 25·025 | 25 | 21·043 | 21 | 17·981 | 18 | 15·589 | 15½ | 47 |
| 47½ | 25·147 | 25¼ | 21·120 | 21 | 18·030 | 18 | 15·620 | 15½ | 47½ |
| 48 | 25·267 | 25¼ | 21·195 | 21¼ | 18·077 | 18 | 15·650 | 15¾ | 48 |
| 48½ | 25·385 | 25½ | 21·269 | 21¼ | 18·123 | 18 | 15·679 | 15¾ | 48½ |
| 49 | 25·502 | 25½ | 21·341 | 21¼ | 18·169 | 18¼ | 15·708 | 15¾ | 49 |
| 49½ | 25·617 | 25⅝ | 21·413 | 21½ | 18·213 | 18¼ | 15·735 | 15¾ | 49½ |
| 50 | 25·730 | 25¾ | 21·482 | 21½ | 18·256 | 18¼ | 15·762 | 15¾ | 50 |
| 51 | 25·951 | 26 | 21·617 | 21½ | 18·339 | 18¼ | 15·813 | 15¾ | 51 |
| 52 | 26·166 | 26¼ | 21·748 | 21¾ | 18·418 | 18½ | 15·861 | 15¾ | 52 |
| 53 | 26·375 | 26¼ | 21·873 | 21¾ | 18·493 | 18½ | 15·907 | 16 | 53 |
| 54 | 26·578 | 26½ | 21·993 | 22 | 18·565 | 18½ | 15·950 | 16 | 54 |
| 55 | 26·774 | 26¾ | 22·109 | 22 | 18·633 | 18¾ | 15·991 | 16 | 55 |
| 56 | 26·965 | 27 | 22·220 | 22¼ | 18·699 | 18¾ | 16·029 | 16 | 56 |
| 57 | 27·151 | 27¼ | 22·327 | 22¼ | 18·761 | 18¾ | 16·065 | 16 | 57 |
| 58 | 27·331 | 27¼ | 22·430 | 22½ | 18·820 | 18¾ | 16·099 | 16 | 58 |
| 59 | 27·506 | 27½ | 22·528 | 22½ | 18·876 | 19 | 16·131 | 16¼ | 59 |
| 60 | 27·676 | 27¾ | 22·623 | 22½ | 18·929 | 19 | 16·161 | 16¼ | 60 |
| 65 | 28·453 | 28½ | 23·047 | 23 | 19·161 | 19¼ | 16·289 | 16¼ | 65 |
| 70 | 29·123 | 29 | 23·395 | 23½ | 19·343 | 19¼ | 16·385 | 16⅜ | 70 |
| 75 | 29·702 | 29¾ | 23·680 | 23¾ | 19·485 | 19½ | 16·456 | 16½ | 75 |
| 80 | 30·201 | 30¼ | 23·915 | 24 | 19·596 | 19½ | 16·509 | 16½ | 80 |
| 85 | 30·631 | 30¾ | 24·109 | 24 | 19·684 | 19¾ | 16·549 | 16½ | 85 |
| 90 | 31·002 | 31 | 24·267 | 24¼ | 19·752 | 19¾ | 16·579 | 16½ | 90 |
| 95 | 31·323 | 31¼ | 24·398 | 24½ | 19·806 | 19¾ | 16·601 | 16½ | 95 |
| 100 | 31·599 | 31½ | 24·505 | 24½ | 19·848 | 19¾ | 16·618 | 16½ | 100 |
| Perp. | 33·333 | 33⅓ | 25·000 | 25 | 20·000 | 20 | 16·667 | 16⅔ | Perp. |

## TABLE FOR DETERMINING THE AMORTIZATION OF LEASES, &c.

*Continued.*

| Years. | Years Pur. 7 per Cent. | | Years Pur. 8 per Cent. | | Years Pur. 9 per Cent. | | Years Pur. 10 per Cent. | | Years. |
|---|---|---|---|---|---|---|---|---|---|
| 40½ | 13·363 | 13¼ | 11·946 | 12 | 10·772 | 10¾ | 9·789 | 9¾ | 40½ |
| 41 | 13·394 | 13½ | 11·967 | 12 | 10·787 | 10¾ | 9·799 | 9¾ | 41 |
| 41½ | 13·424 | 13½ | 11·987 | 12 | 10·800 | 10¾ | 9·808 | 9¾ | 41½ |
| 42 | 13·452 | 13½ | 12·007 | 12 | 10·813 | 10¾ | 9·817 | 9¾ | 42 |
| 42½ | 13·480 | 13½ | 12·025 | 12 | 10·826 | 10¾ | 9·826 | 9¾ | 42½ |
| 43 | 13·507 | 13½ | 12·043 | 12 | 10·838 | 10¾ | 9·834 | 9¾ | 43 |
| 43½ | 13·533 | 13½ | 12·060 | 12 | 10 849 | 10¾ | 9·842 | 9¾ | 43½ |
| 44 | 13·558 | 13½ | 12·077 | 12 | 10·861 | 10¾ | 9·849 | 9¾ | 44 |
| 44½ | 13·582 | 13½ | 12·093 | 12 | 10·871 | 10¾ | 9·856 | 9¾ | 44½ |
| 45 | 13·606 | 13½ | 12·108 | 12 | 10·881 | 11 | 9·863 | 9¾ | 45 |
| 45½ | 13·628 | 13¾ | 12·123 | 12 | 10·891 | 11 | 9·869 | 9¾ | 45½ |
| 46 | 13·650 | 13¾ | 12·137 | 12¼ | 10·900 | 11 | 9·875 | 10 | 46 |
| 46½ | 13·671 | 13¾ | 12·151 | 12¼ | 10·909 | 11 | 9·881 | 10 | 46½ |
| 47 | 13·692 | 13¾ | 12·164 | 12¼ | 10·918 | 11 | 9·887 | 10 | 47 |
| 47½ | 13·711 | 13¾ | 12·177 | 12¼ | 10·926 | 11 | 9·892 | 10 | 47½ |
| 48 | 13·730 | 13¾ | 12·189 | 12¼ | 10·934 | 11 | 9·897 | 10 | 48 |
| 48½ | 13·749 | 13¾ | 12·201 | 12¼ | 10·941 | 11 | 9·902 | 10 | 48½ |
| 49 | 13·767 | 13¾ | 12·212 | 12¼ | 10·948 | 11 | 9·906 | 10 | 49 |
| 49½ | 13·784 | 13¾ | 12·223 | 12¼ | 10·955 | 11 | 9·911 | 10 | 49½ |
| 50 | 13·801 | 13¾ | 12·233 | 12¼ | 10·962 | 11 | 9·915 | 10 | 50 |
| 51 | 13·832 | 13¾ | 12·253 | 12¼ | 10·974 | 11 | 9·921 | 10 | 51 |
| 52 | 13·862 | 13¾ | 12·272 | 12¼ | 10·985 | 11 | 9·930 | 10 | 52 |
| 53 | 13·890 | 14 | 12·288 | 12¼ | 10·996 | 11 | 9·936 | 10 | 53 |
| 54 | 13·916 | 14 | 12·304 | 12¼ | 11·005 | 11 | 9·942 | 10 | 54 |
| 55 | 13·940 | 14 | 12·319 | 12¼ | 11·014 | 11 | 9·947 | 10 | 55 |
| 56 | 13·963 | 14 | 12·332 | 12¼ | 11·022 | 11 | 9·952 | 10 | 56 |
| 57 | 13·984 | 14 | 12·344 | 12¼ | 11·029 | 11 | 9·956 | 10 | 57 |
| 58 | 14·003 | 14 | 12·356 | 12¼ | 11·036 | 11 | 9·960 | 10 | 58 |
| 59 | 14·022 | 14 | 12·367 | 12¼ | 11·042 | 11 | 9·964 | 10 | 59 |
| 60 | 14·039 | 14 | 12·377 | 12½ | 11·048 | 11 | 9·967 | 10 | 60 |
| 65 | 14·110 | 14 | 12·416 | 12½ | 11·070 | 11 | 9·980 | 10 | 65 |
| 70 | 14·160 | 14¼ | 12·443 | 12½ | 11·084 | 11 | 9·987 | 10 | 70 |
| 75 | 14·196 | 14¼ | 12·461 | 12½ | 11·094 | 11 | 9·992 | 10 | 75 |
| 80 | 14·222 | 14¼ | 12·474 | 12½ | 11·100 | 11 | 9·995 | 10 | 80 |
| 85 | 14·240 | 14¼ | 12·482 | 12½ | 11·104 | 11 | 9·997 | 10 | 85 |
| 90 | 14·253 | 14¼ | 12·488 | 12½ | 11·106 | 11 | 9·998 | 10 | 90 |
| 95 | 14·263 | 14¼ | 12·492 | 12½ | 11·108 | 11 | 9·999 | 10 | 95 |
| 100 | 14·269 | 14¼ | 12·494 | 12½ | 11·109 | 11 | 9·999 | 10 | 100 |
| Perp. | 14·286 | 14¼ | 12·500 | 12½ | 11·111 | 11 | 10·000 | 10 | Perp. |

## EXAMPLES.

The foregoing table is reproduced from the twenty-second edition of Inwood's "Tables for the Purchasing of Estates, &c.," by kind permission of the publishers, Messrs. Crosby Lockwood and Son, and shows the annual amounts to be debited to Profit and Loss Account, and credited to account of Lease or other object to be amortized in a given number of years with interest at 3, 4, 5, 6, 7, 8, 9, and 10 per cent. per annum. The table is also serviceable for ascertaining the value of a Lease at the several rates of interest.

EXAMPLE :—A Lease or Annuity for 14 years, to make 3 per cent. and to get back the principal, is worth 11·296 or 11¼ years' purchase of the clear annual rent; at 4 per cent., 10·563, or 10½ years' purchase; at 5 per cent., 9·899, or 10 years' purchase; at 6 per cent., 9·295, or 9¼ years' purchase. In calculating the value of Annuities, Leases, &c., *Compound* Interest is always reckoned and allowed.

A hypothetical Ledger Account, showing the amortization of a Lease at 5 per cent. per annum, will, with a description, be found in Chapter VI., p. 108.

# GLOSSARY OF SOME OF THE TERMS USED.

*The definitions do not extend to terms used in quotations or in the Appendices.*

**Amortization.**—The process by which provision is made for the expiration of value in an asset.

**Appreciation.**—The increase in value of assets either through special or general causes. (Opposed to Depreciation, *q. v.*)

**Assets.**—Property of all kinds, possessed or in reversion. (Opposed to Liabilities, *q. v.*)

**Balance Sheet.**—A complete summary of debit and credit balances as they appear in the accounts of the Ledger at a given date.

**Book Value.**—The monetary value of any asset according to the books of account. (Distinguished from Market Value, *q. v.*)

**Capital.**—The money or properties invested in the business. Assets applied to production of further wealth, or assets used as a source of income.

**Cash Book.**—A commercial book recording the cash transactions.

**Commercial Books.**—The books pertaining to the counting-house, such as the Ledger, Journal, Cash Book, recording mercantile transactions, as distinguished from Factory Books treating of merchandise.

**Commercial Ledger.**—The Mercantile Ledger (as distinguished from the Stores, Stock, and Plant Ledgers).

**Cost of Production.**—The total expenditure incurred in the production of a commodity. (Distinguished from Prime Cost, *q. v.*)

**Counting-House.**—The place in which the mercantile bookkeeping is conducted.

**Craft Register.**—The book recording the work done by, and the earnings of, each of the Craft.

**Credit Note.**—If received, an advice of indebtedness to the firm. If issued, an advice of indebtedness by the firm.

**Credit Note Register.**—A commercial book in which the credit notes received are registered.

## GLOSSARY OF TERMS.

**Day Book.**—A commercial book in which the sales of stock are recorded.

**Delivery Note.**—A request to receive, and a description of, material tendered.

**Depreciation.**—The falling off in the value of buildings, machinery, plant, and other assets. (Distinguished from Appreciation, *q. v.*)

**Dilapidations.**—Those defects in a tenement which have arisen from neglect or misuse; and of use or age, if the efficiency of the structure is destroyed.

**Establishment Expenses—General Charges.**—The general expenses which cannot be *directly* charged to any particular process or branch of a business.

**Estimate of Cost.**—A calculation of the probable cost of a commodity.

**Factory.**—The place in which manufacturing operations are carried on.

**Factory Accounts.**—The systematic registration for purposes of account of transactions appertaining to manufacture.

**Factory General Charges.**—The general expenses incurred in the factory which cannot be directly charged to any particular Order No.

**Factory General Charges Book.**—The book in which the Factory General Charges are collected.

**Fixed Capital.**—That part of the capital of a firm which consists of the instruments of production of a more or less permanent character.

**Fixed Plant.**—The machinery and appurtenances required for the purpose of manufacture, and permanently located in one position in a factory. (Distinguished from Loose Plant and Tools, *q. v.*)

**Foreman.**—A superintendent of a floor, wing, or shop in a factory, or of a set of men.

**Fuel Summary Form.**—A form summarising the various items of cost in the delivered price of fuel.

**General Charges.**—(*See* ESTABLISHMENT EXPENSES.)

**General Stores Account.**—The account in the Commercial Ledger in which the receipts and issues of stores, as recorded in the Commercial Books, are collected.

**Going Concern.**—A business the efficiency of which, for the purpose of profit, is maintained.

**Goodwill.**—The value pertaining to the *clientèle*, or interest in the business.

## GLOSSARY OF TERMS. 235

**Indirect Expenses.**—Outlays not directly remunerative. (Distinguished from General Charges and Establishment Expenses, *q. v.*)

**Indirect Factory Expenses.**—Outlays made in the factory which are not directly remunerative. (Distinguished from Factory General Charges.)

**Inventory.**—A detailed and descriptive catalogue of properties.

**Invoice.**—If received, an advice of indebtedness by the firm. If issued, an advice of indebtedness to the firm.

**Invoice Allocation (or Bought Day) Book.**—A commercial book in which invoices for goods purchased are entered and analysed.

**Invoice Register Book.**—A commercial book in which the invoices received are registered.

**Joint Stock Company.**—An association of individuals who combine by the subscription of capital to carry on a business.

**Labour.**—That factor in the cost of production which in a given trade represents the work of adapting materials.

**Leading Hand.**—The senior hand of a floor, wing, or shop in a factory, or of a gang of men.

**Liabilities.**—The debts and obligations of a firm. (Opposed to Assets, *q. v.*)

**Loose Plant and Tools.**—The machinery, tools, and appurtenances required for the purpose of manufacture temporarily located in any position in a factory. (Distinguished from Fixed Plant, *q. v.*)

**Magazine.**—(*See* STORES.)

**Maintenance.**—The preservation of the efficiency of fixed capital.

**Manufactory.**—(*See* FACTORY.)

**Manufacturing Account.**—The Account in the Commercial Ledger which shows the value of the Stock Orders or goods in course of manufacture.

**Manufacturing Order.**—(*See* STOCK ORDER.)

**Market Price.**—The price at or about which all other similar commodities are being sold in the same place. (Distinguished from Book Value, *q. v.*)

**Material—Stores.**—That factor in the cost of production which represents the raw material of trade employed in the manufacture of commodities.

**Obsolescence.**—The process by which an article before it is worn out falls either wholly or in part into desuetude in a certain trade, and as a result is no longer of current application in that trade.

**Order Form.**—An instruction to a vendor to supply material or do work.

**Orders Received Book.**—A commercial book recording the orders received.

**Outworks Time Record.**—A form used by employés engaged outside the factory, showing how their time has been spent.

**Overlooker.**—A supervisor of labour.

**Overtime.**—Time worked beyond the normal period of employment in the factory.

**Overtime Book.**—A factory book in which the timekeeper records the overtime made.

**Overtime Comparison Book.**—A book in which comparison is made between the cost of ordinary time and overtime.

**Overtime Return.**—A return showing the overtime worked in the factory during a certain period.

**Patents Account.**—The account in the commercial books which records the book value of patents.

**Patterns.**—The types to and from which articles are made.

**Petty Cash Book.**—A commercial book recording small cash transactions.

**Piece Work.**—Work paid for by the piece or job. (Distinguished from work paid by time.)

**Piece Work Analysis Book.**—A book in which the piece work returns are analysed and a comparison instituted as to the relative value, as regards the product, of time and piece wages.

**Piece Work Return.**—A factory form used by employés engaged on piece work.

**Plant.**—The machinery and appurtenances required for the purpose of manufacture. (*Vide* Fixed Capital, Fixed Plant, Loose Plant.)

**Plant and Buildings Ledger.**—A book in which are collected all entries relating to fixed and loose plant and buildings.

**Plant Debit Note.**—A factory form used to record the employment of plant.

**Plant Debit Summary.**—The form on which Plant Debit Notes are summarised.

**Prime Cost.**—The original or direct cost of an article. (Distinguished from Cost of Production, *q. v.*)

**Prime Cost Journal.**—The book in which adjusting entries as to cost are made.

**Prime Cost Ledger—Prime Cost Book.**—The book in which are collected all entries relating to prime cost, or contingently to cost of production.

**Profit and Loss Account.**—The statement which shows the pecuniary result of the business effected. (Distinguished from Revenue, *q. v.*)

**Railway Rates Book.**—The book in which railway rates are recorded under the headings of the various charges making up the rate.

**Rate Book.**—(*See* WAGES RATE BOOK.)

**Raw Material.**—The unadapted materials employed in the production of commodities of a particular trade. The manufactured articles of one trade may be the raw materials of another.

**Renewal.**
**Renovation.** } (*See* MAINTENANCE.)
**Repairs.**

**Reserve Fund.**—A provision for contingencies.

**Residual Value.**—The ultimate selling value of assets when worn out or superseded.

**Retail Warehouse.**—The repository for commodities which have been purchased from the makers or other vendors for reselling.

**Revenue.**—The gross return from capital employed. (Distinguished from Profit and Loss, *q. v.*)

**Sales Analysis Book.**—A commercial book in which an analysis is made of the sale of stock.

**Sales Cancelled Book.**—A commercial book in which the credit notes given to customers in respect of stock returned are entered.

**Scrap.**—The minimum value of articles, *i.e.* the price that may be depended on for waste material.

**Shop Returns Book.**—A book in which are recorded the Stores Debit Notes.

**Sinking Fund.**—A fund invested in order to provide for an eventual loss or claim.

**Stock—Stock-in-Trade.**—Those commodities which, having been manufactured or purchased, constitute the objects of the trade; manufactured commodities on hand; contingently, articles purchased for retailing. (Distinguished from Stores, *q. v.*)

## GLOSSARY OF TERMS.

**Stock Account.**—The account in the Commercial Ledger in which are summarised the monetary transactions relating to stock.

**Stock Books.**—Books relating to the receipt and issue of stock.

**Stock Debit Note.**—A factory form used to record the completion of articles manufactured for stock, and their transfer from the factory to the warehouse.

**Stock Issued Book.**—A factory book in which the stock requisitions are recorded.

**Stock Ledger.**—The book in which all entries relating to stock are collected. (Distinguished from Stores, Plant, and Commercial Ledgers.)

**Stock Order.**—The instruction to manufacture commodities for stock and to record the expenditure. (Distinguished from Working Order, *q. v.*)

**Stock Order No.**—The number given to a Stock Order. (Distinguished from Working Order No., *q. v.*)

**Stock Received Book.**—A factory book recording the receipts of stock.

**Stock Requisition.**—A form used to record the withdrawal of stock from the warehouse.

**Stock Returned by Customers Analysis Book.**—A commercial book in which the Stock Returned Debit Notes are analysed.

**Stock Returned by Customers Book.**—A factory book in which the Stock Returned Debit Notes are recorded.

**Stock Returned Debit Note.**—A factory form used to record the return of stock to the warehouse by customers.

**Stock taking.**—(*See* SURVEY.)

**Stock Uncompleted.**—Articles in course of manufacture for stock.

**Store.**—The repository for stores.

**Stores.**—The raw material employed in manufacture or other purposes. (Distinguished from Stock, *q. v.*)

**Stores Account.**—(*See* GENERAL STORES ACCOUNT.)

**Stores Debit Note.**—A factory form recording the return to store of waste or surplus material.

**Stores Issued Book.**—A factory book in which the Stores Warrants are entered.

**Storekeeper.**—The officer in charge of stores. (Distinguished from Warehouseman, *q. v.*)

**Stores Ledger.**—The book in which all entries relating to stores are collected. (Distinguished from Stock, Plant, and Commercial Ledgers.)

**Stores Received Book.**—A factory book in which the invoices for goods purchased are entered.

**Stores Rejected Book.**—A factory book in which are recorded all the credit-notes received from vendors of goods returned.

**Stores Requisition.**—A requisition from the storekeeper for the purchase of material.

**Stores Requisition Book.**—The book in which stores requisitions are entered.

**Stores Warrant.**—A factory form used for the withdrawal of stores.

**Survey—Stock-taking.**—The process of taking an inventory and of examining the condition, &c., of properties. (*See* VALUATION.)

**Suspense Account.**—An impersonal account in the Commercial Ledger to which items in abeyance are charged.

**Symbolic Nomenclature.**—The designation by symbols of machines and parts.

**Time Allocation Book.**—The book in which the time records are entered, and in which their apportionment to the various orders is carried out.

**Time Book.**—A factory book used by the timekeeper to record the time made by the employés.

**Time Clerk.**—The clerk who enters the employés' records of time, and analyses the same under the various working orders.

**Timekeeper or Gatekeeper.**—The employé whose duty it is to record the time the other employés enter and leave the factory.

**Time Record.**—A factory form used by the employés, recording how their time has been spent.

**Time Sheet.**—A form used to record the time of lighters, barges, or boats on their journeys.

**Trading Account.**—The account in the Commercial Ledger which represents the trading transactions. The debit side of the account records the cost of stock issued, and the credit the proceeds of sales.

**Transfer Analysis Book.**—A commercial book analysing the transfer from stores to warehouse, and *vice versâ*.

**Transfer Book.**—A factory book used to record Transfer Notes.

## GLOSSARY OF TERMS.

**Transfer Note.**—A form employed to record transfer of commodities from store to warehouse, or *vice versâ*.

**Tools.**—Instruments or implements of production of a more or less permanent nature.

**Tool Order.**—An instruction (subsidiary to a Stock Order) to manufacture tools, and by means of which the cost of those to be used in the manufacture of a commodity is ascertained.

**Tool Order No.**—The number given to a Tool Order.

**Unclaimed Wages Book.**—The book in which are entered the names and wages of those employés who are not paid in regular course.

**Valuation.**—The process of ascertaining by examination and survey the present and prospective value of properties or the earning power of any asset.

**Viewer.**—The examiner of manufactured articles or parts.

**Wages.**—Payment for labour.

**Wages Account.**—The account in the Commercial Ledger in which are collected all the entries relating to wages.

**Wages Advice.**—The form used to record the engagement, or dismissal, or resignation of employés, any alteration in their rates, fines levied, or premiums allowed.

**Wages Book.**—The book which records the amounts payable to each employé.

**Wages Rate Book.**—The book in which the rates of wages paid to employés are entered.

**Wagon and Van Statement Form.**—The form on which the earnings of the wagons and vans are shown.

**Wagon Journey Repairs Book.**—The book recording the repairs done to wagons whilst on journeys.

**Warehouse.**—The repository for stock.

**Warehouseman.**—The custodian of the stock. (Distinguished from Storekeeper.)

**Wear and Tear.**—The gradual and normal deterioration of plant and buildings.

**Working Order.**—An instruction to expend labour and material in the maintenance, repair, and renewal of plant and buildings, and to record this expenditure. (Distinguished from Stock Order, *q. v.*)

**Working Order No.**—The number given to a Working Order.

**Writing Down—Writing-off.**—The process by which the book value of an article is reduced.

# INDEX.

*ABSENTEE BOOK*, 18
— Accidents, and Factory Acts, 186, 192
Accidents, records of, 138, 140
— as to Scotland, 191
Accountancy, simple form of, 1
"Accountant, The," on sphere and duties of accountants, 3
Accountants, and commercial ledger, 7
— accuracy in accounts, 6
— as sworn investigators, 148
— concentration of transfer books, 80
— demonstration of economic results, 149
— tendency of factory system, 144
— views of duties of, 3, 149
Accounts, accuracy in preparation of, 144
— accurate adjustment of, 4
— and insurance, 103, 104, 185
— applicable to factories, 3
— assimilation of, 7, 10, 130
— commercial, 9
— concentration of, 7, 10, 130
— converging of, 10
— cost of manufacture, 9
— depreciation sometimes ignored in, 95
— elementary knowledge of, 9

Accounts, fear of extra trouble in, 149
— fundamental principles of, 3
— in Government factories, 126, 130
— in municipal workshops, 126, 130
— investigation of, 148
— purchase-hire system, 127
— statements of, 46
— subdivision and localisation of, 9, 10
— surveys, 115
— utility of system of, 7, 8, 9
*Address Book*, 41
Adjustment of loss under insurance, 181
Administration, extension and economy of, 2
Advertising, and income tax, 161, 162
*Advice Note*, 46
*Advice to Warehouseman*, 82
Agent, insurance, 176
Alteration in fire risk, 179
Amortization, definition, 233
— of leases, 106—108
— table for, 226—232
Appendices, 13, 150, 241
Appreciation, definition, 233
— direct mode of determining, 98
— practical view of, 102
— reserve fund, 103

R

## INDEX.

Arbitration, boards of, 148, 218
— Factory Acts, 218—220, 224
Arsenals, expenditure in, 131
Articles (see Commodities)
Art of book-keeping, 8
Assessments for income tax, 158—164
— for rating, 165—173
Assets, appreciation of, 98
— available, 124
— capital account, 102
— Companies' Act of 1877, 124
— copyright designs as, 114
— definition, 233
— depreciation of, 98
— determination of life of, 105
— goodwill and patents as, 114
— Income Tax Acts, 104, 105, 108
— opportunities for writing down, 123, 124
— periodical valuation of, 98
— profit and loss account, 102, 103
— reserve funds, 103
— sinking funds, 102
— stock as, 124
— stores as, 124
— trade marks as, 114
— valuation of, in going concern, 99
Auctions, and insurance, 183, 184
Audit, and surveys, 117
"Auditors, their Duties and Responsibilities," 106

BABBAGE, Charles, 62
Bad debts, and industrial partnerships, 146
— income tax, 160
Bakehouses and Factory Acts, 188, 216, 222
Balance sheets, advantages of frequent, 116
— definition, 233
— element of uncertainty in, removed, 51

Balance sheets, special assets, 114
— without survey, 115
*Barge Register*, 135, 136
Basis of insurance, 174
Blue Book on Co-operation in Foreign Countries, 149
Boards of arbitration, 148
— conciliation, 157
Boiler insurance, 184
Book gains, and writing down, 124
Book-keepers, 8
Book-keeping, bases as regards stores and stock, 12
— cash, 5
— double entry, 9
— economy and efficiency, 8—9
— fixed capital, 93—114, 129
— fundamental principles, 3
— labour, 14, 42
— localisation in, 9
— ordinary commercial, 3, 42
— prime cost, 11, 59, 68
— purchase - hire system, 126, 127
— recording production and distribution, 75
— science and art of, 8
— special methods, 4
— stock, 75—92
— stores, 43—58
— surveys, 116
— treatises on general, 9
Books, concentration, 87
— exteriors, 10, 77
— merging in commercial ledgers, 12
Book value, definition, 233
Brassey, Lord, 144
Brewers' accounts, 10
*Brigade (Fire) books*, 138
Broker, insurance, 176

## INDEX.

Buildings, depreciation, 13, 105
— evidence of deterioration, 6, 93
— insurance of, 103
— interest on capital, 42
— leases of, 105
— *Ledgers*, 64, 106, 107
— life of, 105
— maintenance, 11, 63, 64, 93, 94
— repairs and renewals, 11, 63, 64, 93
— surveys and valuation of, 98, 99
Buckley, Mr. H. Burton, Q.C., 100—102
Bunyon, Mr. C. J., and Insurance, 174, 177, 179, 180, 183
Business, appearing profitable, 123
— conversion of, 6
— disposal of, 6
— profit or loss on branches, 5
— volume of, 128

CAPITAL, buildings, and machinery, 93
— conflict with labour, 144—145
— co-operative industry, 145
— definition, 233
— fixed (see Fixed Capital)
— income tax, 161
— industrial partnerships, 146
— interdependence with revenue account, 99—102
— loss of, 100—103
— maintenance and depreciation, 99
— profit-sharing, 142
— purchase-hire system, 127, 128
— rating, 170, 171
— reduction of, 124

Capital, repairs charged to, 95
— water companies, 96
— vehicles and horses, 131
Capitalists, 143, 148
Cards as records of expenditure, 130
Carriage of goods, 46, 131—136
Carriers' receipts, 138
Cartage, 127, 131
— *Advice*, 132
— *Book*, 132, 133
— contractor for, 131
— cost of, 131
— gatekeepers' check on, 131
— goods bought, 45
— goods sold, 131
— incidence of cost, 131
Carters, wages of, 132
— *Weekly Returns*, 132
Cash, balance of, 5
— purchase-hire system, 129
— *Sheet*, 37, 38
— wages, 38
Cash book, definition, 233
Cashier, comparison with storekeeper, 121
— wages, 15, 36, 39
Castle, Mr. E. J., on rating, 166, 167, 171
*Casualty Book*, 138
Chambers of Commerce and rating, 168
*Character Book*, 41
— *Form*, 41
Chard Assessment Committee, 170
Chattels, non-rating of, 166
Checks, time, 16
Chemists, manufacturing, accounts of, 10
Children, employment of, 2, 139
— Factory Acts, 186—192, 205, 206, 210
— registers of, 41
Classification of fire risks, 175
Cleaning factory, 71, 186, 187
Clerks, 9, 10, 46

Clerks, invoicing, 85
— prime cost ledger, 61, 65—67, 70
— salaries and prime cost, 71
Coal, consumption of, 137
— *Book*, 137
— *Contract Book*, 137
— factors' accounts, 137
Co-insurers, 182
Commercial books, definition, 233
— — factory books, 7, 8
— — inadequacy of, 6
— — manufacture and sales, 76
— — petty-cash and prime cost, 67
— — stores ledgers, 50
— — stores warrants, and prime cost, 54
— — substantiation of, 7
— — surveys, 116
— Ledger, cash, 6
— — converging of accounts, 10
— — definition, 233
— — depreciation of stock, 125
— — depreciation of stores, 125
— — leases, 106
— — merging of departmental books, 8, 12
— — retail transactions, 90
— — sale of stock, 76, 78
— — securities, 5
— — stock account, 77
— — stock debit notes, 78
— — stores, 11
— — stores account, 67
— — sundry disbursements, 66, 67
— — surveys, 88, 116, 118

Commercial Ledger, wages account, 67
Commodities, classes of expenditure, 11
— cost of manufacture, 4, 70
— production of, 10, 59—74
— sale of, 10, 12, 59, 75, 82—92
— wages and material, 4
Companies' Acts, 124
Conciliation, Boards of, 148
Conditions of average, 178
Consequential losses, 182
Contract insurance, 176
Co-operative production, 127
— blue-book on, 149
— Lord Brassey on, 144
— returns of societies, 146
— (see also Industrial Partnerships)
— trials of systems, 146
Copyright designs, 114
Cost-book and symbolic nomenclature, 150
Cost of production, aggregated and recorded, 65
— — ascertainable, 5
— — definition, 233
— — depreciation, 140
— — employés' rent, 42
— — establishment charges, 71, 122
— — estimate of expenditure, 51
— — fixed capital, 140
— — material, 57
— — parts, 60, 61, 91
— — pressure to minimise, 61
— — prime, 59—69
— — skill of labour, 147
— — standing charges, 6, 65, 122
— — when not for profit, 127, 129—131

## INDEX.

Cost of production, valuations, 122—125
Cotsworth, Mr. M. B., 133
Cotton cloth factories, 223
Counting-house, check on excess supplies, 122
— credit notes from vendors, 55
— definition, 233
— factory, 9
— forwarding of goods, 85
— invoices, 47
— invoice allocation book, 50
— invoicing of goods, 87
— records of depreciation, 112
— requisition book, 44
— retail trading, 89, 90
— sales, 77, 88
— stock, 85
— stock returned debit notes, 85
— stores debit note, 56
Craft Register, 135, 136
Credit Notes, definition, 234
— from vendors, 55
— references on, 55
— register, 55
— — definition, 234
— their registration, 55
— to customer, 77, 87
Customers, cartage of goods to, 131
— delivery of goods to, 133

DAY-BOOK, analysis of sales, 87
— definition, 234
— invoices rendered, 77
— trading account, 89
Deductions for income tax, 160
*Delivery Books*, 138
Delivery of goods from vendors, 47
— to customers, 134

*Delivery Note*, 47, 234
Demurrage, 135
Departments, accounts for, 8, 10
— depreciation in, 98, 107
— localisation of cost in, 8
— subdivision of, 7
Depreciation, actual, rarely charged, 98
— buildings, 6, 13, 94
— classification of objects, 109
— charge per journey on tramway, 106
— cost, 6, 12, 72
— definition, 234
— direct way of determining, 98
— engines and boilers, 113
— factors in determination of, 94
— fixed capital, 93—114, 140
— horse account, 132
— ideal way, 105, 106
— Income Tax Acts, 104, 161
— industrial partnerships, 146
— life of object, 96, 97
— loose plant and tools, 109
— methods in vogue of charging, 97, 98
— of factories, 94
— patterns, 109, 110
— periodical valuation, 99
— plant, 6, 12, 93—114
— purchase-hire system, 127
— railway companies' accounts, 95
— rate of, 12, 95
— rate of, for leases, 106
— ratio between, and expenditure, 96
— stock, 13, 124, 125
— stores, 13, 124, 125
— tools, 6, 13, 109
— trucks accounts, 133
— van accounts, 132
— volume of trade, 98

## INDEX.

Depreciation, water companies' accounts, 96
Details (machine), nomenclature for, 150—157
Deterioration (see Depreciation)
Diagrams, 10
Dilapidations, 107, 234
Distillers, accounts of, 10
Dividends, capital and revenue accounts, 99—103
— depreciation, 95
Dockyards, accounts in, 130
Double shifts, economics of, 140
Drawings and symbolic nomenclature, 151
"Dummy men," 15

"ECONOMICS of Industry," 29, 63
Economics, double shifts, 140
— overtime, 140
— piece-work, 140—143
Economists, division and specialization of labour, 62
— the labour question, 143—148
— unproductive workers, 9
Economy, in division of labour, 62
— " of Machinery and Manufactures," 62
— specialization of labour, 9
Education and Factory Acts, 186, 206—209
Electricity and fire risks, 181
Employés absenting themselves, 18
— address book, 41
— addresses of, 16
— allowances to, 30
— capitalists, 143
— change of address, 41
— character book, 41
— characters of, 16
— confidence in accounts, 6, 14, 149

Employés, co-operators, 144—149
— deductions for rent, 15, 16, 42
— deductions under Factory Acts, 207, 209
— dismissal of, 30
— disposal of fines, 139
— double shifts, 140
— engaged outside factory, 15, 22, 23
— engagement of, 30
— entry and exit, 16—18
— Factory Acts (see Factory Acts)
— factory rules, 41
— fines of, 15, 30, 33, 139
— interest in work, 141
— interdependence of, 24
— leaving work at irregular times, 18
— length of service, 32
— mode of paying wages, 30—42
— moral effects of accurate accounts, 7
— occupying houses of firm, 16, 42
— overtime minimised, 15, 23, 24
— overtime of, 20
— overtime of, outside factory, 22
— payment by time, 14
— payment to deputies, 36
— piece-work, 26, 28, 142
— piece-work balances, 15, 16, 26
— premiums, 30, 35
— profit-sharing, 144, 146, 147
— prohibition of overtime, 140, 141
— provision of mess-room for, 16
— punctuality of, how secured, 24

# INDEX. 247

Employés, rates of pay, 15, 30, 32, 33, 42
— receipts, 16, 34
— remittance of wages, 37
— resignation of, 30
— savings bank funds, 15, 35, 42, 139
— sick funds, 15, 35, 42, 139
— subsistence money, 145
— superannuation funds, 15, 35, 42, 139
— tendency to demand excess time and material, 51
— time checks, 16
— time records and boards, 15, 18, 21
— transference to other departments, 29
— transitory opposition to piece-work, 141
— unclaimed wages, 35
— unpunctuality of, 18, 24
— wages as subsistence money, 145
— wages of, 16, 42, 140, 145
— wages receipt forms, 37
— working in more than one shift, 17
— working hours of, 140
— work requires registration, 4
Employment under Factory Acts, 186, 192—205, 210, 222
*Empties Book*, 137
Establishment expenses, definition, 234
— profit and loss, 73
— valuations, 122
Estimate of cost, 234
— of expenditure on fixed capital, 64
— should precede manufacture, 51
Estimated values in relation to surveys, 118
Evolution of industrial organisations, 2, 144

Expenditure, analysis of, required, 4
— auxiliary operations, 127
— average, per mile on railways, 95
— labour and material analysed, 11
— maintenance of fixed capital, 64
— making good rejected stock, 79
— not for profit, 129, 130
— plant and machinery, 111
— recorded on cards, 130
— repairs and renewals on railways, 96
— vigilance as to, 9
Explosives and fire risks, 180

FACTORIES, cost of gas and water in, 138
— definition, 234
— depreciation of, 94
— duties of occupiers of, 139, 186—225
— economy of, 126
— initial step in organisation of, 14
— legislation as to, 2
— municipal, 126
— national, 126
— railway, 126
— rating of, 13, 165, 173
— rent of, 70
— routine in, 126
— rules of, 41
— solidarity of labour in, 24
— subsidiary books in, 126
— regulation by empirical methods, 3
— warehouses and, 78, 79

# INDEX.

Factories, working for profit, 129
Factory accounts (see contents generally)
— — definition, 3, 234
— — demonstration of economic results, 149
— — essential books in system, 12
— — moral effect of proper system, 6
— — need of systematic, 149
— — non-competitive concerns, 130
— — proper system not memoranda, 8, 116
— — scientific basis, 149
— — subsidiary books, 126
Factory Acts, 186—225
— — accidents, 188—192
— — administration, 186
— — arbitration, 218—220, 224
— — bakehouses, 188, 216, 222
— — children, 205, 192—205, 209, 215, 217
— — definitions, 186
— — education, 186, 205, 209
— — employment, 186, 193, 196, 210
— — fines, 186, 210
— — fire, provision against, 191
— — fitness for employment, 186, 205, 209
— — holidays, 186, 205
— — inspection, 186, 187
— — inspectors, 212, 213
— — legal proceedings, 186
— — meal hours, 186, 193—196
— — miscellaneous regulations, 214—217
— — night-work, 204, 205
— — notices, 216
— — out-workers, 217

Factory Acts, overtime, 201—205
— — parents, 210
— — penalties, 186, 210
— — register of children, 215
— — safety, 186, 188—192
— — sanitation, 186, 187
— — surgeon, 186, 191, 209
— — weights and measures, 216
— — white lead factories, 220
— — women, 192—205
— — young persons, 192—205
— and Workshop Acts, 2, 13, 139, 186—225
— books and registers under, 15, 41, 139, 206—209
— provisions of, 186—225
Factory books, advantages, 7
— — assimilation of, 10
— — assimilation with commercial books, 8
— — exteriors, 10, 77
— — methods of keeping, 9
— — misconceptions as to, 3
— — nature of, 10
— — need for system, 6
— — relation of, 10
— — relation to memoranda books, 8, 116
— — relation to subsidiary questions, 126
— — represent state of affairs, 7
— — special columns, 7
— — specimen rulings of, 10, 11, 18, 19, 20, 22, 23, 24, 27, 29, 30, 32, 34, 36, 37, 38, 39, 40, 45, 46, 48, 49, 50, 52, 53, 55, 56, 57, 66, 67, 68, 69, 81, 83, 84, 86, 87, 108, 110, 111, 112, 118, 132, 134, 135, 136, 138
— — substantiating commercial books, 7
— — utility in cases of fire, 7

INDEX. 249

Factory Books and Forms :—
 Absentee Book, 18
 Address Book, 41
 Advice Note, 47
 Advice to Warehouseman, 82
 Barge Return, 136
 Brigade (Fire) Books, 139
 Buildings Ledger, 64
 Cartage Advice, 132
 Cartage Book, 131, 132
 Carters' Weekly Returns, 132
 Cash Sheet, 38, 39
 Casualty Book, 139
 Character Book, 41
 Character Form, 41
 Coal Book, 138
 Coal Contract Book, 138
 Craft Register, 136
 Delivery Book, 139
 Delivery Note, 47, 234
 Empties Book, 138
 Estimate of Cost, 51, 64, 234
 Factory General Charges Book, 65, 71, 122, 234
 Fines Book, 35
 Fire Hose Book, 139
 Fuel Summary Form, 138
 Gas Meter Reading Books, 138
 Insurance Register, 184
 Invoice Register, 47, 48
 Lighter Return, 136
 Orders Received Book, 82, 85, 236
 Outworks Time Sheet, 23, 24, 236
 Overtime Book, 20, 236
 Overtime Comparison Book, 20, 25, 26, 236
 Overtime Return, 20, 24, 25, 26, 236
 Patterns Book, 138, 236
 Pay Bills, 36
 Pay Sheets, 36
 Piece-work Analysis Book, 29, 236
 Piece-work Log Book, 29
 Piece-work Register, 29

Factory Books and Forms :
 Piece-work Return, 26, 27, 29, 236
 Plant Debit Note, 112, 237
 Plant Debit Summary, 113, 237
 Plant Journal, 112
 Plant Ledgers, 64, 110, 113, 237
 Prime Cost Journal, 70, 237
 Prime Cost Ledger, 11, 40, 65, 66, 67, 68, 69, 70, 74, 79, 110, 113, 237
 Railway Rate Book, 134
 Rate Book, 32, 33, 35, 240
 Registers under Factory Acts, 41, 42, 215
 Sanitation, 187
 Shop Returns Book, 57, 238
 Stock Debit Note, 67, 69, 78, 92, 238
 Stock Issued Book, 78, 84, 85, 90, 125, 238
 Stock Ledger, 5—7, 68, 69, 76, 78, 80, 85, 88, 90, 116, 117, 118, 122
 Stock Order, 21, 40, 51, 52, 54, 60, 62, 63, 64, 65, 68, 70, 92, 238
 Stock Received Book, 68, 78, 90, 238
 Stock Requisition Book, 76, 82, 83, 85, 87, 88, 90, 239
 Stock Returned by Customers Book, 77, 87, 88, 89, 238
 Stock Returned Debit Note, 77, 85, 87, 88, 238
 Stock Transfer Book, 81
 Stores Debit Note, 56, 57, 239
 Stores Issued Book, 53, 239
 Stores Ledger, 5, 8, 10, 48, 49, 53, 57, 58, 80, 115, 116, 117, 118, 120, 239
 Stores Received Book, 48, 50, 68, 239
 Stores Rejected Book, 55, 56, 239
 Stores Requisitions, 44, 45, 239
 Stores Requisition Book, 44, 45, 46, 47, 55, 56, 239

# INDEX.

Factory Books and Forms:—
  Stores Transfer Book, 79, 80
  Stores Warrants, 52, 53, 54, 66, 92, 239
  Survey Sheets, 118
  Time Allocation Book, 21, 22, 23, 26, 40, 41, 239
  Time Boards, 20, 21
  Time Book, 17, 18, 19, 20, 24, 239
  Time Records, 14, 21, 24, 239
  Tool Order, 65, 240
  Transfer Book, 58, 79, 91, 92, 240
  Transfer Notes, 79, 81, 82, 240
  Unclaimed Wages Book, 36, 240
  Wages Abstract, 40, 41
  Wages Advice, 30, 31, 240
  Wages Book, 14, 16, 22, 24, 29, 33, 34, 35, 38, 40, 240
  Wages Rate Book, 32, 33, 34, 240
  Wages Receipts, 35, 36
  Wages Remittance, 36
  Wagon and Van Books, 135
  Water Meter Books, 138
  Working Orders, 20, 46, 54, 112, 113, 114, 137, 241
Factory general charges, 65, 234
  — Book for, 65, 234
  — their allocation, 72
  — their relation to valuations, 122
"Factory System, A History of the," 2
  — — development of the modern, 1, 127, 143
  — — extension of, 2
  — — industrial conditions, 2
  — — new power in civilisation, 2
  — — specialisation of labour, 61
  — — tendency of, 143
Fawcett, Professor Henry, 143
Fines, appropriation, 42
  — change of address, 41

Fines, recorded and deducted, 13, 29, 35
  — under Factory Acts, 186, 210
  — unpunctuality, 24
Fire Insurance (see Insurance)
*Fire Hose Books*, 138
Fixed capital (see generally Chapter vi., 93—114)
  — — definition, 234
  — — depreciation of, 140
  — — interest on, 140
  — — machinery, 64
  — — Mill's definition of, 93
  — — ordinary time, 139
  — — overtime, 24, 140
  — — piece-work, 140
  — — purchase-hire, 127
  — — surveys, 118
Fixed plant, 234
Fletcher, Mr. Banister, 107
Forage, cost of, 132
Foreman, clerical work, 9, 10
  — definition, 234
  — dummy men, 15
  — exchange of material, 52
  — instructions to manufacture, 61
  — overtime, 24, 26
  — payment of wages, 35
  — permits, 18
  — piece-work, 29
  — plant, 112
  — purchase of material, 43
  — stores warrants, 54
  — surplus material, 56
  — time records, 20, 21
  — wages of, 65, 70
  — wages advice, 30
Fraud, chances of, minimised, 14
  — instance of, 15
Freightage, 127, 133
Fuel, cost of, 71
  — its allocation, 113
  — records of, 127, 137, 138
Furniture, manufacture of, 60, 61

INDEX. 251

GAS and fire risks, 180
— Gas companies, expenditure in workshops, 130
Gas companies, factory books required for, 7
— — *Meter Reading, Books of*, 137
Gas, consumption of, how checked and localised, 138
Gatekeeper (see Timekeeper)
— cartage, 131
— permit to remove goods, 121
— wages of, 65
General charges, 6, 123, 124, 234 (see Factory General Charges)
General stores account, 235
Glossary, 13, 232—240
Going concern, definition, 235
— — valuations, 99, 102, 114
Goodwill, definition, 235
— valuation of, 114
Government factories, 126, 129

HALSTEAD Silk Factory, rating, 166
Handling, in surveys, 118
Heating factories, cost of, 70
Hedley, Mr., on rating, 165, 168
"Hints on the Administration of the Factory and Workshop Acts," 225
Hire (see also Purchase-Hire), horses and vehicles, 131—133
— trucks, 135
Horse account, 132
Hunslet Assessment Committee, 165

IMPLEMENTS (see Machinery, Plant, Tools, &c.)
"Incidence of Local Taxation," 165
Income tax, 13, 158—164
— advertising, 160
— assessments to, 158
— capital, 160
— debts, 160

Income tax, deductions allowable, 160
— depreciation, 104, 161
— hired machinery, 161
— insurance, 161
— interest, 160
— liquidations, 163
— new machinery, 160
— partnerships, 160, 163
— profits, 105, 158, 161, 163
— repairs, 161
— return of tax, 162
— three years' average, 159, 163
— valuations, 104
Indemnity insurance, 176
Indirect expenses, cost of production, 12, 42, 70—73
— definition, 235
— loose plant and tools, 109
— profit and loss, 70
— ratio to direct, 70—73
— skilled labour, 72
— wages, 70, 72
— working orders, 70—73
Industrial organisations, relation of factory accounts to, 149
— their evolution, 1—3, 144, 186
Industrial partnerships, 127, 145—148
"Industrial Remuneration Conference," 147
"Industry, The Economics of," 62
Inspection under Factory Acts, 186, 187, 202, 203, 212, 213
Instalments on purchase-hire, 127—129
Insurance, 12, 103, 174—185
— accounts, utility, 181
— adjustment of loss, 181
— agent, 176
— alterations in risk, 179
— auctions, 182
— basis of, 174
— boiler insurance, 184

## INDEX.

Insurance, broker, 176
— cause of fire, 180
— claims on companies, 7
— classification of risks, 175
— co-insurers, 182
— common form of policies, 175
— conditions of average, 178
— consequential losses, 182
— contract, 176
— electricity, 181
— explosives, 181
— gas, 181
— income tax, 161
— indemnity, 176
— joint, 184
— "Law of Fire Insurance," 174, 177, 179, 180, 183
— machinery, 179
— merchandise, 183
— oil, 180
— Phœnix fire rules, 180
— policy, 174—176, 177
— premiums, 177
— profit and loss, 103
— proof of loss, 181
— proposal, 174—176
— Register, 185
— reinstatement, 183
— rent, 182
— renewal of policy, 175
— repairs, 179
— representations, 174
— rights of insurers, 181
— risk, 176
— salvage, 183
— Society of Telegraph Engineers, 181
— specific insurances, 178
— stock, 179, 182
— subrogation, 177
— tariff system, 175
— transfer of properties, 177
— uninsured ships, 99—102
— warranties, 174

Insurance, valuation of properties, 182
— valued policies, 178
Interest and income tax, 161
— and rating, 172
— cost of production, 12, 124
— depreciation, 106
— fixed capital, 140, 148
— horse and vehicle account, 131
— leases, 106
— on capital in employés' houses, 42
— purchase-hire system, 128—130
— wages as subsistence money, 145
Inventory (see Surveys), 235
Invitation to tender forms, 44
Invoice Allocation Book, 50, 235
*Invoice Register*, 46, 47, 235
Invoices, definition, 235
— directions to vendors, 46
— examination, 47
— goods loaned, 88
— goods purchased, 11, 47, 53, 92
— goods retailed, 91
— goods sold direct, 76, 77, 85, 88
— references, 50
— registration, 47
— *Stores Requisition Book*, 45
"Inwood's Tables," 232
Issuer of material, duties, 119—122


JEVONS, Professor W. Stanley, 145
Joint-stock companies, definition, 235
— conversion of private firms, 6
— depreciation, 95
— labour question, 144, 145
— law, capital, and revenue, 99—102
— reduction of capital, 124, 125
— valuation of assets, 114
Joint insurance, 184

INDEX.  253

LABOUR, combination, 2
— definition, 235
— division, 62
— economy in clerical, 8
— employment, 4, 11
— expenditure, 40
— its conflict with capital, 143—146
— maintenance of buildings, 64
— maintenance of machinery, 64
— overtime, 140
— profit-sharing, 142
— rejected stock, 79
— skilled and unskilled, 72
— solidarity, 24, 141
— specialization, 1, 10, 61
— the question of, 127, 148—149
Laing case, rating, 167
"Law of Fire Insurance, The," 174, 177, 179, 180, 183
*Law Times*, and rating, 170
Leading hand, definition, 235
— outside work, 22—24
— piece-work, 29
— stock debit notes, 67
— store warrants, 54
— time records, 14, 21, 22
Leases, amortization of, 106, 109, 226—232
— buildings, 97, 105
— *Ledger Account*, 108
— Table for amortizing, 226—232
Ledgers (see under Commercial Ledger)
Legal decisions on rating, 166—172
Legal proceedings under Factory Acts, 186
Legislation (see under Factory and Workshop Acts)
— rating of machinery, 165, 168—170
Lessees, liabilities of, 109
Liabilities, definition, 235

Lighter Register, 135, 136
Lighting of factory, 70 (see also under Gas)
Liquidations and income tax, 165
Liquid trades, accounts of, 11
Localisation of cost, 8, 56, 61, 64
Loose plant and tools, 109, 235
Loss (see under Profit and Loss)

MACHINE name, 152
Machine symbol, 152
Machinery, charges for use, 64
— checker, 112
— cost of setting, 64
— depreciation, 94, 105
— details, 150—157
— expenditure, 111
— fixed capital, 93—114
— income tax, 160, 161
— hire of, 161
— increased wages, 140
— insurance of, 180
— labour on, 64
— life of, 64, 106, 112
— maintenance of, 94
— numbering of objects, 111
— obsolescence, 96, 172
— purchase-hire system, 126—129
— rating of, 165—171, 173
— record of working hours, 112—114
— residual value, 113
— sinking funds, 102
— specialization of labour, 1
— symbolic nomenclature for, 150—158
— assessment of, 13, 165—173
— the economy of, 61
— the economy of double shifts, 140
— valuation of, 99, 100
— wear and tear of, 98
— yearly replacement of, 98

Magazine (see Store), 235
Maintenance, definition, 235
Manufactory (see Factory)
Manufacture, checks upon wastefulness
— in, 9
— material for, 11
Manufacturer, distinction between re-
— tailer and, 90
Manufacturing account, 66, 67, 131, 235
Market price, 99, 123, 124, 236
— value, 102, 122
Marshall, Alfred, and Mary Paley, 26, 62
Master of the Rolls' decision on rating, 170, 171
Material, cartage, 131
— definition, 236, 237
— distinction between raw and manufactured, 12
— economy in purchasing, 43
— economy in use, 43, 147
— employer sanctioning purchase, 44
— estimated expenditure, 51
— expenditure on rejected stock, 79
— implements and buildings becoming, 93
— indirect charges, 72
— initiative in expenditure, 51
— initiative in purchase, 43
— issuer of, pricing, 120
— issuer of, receiving warrant, 120
— keeping stock, 120
— limitation of issue, 52
— pricing, 122, 123
— purchase, 4, 11, 43
— receipt and issue, 43—58, 90, 117
— requisition from storekeeper, 43
— reserve store, 48
— return to store, 56, 57

Material, returned to vendors, 54
— scrap, 68
— storage, 4
— store of, 5, 121
— surplus, 52, 68
— survey, 118, 125
— used for tools, 64
— used in manufacture, 59, 70
— use of, 4, 11, 51
— used on plant and machinery, 112
— weights in factory books, 7
Matheson, Mr. Ewing, 97
Meal hours under Factory Acts, 186, 192—205
Memoranda books and factory books, 7
Merchandise, insurance of, 183
Mess-room, 16
Metcalfe, Captain H., 130
Mill, J. S., 93
Mixing trades, accounts of, 10
Money trays, 38
Monopolies, 114

NEUCHATEL Asphalte Company, 100
Nomenclature, symbolic, for machine details, 13, 63, 130, 150—157

OBSOLESCENCE, definition, 236
— comparative risk of, 91
— in relation to profit and loss, 96
— in relation to purchase-hire, 128
— of machinery and tools, 97
— of patterns, 111
— of stock, 124, 125
— of stores, 124, 125
— risk of, universal, 97
Office, organisation of, 9
— rent of, 70
— routine of, 9

## INDEX. 255

Oil and fire risk, 180
Orders to manufacture (see Stock Order)
— to vendors, 45, 46, 236
*Orders Received Book*, 83, 85, 236
*Out Works Time Record*, 23, 24, 236
— specimen ruling, 23, 24
Overlooker, definition, 236
— purchase of material, 43
— return of material, 56
Overtime, 17, 18, 236
— *Book*, 18, 236
— check upon, 24
— *Comparison Book*, 26, 27, 236
— comparison with ordinary, 26
— depreciation, 98
— economic aspect of, 127, 139, 140
— Factory Acts, 139, 201—205
— fixed capital, 140
— made outside factory, 24
— minimising amount of, 15, 24
— *Return*, 24, 26, 236
— specimen ruling of forms for, 20, 25
— time records, 21
— Trades Union Congress and, 142

PACKING, 45, 131
— Packing account, 127
Packing cases, 127
Paper trades accounts, 10
Partnerships and income tax, 160, 162
Partnership, change of, 117
Partnerships, industrial, 126, 144—149
Parts, cost should be known, 60, 91
— supply and sale, 121
— symbolic nomenclature, 63, 150—157
Patents, 114, 236
Patents Accounts, 236
Patterns, *Book*, 138
— definition, 236

Patterns, depreciation, 110, 111
— symbolic nomenclature, 151
Pauperism, Professor Fawcett on, 143
*Pay Bills*, 36
Pay clerk, "dummy men," 15
— payment of wages, 35—40
— unclaimed wages, 37
Payment by results (see Piece-work)
Payment of wages, how made, 16, 29—40
— — minimising errors in, 14
— — to deputies, 36
Pay, rates of, altered, 15, 29—32
— — recorded, 15, 29—32
*Pay Sheets*, 36
Penalties under Factory Acts, 186, 210—212
Personal Accounts, 76, 129
Petty Cash Book, 66, 236
Phœnix fire rules, 180
Phœnix Gas Company, 167
Piece name, 155
Piece symbol, 155
*Piece-work Analysis Book*, 29, 236
— — specimen ruling, 29
— balances, how recorded, 15, 26, 29
— compared with day work, 29, 142, 143
— definition, 236
— economic aspects, 26, 126, 139, 141
— *Log Book* for, 29
— method of recording, 26
— non-continuous working, 29
— quality of work, 141
— *Register Book*, 29
— regulating and recording rates, 15, 29, 142
— *Return Form*, 26—29, 236
— — specimen ruling, 27
— solidarity of labour, 141

## INDEX.

Piece-work, trades union views on, 142
— transitory opposition to, 140
— viewer, duties, 26, 29, 142
Pins, manufacture of, 62
Pixley, Mr. F. W., 106
Plant, 3, 4, 42, 93—114, 236
— cost of maintenance, 64
— current value, 94
— *Debit Note*, 112, 237
— — specimen ruling, 112
— *Debit Summary*, 113, 237
— — specimen ruling, 112
— definition, 236
— depreciation, 13, 93, 94, 99
— deterioration on railways, 95
— incidence of deterioration, 6
— *Journal*, 112
— *Ledgers*, 64, 110, 112, 237
— — specimen ruling, 111
— loose, 110, 111
— maintenance, 11, 63, 94
— material expended, 111
— numbering objects, 111
— piece-work, 141
— purchase, 126, 127, 128
— *Recovered Note*, 58
— repairs and renewals, 11, 63
— residual value, 113
— sinking fund, 102
— surveys, 119
— valuation, 98, 99
— wages expended, 111
— wear and tear, 93
— working numbers for, 112
— yearly replacement, 97
Policy of insurance, 174, 176, 177
Potts, Mr. Joseph, on rating, 168
"Practical Treatise on Rating," 166, 167, 168
Premises, waste of, 107
Premiums to employés, 24
— how recorded, 35
— on fire insurance, 176
Price sheets, symbolic nomenclature, 151

Prime cost, 11, 59—74, 218
— admits of varied treatment, 6
— books, 11, 54
— definition, 237
— employés' rent, 42
— Journal, 70, 237
— Ledger, definition, 237
— — clerk keeping the, 61
— — factory general charges, 65
— — functions of, 12, 65
— — goods in manufacture, 69
— — indirect charges, 73
— — manufacture of parts, 63
— — material, 57, 59
— — materials in, 66, 67, 68, 69
— — parts, 63
— — petty cash, 66, 67
— — Petty Cash Book, 66
— — plant charges, 110—112
— — pricing stock from, 68, 70
— — stock, 79
— — stock account, 69
— — time records, 21
— — valuations, 122, 123
— — wages, 16, 40, 59
— — wages entries, 40, 66, 67
"Principles of Political Economy, The," 93, 94
Processes, cost should be known, 61
— profit or loss on, 5
Production as an auxiliary operation, 126

INDEX. 257

Production, co-operative, 126, 144—149
— cost of (see Cost of Production)
— expenses of, 146
— evolution of methods of, 3
— of tools, 65
— organisation of, 3
— without industrial organisation, 1
Profit, income tax, 104, 159, 161, 162
— publication of, 144
— sharing, 141—147
— surplus, 147
— valuations, 122—124
Profit and loss, 5, 76, 237
— — cartage account, 131
— — departmental depreciation, 109
— — depreciation, 71, 94, 96, 98, 114
— — establishment expenses, 71
— — estimated increments, 114
— — income tax, 104, 159, 162
— — indirect charges, 71
— — insurance, 102
— — leases, 106
— — loaned goods, 89
— — loose plant, 107, 109
— — market price, 124
— — Mr. Buckley on, 100—104
— — on branches, 5
— — on individual transactions, 4
— — patterns, 107—109
— — purchase-hire system, 127—129
— — railway accounts, 95
— — receipts and expenditure, 94
— — residual values, 112

Profit and loss, retail trading, 90
— — revenue and capital, 99 —103
— — sales, 123
— — trading account, 89
— — water companies' accounts, 96
— — yearly valuations, 98
Proof of loss by fire, 181
Proposal of fire insurance, 174—181
Punctuality, premiums for, 24
Purchase-hire system, 126, 127
— book-keeping entries, 127
— capital account, 127
— instalments, 127—129
— interest account, 128
— non-completion, 129
— obsolescence, 128
— plant account, 128
— profit and loss, 127

RAILWAY and Canal Traffic Act, 133
— Companies' Clearing House, 133
— deterioration of plant, 95
— factory books required for, 7
— factories, 126, 129
— Order Confirmation Acts, 133
— rates charged by, 133
— sidings, 133
Rate Book, 32, 33, 35, 237, 240
Rating of factories and machinery, 13, 165—173
— assessments, 165, 172
— capital account, 172
— Chambers of Commerce, 167
— Chard Assessment Committee, 170
— chattels, 166
— checks on assessment, 172
— court of appeal, 168

S

Rating of factories, legislation proposed, 167, 169, 170
— Halstead Silk Factory, 167
— interest account, 172
— Laing case, 167
— Law Times, 170
— legal decisions, 166, 167, 168
— Lord Chief Justice Cockburn, 167
— machinery, 166, 167, 170, 171, 172
— Master of the Rolls, 169
— mode of computing assessments, 165
— Mr. Hedley, 165, 168
— Mr. Potts, 168
— Phœnix Gas Company, 167
— "Practical Treatise on," 167, 171
— Rating Bill, 168, 169
— recent decision, 169
— rule of rating, 170
— Tyne Boiler Works, 169
Raw material (see Material)
Records, differentiation of, 10
Redgrave, Mr. C. B., 225
*Register of Children under Factory Acts*, 42, 215
Registration, economy of methods of, 2
— of expenditure, 4
Regulations as to periods and conditions of employment, 1
Reinstatement under fire insurance, 183
Renewals and income tax, 161
— and fire insurance, 180
— and repairs, 237
Rent, deduction from wages, 15, 42
— factory, 71
— fire insurance, 182
— houses occupied by employés, 42
— office, 71
Repairs (see Renewals and Maintenance)
Representations in fire proposals, 174

Reserve funds, appreciation of assets, 103
— definition, 237
— profits of water companies, 96
— provision for insurance, 104
— residual values, 113
Residual value, definition, 237
— depreciation, 94, 105
— profit and loss account, 113
Retail transactions, store and stock, 80, 90
— warehouse, 90, 219
Return of income tax, 163
Revenue, capital account, 99—102
— definition, 237
— fluctuations of market value, 102
— Government factories, 127
— Income Tax Acts, 104, 158—164
— opinion of Mr. Buckley on, 100, 101
— sinking and reserve funds, 103
Rules and regulations in factories, 41

SAFETY, legislation as to, 186, 187, 188
Sales analysis book, definition, 237
— converse of, 87
— purpose, 76, 77, 85, 89
— stock requisitions, 85
Sales and symbolic nomenclature, 151
— book, 88
— — purpose, 76, 77, 88, 89
— Cancelled book, definition, 237
— goods on loan, 88
Sale of parts, 121
Salvage, 183
Sanitation and Factory Acts, 186, 192
Savings bank fund, 15, 34, 139
Science of book-keeping, 8

# INDEX. 259

Scrap (see Residual Value), 237
Selling prices and cost of tools, 65
Shipment of goods, 83
*Shop Returns Book*, definition, 238
— — purpose and specimen ruling, 57
Shops, cleansing and whitewashing, 42, 186, 187
— expenses in, 70
Sick fund, employés', 15, 34, 42, 139
— books, 139
Sidings, railway, 133
Sinking fund, 102, 107, 238
Sliding scales, 6, 148
Smith, Mr. Oberlin and nomenclature, 63, 150—157
Society of Telegraph Engineers, 181
Specific insurances, 178
Specimens of rulings (see Factory Books)
Stable expenses, 131
— men, 131
Standard of efficiency in stock-taking, 117
Standing charges (see General Charges)
Stationery, cost of, 71
Statistical Society and sliding scales, 148
Stock account, 238
Stock, 75—92
— amalgamation with stores, 119
— balancing prime cost book, 68, 69
— books, 3, 76, 91, 119, 238
— cost of parts, 63
— cost of setting tools, 64
— cost value of, shown in ledger, 76
— definition of, 12, 238
— depreciation of, 13, 124, 125
— efficiency of control, 120
— generally kept till demand arises, 124
— in relation to prime cost, 12
— in relation to solvency, 122
— in relation to stores, 12, 59, 60
— in relation to surveys, 119

Stock, insurance, 103, 178, 182
— in warehouse known to storekeeper, 121
— knowable without survey, 5
— losses on, 125
— manufacture for, 51
— obsolescence, 124, 125
— packing cases, 137
— posting, to ledger, 78
— pricing of, at surveys, 122, 123, 124
— production should be for, 59
— reduction in value of, 125
— rejected by customers, 87, 89
— responsibility for, compared with cash, 121
— retail transactions, 90
— return of — to factory, 76
— return of — to warehouse, 76, 87
— sale or distribution of, 76
— sent out on loan, 88
— sent out on loan, invoicing of, 88, 89
— surplus material, 51, 52
— taking (see Surveys)
— transfer to stores, 57, 58
— uncompleted, 69, 238
— value of — ready for sale, how ascertained, 90
— when realisable at market rates, 123
*Stock Debit Note*, definition, 238
— function of, 78, 92
— manufacture of parts, 92
— pricing of, 70
— specimen ruling, 67
*Stock Issued Book*, alternate, 85
— definition, 238
— losses on stock, 125
— purpose of, 76, 84
— specimen of, 84
— retail transactions, 89
*Stock Ledger*, commercial books, 5, 7
— definition, 238

*Stock Ledger*, losses on stock, 125
— posting of, 68, 78, 80, 87, 88
— prices of articles in, 76
— specimen ruling of, 69
— stock in hand, 5
— subdivision of warehouse, 120
— substantiation of balances in, 117
— surveys, 117, 118, 119
— retail transactions, 89
— transfer books, 58, 79, 92
— utility of, as regards stock-in-trade, 115
*Stock Order*, account, 69
— balances, 69
— booking time and material, 51, 52, 59, 63, 92
— definition, 238
— estimate, 51, 65
— general charges, 65, 71
— initiation, 51—54
— number, 20, 21, 54, 238
— plant, 65, 112
— time allocation book, 40
— tools, 65
— uncompleted, 69
*Stock Received Book*, definition, 238
— purpose of, 68, 78, 90
— retail transactions, 90
— Debit Note, 78
*Stock Requisition*, definition, 238
— orders received, 84
— retail transactions, 89
— sales, 77, 84, 85, 87
— specimen ruling of, 83, 86
Stock Returned by Customers' Analysis Book, 238
— purpose of, 77, 88, 89
*Stock Returned by Customers' Book*, 238
— purpose of, 77, 88, 89
— specimen ruling, 87

*Stock Returned Debit Notes*, definition, 238
— purpose, 77, 87, 88
— specimen ruling, 86
Stock system, essential condition, 120
Stock-taking (see Surveys)
*Stock Transfer Book*, 81
Stoppages Agreement Form, 33
Store, 238, 239
Stores, account, 239
— amalgamation with warehouse, 119
— and insurance, 178, 184
— and warehouseman, 121
— articles retailed, 89
— book-keeping, 43—58, 119
— definition, 12, 59, 239
— depreciation, 13, 125
— excess supply, 121
— insurance, 178—184
— losses, 125
— mechanical divisions, 120
— obsolescence, 124
— parts in, 121
— pricing, 120, 122—124
— reduction in value, 124, 125
— relation to prime cost, 12, 66
— relation to stock, 59, 60
— subdivisions, 120
— surveys, 5, 115—125
— transfers of, 57, 79, 91, 92, 121
— wages of distributing, 65
— warrants, 52, 53, 54
Stores Contract Book, 45
*Stores Debit Note*, definition, 239
— — purpose, 56, 57
— — specimen ruling, 56
*Stores Issued Book*, 53, 239
*Stores Ledger*, account, 49
— agreement with commercial ledger, 49
— commercial and subsidiary books, 8, 11, 48

*Stores Ledger*, commercial ledger, 5, 49, 116
— definition, 239
— duty of clerk keeping, 48
— posting of, 48, 57, 58
— pricing warrants, 120
— specimen, 49, 80
— stores in hand, 5
— Stores Issued Book, 53
— Stores Received Book 48, 49
— subdivision of stores, 120
— surveys, 116, 117, 118
— Transfer Books, 79
— utility as regards quantity on hand, 115
Storekeeper, adjustment of accounts, 80
— cartage, 131
— definition, 239
— effects of survey, 117
— efficiency of control, 121
— estimates of cost, 50
— goods retailed, 89
— invoices, 47
— mechanical aids, 120
— numbering warrants, 54
— purchase of material, 42
— quantities on hand, 5
— receipt of goods, 56
— rejection of goods, 56
— removal of goods, 121
— requisition for material, 52
— responsibility, 120, 121
— scrap material, 56
— Shop Returns Book, 57
— Stores Issued Book, 53
— Stores Ledger, 115
— Stores Received Book, 48
— surplus material, 52, 56
— surveys, 119
— transfers, 57, 58, 79, 91, 92
— Transfer Book, 58

*Stores Received Book*, definition, 239
— form, 47
— invoices, 47
— purpose of, 48, 50
— specimen, 48
— stock, 68
*Stores Rejected Book*, 54, 239
— — specimen of, 55
*Stores Requisition*, definition, 239
— how entered, 44
— specimen of, 45
*Stores Requisition Book*, definition, 239
— Credit Notes, 55, 56
— description of, 44
— need of, 47
— purpose, 43
— specimen, 45
*Stores Sent Away form*, 55
*Stores Sold Analysis Book*, 90
Stores Survey, 124
Stores system, essential conditions of, 120
*Stores Transfer Book*, 80, 81
*Stores Warrants*, definition, 239
— distinguished from Stores Requisition, 53
— numbering, 54
— prime cost, 54, 65
— specimen, 53
— transfer books, 92
Strikes, utility of factory books in case of, 7, 149
Subdivision of departments, 8
Sundry disbursements, 65, 66
Superintendence, 70, 146, 147
Supervision, economy of methods, 2, 44
Surgeons and Factory Acts, 186, 188, 208, 209
Surveys, 5, 13, 115—125, 239
— agreement with commercial ledger, 50, 51, 88, 116
Suspense account, 239
Suspension of business in connection with surveys, 117

Surveys, agreement with stores and stock ledgers, 50, 51, 88, 118
— and single entry, 116
— and valuation, 118, 122
— at one time, 117
— based on "handling," 118
— by degrees, 117
— efficiency of, 117
— epitome of, 118
— periodical, 116
— *Sheets*, 118
— transactions during, 117
Symbolic nomenclature, 13, 63, 150—157, 239

TAYLOR, Mr. R. Whateley Cooke, 3
Taylor, Mr. Sedley, industrial partnerships, 147, 148
— — piece-work, 142
Tenders, invitations for, 45
*Time Allocation Book*, 21, 22, 23, 239
— *Boards*, 20, 21
— *Book*, 3, 17, 18, 19, 20, 24, 239
— checks, 16, 17
— contracts, 98
— how recorded, 17—23
— lost, 20
— office, 16, 17
— outside factory, 15, 22, 24
— *Records*, 14, 21, 24, 239
— *Sheet*, 136
Time clerk, definition, 239
— *Allocation Book*, 21, 22, 26, 39—41
— allocation of wages, 15
— duties, 16, 21—23, 24, 26, 35, 40, 111
— interruptions to piece-work, 29
— machine hours, 111
— outworks time sheet, 22
— overtime return, 24

Time clerk, piece-work returns, 26, 29
— possibility of fraud by, 14
— receipts for wages, 35
Timekeeper, definition, 239
— duties, 16, 17—19, 21, 22, 41
— entry and exit of employés, 15, 16
— possibility of fraud by, 14
— summary of time-book, 20
— time records, 22
— wages of, 65
Tools, ascertainment of cost, 65
— cost of setting, 64
— definition, 240
— depreciation, 4, 13, 93
— economy in use, 147
— incidence of cost, 6, 93
— loose, 109
— manufacture, 4, 65
— obsolescence, 97
— *Order*, 65, 240
— piece-work, 141
— surveys of, 119
— symbolic nomenclature, 151
Trade expenses, purchase-hire, 128
Trade, volume of, and depreciation, 98
Trade marks, 114
Trades unions, overtime, 142
— piece-work, 26, 142
Trading account, 70, 90, 91, 240
Tramway companies, expenditure in shops, 131
Transfer Analysis Book, 80, 240
*Transfer Book*, 58, 79, 81, 92, 240
— articles retailed, 91
*Transfer Notes*, 79, 81, 82, 240
Transfer of properties, 177
Truck Acts, 33
Tyne Boiler Works, rating, 169

UNCLAIMED *Wages Book*, 36, 240
Unpunctuality, fines, 24

# INDEX.

Unhealthy employment, special rules, 189

VALUATION, and insurance, 182
— assets, 103
— definition, 240
— depreciation, 98
— Income Tax Acts, 104
— loose plant and tools, 109
— stock and stores, 118, 122
— surveys, 118
Valued Policies, 178
Vehicles account, 131
Viewer (see Piece-work), 240

WAGES, Abstract, 40, 41
— account, 240
Wages, Advice, 29, 32, 240
— specimen ruling, 31
— allocation of, 15, 40, 66
— banking account, 35
— and accountants, 3
— Book, 14, 16, 21, 32—37, 38, 40, 240
— — and piece-work balances, 29
— — and overtime, 23
— — and rents, 42
— — clerk, 22, 23, 29
— — commercial ledger, 67
— cost of production, 6
— deductions from, 15, 16, 139, 209
— definition, 240
— "dummy men," 16
— estimate, 51
— factory general charges, 65
— foremen, 65
— frauds in, 16
— gatekeepers, 65
— general charges, 65

Wages, loose plant and tools, 109
— machinery, 140
— mode of payment, 17, 35—41
— payment, 4
— peculation, 35
— piece-work rates, 142
— plant and machinery, 110
— prime cost, 12, 67
— Rate Book, 32, 35, 240
— — specimen ruling, 32
— record of rate, 32
— Remittance, 37]
— — form, 37
— Receipts, 35, 36
— reduction of, 7
— rent, 42
— registration of, 4
— sliding scale, 7, 148
— subsistence money, 145
— Summary, 15, 34, 35
— superintendence, 146
— system, 10, 14—42
— timekeeper, 65
— Truck Acts, 33
— unclaimed, 15, 36
— — book, 36
Wagons and purchase-hire system, 128
Wagon and Van Book, 133
Wagons Repaired Book, 135
Warehouse, advice, 82
— definition, 240
— excess supplies, 121
— orders received, 82
— records of issues, 85
— repairs of, 64
— repository of parts for sale, 92
— retail, 90
— return of loaned goods, 76, 87
— return of rejected goods, 76, 87
— Stock Issued Book, 85
— stock received, 69

Warehouse, storekeeper and stock, 121
— subdivisions, 120
— subsidiary books, 124
— supply of parts, 121
— transfers to and from factory, 78, 79, 80
— transfers to stores, 57
Warehouseman, adjustments with store, 58, 80
— cartage, 131
— daily return, 85
— definition, 240
— effect of surveys, 117
— efficiency of control, 121
— *Empties Book*, 137
— goods retailed, 91
— material, 121
— mechanical aids, 120
— permits, 121
— responsibilities, 121
— schedule of stores, 122
— stock, 5
— Stock Issued Book, 77
— Stock Ledger, 115
— Stock Received Book, 68

Warehouseman, stock returned, 77
— subdivisions, 120
— surveys, 120
Warranties in fire policies, 174
Waste of premises, 107
Watchman and permits, 121
Water companies' accounts, 7, 96, 129
— — factory books, 7
Water consumption, 138
*Water Meter Reading Books*, 138
Wealth, production, 9, 143
Wear and tear, 98, 128, 241
Weights and measures, 216
White lead factories, 220, 221
Women and Factory Acts, 192—205
— regulations as to employment, 2
*Working Orders*, 20, 40, 54, 112, 113, 114, 137, 241
Workpeople (see Employés)
Works Manager, 47, 50, 51, 61, 64
Workshops (see Factories)
Writing off, 6, 94, 114, 125, 241

YOUNG Persons and Factory Acts, 192—205

THE END.

PRINTED BY J. S. VIRTUE AND CO., LIMITED, CITY ROAD, LONDON.

7, STATIONERS' HALL COURT, LONDON, E.C.
*January*, 1901.

# CROSBY LOCKWOOD & SON'S
## Catalogue of
# Scientific, Technical and Industrial Books.

| | PAGE | | PAGE |
|---|---|---|---|
| MECHANICAL ENGINEERING | 1 | CARPENTRY & TIMBER | 28 |
| CIVIL ENGINEERING | 10 | DECORATIVE ARTS | 30 |
| MARINE ENGINEERING, &c. | 17 | NATURAL SCIENCE | 32 |
| MINING & METALLURGY | 19 | CHEMICAL MANUFACTURES | 34 |
| COLLIERY WORKING, &c. | 21 | INDUSTRIAL ARTS | 36 |
| ELECTRICITY | 23 | COMMERCE, TABLES, &c. | 41 |
| ARCHITECTURE & BUILDING | 25 | AGRICULTURE & GARDENING | 43 |
| SANITATION & WATER SUPPLY | 27 | AUCTIONEERING, VALUING, &c. | 46 |
| LAW & MISCELLANEOUS | 47 | | |

## MECHANICAL ENGINEERING, &c.

**THE MECHANICAL ENGINEER'S POCKET-BOOK.**
Comprising Tables, Formulæ, Rules, and Data: A Handy Book of Reference for Daily Use in Engineering Practice. By D. KINNEAR CLARK, M. Inst. C.E., Fourth Edition. Small 8vo, 700 pp., bound in flexible Leather Cover, rounded corners . . . . . . . . . . . . . . **6/0**

SUMMARY OF CONTENTS:—MATHEMATICAL TABLES.—MEASUREMENT OF SURFACES AND SOLIDS.—ENGLISH AND FOREIGN WEIGHTS AND MEASURES.—MONEYS.—SPECIFIC GRAVITY, WEIGHT, AND VOLUME.—MANUFACTURED METALS.—STEEL PIPES—BOLTS AND NUTS.—SUNDRY ARTICLES IN WROUGHT AND CAST IRON, COPPER BRASS, LEAD, TIN, ZINC.—STRENGTH OF TIMBER.—STRENGTH OF CAST IRON.—STRENGTH OF WROUGHT IRON.—STRENGTH OF STEEL.—TENSILE STRENGTH OF COPPER, LEAD, &c.—RESISTANCE OF STONES AND OTHER BUILDING MATERIALS.—RIVETED JOINTS IN BOILER PLATES.—BOILER SHELLS.—WIRE ROPES AND HEMP ROPES.—CHAINS AND CHAIN CABLES.—FRAMING.—HARDNESS OF METALS, ALLOYS, AND STONES.—LABOUR OF ANIMALS.—MECHANICAL PRINCIPLES.—GRAVITY AND FALL OF BODIES.—ACCELERATING AND RETARDING FORCES.—MILL GEARING, SHAFTING, &c.—TRANSMISSION OF MOTIVE POWER.—HEAT.—COMBUSTION: FUELS.—WARMING, VENTILATION, COOKING STOVES.—STEAM.—STEAM ENGINES AND BOILERS.—RAILWAYS.—TRAMWAYS.—STEAM SHIPS.—PUMPING STEAM ENGINES AND PUMPS.—COAL GAS, GAS ENGINES, &c.—AIR IN MOTION.—COMPRESSED AIR.—HOT AIR ENGINES.—WATER POWER.—SPEED OF CUTTING TOOLS.—COLOURS.—ELECTRICAL ENGINEERING.

"Mr. Clark manifests what is an innate perception of what is likely to be useful in a pocket-book, and he is really unrivalled in the art of condensation. It is very difficult to hit upon any mechanical engineering subject concerning which this work supplies no information, and the excellent index at the end adds to its utility. In one word, it is an exceedingly handy and efficient tool, possessed of which the engineer will be saved many a wearisome calculation, or yet more wearisome hunt through various text-books and treatises, and, as such, we can heartily recommend it to our readers."—*The Engineer.*

"It would be found difficult to compress more matter within a similar compass, or produce a book of 650 pages which should be more compact or convenient for pocket reference. . . . Will be appreciated by mechanical engineers of all classes."—*Practical Engineer.*

## MR. HUTTON'S PRACTICAL HANDBOOKS.

### THE WORKS' MANAGER'S HANDBOOK.

Comprising Modern Rules, Tables, and Data. For Engineers, Millwrights, and Boiler Makers; Tool Makers, Machinists, and Metal Workers; Iron and Brass Founders, &c. By W. S. HUTTON, Civil and Mechanical Engineer, Author of "The Practical Engineer's Handbook." Sixth Edition, carefully Revised, with Additions. In One handsome Volume, medium 8vo, strongly bound. [*Just Published.* **15/0**

☛ *The Author having compiled Rules and Data for his own use in a great variety of modern engineering work, and having found his notes extremely useful, decided to publish them—revised to date—believing that a practical work, suited to the* DAILY REQUIREMENTS OF MODERN ENGINEERS, *would be favourably received.*

"Of this edition we may repeat the appreciative remarks we made upon the first and third. Since the appearance of the latter very considerable modifications have been made, although the total number of pages remains almost the same. It is a very useful collection of rules, tables, and workshop and drawing office data."—*The Engineer,* May 10, 1895.
"The author treats every subject from the point of view of one who has collected workshop notes for application in workshop practice, rather than from the theoretical or literary aspect. The volume contains a great deal of that kind of information which is gained only by practical experience, and is seldom written in books."—*The Engineer,* June 5, 1885.
"The volume is an exceedingly useful one, brimful with engineer's notes, memoranda, and rules, and well worthy of being on every mechanical engineer's bookshelf."—*Mechanical World.*
"The information is precisely that likely to be required in practice. . . . The work forms a desirable addition to the library not only of the works' manager, but of any one connected with general engineering."—*Mining Journal.*
"Brimful of useful information, stated in a concise form, Mr. Hutton's books have met a pressing want among engineers. The book must prove extremely useful to every practical man possessing a copy."—*Practical Engineer.*

### THE PRACTICAL ENGINEER'S HANDBOOK.

Comprising a Treatise on Modern Engines and Boilers, Marine, Locomotive, and Stationary. And containing a large collection of Rules and Practical Data relating to Recent Practice in Designing and Constructing all kinds of Engines, Boilers, and other Engineering work. The whole constituting a comprehensive Key to the Board of Trade and other Examinations for Certificates of Competency in Modern Mechanical Engineering. By WALTER S. HUTTON, Civil and Mechanical Engineer, Author of "The Works' Manager's Handbook for Engineers," &c. With upwards of 370 Illustrations. Fifth Edition, Revised with Additions. Medium 8vo, nearly 500 pp., strongly bound. [*Just Published.* **18/0**

☛ *This Work is designed as a companion to the Author's* "WORKS' MANAGER'S HANDBOOK." *It possesses many new and special features, and contains, like its predecessor, a quantity of matter not originally intended for publication, but collected by the Author for his own use in the construction of a great variety of* MODERN ENGINEERING WORK.

*The information is given in a condensed and concise form, and is illustrated by upwards of 370 Woodcuts; and comprises a quantity of tabulated matter of great value to all engaged in designing, constructing, or estimating for* ENGINES, BOILERS, *and* OTHER ENGINEERING WORK.

"We have kept it at hand for several weeks, referring to it as occasion arose, and we have not on a single occasion consulted its pages without finding the information of which we were in quest."—*Athenæum.*
"A thoroughly good practical handbook, which no engineer can go through without learning something that will be of service to him."—*Marine Engineer.*
"An excellent book of reference for engineers, and a valuable text-book for students of engineering."—*Scotsman.*
"This valuable manual embodies the results and experience of the leading authorities on mechanical engineering."—*Building News.*
"The author has collected together a surprising quantity of rules and practical data, and has shown much judgment in the selections he has made. . . . There is no doubt that this book is one of the most useful of its kind published, and will be a very popular compendium."—*Engineer.*
"A mass of information set down in simple language, and in such a form that it can be easily referred to at any time. The matter is uniformly good and well chosen, and is greatly elucidated by the illustrations. The book will find its way on to most engineers' shelves, where it will rank as one of the most useful books of reference."—*Practical Engineer.*
"Full of useful information, and should be found on the office shelf of all practical engineers."—*English Mechanic.*

## MR. HUTTON'S PRACTICAL HANDBOOKS—*continued.*

### STEAM BOILER CONSTRUCTION.

A Practical Handbook for Engineers, Boiler-Makers, and Steam Users. Containing a large Collection of Rules and Data relating to Recent Practice in the Design, Construction, and Working of all Kinds of Stationary, Locomotive, and Marine Steam-Boilers. By WALTER S. HUTTON, Civil and Mechanical Engineer, Author of "The Works' Manager's Handbook," "The Practical Engineer's Handbook," &c. With upwards of 500 Illustrations. Third Edition, Revised and much Enlarged, medium 8vo, cloth . . **18/0**

☞ THIS WORK *is issued in continuation of the Series of Handbooks written by the Author, viz.* :—"THE WORKS' MANAGER'S HANDBOOK" *and,* "THE PRACTICAL ENGINEER'S HANDBOOK," *which are so highly appreciated by engineers for the practical nature of their information; and is consequently written in the same style as those works.*

*The Author believes that the concentration, in a convenient form for easy reference, of such a large amount of thoroughly practical information on Steam-Boilers, will be of considerable service to those for whom it is intended, and he trusts the book may be deemed worthy of as favourable a reception as has been accorded to its predecessors.*

"One of the best, if not the best, books on boilers that has ever been published. The information is of the right kind, in a simple and accessible form. So far as generation is concerned, this is, undoubtedly, the standard book on steam practice."—*Electrical Review.*

"Every detail, both in boiler design and management, is clearly laid before the reader. The volume shows that boiler construction has been reduced to the condition of one of the most exact sciences; and such a book is of the utmost value to the *fin de siècle* Engineer and Works Manager.'—*Marine Engineer.*

"There has long been room for a modern handbook on steam boilers; there is not that room now, because Mr. Hutton has filled it. It is a thoroughly practical book for those who are occupied in the construction, design, selection, or use of boilers."—*Engineer.*

"The book is of so important and comprehensive a character that it must find its way into the libraries of every one interested in boiler using or boiler manufacture if they wish to be thoroughly informed. We strongly recommend the book for the intrinsic value of its contents."—*Machinery Market.*

### PRACTICAL MECHANICS' WORKSHOP COMPANION.

Comprising a great variety of the most useful Rules and Formulæ in Mechanical Science, with numerous Tables of Practical Data and Calculated Results for Facilitating Mechanical Operations. By WILLIAM TEMPLETON, Author of "The Engineer's Practical Assistant," &c., &c. Eighteenth Edition, Revised, Modernised, and considerably Enlarged by WALTER S. HUTTON, C.E., Author of "The Works' Manager's Handbook," "The Practical Engineer's Handbook," &c. Fcap. 8vo, nearly 500 pp., with 8 Plates and upwards of 250 Illustrative Diagrams, strongly bound for workshop or pocket wear and tear. **6/0**

"In its modernised form Hutton's 'Templeton' should have a wide sale, for it contains much valuable information which the mechanic will often find of use, and not a few tables and notes which he might look for in vain in other works. This modernised edition will be appreciated by all who have learned to value the original editions of 'Templeton.'"—*English Mechanic.*

"It has met with great success in the engineering workshop, as we can testify; and there are a great many men who, in a great measure, owe their rise in life to this little book."—*Building News.*

"This familiar text-book—well known to all mechanics and engineers—is of essential service to the every-day requirements of engineers, millwrights, and the various trades connected with engineering and building. The new modernised edition is worth its weight in gold."—*Building News.* (Second Notice.)

"This well-known and largely-used book contains information, brought up to date, of the sort so useful to the foreman and draughtsman. So much fresh information has been introduced as to constitute it practically a new book. It will be largely used in the office and workshop."—*Mechanical World.*

"The publishers wisely entrusted the task of revision of this popular, valuable, and useful book to Mr. Hutton, than whom a more competent man they could not have found."—*Iron.*

### ENGINEER'S AND MILLWRIGHT'S ASSISTANT.

A Collection of Useful Tables, Rules, and Data. By WILLIAM TEMPLETON. Eighth Edition, with Additions. 18mo, cloth . . . . **2/6**

"Occupies a foremost place among books of this kind. A more suitable present to an apprentice to any of the mechanical trades could not possibly be made."—*Building News.*

"A deservedly popular work. It should be in the 'drawer' of every mechanic."—*English Mechanic.*

A 2

4    CROSBY LOCKWOOD & SON'S CATALOGUE.

## THE MECHANICAL ENGINEER'S REFERENCE BOOK.
For Machine and Boiler Construction. In Two Parts. Part I. GENERAL ENGINEERING DATA. Part II. BOILER CONSTRUCTION. With 51 Plates and numerous Illustrations. By NELSON FOLEY, M.I.N.A. Second Edition, Revised throughout and much Enlarged. Folio, half-bound, net . **£3 3s.**
PART I.—MEASURES.—CIRCUMFERENCES AND AREAS, &c., SQUARES, CUBES FOURTH POWERS.—SQUARE AND CUBE ROOTS.—SURFACE OF TUBES.—RECIPROCALS.—LOGARITHMS. — MENSURATION. — SPECIFIC GRAVITIES AND WEIGHTS.—WORK AND POWER. — HEAT. — COMBUSTION. — EXPANSION AND CONTRACTION. — EXPANSION OF GASES.—STEAM.— STATIC FORCES.—GRAVITATION AND ATTRACTION.—MOTION AND COMPUTATION OF RESULTING FORCES.—ACCUMULATED WORK.—CENTRE AND RADIUS OF GYRATION.—MOMENT OF INERTIA.—CENTRE OF OSCILLATION.—ELECTRICITY.—STRENGTH OF MATERIALS.—ELASTICITY.—TEST SHEETS OF METALS.—FRICTION.—TRANSMISSION OF POWER.—FLOW OF LIQUIDS.—FLOW OF GASES.—AIR PUMPS, SURFACE CONDENSERS, &c.—SPEED OF STEAMSHIPS.—PROPELLERS.—CUTTING TOOLS.—FLANGES. —COPPER SHEETS AND TUBES.—SCREWS, NUTS, BOLT HEADS, &c.—VARIOUS RECIPES AND MISCELLANEOUS MATTER.—WITH DIAGRAMS FOR VALVE-GEAR, BELTING AND ROPES, DISCHARGE AND SUCTION PIPES, SCREW PROPELLERS, AND COPPER PIPES.
PART II.—TREATING OF POWER OF BOILERS.—USEFUL RATIOS.—NOTES ON CONSTRUCTION. — CYLINDRICAL BOILER SHELLS. — CIRCULAR FURNACES. — FLAT PLATES.—STAYS. — GIRDERS.—SCREWS. — HYDRAULIC TESTS. — RIVETING. — BOILER SETTING, CHIMNEYS, AND MOUNTINGS.—FUELS, &c.—EXAMPLES OF BOILERS AND SPEEDS OF STEAMSHIPS.—NOMINAL AND NORMAL HORSE POWER.—WITH DIAGRAMS FOR ALL BOILER CALCULATIONS AND DRAWINGS OF MANY VARIETIES OF BOILERS.
"The book is one which every mechanical engineer may, with advantage to himself, add to his library."—*Industries.*
"Mr. Foley is well fitted to compile such a work. . . . The diagrams are a great feature of the work. . . . Regarding the whole work, it may be very fairly stated that Mr. Foley has produced a volume which will undoubtedly fulfil the desire of the author and become indispensable to all mechanical engineers."—*Marine Engineer.*
"We have carefully examined this work, and pronounce it a most excellent reference book for the use of marine engineers."—*Journal of American Society of Naval Engineers.*

## COAL AND SPEED TABLES.
A Pocket Book for Engineers and Steam Users. By NELSON FOLEY, Author of "The Mechanical Engineer's Reference Book." Pocket-size, cloth . **3/6**
"These tables are designed to meet the requirements of every-day use; are of sufficient scope for most practical purposes, and may be commended to engineers and users of steam."—*Iron.*

## TEXT-BOOK ON THE STEAM ENGINE.
With a Supplement on GAS ENGINES, and PART II. on HEAT ENGINES. By T. M. GOODEVE, M.A., Barrister-at-Law, Professor of Mechanics at the Royal College of Science, London ; Author of " The Principles of Mechanics," " The Elements of Mechanism," &c. Fourteenth Edition. Crown 8vo, cloth . **6/0**
"Professor Goodeve has given us a treatise on the steam engine which will bear comparison with anything written by Huxley or Maxwell, and we can award it no higher praise."—*Engineer.*
"Mr. Goodeve's text-book is a work of which every young engineer should possess himself."—*Mining Journal.*

## ON GAS ENGINES.
With Appendix describing a Recent Engine with Tube Igniter. By T. M. GOODEVE, M.A. Crown 8vo, cloth . . . . . . . **2/6**
"Like all Mr. Goodeve's writings, the present is no exception in point of general excellence. It is a valuable little volume."—*Mechanical World.*

## A TREATISE ON STEAM BOILERS.
Their Strength, Construction, and Economical Working. By R. WILSON, C.E. Fifth Edition. 12mo, cloth . . . . . . . . **6/0**
"The best treatise that has ever been published on steam boilers. —*Engineer.*
"The author shows himself perfect master of his subject, and we heartily recommend all employing steam power to possess themselves of the work."—*Ryland's Iron Trade Circular.*

## THE MECHANICAL ENGINEER'S COMPANION
of Areas, Circumferences, Decimal Equivalents, in inches and feet, millimetres squares, cubes, roots, &c. ; Weights, Measures, and other Data. Also Practical Rules for Modern Engine Proportions. By R. EDWARDS, M.Inst.C.E. Fcap. 8vo, cloth. [*Just Published.* **3/6**
"A very useful little volume. It contains many tables, classified data and memoranda, generally useful to engineers."—*Engineer.*
"This small book is what it professes to be, viz. :—' a handy office companion,' giving as it does, in a succinct form, a variety of information likely to be required by mechanical engineers in their everyday office work."—*Nature.*

## A HANDBOOK ON THE STEAM ENGINE.

With especial Reference to Small and Medium-sized Engines. For the Use of Engine Makers, Mechanical Draughtsmen, Engineering Students, and users of Steam Power. By HERMAN HAEDER, C.E. Translated from the German with considerable additions and alterations, by H. H. P. POWLES, A.M.I.C.E., M.I.M.E. Second Edition, Revised. With nearly 1,100 Illustrations. Crown 8vo, cloth . . . . . . . . . . **9/0**

"A perfect encyclopædia of the steam engine and its details, and one which must take a permanent place in English drawing-offices and workshops."—*A Foreman Pattern-maker.*
"This is an excellent book, and should be in the hands of all who are interested in the construction and design of medium-sized stationary engines. . . . A careful study of its contents and the arrangement of the sections leads to the conclusion that there is probably no other book like it in this country. The volume aims at showing the results of practical experience, and it certainly may claim a complete achievement of this idea."—*Nature.*
"There can be no question as to its value. We cordially commend it to all concerned in the design and construction of the steam engine."—*Mechanical World.*

## BOILER AND FACTORY CHIMNEYS.

Their Draught-Power and Stability. With a chapter on *Lightning Conductors*. By ROBERT WILSON, A.I.C.E., Author of "A Treatise on Steam Boilers," &c. Crown 8vo, cloth . . . . . . . . . **3/6**

"A valuable contribution to the literature of scientific building."—*The Builder.*

## BOILER MAKER'S READY RECKONER & ASSISTANT.

With Examples of Practical Geometry and Templating, for the Use of Platers, Smiths, and Riveters. By JOHN COURTNEY, Edited by D. K. CLARK, M.I.C.E. Third Edition, 480 pp., with 140 Illustrations. Fcap. 8vo . **7/0**

"No workman or apprentice should be without this book."—*Iron Trade Circular.*

## REFRIGERATING & ICE-MAKING MACHINERY.

A Descriptive Treatise for the Use of Persons Employing Refrigerating and Ice-Making Installations, and others. By A. J. WALLIS-TAYLER, A.-M. Inst. C.E. Second Edition, Revised and Enlarged. With Illustrations. Crown 8vo, cloth. [*Just Published.*] **7/6**

"Practical, explicit, and profusely illustrated."—*Glasgow Herald.*
"We recommend the book, which gives the cost of various systems and illustrations showing details of parts of machinery and general arrangements of complete installations."—*Builder.*
"May be recommended as a useful description of the machinery, the processes, and of the facts, figures, and tabulated physics of refrigerating. It is one of the best compilations on the subject."—*Engineer.*

## TEA MACHINERY AND TEA FACTORIES.

A Descriptive Treatise on the Mechanical Appliances required in the Cultivation of the Tea Plant and the Preparation of Tea for the Market. By A. J. WALLIS-TAYLER, A.-M. Inst. C.E. Medium 8vo, 468 pp. With 218 Illustrations. [*Just Published.*] *Net* **25/0**

SUMMARY OF CONTENTS :—MECHANICAL CULTIVATION OR TILLAGE OF THE SOIL.—PLUCKING OR GATHERING THE LEAF.—TEA FACTORIES.—THE DRESSING, MANUFACTURE OR PREPARATION OF TEA BY MECHANICAL MEANS.—ARTIFICIAL WITHERING OF THE LEAF.—MACHINES FOR ROLLING OR CURLING THE LEAF.—FERMENTING PROCESS.—MACHINES FOR THE AUTOMATIC DRYING OR FIRING OF THE LEAF.—MACHINES FOR NON-AUTOMATIC DRYING OR FIRING OF THE LEAF.—DRYING OR FIRING MACHINES.—BREAKING OR CUTTING, AND SORTING MACHINES.—PACKING THE TEA.—MEANS OF TRANSPORT ON TEA PLANTATIONS.—MISCELLANEOUS MACHINERY AND APPARATUS.—FINAL TREATMENT OF THE TEA.—TABLES AND MEMORANDA.

"The subject of tea machinery is now one of the first interest to a large class of people, to whom we strongly commend the volume."—*Chamber of Commerce Journal.*
"When tea planting was first introduced into the British possessions little, if any, machinery was employed, but now its use is almost universal. This volume contains a very full account of the machinery necessary for the proper outfit of a factory, and also a description of the processes best carried out by this machinery."—*Journal Society of Arts.*

## ENGINEERING ESTIMATES, COSTS, AND ACCOUNTS.

A Guide to Commercial Engineering. With numerous examples of Estimates and Costs of Millwright Work, Miscellaneous Productions, Steam Engines and Steam Boilers; and a Section on the Preparation of Costs Accounts. By A GENERAL MANAGER. Second Edition. 8vo, cloth. [*Just Published.*] **12/0**

"This is an excellent and very useful book, covering subject-matter in constant requisition in every factory and workshop. . . . The book is invaluable, not only to the young engineer, but also to the estimate department of every works."—*Builder.*
"We accord the work unqualified praise. The information is given in a plain, straightforward manner, and bears throughout evidence of the intimate practical acquaintance of the author with every phase of commercial engineering."—*Mechanical World.*

## AERIAL OR WIRE-ROPE TRAMWAYS.

Their Construction and Management. By A. J. WALLIS-TAYLER, A.M.Inst.C.E. With 81 Illustrations. Crown 8vo, cloth. [*Just Published.* **7/6**

"This is in its way an excellent volume. Without going into the minutiæ of the subject, it yet lays before its readers a very good exposition of the various systems of rope transmission in use, and gives as well not a little valuable information about their working, repair, and management. We can safely recommend it as a useful general treatise on the subject."—*The Engineer.*

"Mr. Tayler has treated the subject as concisely as thoroughness would permit. The book will rank with the best on this useful topic, and we recommend it to those whose business is the transporting of minerals and goods."—*Mining Journal.*

## MOTOR CARS OR POWER-CARRIAGES FOR COMMON ROADS.

By A. J. WALLIS-TAYLER, Assoc. Memb. Inst. C.E., Author of "Modern Cycles," &c. 212 pp., with 76 Illustrations. Crown 8vo, cloth . . **4/6**

"Mr. Wallis-Tayler's book is a welcome addition to the literature of the subject, as it is the production of an Engineer, and has not been written with a view to assist in the promotion of companies. . . . The book is clearly expressed throughout, and is just the sort of work that an engineer, thinking of turning his attention to motor-carriage work, would do well to read as a preliminary to starting operations."—*Engineering.*

## PLATING AND BOILER MAKING.

A Practical Handbook for Workshop Operations. By JOSEPH G. HORNER, A.M.I.M.E. 380 pp. with 338 Illustrations. Crown 8vo, cloth . . **7/6**

"The latest production from the pen of this writer is characterised by that evidence of close acquaintance with workshop methods which will render the book exceedingly acceptable to the practical hand. We have no hesitation in commending the work as a serviceable and practical handbook on a subject which has not hitherto received much attention from those qualified to deal with it in a satisfactory manner."—*Mechanical World.*

## PATTERN MAKING.

A Practical Treatise, embracing the Main Types of Engineering Construction, and including Gearing, both Hand and Machine-made, Engine Work, Sheaves and Pulleys, Pipes and Columns, Screws, Machine Parts, Pumps and Cocks, the Moulding of Patterns in Loam and Greensand, &c., together with the methods of estimating the weight of Castings; with an Appendix of Tables for Workshop Reference. By JOSEPH G. HORNER, A.M.I.M.E. Second Edition, Enlarged. With 450 Illustrations. Crown 8vo, cloth . . . . **7/6**

"A well-written technical guide, evidently written by a man who understands and has practised what he has written about. . . . We cordially recommend it to engineering students, young journeymen, and others desirous of being initiated into the mysteries of pattern-making."—*Builder.*

"An excellent *vade mecum* for the apprentice who desires to become master of his trade.'—*English Mechanic.*

## MECHANICAL ENGINEERING TERMS

(Lockwood's Dictionary of). Embracing those current in the Drawing Office, Pattern Shop, Foundry, Fitting, Turning, Smiths', and Boiler Shops, &c., &c. Comprising upwards of 6,000 Definitions. Edited by JOSEPH G. HORNER, A.M.I.M.E. Second Edition, Revised, with Additions. Crown 8vo, cloth **7/6**

"Just the sort of handy dictionary required by the various trades engaged in mechanical engineering. The practical engineering pupil will find the book of great value in his studies, and every foreman engineer and mechanic should have a copy."—*Building News.*

## TOOTHED GEARING.

A Practical Handbook for Offices and Workshops. By JOSEPH HORNER, A.M.I.M.E. With 184 Illustrations. Crown 8vo, cloth . . . **6/0**

"We must give the book our unqualified praise for its thoroughness of treatment, and we can heartily recommend it to all interested as the most practical book on the subject yet written."—*Mechanical World.*

## FIRE PROTECTION.

A Complete Manual of the Organisation, Machinery, Discipline and General Working of the Fire Brigade of London. By CAPTAIN EYRE M. SHAW, C.B., Chief Officer, Metropolitan Fire Brigade. New and Revised Edition, Demy 8vo, cloth. . . . . . . . . . *Net* **5/0**

## FIRES, FIRE-ENGINES, AND FIRE BRIGADES.

With a History of Fire-Engines, their Construction, Use, and Management; Foreign Fire Systems; Hints on Fire-Brigades, &c. By CHARLES F. T. YOUNG, C.E. 8vo, cloth . . . . . . . **£1 4s.**

"To such of our readers as are interested in the subject of fires and fire apparatus we can most heartily commend this book."—*Engineering.*

## STONE-WORKING MACHINERY.

A Manual dealing with the Rapid and Economical Conversion of Stone. With Hints on the Arrangement and Management of Stone Works. By M. POWIS BALE, M.I.M.E. Second Edition, enlarged. With Illustrations. Crown 8vo, cloth. [*Just Published.* **9/0**

"The book should be in the hands of every mason or student of stonework."—*Colliery Guardian.*
"A capital handbook for all who manipulate stone for building or ornamental purposes."—*Machinery Market.*

## PUMPS AND PUMPING.

A Handbook for Pump Users. Being Notes on Selection, Construction, and Management. By M. POWIS BALE, M.I.M.E. Third Edition, Revised. Crown 8vo, cloth. [*Just Published.* **2/6**

"The matter is set forth as concisely as possible. In fact, condensation rather than diffuseness has been the author's aim throughout; yet he does not seem to have omitted anything likely to be of use."—*Journal of Gas Lighting.*
"Thoroughly practical and simply and clearly written."—*Glasgow Herald.*

## MILLING MACHINES AND PROCESSES.

A Practical Treatise on Shaping Metals by Rotary Cutters. Including Information on Making and Grinding the Cutters. By PAUL N. HASLUCK, Author of "Lathe-Work." 352 pp. With upwards of 300 Engravings. Large crown 8vo, cloth . . . . . . . . . . **12/6**

"A new departure in engineering literature. . . . We can recommend this work to all interested in milling machines; it is what it professes to be—a practical treatise."—*Engineer.*
"A capital and reliable book which will no doubt be of considerable service both to those who are already acquainted with the process as well as to those who contemplate its adoption."—*Industries.*

## LATHE-WORK.

A Practical Treatise on the Tools, Appliances, and Processes employed in the Art of Turning. By PAUL N. HASLUCK. Sixth Edition. Crown 8vo, cloth . . . . . . . . . . **5/0**

"Written by a man who knows not only how work ought to be done, but who also knows how to do it, and how to convey his knowledge to others. To all turners this book would be valuable."—*Engineering.*
"We can safely recommend the work to young engineers. To the amateur it will simply be invaluable. To the student it will convey a great deal of useful information."—*Engineer.*

## SCREW-THREADS,

And Methods of Producing Them. With numerous Tables and complete Directions for using Screw-Cutting Lathes. By PAUL N. HASLUCK, Author of "Lathe-Work," &c. With Seventy-four Illustrations. Fifth Edition. Waistcoat-pocket size . . . . . . . . **1/6**

"Full of useful information, hints and practical criticism. Taps, dies, and screwing tools generally are illustrated and their actions described."—*Mechanical World.*
"It is a complete compendium of all the details of the screw-cutting lathe; in fact a *multum-in-parvo* on all the subjects it treats upon."—*Carpenter and Builder.*

## TABLES AND MEMORANDA FOR ENGINEERS, MECHANICS, ARCHITECTS, BUILDERS, &c.

Selected and Arranged by FRANCIS SMITH. Sixth Edition, Revised, including ELECTRICAL TABLES, FORMULÆ, and MEMORANDA. Waistcoat-pocket size, limp leather. [*Just Published.* **1/6**

"It would, perhaps, be as difficult to make a small pocket-book selection of notes and formulæ to suit ALL engineers as it would be to make a universal medicine; but Mr. Smith's waistcoat-pocket collection may be looked upon as a successful attempt."—*Engineer.*
"The best example we have ever seen of 270 pages of useful matter packed into the dimensions of a card-case."—*Building News.* "A veritable pocket treasury of knowledge."—*Iron.*

## POCKET GLOSSARY OF TECHNICAL TERMS.

English-French, French-English; with Tables suitable for the Architectural, Engineering, Manufacturing, and Nautical Professions. By JOHN JAMES FLETCHER, Engineer and Surveyor. Second Edition, Revised and Enlarged. 200 pp. Waistcoat-pocket size, limp leather . . . . . . **1/6**

"It is a very great advantage for readers and correspondents in France and England to have so large a number of the words relating to engineering and manufacturers collected in a lilliputian volume. The little book will be useful both to students and travellers."—*Architect.*
"The glossary of terms is very complete, and many of the Tables are new and well arranged. We cordially commend the book."—*Mechanical World.*

8   CROSBY LOCKWOOD & SON'S CATALOGUE.

## THE ENGINEER'S YEAR BOOK FOR 1900.

Comprising Formulæ, Rules, Tables, Data and Memoranda in Civil, Mechanical, Electrical, Marine and Mine Engineering. By H. R. KEMPE, A.M. Inst. C.E., M.I.E.E., Technical Officer of the Engineer-in-Chief's Office, General Post Office, London, Author of "A Handbook of Electrical Testing." "The Electrical Engineer's Pocket-Book," &c. With about 1,000 Illustrations, specially Engraved for the work. Crown 8vo, 800 pp., leather.   [*Just Published.*   **8/0**

"Represents an enormous quantity of work, and forms a desirable book of reference."—*The Engineer.*
"The volume is distinctly in advance of most similar publications in this country."—*Engineering.*
"This valuable and well-designed book of reference meets the demands of all descriptions of engineers."—*Saturday Review.*
"Teems with up-to-date information in every branch of engineering and construction."—*Building News.*
"The needs of the engineering profession could hardly be supplied in a more admirable, complete and convenient form. To say that it more than sustains all comparisons is the effect of the highest sort, and that may justly be said of it."—*Mining Journal.*
"There is certainly room for the newcomer, which supplies explanations and directions, as well as formulæ and tables. It deserves to become one of the most successful of the technical annuals."—*Architect.*
"Brings together with great skill all the technical information which an engineer has to use day by day. It is in every way admirably equipped, and is sure to prove successful."—*Scotsman.*
"The up-to-dateness of Mr. Kempe's compilation is a quality that will not be lost on the busy people for whom the work is intended."—*Glasgow Herald.*

## THE PORTABLE ENGINE.

A Practical Manual on its Construction and Management. For the use of Owners and Users of Steam Engines generally. By WILLIAM DYSON WANSBROUGH. Crown 8vo, cloth   .   .   .   .   .   .   **3/6**

"This is a work of value to those who use steam machinery. . . . Should be read by every one who has a steam engine, on a farm or elsewhere."—*Mark Lane Express.*
"We cordially commend this work to buyers and owners of steam-engines, and to those who have to do with their construction or use."—*Timber Trades Journal.*
"Such a general knowledge of the steam-engine as Mr. Wansbrough furnishes to the reader should be acquired by all intelligent owners and others who use the steam-engine."—*Building News.*
"An excellent text-book of this useful form of engine. The 'Hints to Purchasers' contain a good deal of common-sense and practical wisdom."—*English Mechanic.*

## IRON AND STEEL.

A Work for the Forge, Foundry, Factory, and Office. Containing ready, useful, and trustworthy Information for Ironmasters and their Stock-takers; Managers of Bar, Rail, Plate, and Sheet Rolling Mills; Iron and Metal Founders; Iron Ship and Bridge Builders; Mechanical, Mining, and Consulting Engineers; Architects, Contractors, Builders, &c. By CHARLES HOARE, Author of "The Slide Rule," &c.   Ninth Edition.   32mo, leather   .   **6/0**

"For comprehensiveness the book has not its equal."—*Iron.*
"One of the best of the pocket books."—*English Mechanic.*

## CONDENSED MECHANICS.

A Selection of Formulæ, Rules, Tables, and Data or the Use of Engineering Students, Science Classes, &c. In accordance with the Requirements of the Science and Art Department. By W. G. CRAWFORD HUGHES, A.M.I.C.E. Crown 8vo, cloth   .   .   .   .   .   .   .   .   **2/6**

"The book is well fitted for those who are either confronted with practical problems in their work, or are preparing for examination and wish to refresh their knowledge by going through their formulæ again."—*Marine Engineer.*
"It is well arranged, and meets the wants of those for whom it is intended."—*Railway News.*

## THE SAFE USE OF STEAM.

Containing Rules for Unprofessional Steam Users. By an ENGINEER. Seventh Edition. Sewed   .   .   .   .   .   .   .   .   .   **6d.**

"If steam-users would but learn this little book by heart, boiler explosions would become sensations by their rarity."—*English Mechanic.*

## HEATING BY HOT WATER.

With Information and Suggestions on the best Methods of Heating Public, Private and Horticultural Buildings. By WALTER JONES. Second Edition. With 96 Illustrations, crown 8vo, cloth   .   .   .   .   .   Net **2/6**

"We confidently recommend all interested in heating by hot water to secure a copy of this valuable little treatise."—*The Plumber and Decorator.*

## MECHANICAL ENGINEERING, &c.

### THE LOCOMOTIVE ENGINE.
The Autobiography of an Old Locomotive Engine. By ROBERT WEATHERBURN, M.I.M.E. With Illustrations and Portraits of GEORGE and ROBERT STEPHENSON. Crown 8vo, cloth. [*Just Published.* Net **2/6**

SUMMARY OF CONTENTS:—PROLOGUE.—CYLINDERS.—MOTIONS.—CONNECTING RODS.—FRAMES.—WHEELS.—PUMPS, CLACKS, &c.—INJECTORS.—BOILERS.—SMOKE BOX.—CHIMNEY.—WEATHER BOARD AND AWNING.—INTERNAL DISSENSIONS.—ENGINE DRIVERS, &c.

"It would be difficult to imagine anything more ingeniously planned, more cleverly worked out, and more charmingly written. Readers cannot fail to find the volume most enjoyable."—*Glasgow Herald.*

### THE LOCOMOTIVE ENGINE AND ITS DEVELOPMENT.
A Popular Treatise on the Gradual Improvements made in Railway Engines between 1803 and 1896. By CLEMENT E. STRETTON, C.E. Fifth Edition, Enlarged. With 120 Illustrations. Crown 8vo, cloth. [*Just Published.* **3/6**

"Students of railway history and all who are interested in the evolution of the modern locomotive will find much to attract and entertain in this volume."—*The Times.*

### LOCOMOTIVE ENGINE DRIVING.
A Practical Manual for Engineers in Charge of Locomotive Engines. By MICHAEL REYNOLDS, Member of the Society of Engineers, formerly Locomotive Inspector, L. B. & S. C. R. Ninth Edition. Including a KEY TO THE LOCOMOTIVE ENGINE. Crown 8vo, cloth . . . . . **4/6**

"Mr. Reynolds has supplied a want, and has supplied it well. We can confidently recommend the book not only to the practical driver, but to everyone who takes an interest in the performance of locomotive engines."—*The Engineer.*
"Mr. Reynolds has opened a new chapter in the literature of the day. His treatise is admirable."—*Athenæum.*

### THE MODEL LOCOMOTIVE ENGINEER,
Fireman, and Engine-Boy. Comprising a Historical Notice of the Pioneer Locomotive Engines and their Inventors. By MICHAEL REYNOLDS. Second Edition, with Revised Appendix. Crown 8vo, cloth. [*Just Published.* **4/6**

"From the technical knowledge of the author, it will appeal to the railway man of to-day more forcibly than anything written by Dr. Smiles. . . . The volume contains information of a technical kind, and facts that every driver should be familiar with."—*English Mechanic.*
"We should be glad to see this book in the possession of everyone in the kingdom who has ever laid, or is to lay, hands on a locomotive engine."—*Iron.*

### CONTINUOUS RAILWAY BRAKES.
A Practical Treatise on the several Systems in Use in the United Kingdom; their Construction and Performance. With copious Illustrations and numerous Tables. By MICHAEL REYNOLDS. 8vo, cloth . . . . . **9/0**

"A popular explanation of the different brakes. It will be of great assistance in forming public opinion, and will be studied with benefit by those who take an interest in the brake."—*English Mechanic.*

### STATIONARY ENGINE DRIVING.
A Practical Manual for Engineers in Charge of Stationary Engines. By MICHAEL REYNOLDS. Sixth Edition. Crown 8vo, cloth . . . **4/6**

"The author is thoroughly acquainted with his subjects, and his advice on the various points treated is clear and practical. . . . He has produced a manual which is an exceedingly useful one for the class for whom it is specially intended."—*Engineering.*
"Our author leaves no stone unturned. He is determined that his readers shall not only know something about the stationary engine, but all about it."—*Engineer.*

### ENGINE-DRIVING LIFE.
Stirring Adventure and Incidents in the Lives of Locomotive Engine-Drivers. By MICHAEL REYNOLDS. Third Edition. Crown 8vo, cloth . **1/6**

"Perfectly fascinating. Wilkie Collins's most thrilling conceptions are thrown into the shade by true incidents, endless in their variety, related in every page."—*North British Mail.*

### THE ENGINEMAN'S POCKET COMPANION,
And Practical Educator for Enginemen, Boiler Attendants, and Mechanics. By MICHAEL REYNOLDS. With 45 Illustrations and numerous Diagrams. Fourth Edition, Revised. Royal 18mo, strongly bound for pocket wear **3/6**

"This admirable work is well suited to accomplish its object, being the honest workmanship of a competent engineer."—*Glasgow Herald.*

10   CROSBY LOCKWOOD & SON'S CATALOGUE.

## CIVIL ENGINEERING, SURVEYING, &c.

### LIGHT RAILWAYS FOR THE UNITED KINGDOM, INDIA, AND THE COLONIES.

A Practical Handbook setting forth the Principles on which Light Railways should be Constructed, Worked, and Financed; and detailing the Cost of Construction, Equipment, Revenue and Working Expenses of Local Railways already established in the above-mentioned countries, and in Belgium, France, Switzerland, &c. By J. C. MACKAY, F.G.S., A.M. Inst. C.E. Illustrated with Plates and Diagrams. Medium 8vo, cloth. [*Just Published.* **15/0**

"Mr. Mackay's volume is clearly and concisely written, admirably arranged, and freely illustrated. The book is exactly what has been long wanted. We recommend it to all interested in the subject. It is sure to have a wide sale."—*Railway News.*

"Those who desire to have within reach general information concerning almost all the light railway systems in the world will do well to buy Mr. Mackay's book."—*Engineer.*

"This work appears very opportunely, when the extension of the system on a large scale to England is at last being mooted. In its pages we find all the information that the heart of man can desire on the subject. . . . every detail in its story, founded on the experience of other countries and applied to the possibilities of England, is put before us."—*Spectator.*

### PRACTICAL TUNNELLING.

Explaining in detail Setting-out the Works, Shaft-sinking, and Heading-driving, Ranging the Lines and Levelling underground, Sub-Excavating, Timbering and the Construction of the Brickwork of Tunnels, with the amount of Labour required for, and the Cost of, the various portions of the work. By FREDERICK W. SIMMS, M. Inst. C.E. Fourth Edition, Revised and Further Extended, including the most recent (1895) Examples of Sub-aqueous and other Tunnels, by D. KINNEAR CLARK, M. Inst. C.E. Imperial 8vo, with 34 Folding Plates and other Illustrations. Cloth. [*Just Published.* **£2 2s.**

"The present (1896) edition has been brought right up to date, and is thus rendered a work to which civil engineers generally should have ready access, and to which engineers who have construction work can hardly afford to be without, but which to the younger members of the profession is invaluable, as from its pages they can learn the state to which the science of tunnelling has attained."—*Railway News.*

"The estimation in which Mr. Simms's book has been held for many years cannot be more truly expressed than in the words of the late Prof. Rankine: 'The best source of information on the subject of tunnels is Mr. F. W. Simms's work on Practical Tunnelling.'"—*Architect.*

### THE WATER SUPPLY OF TOWNS AND THE CONSTRUCTION OF WATER-WORKS.

A Practical Treatise for the Use of Engineers and Students of Engineering. By W. K. BURTON, A.M. Inst. C.E., Professor of Sanitary Engineering in the Imperial University, Tokyo, Japan, and Consulting Engineer to the Tokyo Water-works. Second Edition, Revised and Extended. With numerous Plates and Illustrations. Super-royal 8vo, buckram. [*Just Published.* **25/0**

I. INTRODUCTORY.—II. DIFFERENT QUALITIES OF WATER.—III. QUANTITY OF WATER TO BE PROVIDED.—IV. ON ASCERTAINING WHETHER A PROPOSED SOURCE OF SUPPLY IS SUFFICIENT.—V. ON ESTIMATING THE STORAGE CAPACITY REQUIRED TO BE PROVIDED.—VI. CLASSIFICATION OF WATER-WORKS.—VII. IMPOUNDING RESERVOIRS.—VIII. EARTHWORK DAMS.—IX. MASONRY DAMS.—X. THE PURIFICATION OF WATER.—XI. SETTLING RESERVOIRS.—XII. SAND FILTRATION.—XIII. PURIFICATION OF WATER BY ACTION OF IRON, SOFTENING OF WATER BY ACTION OF LIME, NATURAL FILTRATION.—XIV. SERVICE OR CLEAN WATER RESERVOIRS—WATER TOWERS—STAND PIPES.—XV. THE CONNECTION OF SETTLING RESERVOIRS, FILTER BEDS AND SERVICE RESERVOIRS.—XVI. PUMPING MACHINERY.—XVII. FLOW OF WATER IN CONDUITS—PIPES AND OPEN CHANNELS.—XVIII. DISTRIBUTION SYSTEMS.—XIX. SPECIAL PROVISIONS FOR THE EXTINCTION OF FIRE.—XX. PIPES FOR WATER-WORKS.—XXI. PREVENTION OF WASTE OF WATER.—XXII. VARIOUS APPLICATIONS USED IN CONNECTION WITH WATER-WORKS.

APPENDIX I. By PROF. JOHN MILNE, F.R.S.—CONSIDERATIONS CONCERNING THE PROBABLE EFFECTS OF EARTHQUAKES ON WATER-WORKS, AND THE SPECIAL PRECAUTIONS TO BE TAKEN IN EARTHQUAKE COUNTRIES.

APPENDIX II. By JOHN DE RIJKE, C.E.—ON SAND DUNES AND DUNE SAND AS A SOURCE OF WATER SUPPLY.

"The chapter upon filtration of water is very complete, and the details of construction well illustrated. . . . The work should be specially valuable to civil engineers engaged in work in Japan, but the interest is by no means confined to that locality."—*Engineer.*

"We congratulate the author upon the practical commonsense shown in the preparation of this work. . . . The plates and diagrams have evidently been prepared with great care, and cannot fail to be of great assistance to the student."—*Builder.*

"The whole art of water-works construction is dealt with in a clear and comprehensive fashion in this handsome volume. . . . Mr. Burton's practical treatise shows in all its sections the fruit of independent study and individual experience. It is largely based upon his own practice in the branch of engineering of which it treats."—*Saturday Review.*

## THE WATER SUPPLY OF CITIES AND TOWNS.

By WILLIAM HUMBER, A. M. Inst. C.E., and M. Inst M E., Author of "Cast and Wrought Iron Bridge Construction," &c., &c. Illustrated with 50 Double Plates, 1 Single Plate, Coloured Frontispiece, and upwards of 250 Woodcuts, and containing 400 pp. of Text. Imp. 4to, elegantly and substantially half-bound in morocco . . . . . . . . *Net* **£6 6s.**

LIST OF CONTENTS.

I. HISTORICAL SKETCH OF SOME OF THE MEANS THAT HAVE BEEN ADOPTED FOR THE SUPPLY OF WATER TO CITIES AND TOWNS.—II. WATER AND THE FOREIGN MATTER USUALLY ASSOCIATED WITH IT.—III. RAINFALL AND EVAPORATION.—IV. SPRINGS AND THE WATER-BEARING FORMATIONS OF VARIOUS DISTRICTS.—V. MEASUREMENT AND ESTIMATION OF THE FLOW OF WATER.—VI. ON THE SELECTION OF THE SOURCE OF SUPPLY.—VII. WELLS.—VIII. RESERVOIRS.—IX. THE PURIFICATION OF WATER.—X. PUMPS.—XI. PUMPING MACHINERY.—XII. CONDUITS.—XIII. DISTRIBUTION OF WATER. —XIV. METERS, SERVICE PIPES, AND HOUSE FITTINGS.—XV. THE LAW OF ECONOMY OF WATER-WORKS.—XVI. CONSTANT AND INTERMITTENT SUPPLY.—XVII. DESCRIPTION OF PLATES.—APPENDICES, GIVING TABLES OF RATES OF SUPPLY, VELOCITIES, &c., &c., TOGETHER WITH SPECIFICATIONS OF SEVERAL WORKS ILLUSTRATED, AMONG WHICH WILL BE FOUND: ABERDEEN, BIDEFORD, CANTERBURY, DUNDEE, HALIFAX, LAMBETH, ROTHERHAM, DUBLIN, AND OTHERS.

"The most systematic and valuable work upon water supply hitherto produced in English, or in any other language. It is characterised almost throughout by an exhaustiveness much more distinctive of French and German than of English technical treatises."—*Engineer.*

## RURAL WATER SUPPLY.

A Practical Handbook on the Supply of Water and Construction of Waterworks for small Country Districts. By ALLAN GREENWELL, A.M.I.C.E., and W. T. CURRY, A.M.I.C.E., F.G.S. With Illustrations. Second Edition, Revised. Crown 8vo, cloth. [*Just Published.* **5/0**

"We conscientiously recommend it as a very useful book for those concerned in obtaining water for small districts, giving a great deal of practical information in a small compass."—*Builder.*
"The volume contains valuable information upon all matters connected with water supply. . . . Full of details on points which are continually before water-works engineers."—*Nature.*

## HYDRAULIC POWER ENGINEERING.

A Practical Manual on the Concentration and Transmission of Power by Hydraulic Machinery. By G. CROYDON MARKS, A.M. Inst. C.E. With nearly 200 Illustrations. 8vo, cloth. [*Just Published. Net* **9/0**

SUMMARY OF CONTENTS:—PRINCIPLES OF HYDRAULICS.—THE OBSERVED FLOW OF WATER.—HYDRAULIC PRESSURES, MATERIAL.—TEST LOAD PACKINGS FOR SLIDING SURFACES.—PIPE JOINTS.—CONTROLLING VALVES.—PLATFORM LIFTS.—WORKSHOP, FACTORY, AND DOCK CRANES.—HYDRAULIC ACCUMULATORS.—PRESSES.—SHEET METAL WORKING AND FORGING MACHINERY.—HYDRAULIC RIVETTERS.—HAND, POWER, AND STEAM PUMPS.—TURBINES.—IMPULSE AND RE-ACTION TURBINES.—DESIGN OF TURBINES.—WATER WHEELS.—HYDRAULIC ENGINES.—RECENT ACHIEVEMENTS.—TABLES.

"We have nothing but praise for this thoroughly valuable work. The author has succeeded in rendering his subject interesting as well as instructive."—*Practical Engineer.*
"Can be unhesitatingly recommended as a useful and up-to-date manual on hydraulic transmission and utilisation of power."—*Mechanical World.*

## HYDRAULIC TABLES, CO-EFFICIENTS, & FORMULÆ.

For Finding the Discharge of Water from Orifices, Notches, Weirs, Pipes, and Rivers. With New Formulæ, Tables, and General Information on Rain-fall, Catchment-Basins, Drainage, Sewerage, Water Supply for Towns and Mill Power. By JOHN NEVILLE, Civil Engineer, M.R.I.A. Third Edition, revised, with additions. Numerous Illustrations. Crown 8vo, cloth . **14/0**

"It is, of all English books on the subject, the one nearest to completeness."—*Architect.*

## HYDRAULIC MANUAL.

Consisting of Working Tables and Explanatory Text. Intended as a Guide in Hydraulic Calculations and Field Operations. By LOWIS D'A. JACKSON, Author of "Aid to Survey Practice," "Modern Metrology," &c. Fourth Edition, Enlarged. Large crown 8vo, cloth . . . . . **16/0**

"The author has constructed a manual which may be accepted as a trustworthy guide to this branch of the engineer's profession."—*Engineering.*

## WATER ENGINEERING.

A Practical Treatise on the Measurement, Storage, Conveyance, and Utilisation of Water for the Supply of Towns, for Mill Power, and for other Purposes. By C. SLAGG, A. M. Inst. C.E. Second Edition. Crown 8vo, cloth . **7/6**

"As a small practical treatise on the water supply of towns, and on some applications of water-power, the work is in many respects excellent."—*Engineering.*

## THE RECLAMATION OF LAND FROM TIDAL WATERS.

A Handbook for Engineers, Landed Proprietors, and others interested in Works of Reclamation. By ALEXANDER BEAZELEY, M.Inst. C.E. With Illustrations. 8vo, cloth. [*Just Published. Net* **10/6**

"The book shows in a concise way what has to be done in reclaiming land from the sea, and the best way of doing it. The work contains a great deal of practical and useful information which cannot fail to be of service to engineers entrusted with the enclosure of salt marshes, and to land owners intending to reclaim land from the sea."—*The Engineer.*

"The author has carried out his task efficiently and well, and his book contains a large amount of information of great service to engineers and others interested in works of reclamation."—*Nature.*

## MASONRY DAMS FROM INCEPTION TO COMPLETION.

Including numerous Formulæ, Forms of Specification and Tender, Pocket Diagram of Forces, &c. For the use of Civil and Mining Engineers. By C. F. COURTNEY, M. Inst. C.E. 8vo, cloth. [*Just Published.* **9/0**

"The volume contains a good deal of valuable data, and furnishes the engineer with practical advice. The author deals with his subject from the inception to the finish. Many useful suggestions will be found in the remarks on site and position, location of dam, foundations and construction."—*Building News.*

## RIVER BARS.

The Causes of their Formation, and their Treatment by "Induced Tidal Scour;" with a Description of the Successful Reduction by this Method of the Bar at Dublin. By I. J. MANN, Assist. Eng. to the Dublin Port and Docks Board. Royal 8vo, cloth . . . . . . . . . **7/6**

"We recommend all interested in harbour works—and, indeed, those concerned in the improvements of rivers generally—to read Mr. Mann's interesting work."—*Engineer.*

## TRAMWAYS: THEIR CONSTRUCTION AND WORKING.

Embracing a Comprehensive History of the System; with an exhaustive Analysis of the Various Modes of Traction, including Horse Power, Steam, Cable Traction, Electric Traction, &c.; a Description of the Varieties of Rolling Stock; and ample Details of Cost and Working Expenses. New Edition, Thoroughly Revised, and Including the Progress recently made in Tramway Construction, &c., &c. By D. KINNEAR CLARK, M. Inst. C.E. With 400 Illustrations. 8vo, 780 pp., buckram. [*Just Published.* **28/0**

"The new volume is one which will rank, among tramway engineers and those interested in tramway working, with the Author's world-famed book on railway machinery."—*The Engineer.*

## PRACTICAL SURVEYING.

A Text-Book for Students preparing for Examinations or for Survey-work in the Colonies. By GEORGE W. USILL, A.M.I.C.E. With 4 Plates and upwards of 330 Illustrations. Sixth Edition. Including Tables of Natural Sines, Tangents, Secants, &c. Crown 8vo, cloth **7/6**; or, on THIN PAPER, leather, gilt edges, for pocket use. [*Just Published.* **12/6**

"The best forms of instruments are described as to their construction, uses and modes of employment, and there are innumerable hints on work and equipment such as the author, in his experience as surveyor, draughtsman and teacher, has found necessary, and which the student in his inexperience will find most serviceable."—*Engineer.*

"The latest treatise in the English language on surveying, and we have no hesitation in saying that the student will find it a better guide than any of its predecessors. Deserves to be recognised as the first book which should be put in the hands of a pupil of Civil Engineering."—*Architect.*

## SURVEYING WITH THE TACHEOMETER.

A practical Manual for the use of Civil and Military Engineers and Surveyors. Including two series of Tables specially computed for the Reduction of Readings in Sexagesimal and in Centesimal Degrees. By NEIL KENNEDY, M. Inst. C.E. With Diagrams and Plates. Demy 8vo, cloth.
[*Just Published. Net* **10/6**

"The work is very clearly written, and should remove all difficulties in the way of any surveyor desirous of making use of this useful and rapid instrument."—*Nature.*

## AID TO SURVEY PRACTICE.

For Reference in Surveying, Levelling, and Setting-out; and in Route Surveys of Travellers by Land and Sea. With Tables, Illustrations, and Records. By LOWIS D'A. JACKSON, A.M.I.C.E. 8vo, cloth . . . . **12/6**

"A valuable *vade-mecum* for the surveyor. We recommend this book as containing an admirable supplement to the teaching of the accomplished surveyor."—*Athenæum.*

"The author brings to his work a fortunate union of theory and practical experience which, aided by a clear and lucid style of writing, renders the book a very useful one."—*Builder.*

## ENGINEER'S & MINING SURVEYOR'S FIELD BOOK.

Consisting of a Series of Tables, with Rules, Explanations of Systems, and use of Theodolite for Traverse Surveying and plotting the work with minute accuracy by means of Straight Edge and Set Square only; Levelling with the Theodolite, Casting-out and Reducing Levels to Datum, and Plotting Sections in the ordinary manner; Setting-out Curves with the Theodolite by Tangential Angles and Multiples with Right and Left-hand Readings of the Instrument; Setting-out Curves without Theodolite on the System of Tangential Angles by Sets of Tangents and Offsets; and Earthwork Tables to 80 feet deep, calculated for every 6 inches in depth. By W. DAVIS HASKOLL, C.E. With numerous Woodcuts. Fourth Edition, Enlarged. Crown 8vo, cloth . **12/0**

"The book is very handy; the separate tables of sines and tangents to every minute will make it useful for many other purposes, the genuine traverse tables existing all the same."—*Athenæum.*
"Every person engaged in engineering field operations will estimate the importance of such a work and the amount of valuable time which will be saved by reference to a set of reliable tables prepared with the accuracy and fulness of those given in this volume."—*Railway News.*

## LAND AND MARINE SURVEYING.

In Reference to the Preparation of Plans for Roads and Railways; Canals, Rivers, Towns' Water Supplies; Docks and Harbours. With Description and Use of Surveying Instruments. By W. DAVIS HASKOLL, C.E. Second Edition, Revised, with Additions. Large crown 8vo, cloth . . . **9/0**

"This book must prove of great value to the student. We have no hesitation in recommending it, feeling assured that it will more than repay a careful study."—*Mechanical World.*
"A most useful book for the student. We strongly recommend it as a carefully-written and valuable text-book. It enjoys a well-deserved repute among surveyors."—*Builder.*
"This volume cannot fail to prove of the utmost practical utility. It may be safely recommended to all students who aspire to become clean and expert surveyors."—*Mining Journal.*

## PRINCIPLES AND PRACTICE OF LEVELLING.

Showing its Application to Purposes of Railway and Civil Engineering in the Construction of Roads; with Mr. TELFORD'S Rules for the same. By FREDERICK W. SIMMS, F.G.S., M. Inst. C.E. Eighth Edition, with the addition of LAW'S Practical Examples for Setting-out Railway Curves, and TRAUTWINE'S Field Practice of Laying-out Circular Curves. With 7 Plates and numerous Woodcuts, 8vo, cloth . . . . . . . **8/6**
\*\*\* TRAUTWINE on CURVES may be had separate . . . . . **5/0**

"The text-book on levelling in most of our engineering schools and colleges."—*Engineer.*
"The publishers have rendered a substantial service to the profession, especially to the younger members, by bringing out the present edition of Mr. Simms's useful work."—*Engineering.*

## AN OUTLINE OF THE METHOD OF CONDUCTING A TRIGONOMETRICAL SURVEY.

For the Formation of Geographical and Topographical Maps and Plans, Military Reconnaissance, LEVELLING, &c., with Useful Problems, Formulæ, and Tables. By Lieut.-General FROME, R.E. Fourth Edition, Revised and partly Re-written by Major-General Sir CHARLES WARREN, G.C.M.G., R.E. With 19 Plates and 115 Woodcuts, royal 8vo, cloth . . . . **16/0**

"No words of praise from us can strengthen the position so well and so steadily maintained by this work. Sir Charles Warren has revised the entire work, and made such additions as were necessary to bring every portion of the contents up to the present date."—*Broad Arrow.*

## TABLES OF TANGENTIAL ANGLES AND MULTIPLES FOR SETTING-OUT CURVES.

From 5 to 200 Radius. By A. BEAZELEY, M. Inst. C.E. 6th Edition, Revised. With an Appendix on the use of the Tables for Measuring up Curves. Printed on 50 Cards, and sold in a cloth box, waistcoat-pocket size.
[*Just Published.* **3/6**

"Each table is printed on a card, which, placed on the theodolite, leaves the hands free to manipulate the instrument—no small advantage as regards the rapidity of work."—*Engineer.*
"Very handy: a man may know that all his day's work must fall on two of these cards, which he puts into his own card-case, and leaves the rest behind."—*Athenæum.*

## HANDY GENERAL EARTH-WORK TABLES.

Giving the Contents in Cubic Yards of Centre and Slopes of Cuttings and Embankments from 3 inches to 80 feet in Depth or Height, for use with either 66 feet Chain or 100 feet Chain. By J. H. WATSON BUCK, M. Inst. C.E. On a Sheet mounted in cloth case. [*Just Published.* **3/6**

14  *CROSBY LOCKWOOD & SON'S CATALOGUE.*

## EARTHWORK TABLES.
Showing the Contents in Cubic Yards of Embankments, Cuttings, &c., of Heights or Depths up to an average of 80 feet. By JOSEPH BROADBENT, C.E., and FRANCIS CAMPIN, C.E. Crown 8vo, cloth . . . . . . **5/0**
"The way in which accuracy is attained, by a simple division of each cross section into three elements, two in which are constant and one variable, is ingenious."—*Athenæum.*

## A MANUAL ON EARTHWORK.
By ALEX. J. S. GRAHAM, C.E. With numerous Diagrams. Second Edition. 18mo, cloth . . . . . . . . . . . . . . **2/6**

## THE CONSTRUCTION OF LARGE TUNNEL SHAFTS.
A Practical and Theoretical Essay. By J. H. WATSON BUCK, M. Inst. C.E., Resident Engineer, L. and N. W. R. With Folding Plates, 8vo, cloth **12/0**
"Many of the methods given are of extreme practical value to the mason, and the observations on the form of arch, the rules for ordering the stone, and the construction of the templates, will be found of considerable use. We commend the book to the engineering profession."—*Building News.*
"Will be regarded by civil engineers as of the utmost value, and calculated to save much time and obviate many mistakes."—*Colliery Guardian.*

## CAST & WROUGHT IRON BRIDGE CONSTRUCTION
(A Complete and Practical Treatise on), including Iron Foundations. In Three Parts.—Theoretical, Practical, and Descriptive. By WILLIAM HUMBER, A. M. Inst. C.E., and M. Inst. M.E. Third Edition, revised and much improved, with 115 Double Plates (20 of which now first appear in this edition), and numerous Additions to the Text. In 2 vols., imp. 4to, half-bound in morocco . . . . . . . . . . . . . . **£6 16s. 6d.**
"A very valuable contribution to the standard literature of civil engineering. In addition to elevations, plans, and sections, large scale details are given, which very much enhance the instructive worth of those illustrations."—*Civil Engineer and Architect's Journal.*
"Mr. Humber's stately volumes, lately issued—in which the most important bridges erected during the last five years, under the direction of the late Mr. Brunel, Sir W. Cubitt, Mr. Hawkshaw, Mr. Page, Mr. Fowler, Mr. Hemans, and others among our most eminent engineers, are drawn and specified in great detail."—*Engineer.*

## ESSAY ON OBLIQUE BRIDGES
(Practical and Theoretical). With 13 large Plates. By the late GEORGE WATSON BUCK, M.I.C.E. Fourth Edition, revised by his Son, J. H. WATSON BUCK, M.I.C.E.; and with the addition of Description to Diagrams for Facilitating the Construction of Oblique Bridges, by W. H. BARLOW, M.I.C.E. Royal 8vo, cloth . . . . . . . . . . . . . . **12/0**
"The standard text-book for all engineers regarding skew arches is Mr. Buck's treatise, and it would be impossible to consult a better."—*Engineer.*
"Mr. Buck's treatise is recognised as a standard text-book, and his treatment has divested the subject of many of the intricacies supposed to belong to it. As a guide to the engineer and architect, on a confessedly difficult subject, Mr. Buck's work is unsurpassed."—*Building News.*

## THE CONSTRUCTION OF OBLIQUE ARCHES
(A Practical Treatise on). By JOHN HART. Third Edition, with Plates. Imperial 8vo, cloth . . . . . . . . . . . . . . **8/0**

## GRAPHIC AND ANALYTIC STATICS.
In their Practical Application to the Treatment of Stresses in Roofs, Solid Girders, Lattice, Bowstring, and Suspension Bridges, Braced Iron Arches and Piers, and other Frameworks. By R. HUDSON GRAHAM, C.E. Containing Diagrams and Plates to Scale. With numerous Examples, many taken from existing Structures. Specially arranged for Class-work in Colleges and Universities. Second Edition, Revised and Enlarged. 8vo, cloth . **16/0**
"Mr. Graham's book will find a place wherever graphic and analytic statics are used or studied."—*Engineer.*
"The work is excellent from a practical point of view, and has evidently been prepared with much care. The directions for working are simple, and are illustrated by an abundance of well-selected examples. It is an excellent text-book for the practical draughtsman."—*Athenæum.*

## WEIGHTS OF WROUGHT IRON & STEEL GIRDERS.
A Graphic Table for Facilitating the Computation of the Weights of Wrought Iron and Steel Girders, &c., for Parliamentary and other Estimates. By J. H. WATSON BUCK, M. Inst. C.E. On a Sheet . . . . **2/6**

## CIVIL ENGINEERING, SURVEYING, &c. 15

### PRACTICAL GEOMETRY.
For the Architect, Engineer, and Mechanic. Giving Rules for the Delineation and Application of various Geometrical Lines, Figures, and Curves. By E. W. TARN, M.A., Architect. 8vo, cloth . . . . . . . **9/0**

"No book with the same objects in view has ever been published in which the clearness of the rules laid down and the illustrative diagrams have been so satisfactory."—*Scotsman.*

### THE GEOMETRY OF COMPASSES.
Or, Problems Resolved by the mere Description of Circles and the Use of Coloured Diagrams and Symbols. By OLIVER BYRNE. Coloured Plates. Crown 8vo, cloth . . . . . . . . . . **3/6**

### HANDY BOOK FOR THE CALCULATION OF STRAINS
In Girders and Similar Structures and their Strength. Consisting of Formulæ and Corresponding Diagrams, with numerous details for Practical Application, &c. By WILLIAM HUMBER, A. M. Inst. C.E., &c. Fifth Edition. Crown 8vo, with nearly 100 Woodcuts and 3 Plates, cloth . . **7/6**

"The formulæ are neatly expressed, and the diagrams good."—*Athenæum.*
"We heartily commend this really *handy* book to our engineer and architect readers."—*English Mechanic.*

### TRUSSES OF WOOD AND IRON.
Practical Applications of Science in Determining the Stresses, Breaking Weights, Safe Loads, Scantlings, and Details of Construction. With Complete Working Drawings. By WILLIAM GRIFFITHS, Surveyor. 8vo, cloth. **4/6**

"This handy little book enters so minutely into every detail connected with the construction of roof trusses that no student need be ignorant of these matters."—*Practical Engineer.*

### THE STRAINS ON STRUCTURES OF IRONWORK.
With Practical Remarks on Iron Construction. By F. W. SHEILDS, M.I.C.E. 8vo, cloth . . . . . . . . . . . **5/0**

### A TREATISE ON THE STRENGTH OF MATERIALS.
With Rules for Application in Architecture, the Construction of Suspension Bridges, Railways, &c. By PETER BARLOW, F.R.S. A new Edition, revised by his Sons, P. W. BARLOW, F.R.S., and W. H. BARLOW, F.R.S.; to which are added, Experiments by HODGKINSON, FAIRBAIRN, and KIRKALDY; and Formulæ for calculating Girders, &c. Arranged and Edited by WM. HUMBER, A. M. Inst. C.E. 8vo, cloth . . . . . . . . **18/0**

"Valuable alike to the student, tyro, and the experienced practitioner, it will always rank in future as it has hitherto done, as the standard treatise on that particular subject."—*Engineer.*
"As a scientific work of the first class, it deserves a foremost place on the bookshelves of every civil engineer and practical mechanic."—*English Mechanic.*

### STRENGTH OF CAST IRON AND OTHER METALS.
By THOMAS TREDGOLD, C.E. Fifth Edition, including HODGKINSON'S Experimental Researches. 8vo, cloth . . . . . . . **12/0**

### SAFE RAILWAY WORKING.
A Treatise on Railway Accidents, their Cause and Prevention; with a Description of Modern Appliances and Systems. By CLEMENT E. STRETTON, C.E., Vice-President and Consulting Engineer, Amalgamated Society of Railway Servants. With Illustrations and Coloured Plates. Third Edition, Enlarged. Crown 8vo, cloth . . . . . . . . **3/6**

"A book for the engineer, the directors, the managers; and, in short, all who wish for information on railway matters will find a perfect encyclopædia in 'Safe Railway Working.'"— *Railway Review.*
"We commend the remarks on railway signalling to all railway managers, especially where a uniform code and practice is advocated."—*Herepath's Railway Journal.*

### EXPANSION OF STRUCTURES BY HEAT.
By JOHN KEILY, C.E., late of the Indian Public Works Department. Crown 8vo, cloth . . . . . . . . . . . . **3/6**

"The aim the author has set before him, viz., to show the effects of heat upon metallic and other structures, is a laudable one, for this is a branch of physics upon which the engineer or architect can find but little reliable and comprehensive data in books."—*Builder.*

## THE PROGRESS OF MODERN ENGINEERING.

Complete in Four Volumes, imperial 4to, half-morocco, price **£12 12s.**
Each volume sold separately, as follows :—
FIRST SERIES, Comprising Civil, Mechanical, Marine, Hydraulic, Railway, Bridge, and other Engineering Works, &c. By WILLIAM HUMBER, A. M. Inst. C.E., &c. Imp. 4to, with 36 Double Plates, drawn to a large scale, Photographic Portrait of John Hawkshaw, C.E., F.R.S., &c., and copious descriptive Letterpress, Specifications, &c. Half-morocco . . **£3 3s.**

LIST OF THE PLATES AND DIAGRAMS.

VICTORIA STATION AND ROOF, L. B. & S. C. R. (8 PLATES); SOUTHPORT PIER (2 PLATES); VICTORIA STATION AND ROOF, L. C. & D. AND G. W. R. (6 PLATES); ROOF OF CREMORNE MUSIC HALL; BRIDGE OVER G. N. RAILWAY; ROOF OF STATION, DUTCH RHENISH RAIL. (2 PLATES); BRIDGE OVER THE THAMES, WEST LONDON EXTENSION RAILWAY (5 PLATES); ARMOUR PLATES: SUSPENSION BRIDGE, THAMES (4 PLATES); THE ALLEN ENGINE; SUSPENSION BRIDGE, AVON (3 PLATES); UNDERGROUND RAILWAY (3 PLATES).

## HUMBER'S MODERN ENGINEERING.

SECOND SERIES. Imp. 4to, with 3 Double Plates, Photographic Portrait of Robert Stephenson, C.E., M.P., F.R.S., &c., and copious descriptive Letterpress, Specifications, &c. Half-morocco . . . . . . . **£3 3s.**

LIST OF THE PLATES AND DIAGRAMS.

BIRKENHEAD DOCKS, LOW WATER BASIN (15 PLATES); CHARING CROSS STATION ROOF, C. C. RAILWAY (3 PLATES); DIGSWELL VIADUCT, GREAT NORTHERN RAILWAY; ROBBERY WOOD VIADUCT, GREAT NORTHERN RAILWAY; IRON PERMANENT WAY; CLYDACH VIADUCT, MERTHYR, TREDEGAR, AND ABERGAVENNY RAILWAY; EBBW VIADUCT, MERTHYR, TREDEGAR, AND ABERGAVENNY RAILWAY; COLLEGE WOOD VIADUCT, CORNWALL RAILWAY; DUBLIN WINTER PALACE ROOF (3 PLATES); BRIDGE OVER THE THAMES, L. C. & D. RAILWAY (6 PLATES); ALBERT HARBOUR, GREENOCK (4 PLATES).

## HUMBER'S MODERN ENGINEERING.

THIRD SERIES. Imp. 4to, with 40 Double Plates, Photographic Portrait of J. R. M'Clenn, late Pres. Inst. C.E., and copious descriptive Letterpress, Specifications, &c. Half-morocco . . . . . . . **£3 3s.**

LIST OF THE PLATES AND DIAGRAMS.

MAIN DRAINAGE, METROPOLIS.—*North Side*.—MAP SHOWING INTERCEPTION OF SEWERS; MIDDLE LEVEL SEWER (2 PLATES); OUTFALL SEWER, BRIDGE OVER RIVER LEA (3 PLATES); OUTFALL SEWER, BRIDGE OVER MARSH LANE, NORTH WOOLWICH RAILWAY, AND BOW AND BARKING RAILWAY JUNCTION; OUTFALL SEWER, BRIDGE OVER BOW AND BARKING RAILWAY (3 PLATES); OUTFALL SEWER, BRIDGE OVER EAST LONDON WATER-WORKS' FEEDER (2 PLATES); OUTFALL SEWER RESERVOIR (2 PLATES); OUTFALL SEWER, TUMBLING BAY AND OUTLET; OUTFALL SEWER, PENSTOCKS. *South Side*.—OUTFALL SEWER, BERMONDSEY BRANCH (2 PLATES); OUTFALL SEWER, RESERVOIR AND OUTLET (4 PLATES); OUTFALL SEWER, FILTH HOIST; SECTIONS OF SEWERS NORTH AND SOUTH SIDES).
THAMES EMBANKMENT.—SECTION OF RIVER WALL; STEAMBOAT PIER, WESTMINSTER (2 PLATES); LANDING STAIRS BETWEEN CHARING CROSS AND WATERLOO BRIDGES; YORK GATE (2 PLATES); OVERFLOW AND OUTLET AT SAVOY STREET SEWER (3 PLATES); STEAMBOAT PIER, WATERLOO BRIDGE (3 PLATES); JUNCTION OF SEWERS, PLANS AND SECTIONS; GULLIES, PLANS AND SECTIONS; ROLLING STOCK; GRANITE AND IRON FORTS.

## HUMBER'S MODERN ENGINEERING.

FOURTH SERIES. Imp. 4to, with 36 Double Plates, Photographic Portrait of John Fowler, late Pres. Inst. C.E., and copious descriptive Letterpress, Specifications, &c. Half-morocco . . . . . . . **£3 3s.**

LIST OF THE PLATES AND DIAGRAMS.

ABBEY MILLS PUMPING STATION, MAIN DRAINAGE, METROPOLIS (4 PLATES); BARROW DOCKS (5 PLATES); MANQUIS VIADUCT, SANTIAGO AND VALPARAISO RAILWAY, (2 PLATES); ADAM'S LOCOMOTIVE, ST. HELEN'S CANAL RAILWAY (2 PLATES); CANNON STREET STATION ROOF, CHARING CROSS RAILWAY (3 PLATES); ROAD BRIDGE OVER THE RIVER MOKA (2 PLATES); TELEGRAPHIC APPARATUS FOR MESOPOTAMIA; VIADUCT OVER THE RIVER WYE, MIDLAND RAILWAY (3 PLATES); ST. GERMANS VIADUCT, CORNWALL RAILWAY (2 PLATES); WROUGHT-IRON CYLINDER FOR DIVING BELL; MILLWALL DOCKS (6 PLATES); MILROY'S PATENT EXCAVATOR; METROPOLITAN DISTRICT RAILWAY (6 PLATES); HARBOURS, PORTS, AND BREAKWATERS (3 PLATES).

# MARINE ENGINEERING, SHIPBUILDING, NAVIGATION, &c.

### THE NAVAL ARCHITECT'S AND SHIPBUILDER'S
POCKET-BOOK of Formulæ, Rules, and Tables, and Marine Engineer's and Surveyor's Handy Book of Reference. By CLEMENT MACKROW, M.I.N.A. Seventh Edition, 700 pp., with 300 Illustrations. Fcap., leather . . **12/6**

SUMMARY OF CONTENTS:—SIGNS AND SYMBOLS, DECIMAL FRACTIONS.—TRIGONOMETRY.—PRACTICAL GEOMETRY.—MENSURATION.—CENTRES AND MOMENTS OF FIGURES. —MOMENTS OF INERTIA AND RADII OF GYRATION.—ALGEBRAICAL EXPRESSIONS FOR SIMPSON'S RULES.—MECHANICAL PRINCIPLES.—CENTRE OF GRAVITY.—LAWS OF MOTION. —DISPLACEMENT, CENTRE OF BUOYANCY.—CENTRE OF GRAVITY OF SHIP'S HULL.— STABILITY CURVES AND METACENTRES.—SEA AND SHALLOW-WATER WAVES.—ROLLING OF SHIPS.—PROPULSION AND RESISTANCE OF VESSELS.—SPEED TRIALS.—SAILING, CENTRE OF EFFORT.—DISTANCES DOWN RIVERS, COAST LINES.—STEERING AND RUDDERS OF VESSELS.—LAUNCHING CALCULATIONS AND VELOCITIES.—WEIGHT OF MATERIAL AND GEAR.—GUN PARTICULARS AND WEIGHT.—STANDARD GAUGES.— RIVETED JOINTS AND RIVETING.—STRENGTH AND TESTS OF MATERIALS.—BINDING AND SHEARING STRESSES, &c.—STRENGTH OF SHAFTING, PILLARS, WHEELS, &c. —HYDRAULIC DATA, &c.—CONIC SECTIONS, CATENARIAN CURVES.—MECHANICAL POWERS, WORK.—BOARD OF TRADE REGULATIONS FOR BOILERS AND ENGINES.—BOARD OF TRADE REGULATIONS FOR SHIPS.—LLOYD'S RULES FOR BOILERS.—LLOYD'S WEIGHT OF CHAINS.—LLOYD'S SCANTLINGS FOR SHIPS.—DATA OF ENGINES AND VESSELS.— SHIPS' FITTINGS AND TESTS.—SEASONING PRESERVING TIMBER.—MEASUREMENT OF TIMBER.—ALLOYS, PAINTS, VARNISHES.—DATA FOR STOWAGE.—ADMIRALTY TRANSPORT REGULATIONS.—RULES FOR HORSE-POWER, SCREW PROPELLERS, &c.—PERCENTAGES FOR BUTT STRAPS, &c.—PARTICULARS OF YACHTS.—MASTING AND RIGGING VESSELS.—DISTANCES OF FOREIGN PORTS.—TONNAGE TABLES.—VOCABULARY OF FRENCH AND ENGLISH TERMS. — ENGLISH WEIGHTS AND MEASURES. — FOREIGN WEIGHTS AND MEASURES.—DECIMAL EQUIVALENTS.—FOREIGN MONEY.—DISCOUNT AND WAGES TABLES.—USEFUL NUMBERS AND READY RECKONERS.—TABLES OF CIRCULAR MEASURES.—TABLES OF AREAS OF AND CIRCUMFERENCES OF CIRCLES.— TABLES OF AREAS OF SEGMENTS OF CIRCLES.—TABLES OF SQUARES AND CUBES AND ROOTS OF NUMBERS.—TABLES OF LOGARITHMS OF NUMBERS.—TABLES OF HYPERBOLIC LOGARITHMS.—TABLES OF NATURAL SINES, TANGENTS, &c.—TABLES OF LOGARITHMIC SINES, TANGENTS, &c.

"In these days of advanced knowledge a work like this is of the greatest value. It contains a vast amount of information. We unhesitatingly say that it is the most valuable compilation for its specific purpose that has ever been printed. No naval architect, engineer, surveyor, or seaman, wood or iron shipbuilder, can afford to be without this work."—*Nautical Magazine.*

"Should be used by all who are engaged in the construction or design of vessels. . . . Will be found to contain the most useful tables and formulæ required by shipbuilders, carefully collected from the best authorities, and put together in a popular and simple form. The book is one of exceptional merit."—*Engineer.*

"The professional shipbuilder has now, in a convenient and accessible form, reliable data for solving many of the numerous problems that present themselves in the course of his work."—*Iron.*

"There is no doubt that a pocket-book of this description must be a necessity in the shipbuilding trade. . . The volume contains a mass of useful information clearly expressed and presented in a handy form."—*Marine Engineer.*

### WANNAN'S MARINE ENGINEER'S GUIDE
To Board of Trade Examinations for Certificates of Competency. Containing all Latest Questions to Date, with Simple, Clear, and Correct Solutions; Elementary and Verbal Questions and Answers; complete Set of Drawings with Statements completed. By A. C. WANNAN, C.E., and E. W. I. WANNAN, M.I.M.E. Illustrated with numerous Engravings. Crown 8vo, 370 pages, cloth. **8/6**

"The book is clearly and plainly written and avoids unnecessary explanations and formulas and we consider it a valuable book for students of marine engineering."—*Nautical Magazine.*

### WANNAN'S MARINE ENGINEER'S POCKET-BOOK.
Containing the Latest Board of Trade Rules and Data for Marine Engineers. By A. C. WANNAN. Second Edition, carefully Revised. Square 18mo, with thumb Index, leather. **5/0**

"There is a great deal of useful information in this little pocket-book. It is of the rule-of-thumb order, and is, on that account, well adapted to the uses of the sea-going engineer."— *Engineer.*

### MARINE ENGINES AND STEAM VESSELS.
A Treatise on. By ROBERT MURRAY, C.E. Eighth Edition, thoroughly Revised, with considerable Additions by the Author and by GEORGE CARLISLE, C.E., Senior Surveyor to the Board of Trade. 12mo, cloth **4/6**

18   CROSBY LOCKWOOD & SON'S CATALOGUE.

## SEA TERMS, PHRASES, AND WORDS

(Technical Dictionary of) used in the English and French Languages (English-French, French-English). For the Use of Seamen, Engineers, Pilots, Shipbuilders, Shipowners, and Ship-brokers. Compiled by W. PIRRIE, late of the African Steamship Company. Fcap. 8vo, cloth limp . . . **5/0**

"This volume will be highly appreciated by seamen, engineers, pilots, shipbuilders and shipowners. It will be found wonderfully accurate and complete."—*Scotsman.*

"A very useful dictionary, which has long been wanted by French and English engineers, masters, officers and others."—*Shipping World.*

## ELECTRIC SHIP-LIGHTING.

A Handbook on the Practical Fitting and Running of Ships' Electrical Plant, for the Use of Shipowners and Builders, Marine Electricians and Sea-going Engineers in Charge. By J. W. URQUHART, Author of "Electric Light," "Dynamo Construction," &c. Second Edition, Revised and Extended. 326 pp., with 88 Illustrations. Crown 8vo, cloth.  [*Just Published.* **7/6**

## MARINE ENGINEER'S POCKET-BOOK.

Consisting of useful Tables and Formulæ. By FRANK PROCTOR, A.I.N.A. Third Edition. Royal 32mo, leather, gilt edges, with strap . . . **4/0**

"We recommend it to our readers as going far to supply a long-felt want."—*Naval Science.*
"A most useful companion to all marine engineers."—*United Service Gazette.*

## ELEMENTARY ENGINEERING.

A Manual for Young Marine Engineers and Apprentices. In the Form of Questions and Answers on Metals, Alloys, Strength of Materials, Construction and Management of Marine Engines and Boilers, Geometry, &c., &c. With an Appendix of Useful Tables. By J. S. BREWER. Crown 8vo, cloth . **1/6**

"Contains much valuable information for the class for whom it is intended, especially in the chapters on the management of boilers and engines."—*Nautical Magazine.*

## PRACTICAL NAVIGATION.

Consisting of THE SAILOR'S SEA-BOOK, by JAMES GREENWOOD and W. H. ROSSER; together with the exquisite Mathematical and Nautical Tables for the Working of the Problems, by HENRY LAW, C.E., and Professor J. R. YOUNG. Illustrated.  12mo, strongly half-bound . . . . . **7/0**

## MARINE ENGINEER'S DRAWING-BOOK.

Adapted to the Requirements of the Board of Trade Examinations. By JOHN LOCKIE, C.E. With 22 Plates, Drawn to Scale. Royal 8vo, cloth . **3/6**

## THE ART AND SCIENCE OF SAILMAKING.

By SAMUEL B. SADLER, Practical Sailmaker, late in the employment of Messrs. Ratsey and Lapthorne, of Cowes and Gosport. With Plates and other Illustrations. Small 4to, cloth . . . . . . . . **12/6**

"This extremely practical work gives a complete education in all the branches of the manufacture; cutting out, roping, seaming, and goring. It is copiously illustrated, and will form a first-rate text-book and guide."—*Portsmouth Times.*

## CHAIN CABLES AND CHAINS.

Comprising Sizes and Curves of Links, Studs, &c., Iron for Cables and Chains, Chain Cable and Chain Making, Forming and Welding Links, Strength of Cables and Chains, Certificates for Cables, Marking Cables, Prices of Chain Cables and Chains, Historical Notes, Acts of Parliament, Statutory Tests, Charges for Testing, List of Manufacturers of Cables, &c., &c. By THOMAS W. TRAILL, F.E.R.N., M.Inst.C.E., Engineer-Surveyor-in-Chief, Board of Trade, Inspector of Chain Cable and Anchor Proving Establishments, and General Superintendent Lloyd's Committee on Proving Establishments. With numerous Tables, Illustrations, and Lithographic Drawings. Folio, cloth, bevelled boards . . . . . . . . . . **£2 2s.**

"It contains a vast amount of valuable information. Nothing seems to be wanting to make it a complete and standard work of reference on the subject."—*Nautical Magazine.*

## MINING, METALLURGY, AND COLLIERY WORKING.

### THE METALLURGY OF GOLD.
A Practical Treatise on the Metallurgical Treatment of Gold-bearing Ores. Including the Assaying, Melting, and Refining of Gold. By M. EISSLER, Mining Engineer, A.I.M.E., Member of the Institute of Mining and Metallurgy. Author of "Modern High Explosives," "The Metallurgy of Silver," &c., &c. Fifth Edition, Enlarged and Re-arranged. With over 300 illustrations and numerous Folding Plates, Medium 8vo, cloth.
[*Just Published. Net* **21/0**
"This book thoroughly deserves its title of a 'Practical Treatise.' The whole process of gold milling, from the breaking of the quartz to the assay of the bullion, is described in clear and orderly narrative and with much, but not too much, fulness of detail."—*Saturday Review*.
"The work is a storehouse of information and valuable data, and we strongly recommend it to all professional men engaged in the gold-mining industry."—*Mining Journal*.

### THE CYANIDE PROCESS OF GOLD EXTRACTION.
Including its Practical Application on the Witwatersrand Gold Fields in South Africa. By M. EISSLER, M.E., Author of "The Metallurgy of Gold," &c. With Diagrams and Working Drawings. Second Edition, Revised and Enlarged. 8vo, cloth. **7/6**
"This book is just what was needed to acquaint mining men with the actual working of a process which is not only the most popular, but is, as a general rule, the most successful for the extraction of gold from tailings."—*Mining Journal*.
"The work will prove invaluable to all interested in gold mining, whether metallurgists or as investors."—*Chemical News*.

### DIAMOND DRILLING FOR GOLD & OTHER MINERALS.
A Practical Handbook on the Use of Modern Diamond Core Drills in Prospecting and Exploiting Mineral-Bearing Properties, including Particulars of the Costs of Apparatus and Working. By G. A. DENNY, M.N.E. Inst. M.E., M.I.M. and M. Author of "The Klerksdorp Goldfields." Medium 8vo, 168 pp., with Illustrative Diagrams. [*Just Published*. **12/6**
"There is certainly scope for a work on diamond drilling, and Mr. Denny deserves grateful recognition for supplying a decided want. We strongly recommend every board of directors to carefully peruse the pages treating of the applicability of diamond drilling to auriferous deposits, and, under certain conditions, its advantages over shaft sinking for systematic prospecting, both from the surface and underground. The author has given us a valuable volume of eminently practical data that should be in the possession of those interested in mining."—*Mining Journal*.
"Mr. Denny's handbook is the first English work to give a detailed account of the use of modern diamond core-drills in searching for mineral deposits. The work contains much information of a practical character, including particulars of the cost of apparatus and of working."—*Nature*.

### FIELD TESTING FOR GOLD AND SILVER.
A Practical Manual for Prospectors and Miners. By W. H. MERRITT, M.N.E. Inst. M.E., A.R.S.M., &c. With Photographic Plates and other Illustrations. Fcap. 8vo, leather. [*Just Published. Net* **5/0**
"As an instructor of prospectors' classes Mr. Merritt has the advantage of knowing exactly the information likely to be most valuable to the miner in the field. The contents cover all the details of sampling and testing gold and silver ores. The work will be a useful addition to a prospector's kit."—*Mining Journal*.
"It gives the gist of the author's experience as a teacher of prospectors, and is a book which no prospector could use habitually without finding it pan out well."—*Scotsman*.

### THE PROSPECTOR'S HANDBOOK.
A Guide for the Prospector and Traveller in search of Metal-Bearing or other Valuable Minerals. By J. W. ANDERSON, M.A. (Camb.), F.R.G.S., Author of "Fiji and New Caledonia." Eighth Edition, thoroughly Revised and much Enlarged. Small crown 8vo, cloth, **3/6** ; or, leather, pocket-book form, with tuck. [*Just Published*. **4/6**
"Will supply a much-felt want, especially among Colonists, in whose way are so often thrown many mineralogical specimens the value of which it is difficult to determine."—*Engineer*.
"How to find commercial minerals, and how to identify them when they are found, are the leading points to which attention is directed. The author has managed to pack as much practical detail into his pages as would supply material for a book three times its size."—*Mining Journal*.

20   CROSBY LOCKWOOD & SON'S CATALOGUE.

## THE METALLURGY OF SILVER.

A Practical Treatise on the Amalgamation, Roasting, and Lixiviation of Silver Ores. Including the Assaying, Melting, and Refining of Silver Bullion. By M. EISSLER, Author of "The Metallurgy of Gold," &c. Third Edition. Crown 8vo, cloth . . . . . . . . . . . **10/6**

"A practical treatise, and a technical work which we are convinced will supply a long-felt want amongst practical men, and at the same time be of value to students and others indirectly connected with the industries."—*Mining Journal.*
"From first to last the book is thoroughly sound and reliable."—*Colliery Guardian.*
"For chemists, practical miners, assayers, and investors alike we do not know of any work on the subject so handy and yet so comprehensive."—*Glasgow Herald.*

## THE METALLURGY OF ARGENTIFEROUS LEAD.

A Practical Treatise on the Smelting of Silver-Lead Ores and the Refining of Lead Bullion. Including Reports on various Smelting Establishments and Descriptions of Modern Smelting Furnaces and Plants in Europe and America. By M. EISSLER, M.E., Author of "The Metallurgy of Gold," &c. Crown 8vo, 400 pp., with 183 Illustrations, cloth . . . . . . . **12/6**

"The numerous metallurgical processes, which are fully and extensively treated of, embrace all the stages experienced in the passage of the lead from the various natural states to its issue from the refinery as an article of commerce."—*Practical Engineer.*
"The present volume fully maintains the reputation of the author. Those who wish to obtain a thorough insight into the present state of this industry cannot do better than read this volume, and all mining engineers cannot fail to find many useful hints and suggestions in it."—*Industries.*

## METALLIFEROUS MINERALS AND MINING.

By D. C. DAVIES, F.G.S., Mining Engineer, &c., Author of "A Treatise on Slate and Slate Quarrying." Fifth Edition, thoroughly Revised and much Enlarged by his Son, E. HENRY DAVIES, M.E., F.G.S. With about 150 Illustrations. Crown 8vo, cloth . . . . . . . . **12/6**

"Neither the practical miner nor the general reader, interested in mines, can have a better book for his companion and his guide."—*Mining Journal.*
"We are doing our readers a service in calling their attention to this valuable work."—*Mining World.*
"As a history of the present state of mining throughout the world this book has a real value and it supplies an actua want."—*Athenæum.*

## MACHINERY FOR METALLIFEROUS MINES.

A Practical Treatise for Mining Engineers, Metallurgists, and Managers of Mines. By E. HENRY DAVIES, M.E., F.G.S. Crown 8vo, 580 pp., with upwards of 300 Illustrations, cloth. . . . . . . . . **12/6**

"Mr. Davies, in this handsome volume, has done the advanced student and the manager of mines good service. Almost every kind of machinery in actual use is carefully described, and the woodcuts and plates are good."—*Athenæum.*
"From cover to cover the work exhibits all the same characteristics which excite the confidence and attract the attention of the student as he peruses the first page. The work may safely be recommended. By its publication the literature connected with the industry will be enriched and the reputation of its author enhanced."—*Mining Journal.*

## EARTHY AND OTHER MINERALS AND MINING.

By D. C. DAVIES, F.G.S., Author of "Metalliferous Minerals," &c. Third Edition, Revised and Enlarged by his Son, E. HENRY DAVIES, M.E., F.G.S With about 100 Illustrations. Crown 8vo, cloth . . . . . **12/6**

"We do not remember to have met with any English work on mining matters that contains the same amount of information packed in equally convenient form."—*Academy.*
"We should be inclined to rank it as among the very best of the handy technical and trades manuals which have recently appeared."—*British Quarterly Review.*

## BRITISH MINING.

A Treatise on the History, Discovery, Practical Development, and Future Prospects of Metalliferous Mines in the United Kingdom. By ROBERT HUNT, F.R.S., late Keeper of Mining Records. Upwards of 950 pp., with 230 Illustrations. Second Edition, Revised. Super-royal 8vo, cloth **£2 2s.**

"The book is a treasure-house of statistical information on mining subjects, and we know of no other work embodying so great a mass of matter of this kind. Were this the only merit of Mr. Hunt's volume it would be sufficient to render it indispensable in the library of every one interested in the development of the mining and metallurgical industries of this country."—*Athenæum.*

MINING, METALLURGY, & COLLIERY WORKING. 21

## POCKET-BOOK FOR MINERS AND METALLURGISTS.
Comprising Rules, Formulæ, Tables, and Notes for Use in Field and Office Work. By F. DANVERS POWER, F.G.S., M.E. Second Edition, Corrected. Fcap. 8vo, leather. [*Just Published.* **9/0**
"This excellent book is an admirable example of its kind, and ought to find a large sale amongst English-speaking prospectors and mining engineers."—*Engineering.*

## THE MINER'S HANDBOOK.
A Handy Book of Reference on the subjects of Mineral Deposits, Mining Operations, Ore Dressing, &c. For the Use of Students and others interested in Mining Matters. By JOHN MILNE, F.R.S., Professor of Mining in the Imperial University of Japan. Revised Edition. Fcap. 8vo, leather . **7/6**
"Professor Milne's handbook is sure to be received with favour by all connected with mining, and will be extremely popular among students."—*Athenæum.*

## THE IRON ORES of GREAT BRITAIN and IRELAND.
Their Mode of Occurrence, Age and Origin, and the Methods of Searching for and Working Them. With a Notice of some of the Iron Ores of Spain. By J. D. KENDALL, F.G.S., Mining Engineer. Crown 8vo, cloth . . **16/0**
"The author has a thorough practical knowledge of his subject, and has supplemented a careful study of the available literature by unpublished information derived from his own observations. The result is a very useful volume, which cannot fail to be of value to all interested in the iron industry of the country."—*Industries.*

## MINE DRAINAGE.
A Complete Practical Treatise on Direct-Acting Underground Steam Pumping Machinery. By STEPHEN MICHELL. Second Edition, Re-written and Enlarged, 390 pp. With about 250 Illustrations. Royal 8vo, cloth.
[*Just Published.* Net **25/0**
SUMMARY OF CONTENTS:—HORIZONTAL PUMPING ENGINES.—ROTARY AND NON-ROTARY HORIZONTAL ENGINES.—SIMPLE AND COMPOUND STEAM PUMPS.—VERTICAL PUMPING ENGINES.—ROTARY AND NON-ROTARY VERTICAL ENGINES.—SIMPLE AND COMPOUND STEAM PUMPS.—TRIPLE-EXPANSION STEAM PUMPS.—PULSATING STEAM PUMPS.—PUMP VALVES.—SINKING PUMPS, &c., &c.
"This volume contains an immense amount of important and interesting new matter. The book should undoubtedly prove of great use to all who wish for information on the subject, inasmuch as the different patterns of steam pumps are not alone lucidly described and clearly illustrated, but in addition numerous tables are supplied, in which their sizes, capacity, price, &c., are set forth, hence facilitating immensely the rational selection of a pump to suit any purpose that the reader may desire, or, on the other hand, supplying him with useful information about any of the pumps that come within the scope of the volume."—*The Engineer.*

## THE COLLIERY MANAGER'S HANDBOOK.
A Comprehensive Treatise on the Laying-out and Working of Collieries, Designed as a Book of Reference for Colliery Managers, and for the Use of Coal Mining Students preparing for First-class Certificates. By CALEB PAMELY, Mining Engineer and Surveyor; Member of the North of England Institute of Mining and Mechanical Engineers; and Member of the South Wales Institute of Mining Engineers. With 700 Plans, Diagrams, and other Illustrations. Fourth Edition, Revised and Enlarged, medium 8vo, over 900 pp. Strongly bound . . . . . . . . . . **£1 5s.**
SUMMARY OF CONTENTS:—GEOLOGY.—SEARCH FOR COAL.—MINERAL LEASES AND OTHER HOLDINGS.—SHAFT SINKING.—FITTING UP THE SHAFT AND SURFACE ARRANGEMENTS.—STEAM BOILERS AND THEIR FITTINGS.—TIMBERING AND WALLING.—NARROW WORK AND METHODS OF WORKING. — UNDERGROUND CONVEYANCE. —DRAINAGE.—THE GASES MET WITH IN MINES; VENTILATION.—ON THE FRICTION OF AIR IN MINES.—THE PRIESTMAN OIL ENGINE; PETROLEUM AND NATURAL GAS.—SURVEYING AND PLANNING.—SAFETY LAMPS AND FIREDAMP DETECTORS.—SUNDRY AND INCIDENTAL OPERATIONS AND APPLIANCES.—COLLIERY EXPLOSIONS.—MISCELLANEOUS QUESTIONS AND ANSWERS.—*Appendix:* SUMMARY OF REPORT OF H.M. COMMISSIONERS ON ACCIDENTS IN MINES.

"Mr. Pamely has not only given us a comprehensive reference book of a very high order, suitable to the requirements of mining engineers and colliery managers, but has also provided mining students with a class-book that is as interesting as it is instructive."—*Colliery Manager.*
"Mr. Pamely's work is eminently suited to the purpose for which it is intended, being clear, interesting, exhaustive, rich in detail, and up to date, giving descriptions of the latest machines in every department. A mining engineer could scarcely go wrong who followed this work."—*Colliery Guardian.*
"This is the most complete 'all-round' work on coal-mining published in the English language. . . . No library of coal-mining books is complete without it."—*Colliery Engineer* (Scranton, Pa., U.S.A.).

22     CROSBY LOCKWOOD & SON'S CATALOGUE.

## COLLIERY WORKING AND MANAGEMENT.

Comprising the Duties of a Colliery Manager, the Oversight and Arrangement of Labour and Wages, and the different Systems of Working Coal Seams. By H. F. BULMAN and R. A. S. REDMAYNE. 350 pp., with 28 Plates and other Illustrations, including Underground Photographs. Medium 8vo, cloth.     [*Just Published.*  **15/0**

"This is, indeed, an admirable Handbook for Colliery Managers, in fact it is an indispensable adjunct to a Colliery Manager's education, as well as being a most useful and interesting work on the subject for all who in any way have to do with coal mining. The underground photographs are an attractive feature of the work, being very lifelike and necessarily true representations of the scenes they depict."—*Colliery Guardian.*

"Mr. Bulman and Mr. Redmayne, who are both experienced Colliery Managers of great literary ability, are to be congratulated on having supplied an authoritative work dealing with a side of the subject of coal mining which has hitherto received but scant treatment. The authors elucidate their text by 119 woodcuts and 28 plates, most of the latter being admirable reproductions of photographs taken underground with the aid of the magnesium flash-light. These illustrations are excellent."—*Nature.*

## COAL AND COAL MINING.

By the late Sir WARINGTON W. SMYTH, F.R.S., Chief Inspector of the Mines of the Crown. Eighth Edition, Revised and Extended by T. FORSTER BROWN, Mining Engineer, Chief Inspector of the Mines of the Crown and of the Duchy of Cornwall. Crown 8vo, cloth.     [*Just Published.*  **3/6**

"As an outline is given of every known coal-field in this and other countries, as well as of the principal methods of working, the book will doubtless interest a very large number of readers."—*Mining Journal.*

## NOTES AND FORMULÆ FOR MINING STUDENTS.

By JOHN HERMAN MERIVALE, M.A., Late Professor of Mining in the Durham College of Science, Newcastle-upon-Tyne. Fourth Edition, Revised and Enlarged. By H. F. BULMAN, A.M.Inst.C.E. Small crown 8vo, cloth.  **2/6**

"The author has done his work in a creditable manner, and has produced a book that will be of service to students and those who are practically engaged in mining operations."—*Engineer.*

## INFLAMMABLE GAS AND VAPOUR IN THE AIR

(The Detection and Measurement of). By FRANK CLOWES, D.Sc., Lond., F.I.C., Prof. of Chemistry in the University College, Nottingham. With a Chapter on THE DETECTION AND MEASUREMENT OF PETROLEUM VAPOUR by BOVERTON REDWOOD, F.R.S.E., Consulting Adviser to the Corporation of London under the Petroleum Acts. Crown 8vo, cloth.     *Net* **5/0**

"Professor Clowes has given us a volume on a subject of much industrial importance . . . Those interested in these matters may be recommended to study this book, which is easy of comprehension and contains many good things."—*The Engineer.*

"A book that no mining engineer—certainly no coal miner—can afford to ignore or to leave unread."—*Mining Journal.*

## COAL & IRON INDUSTRIES of the UNITED KINGDOM.

Comprising a Description of the Coal Fields, and of the Principal Seams of Coal, with Returns of their Produce and its Distribution, and Analyses of Special Varieties. Also, an Account of the Occurrence of Iron Ores in Veins or Seams; Analyses of each Variety; and a History of the Rise and Progress of Pig Iron Manufacture. By RICHARD MEADE. 8vo, cloth .   . **£1 8s.**

"Of this book we may unreservedly say that it is the best of its class which we have ever met. . . . A book of reference which no one engaged in the iron or coal trades should omit from his library."—*Iron and Coal Trades Review.*

## ASBESTOS AND ASBESTIC.

Their Properties, Occurrence, and Use. By ROBERT H. JONES, F.S.A., Mineralogist, Hon. Mem. Asbestos Club, Black Lake, Canada. With Ten Collotype Plates and other Illustrations. Demy 8vo, cloth.
    [*Just Published.*  **16/0**

"An interesting and invaluable work."—*Colliery Guardian.*

## GRANITES AND OUR GRANITE INDUSTRIES.

By GEORGE F. HARRIS, F.G.S., Membre de la Société Belge de Géologie, Lecturer on Economic Geology at the Birkbeck Institution, &c. With Illustrations. Crown 8vo, cloth   .    .    .    .    .    .    .    .    .    **2/6**

"A clearly and well-written manual for persons engaged or interested in the granite industry."—*Scotsman.*

## TRAVERSE TABLES.

For use in Mine Surveying. By W. LINTERN, Mining Engineer. Crown 8vo, cloth.     [*Just Published.* *Net* **3/0**

# ELECTRICITY, ELECTRICAL ENGINEERING, &c.

### SUBMARINE TELEGRAPHS.
Their History, Construction, and Working. Founded in part on WÜNSCHEN-DORFF's "Traité de Télégraphie Sous-Marine," and Compiled from Authoritative and Exclusive Sources. By CHARLES BRIGHT, F.R.S.E. Super-royal 8vo, about 780 pp., fully Illustrated, including Maps and Folding Plates
[*Just Published. Net* **£3 3s.**

"There are few, if any, persons more fitted to write a treatise on submarine telegraphy than Mr. Charles Bright. The author has done his work admirably, and has written in a way which will appeal as much to the layman as to the engineer. This admirable volume must, for many years to come, hold the position of the English classic on submarine telegraphy."—*Engineer.*

"This book is full of information. It makes a book of reference which should be in every engineer's library."—*Nature.*

"Mr. Bright's interestingly written and admirably illustrated book will meet with a welcome reception from cable men."—*Electrician.*

"The author deals with his subject from all points of view—political and strategical as well as scientific. The work will be of interest, not only to men of science, but to the general public. We can strongly recommend it."—*Athenæum.*

"The work contains a great store of technical information concerning the making and working of submarine telegraphs. In bringing together the most valuable results relating to the evolution of the telegraph, the author has rendered a service that will be very widely appreciated."—*Morning Post.*

### THE ELECTRICAL ENGINEER'S POCKET-BOOK.
Consisting of Modern Rules, Formulæ, Tables, and Data. By H. R. KEMPE, M.Inst.E.E., A.M.Inst.C.E., Technical Officer Postal Telegraphs, Author of "A Handbook of Electrical Testing," "The Engineer's Year-Book," &c. Second Edition, thoroughly Revised, with Additions. With numerous Illustrations. Royal 32mo, oblong, leather . . . . . . . **5/0**

"It is the best book of its kind."—*Electrical Engineer.*
"The Electrical Engineer's Pocket-Book is a good one."—*Electrician.*
"Strongly recommended to those engaged in the electrical industries."—*Electrical Review.*

### ELECTRIC LIGHT FITTING.
A Handbook for Working Electrical Engineers, embodying Practical Notes on Installation Management. By J. W. URQUHART, Electrician, Author of "Electric Light," &c. With numerous Illustrations. Third Edition, Revised, with Additions. Crown 8vo, cloth. [*Just Published.* **5/0**

"This volume deals with what may be termed the mechanics of electric lighting, and is addressed to men who are already engaged in the work, or are training for it. The work traverses a great deal of ground, and may be read as a sequel to the same author's useful work on 'Electric Light.'"—*Electrician.*

"Eminently practical and useful. . . . Ought to be in the hands of every one in charge of an electric light plant."—*Electrical Engineer.*

### ELECTRIC LIGHT.
Its Production and Use, Embodying Plain Directions for the Treatment of Dynamo-Electric Machines, Batteries, Accumulators, and Electric Lamps. By J. W. URQUHART, C.E. Sixth Edition, Revised, with Additions and 145 Illustrations. Crown 8vo, cloth. [*Just Published.* **7/6**

"The whole ground of electric lighting is more or less covered and explained in a very clear and concise manner."—*Electrical Review.*

"A *vade-mecum* of the salient facts connected with the science of electric lighting."—*Electrician.*

"You cannot for your purpose have a better book than 'Electric Light' by Urquhart."—*Engineer.*

### DYNAMO CONSTRUCTION.
A Practical Handbook for the Use of Engineer-Constructors and Electricians-in-Charge. Embracing Framework Building, Field Magnet and Armature Winding and Grouping, Compounding, &c. With Examples of leading English, American, and Continental Dynamos and Motors. By J. W. URQUHART, Author of "Electric Light," &c. Second Edition, Enlarged. With 114 Illustrations. Crown 8vo, cloth . . . . . . **7/6**

"Mr. Urquhart's book is the first one which deals with these matters in such a way that the engineering student can understand them. The book is very readable, and the author leads his readers up to difficult subjects by reasonably simple tests."—*Engineering Review.*

"A book for which a demand has long existed."—*Mechanical World.*

24   CROSBY LOCKWOOD & SON'S CATALOGUE.

## THE MANAGEMENT OF DYNAMOS.

A Handy Book of Theory and Practice for the Use of Mechanics, Engineers, Students, and others in Charge of Dynamos. By G. W. LUMMIS-PATERSON. Second Edition, thoroughly Revised and Enlarged. With numerous Illustrations. Crown 8vo, cloth.   [*Just Published.*  **4/6**

"An example which deserves to be taken as a model by other authors. The subject is treated in a manner which any intelligent man who is fit to be entrusted with charge of an engine should be able to understand. It is a useful book to all who make, tend, or employ electric machinery."—*Architect.*

## THE STANDARD ELECTRICAL DICTIONARY.

A Popular Encyclopædia of Words and Terms Used in the Practice of Electrical Engineering. By T. O'CONOR SLOANE, A.M., Ph.D. Second Edition, with Appendix to date. Crown 8vo, 680 pp., 390 Illustrations, cloth.
[*Just Published.*  **7/6**

"The work has many attractive features in it, and is, beyond doubt, a well put together and useful publication. The amount of ground covered may be gathered from the fact that in the index about 5,600 references will be found."—*Electrical Review.*

## ELECTRIC SHIP-LIGHTING.

A Handbook on the Practical Fitting and Running of Ships' Electrical Plant. For the Use of Shipowners and Builders, Marine Electricians, and Seagoing Engineers-in-Charge. By J. W. URQUHART, C.E. Second Edition, Revised and Extended. 326 pp., with 88 Illustrations, Crown 8vo, cloth.
[*Just Published.*  **7/6**

"The subject of ship electric lighting is one of vast importance, and Mr. Urquhart is to be highly complimented for placing such a valuable work at the service of marine electricians."—*The Steamship.*

## ELECTRIC LIGHT FOR COUNTRY HOUSES.

A Practical Handbook on the Erection and Running of Small Installations, with Particulars of the Cost of Plant and Working. By J. H. KNIGHT. Second Edition, Revised. Crown 8vo, wrapper.   [*Just Published.*  **1/0**

"The book contains excellent advice and many practical hints for the help of those who wish to light their own houses."—*Building News.*

## ELECTRIC LIGHTING (ELEMENTARY PRINCIPLES OF).

By ALAN A. CAMPBELL SWINTON, M.Inst.C.E., M.Inst.E.E. Fourth Edition, Revised. With 16 Illustrations. Crown 8vo, cloth.   [*Just Published.*  **1/6**

"Any one who desires a short and thoroughly clear exposition of the elementary principles of electric lighting cannot do better than read this little work."—*Bradford Observer.*

## DYNAMIC ELECTRICITY AND MAGNETISM.

By PHILIP ATKINSON, A.M., Ph.D., Author of "Elements of Static Electricity," &c. Crown 8vo, 417 pp., with 120 Illustrations, cloth  .  **10/6**

## POWER TRANSMITTED BY ELECTRICITY

And applied by the Electric Motor, including Electric Railway Construction. By P. ATKINSON, A.M., Ph.D. With 96 Illustrations. Crown 8vo, cloth  **7/6**

## HOW TO MAKE A DYNAMO.

A Practical Treatise for Amateurs. Containing numerous Illustrations and Detailed Instructions for Constructing a Small Dynamo to Produce the Electric Light. By ALFRED CROFTS. Sixth Edition, Revised and Enlarged. Crown 8vo, cloth.   [*Just Published.*  **2/0**

"The instructions given in this unpretentious little book are sufficiently clear and explicit to enable any amateur mechanic possessed of average skill and the usual tools to be found in an amateur's workshop to build a practical dynamo machine."—*Electrician.*

## THE STUDENT'S TEXT-BOOK OF ELECTRICITY.

By H. M. NOAD, F.R.S. Cheaper Edition. 650 pp., with 470 Illustrations. Crown 8vo, cloth   .   .   .   .   .   .   .   .   .   **9/0**

## ARCHITECTURE, BUILDING, &c.

### PRACTICAL BUILDING CONSTRUCTION.
A Handbook for Students Preparing for Examinations, and a Book of Reference for Persons Engaged in Building. By JOHN PARNELL ALLEN, Surveyor, Lecturer on Building Construction at the Durham College of Science, Newcastle-on-Tyne. Third Edition, Revised and Enlarged. Medium 8vo, 450 pp., with 1,000 Illustrations, cloth. [*Just Published.* **7/6**

"The most complete exposition of building construction we have seen. It contains all that is necessary to prepare students for the various examinations in building construction."—*Building News.*

"The author depends nearly as much on his diagrams as on his type. The pages suggest the hand of a man of experience in building operations—and the volume must be a blessing to many teachers as well as to students."—*The Architect.*

"The work is sure to prove a formidable rival to great and small competitors alike, and bids fair to take a permanent place as a favourite student's text-book. The large number of illustrations deserve particular mention for the great merit they possess for purposes of reference in exactly corresponding to convenient scales."—*Journal of the Royal Institute of British Architects.*

### PRACTICAL MASONRY.
A Guide to the Art of Stone Cutting. Comprising the Construction, Setting Out, and Working of Stairs, Circular Work, Arches, Niches, Domes, Pendentives, Vaults, Tracery Windows, &c., &c. For the Use of Students, Masons, and other Workmen. By WILLIAM R. PURCHASE, Building Inspector to the Borough of Hove. Third Edition, with Glossary of Terms. Royal 8vo, 142 pp., with 52 Lithographic Plates, comprising nearly 400 separate Diagrams, cloth. [*Just Published.* **7/6**

"Mr. Purchase's 'Practical Masonry' will undoubtedly be found useful to all interested in this important subject, whether theoretically or practically. Most of the examples given are from actual work carried out, the diagrams being carefully drawn. The book is a practical treatise on the subject, the author himself having commenced as an operative mason, and afterwards acted as foreman mason on many large and important buildings prior to the attainment of his present position. It should be found of general utility to architectural students and others, as well as to those to whom it is specially addressed."—*Journal of the Royal Institute of British Architects.*

### CONCRETE: ITS NATURE AND USES.
A Book for Architects, Builders, Contractors, and Clerks of Works. By GEORGE L. SUTCLIFFE, A.R.I.B.A. 350 pp., with numerous Illustrations. Crown 8vo, cloth . . . . . . . . . . . **7/6**

"The author treats a difficult subject in a lucid manner. The manual fills a long-felt gap. It is careful and exhaustive; equally useful as a student's guide and an architect's book of reference."—*Journal of the Royal Institute of British Architects.*

"There is room for this new book, which will probably be for some time the standard work on the subject for a builder's purpose."—*Glasgow Herald.*

### THE MECHANICS OF ARCHITECTURE.
A Treatise on Applied Mechanics, especially Adapted to the Use of Architects. By E. W. TARN, M.A., Author of "The Science of Building," &c. Second Edition, Enlarged. Illustrated with 125 Diagrams. Crown 8vo, cloth **7/6**

"The book is a very useful and helpful manual of architectural mechanics, and really contains sufficient to enable a careful and painstaking student to grasp the principles bearing upon the majority of building problems. . . . Mr. Tarn has added, by this volume, to the debt of gratitude which is owing to him by architectural students for the many valuable works which he has produced for their use."—*The Builder.*

### LOCKWOOD'S BUILDER'S PRICE BOOK for 1900.
A Comprehensive Handbook of the Latest Prices and Data for Builders, Architects, Engineers, and Contractors. Re-constructed, Re-written, and Greatly Enlarged. By FRANCIS T. W. MILLER. 800 closely-printed pages, crown 8vo, cloth . . . . . . . . . . **4/0**

"This book is a very useful one, and should find a place in every English office connected with the building and engineering professions."—*Industries.*

"An excellent book of reference."—*Architect.*

"In its new and revised form this Price Book is what a work of this kind should be—comprehensive, reliable, well arranged, legible, and well bound."—*British Architect.*

### THE DECORATIVE PART OF CIVIL ARCHITECTURE.
By Sir WILLIAM CHAMBERS, F.R.S. With Portrait, Illustrations, Notes, and an EXAMINATION OF GRECIAN ARCHITECTURE, by JOSEPH GWILT, F.S.A. Revised and Edited by W. H. LEEDS. 66 Plates, 4to, cloth . . **21/0**

## A HANDY BOOK OF VILLA ARCHITECTURE.

Being a Series of Designs for Villa Residences in various Styles. With Outline Specifications and Estimates. By C. WICKES, Architect, Author of "The Spires and Towers of England," &c. 61 Plates, 4to, half-morocco, gilt edges . . . . . . . . . . . . **£1 11s. 6d.**
"The whole of the designs bear evidence of their being the work of an artistic architect, and they will prove very valuable and suggestive."—*Building News.*

## THE ARCHITECT'S GUIDE.

Being a Text-book of Useful Information for Architects, Engineers, Surveyors, Contractors, Clerks of Works, &c., &c. By FREDERICK ROGERS, Architect. Third Edition. Crown 8vo, cloth . . . . . . . . **3/6**
"As a text-book of useful information for architects, engineers, surveyors, &c., it would be hard to find a handier or more complete little volume."—*Standard.*

## ARCHITECTURAL PERSPECTIVE.

The whole Course and Operations of the Draughtsman in Drawing a Large House in Linear Perspective. Illustrated by 43 Folding Plates. By F. O. FERGUSON. Second Edition, Enlarged. 8vo, boards . . . . **3/6**
"It is the most intelligible of the treatises on this ill-treated subject that I have met with."—E. INGRESS BELL, ESQ., in the *R.I.B.A. Journal.*

## PRACTICAL RULES ON DRAWING.

For the Operative Builder and Young Student in Architecture. By GEORGE PYNE. 14 Plates, 4to, boards . . . . . . . . . **7/6**

## MEASURING AND VALUING ARTIFICER'S WORK

(The Student's Guide to the Practice of). Containing Directions for taking Dimensions, Abstracting the same, and bringing the Quantities into Bill, with Tables of Constants for Valuation of Labour, and for the Calculation of Areas and Solidities. Originally edited by E. DOBSON, Architect. With Additions by E. W. TARN, M.A. Seventh Edition, Revised. With 8 Plates and 63 Woodcuts. Crown 8vo, cloth. [*Just Published.* **7/6**
"This edition will be found the most complete treatise on the principles of measuring and valuing artificer's work that has yet been published."—*Building News.*

## TECHNICAL GUIDE, MEASURER, AND ESTIMATOR.

For Builders and Surveyors. Containing Technical Directions for Measuring Work in all the Building Trades, Complete Specifications for Houses, Roads, and Drains, and an Easy Method of Estimating the parts of a Building collectively. By A. C. BEATON. Ninth Edition. Waistcoat-pocket size, gilt edges . . . . . . . . . . . . **1/6**
"No builder, architect, surveyor, or valuer should be without his 'Beaton.'"—*Building News.*

## CONSTRUCTIONAL IRON AND STEEL WORK.

As Applied to Public, Private, and Domestic Buildings. A Practical Treatise for Architects, Students, and Builders. By F. CAMPIN. Crown 8vo, cloth. [*Just Published.* **3/6**
"Any one who wants a book on ironwork, as employed in buildings for stanchions, columns, and beams, will find the present volume to be suitable. The author has had long and varied experience in designing this class of work. The illustrations have the character of working drawings. This practical book may be counted a most valuable work."—*British Architect.*

## SPECIFICATIONS FOR PRACTICAL ARCHITECTURE.

A Guide to the Architect, Engineer, Surveyor, and Builder. With an Essay on the Structure and Science of Modern Buildings. Upon the Basis of the Work by ALFRED BARTHOLOMEW, thoroughly Revised, Corrected, and greatly added to by FREDERICK ROGERS, Architect. Third Edition, Revised. 8vo, cloth . . . . . . . . . . . . . **15/0**
"The work is too well known to need any recommendation from us. It is one of the books with which every young architect must be equipped."—*Architect.*

## THE HOUSE-OWNER'S ESTIMATOR.

Or, What will it Cost to Build, Alter, or Repair? A Price Book for Unprofessional People as well as the Architectural Surveyor and Builder. By J. D. SIMON. Edited by F. T. W. MILLER, A.R.I.B.A. Fifth Edition, Carefully Revised. Crown 8vo, cloth. [*Just Published. Net* **3/6**
"In two years it will repay its cost a hundred times over."—*Field.*

## SANITATION AND WATER SUPPLY.

### THE PURIFICATION OF SEWAGE.
Being a Brief Account of the Scientific Principles of Sewage Purification, and their Practical Application. By SIDNEY BARWISE, M.D. (Lond.), M.R.C.S., D.P.H. (Camb.), Fellow of the Sanitary Institute, Medical Officer of Health to the Derbyshire County Council. Crown 8vo, cloth. [*Just Published.* **5/0**
"'What process shall we adopt to purify our sewage?' This question has rarely been treated from so many points of view in one book. This volume teems with practical hints, which show the intimate knowledge the author has of his subject."—*The Engineer.*
"We know of no book of the same size which gives so complete and accurate an account of the principles of sewage purification."—*The Builder.*

### WATER AND ITS PURIFICATION.
A Handbook for the Use of Local Authorities, Sanitary Officers, and others interested in Water Supply. By S. RIDEAL, D.Sc. Lond., F.I.C. With numerous Illustrations and Tables. Crown 8vo, cloth. [*Just Published.* **7/6**
"Dr. Rideal's book is both interesting and accurate, and contains a most useful *résumé* of the latest knowledge upon the subject of which it treats. It ought to be of great service to all who are connected with the supply of water for domestic or manufacturing purposes."—*The Engineer.*
"Dealing as clearly as it does with the various ramifications of such an important subject as water and its purification it may be warmly recommended. Local authorities and all engaged in sanitary affairs, and others interested in water supply, will read its pages with profit."—*Lancet.*

### RURAL WATER SUPPLY.
A Practical Handbook on the Supply of Water and Construction of Waterworks for Small Country Districts. By ALLAN GREENWELL, A.M.I.C.E., and W. T. CURRY, A.M.I.C.E. Revised Edition. Crown 8vo, cloth **5/0**
"We conscientiously recommend it as a very useful book for those concerned in obtaining water for small districts, giving a great deal of practical information in a small compass."—*Builder.*

### THE WATER SUPPLY OF CITIES AND TOWNS.
By WILLIAM HUMBER, A.M. Inst. C.E., and M.Inst. M.E. Imp. 4to, half-bound morocco. (See page 11.) . . . . . . *Net* **£6 6s.**

### THE WATER SUPPLY OF TOWNS AND THE CONSTRUCTION OF WATER-WORKS.
By PROFESSOR W. K. BURTON, A.M. Inst. C.E. Second Edition, Revised and Extended. Royal 8vo, cloth. (See page 10.) . . . . **25/0**

### WATER ENGINEERING.
A Practical Treatise on the Measurement, Storage, Conveyance, and Utilisation of Water for the Supply of Towns, for Mill Power, and for other Purposes. By C. SLAGG, A.M. Inst. C.E. Second Edition. Crown 8vo, cloth . **7/6**

### SANITARY WORK IN SMALL TOWNS AND VILLAGES.
By CHARLES SLAGG, A. M. Inst. C.E. Crown 8vo, cloth . **3/0**

### SANITARY ARRANGEMENT OF DWELLING-HOUSES.
A Handbook for Householders and Owners of Houses. By A. J. WALLIS-TAYLER, A.M.Inst.C.E. Crown 8vo, cloth . . . . . . **2/6**
"This book will be largely read; it will be of considerable service to the public. It is well arranged, easily read, and for the most part devoid of technical terms."—*Lancet.*

### VENTILATION.
A Text-book to the Practice of the Art of Ventilating Buildings. By W. P. BUCHAN, R.P. Crown 8vo, cloth . . . . . . . **3/6**

### PLUMBING.
A Text-book to the Practice of the Art or Craft of the Plumber. By W. P. BUCHAN, R.P. Eighth Edition, Enlarged. Crown 8vo, cloth . . **3/6**

### THE HEALTH OFFICER'S POCKET-BOOK.
A Guide to Sanitary Practice and Law. For Medical Officers of Health, Sanitary Inspectors, Members of Sanitary Authorities, &c. By EDWARD F. WILLOUGHBY, M.D. (Lond.), &c. Fcap. 8vo, cloth . . . **7/6**
"A mine of condensed information of a pertinent and useful kind on the various subjects of which it treats. The matter seems to have been carefully compiled and arranged for facility of reference, and it is well illustrated by diagrams and woodcuts. The different subjects are succinctly but fully and scientifically dealt with."—*The Lancet.*

## CARPENTRY, TIMBER, &c.

### THE ELEMENTARY PRINCIPLES OF CARPENTRY.

A Treatise on the Pressure and Equilibrium of Timber Framing, the Resistance of Timber, and the Construction of Floors, Arches, Bridges, Roofs, Uniting Iron and Stone with Timber, &c. To which is added an Essay on the Nature and Properties of Timber, &c., with Descriptions of the kinds of Wood used in Building; also numerous Tables of the Scantlings of Timber for different purposes, the Specific Gravities of Materials, &c. By THOMAS TREDGOLD, C.E. With an Appendix of Specimens of Various Roofs of Iron and Stone, Illustrated. Seventh Edition, thoroughly Revised and considerably Enlarged by E. WYNDHAM TARN, M.A., Author of "The Science of Building," &c. With 61 Plates, Portrait of the Author, and several Woodcuts. In One large Vol., 4to, cloth . . . . . . . . . . . . **25/0**

"Ought to be in every architect's and every builder's library."—*Builder.*
"A work whose monumental excellence must commend it wherever skilful carpentry is concerned. The author's principles are rather confined than impaired by time. The additional plates are of great intrinsic value."—*Building News.*

### WOODWORKING MACHINERY.

Its Rise, Progress, and Construction. With Hints on the Management of Saw Mills and the Economical Conversion of Timber. Illustrated with Examples of Recent Designs by leading English, French, and American Engineers. By M. POWIS BALE, A.M.Inst.C.E., M.I.M.E. Second Edition, Revised, with large Additions, large crown 8vo, 440 pp., cloth . . . . **9/0**

"Mr. Bale is evidently an expert on the subject, and he has collected so much information that his book is all-sufficient for builders and others engaged in the conversion of timber."—*Architect.*
"The most comprehensive compendium of wood-working machinery we have seen. The author is a thorough master of his subject."—*Building News.*

### SAW MILLS.

Their Arrangement and Management, and the Economical Conversion of Timber. By M. POWIS BALE, A.M.Inst.C.E. Second Edition, Revised. Crown 8vo, cloth. [*Just Published.* **10/6**

"The *administration* of a large sawing establishment is discussed, and the subject examined from a financial standpoint. Hence the size, order, and disposition of saw mills and the like are gone into in detail, and the course of the timber is traced from its reception to its delivery in its converted state. We could not desire a more complete or practical treatise."—*Builder.*

### THE CARPENTER'S GUIDE.

Or, Book of Lines for Carpenters; comprising all the Elementary Principles essential for acquiring a knowledge of Carpentry. Founded on the late PETER NICHOLSON'S standard work. A New Edition, Revised by ARTHUR ASHPITEL, F.S.A. Together with Practical Rules on Drawing, by GEORGE PYNE. With 74 Plates, 4to, cloth . . . . . . . . . . **£1 1s.**

### A PRACTICAL TREATISE ON HANDRAILING.

Showing New and Simple Methods for Finding the Pitch of the Plank, Drawing the Moulds, Bevelling, Jointing-up, and Squaring the Wreath. By GEORGE COLLINGS. Second Edition, Revised and Enlarged, to which is added A TREATISE ON STAIR-BUILDING. With Plates and Diagrams . . **2/6**

"Will be found of practical utility in the execution of this difficult branch of joinery."—*Builder.*
"Almost every difficult phase of this somewhat intricate branch of joinery is elucidated by the aid of plates and explanatory letterpress."—*Furniture Gazette.*

### CIRCULAR WORK IN CARPENTRY AND JOINERY.

A Practical Treatise on Circular Work of Single and Double Curvature. By GEORGE COLLINGS. With Diagrams. Third Edition, 12mo, cloth . **2/6**

"An excellent example of what a book of this kind should be. Cheap in price, clear in definition, and practical in the examples selected."—*Builder.*

### THE CABINET-MAKER'S GUIDE TO THE ENTIRE CONSTRUCTION OF CABINET WORK.

Including the Art of Laying Veneers, &c. By RICHARD BITMEAD. Crown 8vo, with numerous Illustrations. [*Nearly Ready.*

# CARPENTRY, TIMBER, &c.    29

## HANDRAILING COMPLETE IN EIGHT LESSONS.
On the Square-Cut System. By J. S. GOLDTHORP, Head of Building Department, Halifax Technical School. With Eight Plates and over 150 Practical Exercises. 4to, cloth . . . . . . . . . . **3/6**

"Likely to be of considerable value to joiners and others who take a pride in good work. The arrangement of the book is excellent. We heartily commend it to teachers and students "—*Timber Trades Journal*.

## TIMBER MERCHANT'S and BUILDER'S COMPANION.
Containing New and Copious Tables of the Reduced Weight and Measurement of Deals and Battens, of all sizes, from One to a Thousand Pieces, and the relative Price that each size bears per Lineal Foot to any given Price per Petersburgh Standard Hundred; the Price per Cube Foot of Square Timber to any given Price per Load of 50 Feet, &c., &c. By WILLIAM DOWSING. Fourth Edition, Revised and Corrected. Crown 8vo, cloth . . . **3/0**

"We are glad to see a fourth edition of these admirable tables, which for correctness and simplicity of arrangement leave nothing to be desired."—*Timber Trades Journal*.

## THE PRACTICAL TIMBER MERCHANT.
A Guide for the Use of Building Contractors, Surveyors, Builders, &c., comprising useful Tables for all purposes connected with the Timber Trade, Marks of Wood, Essay on the Strength of Timber, Remarks on the Growth of Timber, &c. By W. RICHARDSON. Second Edition. Fcap. 8vo, cloth . **3/6**

"Contains much valuable information for timber merchants, builders, foresters, and all others connected with the growth, sale, and manufacture of timber."—*Journal of Forestry*.

## PACKING-CASE TABLES.
Showing the number of Superficial Feet in Boxes or Packing-Cases, from six inches square and upwards. By W. RICHARDSON, Timber Broker. Third Edition. Oblong 4to, cloth . . . . . . . . . **3/6**

"Invaluable labour-saving tables."—*Ironmonger*.

## GUIDE TO SUPERFICIAL MEASUREMENT.
Tables calculated from 1 to 200 inches in length by 1 to 108 inches in breadth. For the use of Architects, Surveyors, Engineers, Timber Merchants, Builders, &c. By JAMES HAWKINGS. Fourth Edition. Fcap. 8vo, cloth . **3/6**

"A useful collection of tables to facilitate rapid calculation of surfaces. The exact area of any surface of which the limits have been ascertained can be instantly determined. The book will be found of the greatest utility to all engaged in building operations."—*Scotsman*.

## PRACTICAL FORESTRY.
And its Bearing on the Improvement of Estates. By CHARLES E. CURTIS, F.S.I., Professor of Forestry, Field Engineering, and General Estate Management, at the College of Agriculture, Downton. Second Edition, Revised. Crown 8vo, cloth. [*Just Published*. **3/6**

SUMMARY OF CONTENTS:—PREFATORY REMARKS.—OBJECTS OF PLANTING.—CHOICE OF A FORESTER.—CHOICE OF SOIL AND SITE.—LAYING OUT OF LAND FOR PLANTATIONS.—PREPARATION OF THE GROUND FOR PLANTING.—DRAINAGE.—PLANTING.—DISTANCES AND DISTRIBUTION OF TREES IN PLANTATIONS.—TREES AND GROUND GAME.—ATTENTION AFTER PLANTING.—THINNING OF PLANTATIONS — PRUNING OF FOREST TREES.—REALIZATION.—METHODS OF SALE.—MEASUREMENT OF TIMBER.—MEASUREMENT AND VALUATION OF LARCH PLANTATION.—FIRE LINES.—COST OF PLANTING.

"Mr. Curtis has in the course of a series of short pithy chapters afforded much information of a useful and practical character on the planting and subsequent treatment of trees."—*Illustrated Carpenter and Builder*.

## THE ELEMENTS OF FORESTRY.
Designed to afford Information concerning the Planting and Care of Forest Trees for Ornament or Profit, with suggestions upon the Creation and Care of Woodlands. By F. B. HOUGH. Large crown 8vo, cloth . . **10/0**

## THE TIMBER IMPORTER'S, TIMBER MERCHANT'S, AND BUILDER'S STANDARD GUIDE.
By RICHARD E. GRANDY. Comprising:—An Analysis of Deal Standards, Home and Foreign, with Comparative Values and Tabular Arrangements for fixing Net Landed Cost on Baltic and North American Deals, including all intermediate Expenses, Freight, Insurance, &c.; together with copious Information for the Retailer and Builder. Third Edition. 12mo, cloth . . **2/0**

## DECORATIVE ARTS, &c.

### SCHOOL OF PAINTING FOR THE IMITATION OF WOODS AND MARBLES.

As Taught and Practised by A. R. VAN DER BURG and P. VAN DER BURG, Directors of the Rotterdam Painting Institution. Royal folio, 18½ by 12½ in., Illustrated with 24 full-size Coloured Plates; also 12 plain Plates, comprising 154 Figures. Third Edition, cloth. [*Just Published.* **£1 11s. 6d.**

LIST OF PLATES:—1. VARIOUS TOOLS REQUIRED FOR WOOD PAINTING.—2, 3. WALNUT; PRELIMINARY STAGES OF GRAINING AND FINISHED SPECIMEN.—4. TOOLS USED FOR MARBLE PAINTING AND METHOD OF MANIPULATION.—5, 6. ST. REMI MARBLE; EARLIER OPERATIONS AND FINISHED SPECIMEN. — 7. METHODS OF SKETCHING DIFFERENT GRAINS, KNOTS, &c.—8, 9. ASH: PRELIMINAPY STAGES AND FINISHED SPECIMEN.—10. METHODS OF SKETCHING MARBLE GRAINS.—11, 12. BRECHE MARBLE; PRELIMINARY STAGES OF WORKING AND FINISHED SPECIMEN.—13. MAPLE; METHODS OF PRODUCING THE DIFFERENT GRAINS.—14, 15. BIRD'S-EYE MAPLE; PRELIMINARY STAGES AND FINISHED SPECIMEN.—16. METHODS OF SKETCHING THE DIFFERENT SPECIES OF WHITE MARBLE.—17, 18. WHITE MARBLE; PRELIMINARY STAGES OF PROCESS AND FINISHED SPECIMEN.—19. MAHOGANY; SPECIMENS OF VARIOUS GRAINS AND METHODS OF MANIPULATION.—20, 21. MAHOGANY; EARLIER STAGES AND FINISHED SPECIMEN.—22, 23, 24. SIENNA MARBLE; VARIETIES OF GRAIN, PRELIMINARY STAGES AND FINISHED SPECIMEN.—25, 26, 27. JUNIPER WOOD; METHODS OF PRODUCING GRAIN, &c.; PRELIMINARY STAGES AND FINISHED SPECIMEN.—28, 29, 30. VERT DE MER MARBLE; VARIETIES OF GRAIN AND METHODS OF WORKING, UNFINISHED AND FINISHED SPECIMENS.—31, 32, 33. OAK; VARIETIES OF GRAIN, TOOLS EMPLOYED AND METHODS OF MANIPULATION, PRELIMINARY STAGES AND FINISHED SPECIMEN.—34, 35, 36. WAULSORT MARBLE; VARIETIES OF GRAIN, UNFINISHED AND FINISHED SPECIMENS.

"Those who desire to attain skill in the art of painting woods and marbles will find advantage in consulting this book. . . . Some of the Working Men's Clubs should give their young men the opportunity to study it."—*Builder.*

"A comprehensive guide to the art. The explanations of the processes, the manipulation and management of the colours, and the beautifully executed plates will not be the least valuable to the student who aims at making his work a faithful transcript of nature."—*Building News.*

"Students and novices are fortunate who are able to become the possessors of so noble a work."—*The Architect.*

### ELEMENTARY DECORATION.

A Guide to the Simpler Forms of Everyday Art. Together with PRACTICAL HOUSE DECORATION. By JAMES W. FACEY. With numerous Illustrations. In One Vol., strongly half-bound . . . . . . **5/0**

### HOUSE PAINTING, GRAINING, MARBLING, AND SIGN WRITING.

A Practical Manual of. By ELLIS A. DAVIDSON. Eighth Edition. With Coloured Plates and Wood Engravings. 12mo, cloth boards . . . **6/0**

"A mass of information of use to the amateur and of value to the practical man."—*English Mechanic.*

### THE DECORATOR'S ASSISTANT.

A Modern Guide for Decorative Artists and Amateurs, Painters, Writers, Gilders, &c. Containing upwards of 600 Receipts, Rules, and Instructions; with a variety of Information for General Work connected with every Class of Interior and Exterior Decorations, &c. Seventh Edition. 152 pp., cr. 8vo. **1/0**

"Full of receipts of value to decorators, painters, gilders, &c. The book contains the gist of larger treatises on colour and technical processes. It would be difficult to meet with a work so full of varied information on the painter's art."—*Building News.*

### MARBLE DECORATION

And the Terminology of British and Foreign Marbles. A Handbook for Students. By GEORGE H. BLAGROVE, Author of "Shoring and its Application," &c. With 28 Illustrations. Crown 8vo, cloth . . . . **3/6**

"This most useful and much wanted handbook should be in the hands of every architect and builder."—*Building World.*

"A carefully and usefully written treatise: the work is essentially practical."—*Scotsman.*

## DELAMOTTE'S WORKS ON ALPHABETS AND ILLUMINATION.

### ORNAMENTAL ALPHABETS, ANCIENT & MEDIÆVAL.
From the Eighth Century, with Numerals; including Gothic, Church-Text, large and small, German, Italian, Arabesque, Initials for Illumination, Monograms, Crosses, &c., &c., for the use of Architectural and Engineering Draughtsmen, Missal Painters, Masons, Decorative Painters, Lithographers, Engravers, Carvers, &c., &c. Collected and Engraved by F. DELAMOTTE, and printed in Colours. New and Cheaper Edition. Royal 8vo, oblong, ornamental boards . . . . . . . . . . . . **2/6**

"For those who insert enamelled sentences round gilded chalices, who blazon shop legends over shop-doors, who letter church walls with pithy sentences from the Decalogue, this book will be useful."—*Athenæum.*

### MODERN ALPHABETS, PLAIN AND ORNAMENTAL.
Including German, Old English, Saxon, Italic, Perspective, Greek, Hebrew, Court Hand, Engrossing, Tuscan, Riband, Gothic, Rustic, and Arabesque; with several Original Designs, and an Analysis of the Roman and Old English Alphabets, large and small, and Numerals, for the use of Draughtsmen, Surveyors, Masons, Decorative Painters, Lithographers, Engravers, Carvers, &c. Collected and Engraved by F. DELAMOTTE, and printed in Colours. New and Cheaper Edition. Royal 8vo, oblong, ornamental boards . **2/6**

"There is comprised in it every possible shape into which the letters of the alphabet and numerals can be formed, and the talent which has been expended in the conception of the various plain and ornamental letters is wonderful."—*Standard.*

### MEDIÆVAL ALPHABETS AND INITIALS FOR ILLUMINATORS.
By F. G. DELAMOTTE. Containing 21 Plates and Illuminated Title, printed in Gold and Colours. With an Introduction by J. WILLIS BROOKS. Fourth and Cheaper Edition. Small 4to, ornamental boards . . . . **4/0**

"A volume in which the letters of the alphabet come forth glorified in gilding and all the colours of the prism interwoven and intertwined and intermingled."—*Sun.*

### A PRIMER OF THE ART OF ILLUMINATION.
For the Use of Beginners; with a Rudimentary Treatise on the Art, Practical Directions for its Exercise, and Examples taken from Illuminated MSS., printed in Gold and Colours. By F. DELAMOTTE. New and Cheaper Edition. Small 4to, ornamental boards . . : . . . . **6/0**

"The examples of ancient MSS. recommended to the student, which, with much good sense, the author chooses from collections accessible to all, are selected with judgment and knowledge as well as taste."—*Athenæum.*

### THE EMBROIDERER'S BOOK OF DESIGN.
Containing Initials, Emblems, Cyphers, Monograms, Ornamental Borders, Ecclesiastical Devices, Mediæval and Modern Alphabets, and National Emblems. Collected by F. DELAMOTTE, and printed in Colours. Oblong royal 8vo, ornamental wrapper . . . . . . . . . **1/6**

"The book will be of great assistance to ladies and young children who are endowed with the art of plying the needle in this most ornamental and useful pretty work."—*East Anglian Times.*

### INSTRUCTIONS IN WOOD-CARVING FOR AMATEURS.
With Hints on Design. By A LADY. With 10 Plates. New and Cheaper Edition. Crown 8vo, in emblematic wrapper . . . . . . **2/0**

"The handicraft of the wood-carver, so well as a book can impart it, may be learnt from 'A Lady's' publication."—*Athenæum.*

### PAINTING POPULARLY EXPLAINED.
By THOMAS JOHN GULLICK, Painter, and JOHN TIMBS, F.S.A. Including Fresco, Oil, Mosaic, Water-Colour, Water-Glass, Tempera, Encaustic, Miniature, Painting on Ivory, Vellum, Pottery, Enamel, Glass, &c. Fifth Edition. Crown 8vo, cloth . . . . . . . . . **5/0**

\*\*\* *Adopted as a Prize Book at South Kensington.*

"Much may be learned, even by those who fancy they do not require to be taught, from the careful perusal of this unpretending but comprehensive treatise."—*Art Journal.*

32 CROSBY LOCKWOOD & SON'S CATALOGUE.

## NATURAL SCIENCE, &c.

### THE VISIBLE UNIVERSE.
Chapters on the Origin and Construction of the Heavens. By J. E. GORE, F.R.A.S., Author of "Star Groups," &c. Illustrated by 6 Stellar Photographs and 12 Plates. Demy 8vo, cloth . . . . . . . . . **16/0**

"A valuable and lucid summary of recent astronomical theory, rendered more valuable and attractive by a series of stellar photographs and other illustrations."—*The Times.*
"In presenting a clear and concise account of the present state of our knowledge Mr. Gore has made a valuable addition to the literature of the subject."—*Nature.*
"Mr. Gore's 'Visible Universe' is one of the finest works on astronomical science that have recently appeared in our language. In spirit and in method it is scientific from cover to cover, but the style is so clear and attractive that it will be as acceptable and as readable to those who make no scientific pretensions as to those who devote themselves specially to matters astronomical."—*Leeds Mercury.*

### STAR GROUPS.
A Student's Guide to the Constellations. By J. ELLARD GORE, F.R.A.S., M.R.I.A., &c., Author of "The Visible Universe," "The Scenery of the Heavens," &c. With 30 Maps. Small 4to, cloth . . . . . **5/0**

"The volume contains thirty maps showing stars of the sixth magnitude—the usual naked-eye limit—and each is accompanied by a brief commentary adapted to facilitate recognition and bring to notice objects of special interest. For the purpose of a preliminary survey of the 'midnight pomp' of the heavens nothing could be better than a set of delineations averaging scarcely twenty square inches in area and including nothing that cannot at once be identified."—*Saturday Review.*

### AN ASTRONOMICAL GLOSSARY.
Or, Dictionary of Terms used in Astronomy. With Tables of Data and Lists of Remarkable and Interesting Celestial Objects. By J. ELLARD GORE, F.R.A.S., Author of "The Visible Universe," &c. Small crown 8vo, cloth. **2/6**

"A very useful little work for beginners in astronomy, and not to be despised by more advanced students."—*The Times.*
"A very handy book . . . the utility of which is much increased by its valuable tables of astronomical data."—*Athenæum.*

### THE MICROSCOPE.
Its Construction and Management. Including Technique, Photo-micrography, and the Past and Future of the Microscope. By Dr. HENRI VAN HEURCK. Re-Edited and Augmented from the Fourth French Edition, and Translated by WYNNE E. BAXTER, F.G.S. 400 pp., with upwards of 250 Woodcuts, imp. 8vo, cloth . . . . . . . . . . . . **18/0**

"A translation of a well-known work, at once popular and comprehensive."—*Times.*
"The translation is as felicitous as it is accurate."—*Nature.*

### ASTRONOMY.
By the late Rev. ROBERT MAIN, M.A., F.R.S. Third Edition, Revised by WILLIAM THYNNE LYNN, B.A., F.R.A.S., formerly of the Royal Observatory, Greenwich. 12mo, cloth . . . . . . . . . . **2/0**

"A sound and simple treatise, very carefully edited, and a capital book for beginners."—*Knowledge.*
"Accurately brought down to the requirements of the present time by Mr. Lynn "—*Educational Times.*

### A MANUAL OF THE MOLLUSCA.
A Treatise on Recent and Fossil Shells. By S. P. WOODWARD, A.L.S., F.G.S. With an Appendix on RECENT AND FOSSIL CONCHOLOGICAL DISCOVERIES, by RALPH TATE, A.L.S, F.G.S. With 23 Plates and upwards of 300 Woodcuts. Reprint of Fourth Edition (1880). Crown 8vo, cloth . . . . . . . . . . . . . . **7/6**

"A most valuable storehouse of conchological and geological information."—*Science Gossip.*

### THE TWIN RECORDS OF CREATION.
Or, Geology and Genesis, their Perfect Harmony and Wonderful Concord. By G. W. V. LE VAUX. 8vo, cloth . . . . . . . **5/0**

"A valuable contribution to the evidences of Revelation, and disposes very conclusively of the arguments of those who would set God's Works against God's Word. No real difficulty is shirked, and no sophistry is left unexposed."—*The Rock.*

## NATURAL SCIENCE, &c.

### HANDBOOK OF MECHANICS.
By Dr. LARDNER. Enlarged and re-written by BENJAMIN LOEWY, F.R.A.S. 378 Illustrations. Post 8vo, cloth . . . . . . . . . **6/0**
"The perspicuity of the original has been retained, and chapters which had become obsolete have been replaced by others of more modern character. The explanations throughout are studiously popular, and care has been taken to show the application of the various branches of physics to the industrial arts, and to the practical business of life."—*Mining Journal.*

### HANDBOOK OF HYDROSTATICS AND PNEUMATICS.
By Dr. LARDNER. New Edition, Revised and Enlarged by BENJAMIN LOEWY, F.R.A.S. With 236 Illustrations. Post 8vo, cloth . . . **5/0**
"For those 'who desire to attain an accurate knowledge of physical science without the profound methods of mathematical investigation,' this work is well adapted."—*Chemical News.*

### HANDBOOK OF HEAT.
By Dr. LARDNER. Edited and re-written by BENJAMIN LOEWY, F.R.A.S., &c. 117 Illustrations. Post 8vo, cloth . . . . . . . . **6/0**
"The style is always clear and precise, and conveys instruction without leaving any cloudiness or lurking doubts behind."—*Engineering.*

### HANDBOOK OF OPTICS.
By Dr. LARDNER. New Edition. Edited by T. OLVER HARDING, B.A. Lond. With 298 Illustrations. Small 8vo, 448 pp., cloth . . . . . **5/0**
"Written by one of the ablest English scientific writers, beautifully and elaborately illustrated."
—*Mechanics' Magazine.*

### ELECTRICITY, MAGNETISM, AND ACOUSTICS.
By Dr. LARDNER. Edited by GEO. CAREY FOSTER, B.A., F.C.S. With 400 Illustrations. Small 8vo, cloth . . . . . . . . **5/0**
"The book could not have been entrusted to any one better calculated to preserve the terse and lucid style of Lardner, while correcting his errors and bringing up his work to the present state of scientific knowledge."—*Popular Science Review.*

### HANDBOOK OF ASTRONOMY.
By Dr. LARDNER. Fourth Edition. Revised and Edited by EDWIN DUNKIN, F.R.A.S., Royal Observatory, Greenwich. With 38 Plates and upwards of 100 Woodcuts. 8vo, cloth . . . . . . . . . **9/6**
"Probably no other book contains the same amount of information in so compendious and well arranged a form—certainly none at the price at which this is offered to the public."—*Athenæum.*
"We can do no other than pronounce this work a most valuable manual of astronomy, and we strongly recommend it to all who wish to acquire a general—but at the same time correct—acquaintance with this sublime science."—*Quarterly Journal of Science.*

### MUSEUM OF SCIENCE AND ART.
Edited by Dr. LARDNER. With upwards of 1,200 Engravings on Wood. In Six Double Volumes, **£1 1s.** in a new and elegant cloth binding; or handsomely bound in half-morocco . . . . . . **£1 11s. 6d.**
"A cheap and interesting publication, alike informing and attractive. The papers combine subjects of importance and great scientific knowledge, considerable inductive powers, and a popular style of treatment."—*Spectator.*

*Separate books formed from the above.*

| | |
|---|---|
| Common Things Explained. 5s. | Steam and Its Uses. 2s. cloth. |
| The Microscope. 2s. cloth. | Popular Astronomy. 4s. 6d. cloth. |
| Popular Geology. 2s. 6d. cloth. | The Bee and White Ants. 2s. cloth. |
| Popular Physics. 2s. 6d. cloth. | The Electric Telegraph. 1s. 6d. |

### NATURAL PHILOSOPHY FOR SCHOOLS.
By Dr. LARDNER. Fcap. 8vo . . . . . . . . . **3/6**
"A very convenient class book for junior students in private schools."—*British Quarterly Review.*

### ANIMAL PHYSIOLOGY FOR SCHOOLS.
By Dr. LARDNER. Fcap. 8vo . . . . . . . . . **3/6**
"Clearly written, well arranged, and excellently illustrated."—*Gardener's Chronicle.*

### THE ELECTRIC TELEGRAPH.
By Dr. LARDNER. Revised by E. B. BRIGHT, F.R.A.S. Fcap. 8vo. . **2/6**
One of the most readable books extant on the Electric Telegraph."—*English Mechanic.*

## CHEMICAL MANUFACTURES, CHEMISTRY, &c.

### THE GAS ENGINEER'S POCKET-BOOK.
Comprising Tables, Notes and Memoranda relating to the Manufacture, Distribution and Use of Coal Gas and the Construction of Gas Works. By H. O'CONNOR, A.M.Inst.C.E., 450 pp., crown 8vo, fully Illustrated, leather. [*Just Published.* **10/6**

"The book contains a vast amount of information. The author goes consecutively through the engineering details and practical methods involved in each of the different processes or parts of a gas-works. He has certainly succeeded in making a compilation of hard matters of fact absolutely interesting to read."—*Gas World*.

"A useful work of reference for the gas engineer and all interested in lighting or heating by gas, while the analyses of the various descriptions of gas will be of value to the technical chemist. All matter in any way connected with the manufacture and use of gas is dealt with. The book has evidently been carefully compiled, and certainly constitutes a useful addition to gas literature."—*Builder*.

"The volume contains a great quantity of specialised information, compiled, we believe, from trustworthy sources, which should make it of considerable value to those for whom it is specifically produced."—*Engineer*.

### LIGHTING BY ACETYLENE
Generators, Burners, and Electric Furnaces. By WILLIAM E. GIBBS, M.E. With 66 Illustrations. Crown 8vo, cloth. [*Just Published.* **7/6**

### ENGINEERING CHEMISTRY.
A Practical Treatise for the Use of Analytical Chemists, Engineers, Iron Masters, Iron Founders, Students and others. Comprising Methods of Analysis and Valuation of the Principal Materials used in Engineering Work, with Analyses, Examples and Suggestions. By H. J. PHILLIPS, F.I.C., F.C.S. Second Edition, Enlarged. Crown 8vo, 400 pp., with Illustrations, cloth **10/6**

"In this work the author has rendered no small service to a numerous body of practical men. . . . The analytical methods may be pronounced most satisfactory, being as accurate as the despatch required of engineering chemists permits."—*Chemical News*.

"Full of good things. As a handbook of technical analysis, it is very welcome."—*Builder*.

"The analytical methods given are, as a whole, such as are likely to give rapid and trustworthy results in experienced hands. . . . There is much excellent descriptive matter in the work, the chapter on 'Oils and Lubrication' being specially noticeable in this respect."—*Engineer*.

### NITRO-EXPLOSIVES.
A Practical Treatise concerning the Properties, Manufacture, and Analysis of Nitrated Substances, including the Fulminates, Smokeless Powders, and Celluloid. By P. G. SANFORD, F.I.C., Consulting Chemist to the Cotton Powder Company, &c. With Illustrations. Crown 8vo, cloth. [*Just Published.* **9/0**

"Any one having the requisite apparatus and materials could make nitro-glycerine or guncotton, to say nothing of other explosives, by the aid of the instructions in this volume. This is one of the very few text-books in which can be found just what is wanted. Mr. Sanford goes through the whole list of explosives commonly used, names any given explosive, and tells us of what it is composed and how it is manufactured. The book is excellent throughout."—*Engineer*.

### A HANDBOOK ON MODERN EXPLOSIVES.
A Practical Treatise on the Manufacture and Use of Dynamite, Gun-Cotton, Nitro-Glycerine and other Explosive Compounds, including Collodion-Cotton. With Chapters on Explosives in Practical Application. By M. EISSLER, Mining Engineer and Metallurgical Chemist. Second Edition, Enlarged. With 150 Illustrations. Crown 8vo, cloth. [*Just Published.* **12/6**

"Useful not only to the miner, but also to officers of both services to whom blasting and the use of explosives generally may at any time become a necessary auxiliary."—*Nature*.

### DANGEROUS GOODS.
Their Sources and Properties, Modes of Storage and Transport. With Notes and Comments on Accidents arising therefrom, together with the Government and Railway Classifications, Acts of Parliament, &c. A Guide for the Use of Government and Railway Officials, Steamship Owners, Insurance Companies and Manufacturers, and Users of Explosives and Dangerous Goods. By H. JOSHUA PHILLIPS, F.I.C., F.C.S. Crown 8vo, 374 pp., cloth . . **9/0**

"Merits a wide circulation, and an intelligent, appreciative study."—*Chemical News*.

## CHEMICAL MANUFACTURES, CHEMISTRY, &c. 35

### A MANUAL OF THE ALKALI TRADE.

Including the Manufacture of Sulphuric Acid, Sulphate of Soda, and Bleaching Powder. By JOHN LOMAS, Alkali Manufacturer, Newcastle-upon-Tyne and London. 390 pp. of Text. With 232 Illustrations and Working Drawings. Second Edition, with Additions. Super-royal 8vo, cloth . . **£1 10s.**

"This book is written by a manufacturer for manufacturers. The working details of the most approved forms of apparatus are given, and these are accompanied by no less than 232 wood engravings, all of which may be used for the purposes of construction. Every step in the manufacture is very fully described in this manual, and each improvement explained."—*Athenæum.*

"We find not merely a sound and luminous explanation of the chemical principles of the trade, but a notice of numerous matters which have a most important bearing on the successful conduct of alkali works, but which are generally overlooked by even experienced technological authors."—*Chemical Review.*

### THE BLOWPIPE IN CHEMISTRY, MINERALOGY, AND GEOLOGY.

Containing all known Methods of Anhydrous Analysis, many Working Examples, and Instructions for Making Apparatus. By Lieut.-Colonel W. A. ROSS, R.A., F.G.S. With 120 Illustrations. Second Edition, Enlarged. Crown 8vo, cloth . . . . . . . . . . **5/0**

"The student who goes conscientiously through the course of experimentation here laid down will gain a better insight into inorganic chemistry and mineralogy than if he had 'got up' any of the best text-books of the day, and passed any number of examinations in their contents."—*Chemical News.*

### THE MANUAL OF COLOURS AND DYE-WARES.

Their Properties, Applications, Valuations, Impurities and Sophistications. For the Use of Dyers, Printers, Drysalters, Brokers, &c. By J. W. SLATER. Second Edition, Revised and greatly Enlarged. Crown 8vo, cloth . **7/6**

"A complete encyclopædia of the *materia tinctoria*. The information given respecting each article is full and precise, and the methods of determining the value of articles such as these, so liable to sophistication, are given with clearness, and are practical as well as valuable."—*Chemist and Druggist.*

"There is no other work which covers precisely the same ground. To students preparing for examinations in dyeing and printing it will prove exceedingly useful."—*Chemical News.*

### A HANDY BOOK FOR BREWERS.

Being a Practical Guide to the Art of Brewing and Malting. Embracing the Conclusions of Modern Research which bear upon the Practice of Brewing. By HERBERT EDWARDS WRIGHT, M.A. Second Edition, Enlarged. Crown 8vo, 530 pp., cloth. . [*Just Published.*] **12/6**

"May be consulted with advantage by the student who is preparing himself for examinational tests, while the scientific brewer will find in it a *résumé* of all the most important discoveries of modern times. The work is written throughout in a clear and concise manner, and the author takes great care to discriminate between vague theories and well-established facts."—*Brewers' Journal.*

"We have great pleasure in recommending this handy book, and have no hesitation in saying that it is one of the best—if not the best—which has yet been written on the subject of beer-brewing in this country; it should have a place on the shelves of every brewer's library."—*Brewers' Guardian.*

"Although the requirements of the student are primarily considered, an acquaintance of half-an-hour's duration cannot fail to impress the practical brewer with the sense of having found a trustworthy guide and practical counsellor in brewery matters."—*Chemical Trade Journal.*

### FUELS: SOLID, LIQUID, AND GASEOUS.

Their Analysis and Valuation. For the Use of Chemists and Engineers. By H. J. PHILLIPS, F.C.S., formerly Analytical and Consulting Chemist to the G.E. Rlwy. Third Edition, Revised and Enlarged. Crown 8vo, cloth **2/0**

"Ought to have its place in the laboratory of every metallurgical establishment and wherever fuel is used on a large scale."—*Chemical News.*

## THE ARTISTS' MANUAL OF PIGMENTS.

Showing their Composition, Conditions of Permanency, Non-Permanency, and Adulterations; Effects in Combination with Each Other and with Vehicles; and the most Reliable Tests of Purity. By H. C. STANDAGE. Crown 8vo. **2/6**
"This work is indeed *multum-in-parvo*, and we can, with good conscience, recommend it to all who come in contact with pigments, whether as makers, dealers, or users."—*Chemical Review.*

## A POCKET-BOOK OF MENSURATION AND GAUGING.

Containing Tables, Rules, and Memoranda for Revenue Officers, Brewers, Spirit Merchants, &c. By J. B. MANT, Inland Revenue. Second Edition, Revised. 18mo, leather . . . . . . . . . **4/0**
"This handy and useful book is adapted to the requirements of the Inland Revenue Department, and will be a favourite book of reference."—*Civilian.*
"Should be in the hands of every practical brewer."—*Brewers' Journal.*

---

# INDUSTRIAL ARTS, TRADES, AND MANUFACTURES.

## TEA MACHINERY AND TEA FACTORIES.

A Descriptive Treatise on the Mechanical Appliances required in the Cultivation of the Tea Plant and the Preparation of Tea for the Market. By A. J. WALLIS-TAYLER, A. M. Inst. C.E. Medium 8vo, 468 pp. With 218 Illustrations. [*Just Published.*  *Net* **25/0**
SUMMARY OF CONTENTS :—MECHANICAL CULTIVATION OR TILLAGE OF THE SOIL.—PLUCKING OR GATHERING THE LEAF.—TEA FACTORIES.—THE DRESSING, MANUFACTURE, OR PREPARATION OF TEA BY MECHANICAL MEANS.—ARTIFICIAL WITHERING OF THE LEAF.—MACHINES FOR ROLLING OR CURLING THE LEAF.— FERMENTING PROCESS.—MACHINES FOR THE AUTOMATIC DRYING OR FIRING OF THE LEAF.—MACHINES FOR NON-AUTOMATIC DRYING OR FIRING OF THE LEAF.—DRYING OR FIRING MACHINES.—BREAKING OR CUTTING, AND SORTING MACHINES.—PACKING THE TEA.—MEANS OF TRANSPORT ON TEA PLANTATIONS.—MISCELLANEOUS MACHINERY AND APPARATUS.—FINAL TREATMENT OF THE TEA.—TABLES AND MEMORANDA.
"The subject of tea machinery is now one of the first interest to a large class of people, to whom we strongly commend the volume."—*Chamber of Commerce Journal.*
"When tea planting was first introduced into the British possessions little, if any, machinery was employed, but now its use is almost universal. This volume contains a very full account of the machinery necessary for the proper outfit of a factory, and also a description of the processes best carried out by this machinery."—*Journal Society of Arts.*

## FLOUR MANUFACTURE.

A Treatise on Milling Science and Practice. By FRIEDRICH KICK, Imperial Regierungsrath, Professor of Mechanical Technology in the Imperial German Polytechnic Institute, Prague. Translated from the Second Enlarged and Revised Edition with Supplement. By H. H. P. POWLES, Assoc. Memb. Institution of Civil Engineers. Nearly 400 pp. Illustrated with 28 Folding Plates, and 167 Woodcuts. Royal 8vo, cloth . . . . **£1 5s.**
"This valuable work is, and will remain, the standard authority on the science of milling. . . . The miller who has read and digested this work will have laid the foundation, so to speak, of a successful career; he will have acquired a number of general principles which he can proceed to apply. In this handsome volume we at last have the accepted text-book of modern milling in good, sound English, which has little, if any, trace of the German idiom."—*The Miller.*

## COTTON MANUFACTURE.

A Manual of Practical Instruction of the Processes of Opening, Carding, Combing, Drawing, Doubling and Spinning of Cotton, the Methods of Dyeing, &c. For the Use of Operatives, Overlookers, and Manufacturers. By JOHN LISTER, Technical Instructor, Pendleton. 8vo, cloth . . **7/6**
"A distinct advance in the literature of cotton manufacture."—*Machinery.*
"It is thoroughly reliable, fulfilling nearly all the requirements desired."—*Glasgow Herald.*

## MODERN CYCLES.

A Practical Handbook on their Construction and Repair. By A. J. WALLIS-TAYLER, A. M. Inst. C. E. Author of "Refrigerating Machinery," &c. With upwards of 300 Illustrations. Crown 8vo, cloth. [*Just Published.*  **10/6**
"The large trade that is done in the component parts of bicycles has placed in the way of men mechanically inclined extraordinary facilities for building bicycles for their own use. . . . The book will prove a valuable guide for all those who aspire to the manufacture or repair of their own machines."—*The Field.*
"A most comprehensive and up-to-date treatise."—*The Cycle.*
"A very useful book, which is quite entitled to rank as a standard work for students of cycle construction."—*Wheeling.*

INDUSTRIAL AND USEFUL ARTS. 37

## CEMENTS, PASTES, GLUES, AND GUMS.

A Practical Guide to the Manufacture and Application of the various Agglutinants required in the Building, Metal-Working, Wood-Working, and Leather-Working Trades, and for Workshop, Laboratory or Office Use. With upwards of 900 Recipes and Formulæ. By H. C. STANDAGE, Chemist. Third Edition. Crown 8vo, cloth. [*Just Published.* **2/0**

"We have pleasure in speaking favourably of this volume. So far as we have had experience, which is not inconsiderable, this manual is trustworthy."—*Athenæum.*
"As a revelation of what are considered trade secrets, this book will arouse an amount of curiosity among the large number of industries it touches."—*Daily Chronicle.*

## THE ART OF SOAP-MAKING.

A Practical Handbook of the Manufacture of Hard and Soft Soaps, Toilet Soaps, &c. Including many New Processes, and a Chapter on the Recovery of Glycerine from Waste Leys. By ALX. WATT. Fifth Edition, Revised, with an Appendix on Modern Candlemaking. Crown 8vo, cloth . . . **7/6**

"The work will prove very useful, not merely to the technological student, but to the practical soap boiler who wishes to understand the theory of his art."—*Chemical News.*
"A thoroughly practical treatise on an art which has almost no literature in our language. We congratulate the author on the success of his endeavour to fill a void in English technical literature."—*Nature.*

## PRACTICAL PAPER-MAKING.

A Manual for Paper-Makers and Owners and Managers of Paper-Mills. With Tables, Calculations, &c. By G. CLAPPERTON, Paper-Maker. With Illustrations of Fibres from Micro-Photographs. Crown 8vo, cloth . . **5/0**

"The author caters for the requirements of responsible mill hands, apprentices, &c., whilst his manual will be found of great service to students of technology, as well as to veteran paper-makers and mill owners. The illustrations form an excellent feature."—*The World's Paper Trade Review.*
"We recommend everybody interested in the trade to get a copy of this thoroughly practical book."—*Paper Making.*

## THE ART OF PAPER-MAKING.

A Practical Handbook of the Manufacture of Paper from Rags, Esparto, Straw, and other Fibrous Materials. Including the Manufacture of Pulp from Wood Fibre, with a Description of the Machinery and Appliances used. To which are added Details of Processes for Recovering Soda from Waste Liquors. By ALEXANDER WATT, Author of "The Art of Soap-Making." With Illustrations. Crown 8vo, cloth . . . . . . . . . **7/6**

"It may be regarded as the standard work on the subject. The book is full of valuable information. The 'Art of Paper-Making' is in every respect a model of a text-book, either for a technical class, or for the private student."—*Paper and Printing Trades Journal.*

## A TREATISE ON PAPER.

For Printers and Stationers. With an Outline of Paper Manufacture; Complete Tables of Sizes, and Specimens of Different Kinds of Paper. By RICHARD PARKINSON, late of the Manchester Technical School. Demy 8vo, cloth. [*Just Published.* **3/6**

## THE ART OF LEATHER MANUFACTURE.

Being a Practical Handbook, in which the Operations of Tanning, Currying, and Leather Dressing are fully Described, and the Principles of Tanning Explained, and many Recent Processes Introduced ; as also Methods for the Estimation of Tannin, and a Description of the Arts of Glue Boiling, Gut Dressing, &c. By ALEXANDER WATT, Author of "Soap-Making," &c. Fourth Edition. Crown 8vo, cloth . . . . . . . **9/0**

"A sound, comprehensive treatise on tanning and its accessories. The book is an eminently valuable production, which redounds to the credit of both author and publishers."—*Chemical Review.*

## THE ART OF BOOT AND SHOE MAKING.

A Practical Handbook, including Measurement, Last-Fitting, Cutting-Out, Closing and Making, with a Description of the most approved Machinery Employed. By JOHN B. LENO, late Editor of *St. Crispin*, and *The Boot and Shoe-Maker*. 12mo, cloth . . . . . . . . . **2/0**

38   CROSBY LOCKWOOD & SON'S CATALOGUE.

## WOOD ENGRAVING.

A Practical and Easy Introduction to the Study of the Art. By W. N. BROWN. 12mo, cloth . . . . . . . . . . **1/6**

"The book is clear and complete, and will be useful to any one wanting to understand the first elements of the beautiful art of wood engraving."—*Graphic.*

## MODERN HOROLOGY, IN THEORY AND PRACTICE.

Translated from the French of CLAUDIUS SAUNIER, ex-Director of the School of Horology at Macon, by JULIEN TRIPPLIN, F.R.A.S., Besancon Watch Manufacturer, and EDWARD RIGG, M.A., Assayer in the Royal Mint. With Seventy-eight Woodcuts and Twenty-two Coloured Copper Plates. Second Edition. Super-royal 8vo, cloth, **£2 2s.**; half-calf . . . **£2 10s.**

"There is no horological work in the English language at all to be compared to this production of M. Saunier's for clearness and completeness. It is alike good as a guide for the student and as a reference for the experienced horologist and skilled workman."—*Horological Journal.*

"The latest, the most complete, and the most reliable of those literary productions to which continental watchmakers are indebted for the mechanical superiority over their English brethren —in fact, the Book of Books, is M. Saunier's 'Treatise.'"—*Watchmaker, Jeweller, and Silversmith.*

## THE WATCH ADJUSTER'S MANUAL.

A Practical Guide for the Watch and Chronometer Adjuster in Making, Springing, Timing and Adjusting for Isochronism, Positions and Temperatures. By C. E. FRITTS. 370 pp., with Illustrations, 8vo, cloth . . . **16/0**

## THE WATCHMAKER'S HANDBOOK.

Intended as a Workshop Companion for those engaged in Watchmaking and the Allied Mechanical Arts. Translated from the French of CLAUDIUS SAUNIER, and enlarged by JULIEN TRIPPLIN, F.R.A.S., and EDWARD RIGG, M.A., Assayer in the Royal Mint. Third Edition. 8vo, cloth. **9/0**

"Each part is truly a treatise in itself. The arrangement is good and the language is clear and concise. It is an admirable guide for the young watchmaker."—*Engineering.*

"It is impossible to speak too highly of its excellence. It fulfils every requirement in a handbook intended for the use of a workman. Should be found in every workshop."—*Watch and Clockmaker.*

## A HISTORY OF WATCHES & OTHER TIMEKEEPERS.

By JAMES F. KENDAL, M.B.H. Inst. Boards, **1/6**; or cloth, gilt . **2/6**

"The best which has yet appeared on this subject in the English language."—*Industries.*

"Open the book where you may, there is interesting matter in it concerning the ingenious devices of the ancient or modern horologer."—*Saturday Review.*

## ELECTRO-DEPOSITION.

A Practical Treatise on the Electrolysis of Gold, Silver, Copper, Nickel, and other Metals and Alloys. With Descriptions of Voltaic Batteries, Magneto and Dynamo-Electric Machines, Thermopiles, and of the Materials and Processes used in every Department of the Art, and several Chapters on ELECTRO-METALLURGY. By ALEXANDER WATT, Author of "Electro-Metallurgy," &c. Third Edition, Revised. Crown 8vo, cloth . . **9/0**

"Eminently a book for the practical worker in electro-deposition. It contains practical descriptions of methods, processes and materials, as actually pursued and used in the workshop."—*Engineer.*

## ELECTRO-METALLURGY.

Practically Treated. By ALEXANDER WATT. Tenth Edition, including the most recent Processes. 12mo, cloth . . . . . . . . **3/6**

"From this book both amateur and artisan may learn everything necessary for the successful prosecution of electroplating."—*Iron.*

## JEWELLER'S ASSISTANT IN WORKING IN GOLD.

A Practical Treatise for Masters and Workmen, Compiled from the Experience of Thirty Years' Workshop Practice. By GEORGE E. GEE, Author of "The Goldsmith's Handbook," &c. Crown 8vo, cloth . . . . . **7/6**

"This manual of technical education is apparently destined to be a valuable auxiliary to a handicraft which is certainly capable of great improvement."—*The Times.*

## ELECTROPLATING.
A Practical Handbook on the Deposition of Copper, Silver, Nickel, Gold, Aluminium, Brass, Platinum, &c., &c. By J. W. URQUHART, C.E. Fourth Edition, Revised. Crown 8vo, cloth. [*Just Published.* **5/0**
" An excellent practical manual."—*Engineering.*
" An excellent work, giving the newest information."—*Horological Journal.*

## ELECTROTYPING.
The Reproduction and Multiplication of Printing Surfaces and Works of Art by the Electro-Deposition of Metals. By J. W. URQUHART, C.E. Crown 8vo, cloth . . . . . . . . . . . . . **5/0**
" The book is thoroughly practical; the reader is, therefore, conducted through the leading laws of electricity, then through the metals used by electrotypers, the apparatus, and the depositing processes, up to the final preparation of the work."—*Art Journal.*

## GOLDSMITH'S HANDBOOK.
By GEORGE E. GEE, Jeweller, &c. Fifth Edition. 12mo, cloth . . **3/0**
" A good, sound educator, and will be generally accepted as an authority."—*Horological Journal.*

## SILVERSMITH'S HANDBOOK.
By GEORGE E. GEE, Jeweller, &c. Third Edition, with numerous Illustrations. 12mo, cloth . . . . . . . . . . . **3/0**
" The chief merit of the work is its practical character. . . . The workers in the trade will speedily discover its merits when they sit down to study it."—*English Mechanic.*
\*\*\* *The above two works together, strongly half-bound, price 7s.*

## SHEET METAL WORKER'S INSTRUCTOR.
Comprising a Selection of Geometrical Problems and Practical Rules for Describing the Various Patterns Required by Zinc, Sheet-Iron, Copper, and Tin-Plate Workers. By REUBEN HENRY WARN. New Edition, Revised and greatly Enlarged by JOSEPH G. HORNER, A.M.I.M.E. Crown 8vo, 254 pp., with 430 Illustrations, cloth. [*Just Published.* **7/6**

## BREAD & BISCUIT BAKER'S & SUGAR-BOILER'S ASSISTANT.
Including a large variety of Modern Recipes. With Remarks on the Art of Bread-making. By ROBERT WELLS. Third Edition. Crown 8vo, cloth . **2/0**
" A large number of wrinkles for the ordinary cook, as well as the baker."—*Saturday Review.*

## PASTRYCOOK & CONFECTIONER'S GUIDE.
For Hotels, Restaurants, and the Trade in general, adapted also for Family Use. By R. WELLS, Author of " The Bread and Biscuit Baker." Crown 8vo, cloth . . . . . . . . . . . . . **2/0**
" We cannot speak too highly of this really excellent work. In these days of keen competition our readers cannot do better than purchase this book."—*Bakers' Times.*

## ORNAMENTAL CONFECTIONERY.
A Guide for Bakers, Confectioners and Pastrycooks; including a variety of Modern Recipes, and Remarks on Decorative and Coloured Work. With 129 Original Designs. By ROBERT WELLS. Second Edition. Crown 8vo . **5/0**
" A valuable work, practical, and should be in the hands of every baker and confectioner. The illustrative designs are alone worth treble the amount charged for the whole work."—*Bakers' Times.*

## THE MODERN FLOUR CONFECTIONER, WHOLESALE AND RETAIL.
Containing a large Collection of Recipes or Cheap Cakes, Biscuits, &c. With remarks on the Ingredients Used in their Manufacture. By ROBERT WELLS, Author of " The Bread and Biscuit Baker," &c. Crown 8vo, cloth . **2/0**
" The work is of a decidedly practical character, and in every recipe regard is had to economical working."—*North British Daily Mail.*

## RUBBER HAND STAMPS
And the Manipulation of Rubber. A Practical Treatise on the Manufacture of Indiarubber Hand Stamps, Small Articles of Indiarubber, The Hektograph, Special Inks, Cements, and Allied Subjects. By T. O'CONOR SLOANE, A.M., Ph.D. With numerous Illustrations. Square 8vo, cloth . . . **5/0**

40    CROSBY LOCKWOOD & SON'S CATALOGUE.

## HANDYBOOKS FOR HANDICRAFTS.
BY PAUL N. HASLUCK.
Editor of "Work" (New Series), Author of "Lathe Work," "Milling Machines," &c.
Crown 8vo, 144 pp., price 1s. each.

These HANDYBOOKS *have been written to supply information for* WORKMEN, STUDENTS, *and* AMATEURS *in the several Handicrafts, on the actual* PRACTICE *of the* WORKSHOP, *and are intended to convey in plain language* TECHNICAL KNOWLEDGE *of the several* CRAFTS. *In describing the processes employed, and the manipulation of material, workshop terms are used ; workshop practice is fully explained ; and the text is freely illustrated with drawings of modern tools, appliances, and processes.*

### THE METAL TURNER'S HANDYBOOK.
A Practical Manual for Workers at the Foot-Lathe. With over 100 Illustrations.    .    .    .    .    .    .    .    .    .    .    1/0
"The book will be of service alike to the amateur and the artisan turner. It displays thorough knowledge of the subject."—*Scotsman.*

### THE WOOD TURNER'S HANDYBOOK.
A Practical Manual for Workers at the Lathe. With over 100 Illustrations.    1/0
"We recommend the book to young turners and amateurs. A multitude of workmen have hitherto sought in vain for a manual of this special industry."—*Mechanical World.*

### THE WATCH JOBBER'S HANDYBOOK.
A Practical Manual on Cleaning, Repairing, and Adjusting. With upwards of 100 Illustrations    .    .    .    .    .    .    .    .    1/0
"We strongly advise all young persons connected with the watch trade to acquire and study this inexpensive work."—*Clerkenwell Chronicle.*

### THE PATTERN MAKER'S HANDYBOOK.
A Practical Manual on the Construction of Patterns for Founders. With upwards of 100 Illustrations    .    .    .    .    .    .    .    1/0
"A most valuable, if not indispensable manual for the pattern maker."—*Knowledge.*

### THE MECHANIC'S WORKSHOP HANDYBOOK.
A Practical Manual on Mechanical Manipulation, embracing Information on various Handicraft Processes. With Useful Notes and Miscellaneous Memoranda. Comprising about 200 Subjects    .    .    .    .    1/0
"A very clever and useful book, which should be found in every workshop; and it should certainly find a place in all technical schools."—*Saturday Review.*

### THE MODEL ENGINEER'S HANDYBOOK.
A Practical Manual on the Construction of Model Steam Engines. With upwards of 100 Illustrations.    .    .    .    .    .    .    1/0
"Mr. Hasluck has produced a very good little book."—*Builder.*

### THE CLOCK JOBBER'S HANDYBOOK.
A Practical Manual on Cleaning, Repairing, and Adjusting. With upwards of 100 Illustrations    .    .    .    .    .    .    .    .    1/0
"It is of inestimable service to those commencing the trade."—*Coventry Standard.*

### THE CABINET MAKER'S HANDYBOOK.
A Practical Manual on the Tools, Materials, Appliances, and Processes employed in Cabinet Work. With upwards of 100 Illustrations    .    1/0
"Mr. Hasluck's thorough-going little Handybook is amongst the most practical guides we have seen for beginners in cabinet-work."—*Saturday Review.*

### THE WOODWORKER'S HANDYBOOK OF MANUAL INSTRUCTION.
Embracing Information on the Tools, Materials, Appliances and Processes Employed in Woodworking. With 104 Illustrations.    .    .    .    1/0

OPINIONS OF THE PRESS.
"Written by a man who knows, not only how work ought to be done, but how to do it, and how to convey his knowledge to others."—*Engineering.*
"Mr. Hasluck writes admirably, and gives complete Instructions."—*Engineer.*
"Mr. Hasluck combines the experience of a practical teacher with the manipulative skill and scientific knowledge of processes of the trained mechanician, and the manuals are marvels of what can be produced at a popular price."—*Schoolmaster.*
"Helpful to workmen of all ages and degrees of experience."—*Daily Chronicle.*
"Practical, sensible, and remarkably cheap."—*Journal of Education.*
"Concise, clear, and practical."—*Saturday Review.*

# COMMERCE, COUNTING-HOUSE WORK, TABLES, &c.

### LESSONS IN COMMERCE.
By Professor R. GAMBARO, of the Royal High Commercial School at Genoa. Edited and Revised by JAMES GAULT, Professor of Commerce and Commercial Law in King's College, London. Second Edition, Revised. Crown 8vo . **3/6**
"The publishers of this work have rendered considerable service to the cause of commercial education by the opportune production of this volume. . . . The work is peculiarly acceptable to English readers and an admirable addition to existing class books. In a phrase, we think the work attains its object in furnishing a brief account of those laws and customs of British trade with which the commercial man interested therein should be familiar."—*Chamber of Commerce Journal.*
"An invaluable guide in the hands of those who are preparing for a commercial career, and, in fact, the information it contains on matters of business should be impressed on every one."—*Counting House.*

### THE FOREIGN COMMERCIAL CORRESPONDENT.
Being Aids to Commercial Correspondence in Five Languages—English, French, German, Italian, and Spanish. By CONRAD E. BAKER. Second Edition. Crown 8vo, cloth . . . . . . . . . **3/6**
"Whoever wishes to correspond in all the languages mentioned by Mr. Baker cannot do better than study this work, the materials of which are excellent and conveniently arranged. They consist not of entire specimen letters, but—what are far more useful—short passages, sentences, or phrases expressing the same general idea in various forms."—*Athenæum.*
"A careful examination has convinced us that it is unusually complete, well arranged and reliable. The book is a thoroughly good one."—*Schoolmaster.*

### FACTORY ACCOUNTS: their PRINCIPLES & PRACTICE.
A Handbook for Accountants and Manufacturers, with Appendices on the Nomenclature of Machine Details; the Income Tax Acts; the Rating of Factories; Fire and Boiler Insurance; the Factory and Workshop Acts, &c., including also a Glossary of Terms and a large number of Specimen Rulings. By EMILE GARCKE and J. M. FELLS. Fourth Edition, Revised and Enlarged. Demy 8vo, 250 pp., strongly bound . . . . . . . **6/0**
"A very interesting description of the requirements of Factory Accounts. . . . The principle of assimilating the Factory Accounts to the general commercial books is one which we thoroughly agree with."—*Accountants' Journal.*
"Characterised by extreme thoroughness. There are few owners of factories who would not derive great benefit from the perusal of this most admirable work."—*Local Government Chronicle.*

### MODERN METROLOGY.
A Manual of the Metrical Units and Systems of the present Century. With an Appendix containing a proposed English System. By LOWIS D. A. JACKSON, A. M. Inst. C. E., Author of "Aid to Survey Practice," &c. Large crown 8vo, cloth . . . . . . . . . . **12/6**
"We recommend the work to all interested in the practical reform of our weights and measures."—*Nature.*

### A SERIES OF METRIC TABLES.
In which the British Standard Measures and Weights are compared with those of the Metric System at present in Use on the Continent. By C. H. DOWLING, C.E. 8vo, strongly bound . . . . . . . . **10/6**
"Mr. Dowling's Tables are well put together as a ready reckoner for the conversion of one system into the other."—*Athenæum.*

### THE IRON AND METAL TRADES' COMPANION.
For Expeditiously Ascertaining the Value of any Goods bought or sold by Weight, from 1s. per cwt. to 112s. per cwt., and from one farthing per pound to one shilling per pound. By THOMAS DOWNIE. 396 pp., leather . . **9/0**
"A most useful set of tables, nothing like them before existed."—*Building News.*
"Although specially adapted to the iron and metal trades, the tables will be found useful in every other business in which merchandise is bought and sold by weight."—*Railway News.*

## NUMBER, WEIGHT, AND FRACTIONAL CALCULATOR.

Containing upwards of 250,000 Separate Calculations, showing at a Glance the Value at 422 Different Rates, ranging from $\frac{1}{144}$th of a Penny to 20s. each, or per cwt., and £20 per ton, of any number of articles consecutively, from 1 to 470. Any number of cwts., qrs., and lbs., from 1 cwt. to 470 cwts. Any number of tons, cwts., qrs., and lbs., from 1 to 1,000 tons. By WILLIAM CHADWICK, Public Accountant. Third Edition, Revised. 8vo, strongly bound . **18/0**

"It is as easy of reference for any answer or any number of answers as a dictionary. For making up accounts or estimates the book must prove invaluable to all who have any considerable quantity of calculations involving price and measure in any combination to do."—*Engineer.*
"The most perfect work of the kind yet prepared."—*Glasgow Herald.*

## THE WEIGHT CALCULATOR.

Being a Series of Tables upon a New and Comprehensive Plan, exhibiting at one Reference the exact Value of any Weight from 1 lb. to 15 tons, at 300 Progressive Rates, from 1d. to 168s. per cwt., and containing 186,000 Direct Answers, which, with their Combinations, consisting of a single addition (mostly to be performed at sight), will afford an aggregate of 10,266,000 Answers; the whole being calculated and designed to ensure correctness and promote despatch. By HENRY HARBEN, Accountant. Fifth Edition, carefully Corrected. Royal 8vo, strongly half-bound . . . . . . **£1 5s.**

"A practical and useful work of reference for men of business generally."—*Ironmonger.*
"Of priceless value to business men. It is a necessary book in all mercantile offices."—*Sheffield Independent.*

## THE DISCOUNT GUIDE.

Comprising several Series of Tables for the Use of Merchants, Manufacturers, Ironmongers, and Others, by which may be ascertained the Exact Profit arising from any mode of using Discounts, either in the Purchase or Sale of Goods, and the method of either Altering a Rate of Discount, or Advancing a Price, so as to produce, by one operation, a sum that will realise any required Profit after allowing one or more Discounts: to which are added Tables of Profit or Advance from 1¼ to 90 per cent., Tables of Discount from 1¼ to 98¾ per cent., and Tables of Commission, &c., from ⅛ to 10 per cent. By HENRY HARBEN, Accountant. New Edition, Corrected. Demy 8vo, half-bound . **£1 5s.**

"A book such as this can only be appreciated by business men, to whom the saving of time means saving of money. The work must prove of great value to merchants, manufacturers, and general traders."—*British Trade Journal.*

## TABLES OF WAGES.

At 54, 52, 50 and 48 Hours per Week. Showing the Amounts of Wages from One quarter of an hour to Sixty-four hours, in each case at Rates of Wages advancing by One Shilling from 4s. to 55s. per week. By THOS. GARBUTT, Accountant. Square crown 8vo, half-bound . . . . . . **6/0**

## IRON-PLATE WEIGHT TABLES.

For Iron Shipbuilders, Engineers, and Iron Merchants. Containing the Calculated Weights of upwards of 150,000 different sizes of Iron Plates from 1 foot by 6 in. by ¼ in. to 10 feet by 5 feet by 1 in. Worked out on the Basis of 40 lbs. to the square foot of Iron of 1 inch in thickness. By H. BURLINSON and W. H. SIMPSON. 4to, half-bound . . . . . . **£1 5s.**

## MATHEMATICAL TABLES (ACTUARIAL).

Comprising Commutation and Conversion Tables, Logarithms, Cologarithms, Antilogarithms and Reciprocals. By J. W. GORDON. Royal 8vo, mounted on canvas, in cloth case. *Just Published.* **5/0**

# AGRICULTURE, FARMING, GARDENING, &c.

## THE COMPLETE GRAZIER AND FARMER'S AND CATTLE BREEDER'S ASSISTANT.

A Compendium of Husbandry. Originally Written by WILLIAM YOUATT. Fourteenth Edition, entirely Re-written, considerably Enlarged, and brought up to Present Requirements, by WILLIAM FREAM, LL.D., Assistant Commissioner, Royal Commission on Agriculture, 1893, Author of "The Elements of Agriculture," &c. Royal 8vo, 1,100 pp., with over 450 Illustrations, handsomely bound. [*Just Published.* **£1 11s. 6d.**

SUMMARY OF CONTENTS.

BOOK I. ON THE VARIETIES, BREEDING, REARING, FATTENING AND MANAGEMENT OF CATTLE.
BOOK II. ON THE ECONOMY AND MANAGEMENT OF THE DAIRY.
BOOK III. ON THE BREEDING, REARING, AND MANAGEMENT OF HORSES.
BOOK IV. ON THE BREEDING, REARING, AND FATTENING OF SHEEP.
BOOK V. ON THE BREEDING, REARING, AND FATTENING OF SWINE.
BOOK VI. ON THE DISEASES OF LIVE STOCK.
BOOK VII. ON THE BREEDING, REARING, AND MANAGEMENT OF POULTRY.
BOOK VIII. ON FARM OFFICES AND IMPLEMENTS OF HUSBANDRY.
BOOK IX. ON THE CULTURE AND MANAGEMENT OF GRASS LANDS.
BOOK X. ON THE CULTIVATION AND APPLICATION OF GRASSES, PULSE AND ROOTS.
BOOK XI. ON MANURES AND THEIR APPLICATION TO GRASS LAND AND CROPS.
BOOK XII. MONTHLY CALENDARS OF FARMWORK.

\*\*\* OPINIONS OF THE PRESS ON THE NEW EDITION.

"Dr. Fream is to be congratulated on the successful attempt he has made to give us a work which will at once become the standard classic of the farm practice of the country. We believe that it will be found that it has no compeer among the many works at present in existence. . . . The illustrations are admirable, while the frontispiece, which represents the well-known bull, New Year's Gift, owned by the Queen, is a work of art."—*The Times.*

"The book must be recognised as occupying the proud position of the most exhaustive work of reference in the English language on the subject with which it deals."—*Athenæum.*

"The most comprehensive guide to modern farm practice that exists in the English language to-day. . . . The book is one that ought to be on every farm and in the library of every land owner."—*Mark Lane Express.*

"In point of exhaustiveness and accuracy the work will certainly hold a pre-eminent and unique position among books dealing with scientific agricultural practice. It is, in fact, an agricultural library of itself."—*North British Agriculturist.*

"A compendium of authoritative and well-ordered knowledge on every conceivable branch of the work of the live stock farmer; probably without an equal in this or any other country."—*Yorkshire Post.*

## FARM LIVE STOCK OF GREAT BRITAIN.

By ROBERT WALLACE, F.L.S., F.R.S.E., &c., Professor of Agriculture and Rural Economy in the University of Edinburgh. Third Edition, thoroughly Revised and considerably Enlarged. With over 120 Phototypes of Prize Stock. Demy 8vo, 384 pp., with 79 Plates and Maps, cloth. . . **12/6**

"A really complete work on the history, breeds, and management of the farm stock of Great Britain, and one which is likely to find its way to the shelves of every country gentleman's library."—*The Times.*

"The latest edition of 'Farm Live Stock of Great Britain' is a production to be proud of, and its issue not the least of the services which its author has rendered to agricultural science."—*Scottish Farmer.*

"The book is very attractive, . . . and we can scarcely imagine the existence of a farmer who would not like to have a copy of this beautiful and useful work."—*Mark Lane Express.*

## NOTE-BOOK OF AGRICULTURAL FACTS & FIGURES FOR FARMERS AND FARM STUDENTS.

By PRIMROSE MCCONNELL, B.Sc., Fellow of the Highland and Agricultural Society, Author of "Elements of Farming." Sixth Edition, Re-written, Revised, and greatly Enlarged. Fcap. 8vo, 480 pp., leather. [*Just Published.* **6/0**

SUMMARY OF CONTENTS: SURVEYING AND LEVELLING.— WEIGHTS AND MEASURES.— MACHINERY AND BUILDINGS.— LABOUR.— OPERATIONS.— DRAINING.— EMBANKING.— GEOLOGICAL MEMORANDA.— SOILS.— MANURES.— CROPPING.— CROPS.— ROTATIONS. — WEEDS.— FEEDING.— DAIRYING.— LIVE STOCK. — HORSES. — CATTLE.— SHEEP.—PIGS.—POULTRY.—FORESTRY.—HORTICULTURE.—MISCELLANEOUS.

"No farmer, and certainly no agricultural student, ought to be without this *multum-in-parvo* manual of all subjects connected with the farm."—*North British Agriculturist.*

"This little pocket-book contains a large amount of useful information upon all kinds of agricultural subjects. Something of the kind has long been wanted."—*Mark Lane Express.*

"The amount of information it contains is most surprising; the arrangement of the matter is so methodical—although so compressed—as to be intelligible to everyone who takes a glance through its pages. They teem with information."—*Farm and Home.*

44     CROSBY LOCKWOOD & SON'S CATALOGUE.

## BRITISH DAIRYING.

A Handy Volume on the Work of the Dairy-Farm. For the Use of Technical Instruction Classes, Students in Agricultural Colleges and the Working Dairy-Farmer. By Prof. J. P. SHELDON. With Illustrations. Second Edition, Revised. Crown 8vo, cloth.   [*Just Published.*   **2/6**
"Confidently recommended as a useful text-book on dairy farming."—*Agricultural Gazette.*
"Probably the best half-crown manual on dairy work that has yet been produced."—*North British Agriculturist.*
"It is the soundest little work we have yet seen on the subject."—*The Times.*

## MILK, CHEESE, AND BUTTER.

A Practical Handbook on their Properties and the Processes of their Production. Including a Chapter on Cream and the Methods of its Separation from Milk. By JOHN OLIVER, late Principal of the Western Dairy Institute, Berkeley. With Coloured Plates and 200 Illustrations. Crown 8vo, cloth.
**7/6**
"An exhaustive and masterly production. It may be cordially recommended to all students and practitioners of dairy science."—*North British Agriculturist.*
"We recommend this very comprehensive and carefully-written book to dairy-farmers and students of dairying. It is a distinct acquisition to the library of the agriculturist."—*Agricultural Gazette.*

## SYSTEMATIC SMALL FARMING.

Or, The Lessons of My Farm. Being an Introduction to Modern Farm Practice for Small Farmers. By R. SCOTT BURN, Author of "Outlines of Modern Farming," &c. Crown 8vo, cloth.   .   .   .   .   .   .   **6/0**
"This is the completest book of its class we have seen, and one which every amateur farmer will read with pleasure, and accept as a guide."—*Field.*

## OUTLINES OF MODERN FARMING.

By R. SCOTT BURN. Soils, Manures, and Crops—Farming and Farming Economy—Cattle, Sheep, and Horses—Management of Dairy, Pigs, and Poultry—Utilisation of Town-Sewage, Irrigation, &c. Sixth Edition. In One Vol., 1,250 pp., half-bound, profusely Illustrated   .   .   .   .   **12/0**

## FARM ENGINEERING, The COMPLETE TEXT-BOOK of.

Comprising Draining and Embanking; Irrigation and Water Supply; Farm Roads, Fences and Gates; Farm Buildings; Barn Implements and Machines; Field Implements and Machines; Agricultural Surveying, &c. By Professor JOHN SCOTT. In One Vol., 1,150 pp., half-bound, with over 600 Illustrations.
**12/0**
"Written with great care, as well as with knowledge and ability. The author has done his work well; we have found him a very trustworthy guide wherever we have tested his statements. The volume will be of great value to agricultural students."—*Mark Lane Express.*

## THE FIELDS OF GREAT BRITAIN.

A Text-Book of Agriculture. Adapted to the Syllabus of the Science and Art Department. For Elementary and Advanced Students. By HUGH CLEMENTS (Board of Trade). Second Edition, Revised, with Additions. 18mo, cloth   .   .   .   .   .   .   .   .   .   .   .   .   **2/6**
"It is a long time since we have seen a book which has pleased us more, or which contains such a vast and useful fund of knowledge."—*Educational Times.*

## TABLES and MEMORANDA for FARMERS, GRAZIERS, AGRICULTURAL STUDENTS, SURVEYORS, LAND AGENTS, AUCTIONEERS, &c.

With a New System of Farm Book-keeping. By SIDNEY FRANCIS. Fifth Edition. 272 pp., waistcoat-pocket size, limp leather   .   .   .   **1/6**
"Weighing less than 1 oz., and occupying no more space than a match-box, it contains a mass of facts and calculations which has never before, in such handy form, been obtainable. Every operation on the farm is dealt with. The work may be taken as thoroughly accurate, the whole of the tables having been revised by Dr. Fream. We cordially recommend it."—*Bell's Weekly Messenger.*

## THE ROTHAMSTED EXPERIMENTS AND THEIR PRACTICAL LESSONS FOR FARMERS.

Part I. STOCK. Part II. CROPS. By C. J. R. TIPPER. Crown 8vo, cloth.
[*Just Published.*   **3/6**
"We have no doubt that the book will be welcomed by a large class of farmers and others interested in agriculture."—*Standard.*

## AGRICULTURE, FARMING, GARDENING, &c. 45

### FERTILISERS AND FEEDING STUFFS.
A Handbook for the Practical Farmer. By BERNARD DYER. D.Sc. (Lond.) With the Text of the Fertilisers and Feeding Stuffs Act of 1893, &c. Third Edition, Revised. Crown 8vo, cloth. [*Just Published.* **1/0**
"This little book is precisely what it professes to be—'A Handbook for the Practical Farmer.' Dr. Dyer has done farmers good service in placing at their disposal so much useful information in so intelligible a form."—*The Times.*

### BEES FOR PLEASURE AND PROFIT.
A Guide to the Manipulation of Bees, the Production of Honey, and the General Management of the Apiary. By G. GORDON SAMSON. With numerous Illustrations. Crown 8vo, cloth . . . . . . **1/0**

### BOOK-KEEPING for FARMERS and ESTATE OWNERS.
A Practical Treatise, presenting, in Three Plans, a System adapted for all Classes of Farms. By JOHNSON M. WOODMAN, Chartered Accountant. Second Edition, Revised. Crown 8vo, cloth . . . . . **2/6**
"The volume is a capital study of a most important subject."—*Agricultural Gazette.*

### WOODMAN'S YEARLY FARM ACCOUNT BOOK.
Giving Weekly Labour Account and Diary, and showing the Income and Expenditure under each Department of Crops, Live Stock, Dairy, &c., &c. With Valuation, Profit and Loss Account, and Balance Sheet at the End of the Year. By JOHNSON M. WOODMAN, Chartered Accountant. Second Edition. Folio, half-bound . . . . . . . . . . *Net* **7/6**
"Contains every requisite form for keeping farm accounts readily and accurately."—*Agriculture.*

### THE FORCING GARDEN.
Or, How to Grow Early Fruits, Flowers and Vegetables. With Plans and Estimates for Building Glasshouses, Pits and Frames. With Illustrations. By SAMUEL WOOD. Crown 8vo, cloth . . . . . . **3/6**
"A good book, containing a great deal of valuable teaching."—*Gardeners' Magazine.*

### A PLAIN GUIDE TO GOOD GARDENING.
Or, How to Grow Vegetables, Fruits, and Flowers. By S. WOOD. Fourth Edition, with considerable Additions, and numerous Illustrations. Crown 8vo, cloth . . . . . . . . . . . . **3/6**
"A very good book, and one to be highly recommended as a practical guide. The practical directions are excellent."—*Athenæum.*

### MULTUM-IN-PARVO GARDENING.
Or, How to Make One Acre of Land produce £620 a year, by the Cultivation of Fruits and Vegetables; also, How to Grow Flowers in Three Glass Houses, so as to realise £176 per annum clear Profit. By SAMUEL WOOD, Author of "Good Gardening," &c. Sixth Edition, Crown 8vo, sewed . . . **1/0**
"We are bound to recommend it as not only suited to the case of the amateur and gentleman's gardener, but to the market grower."—*Gardeners' Magazine.*

### THE LADIES' MULTUM-IN-PARVO FLOWER GARDEN.
And Amateur's Complete Guide. By S. WOOD. Crown 8vo, cloth . **3/6**
"Full of shrewd hints and useful instructions, based on a lifetime of experience."—*Scotsman.*

### POTATOES: HOW TO GROW AND SHOW THEM.
A Practical Guide to the Cultivation and General Treatment of the Potato. By J. PINK. Crown 8vo . . . . . . . . . **2/0**

### MARKET AND KITCHEN GARDENING.
By C. W. SHAW, late Editor of *Gardening Illustrated.* Cloth . . **3/6**
"The most valuable compendium of kitchen and market-garden work published."—*Farmer.*

## AUCTIONEERING, VALUING, LAND SURVEYING, ESTATE AGENCY, &c.

**INWOOD'S TABLES FOR PURCHASING ESTATES AND FOR THE VALUATION OF PROPERTIES,**
Including Advowsons, Assurance Policies, Copyholds, Deferred Annuities, Freeholds, Ground Rents, Immediate Annuities, Leaseholds, Life Interests, Mortgages, Perpetuities, Renewals of Leases, Reversions, Sinking Funds, &c., &c. 26th Edition, Revised and Extended by WILLIAM SCHOOLING, F.R.A.S., with Logarithms of Natural Numbers and THOMAN'S Logarithmic Interest and Annuity Tables. 360 pp., Demy 8vo, cloth.
[*Just Published.* Net **8/0**

"Those interested in the purchase and sale of estates, and in the adjustment of compensation cases, as well as in transactions in annuities, life insurances, &c., will find the present edition of eminent service."—*Engineering.*
"This valuable book has been considerably enlarged and improved by the labours of Mr. Schooling, and is now very complete indeed."—*Economist.*
"Altogether this edition will prove of extreme value to many classes of professional men in saving them many long and tedious calculations."—*Investors' Review.*

**THE APPRAISER, AUCTIONEER, BROKER, HOUSE AND ESTATE AGENT AND VALUER'S POCKET ASSISTANT.**
For the Valuation for Purchase, Sale, or Renewal of Leases, Annuities, and Reversions, and of Property generally; with Prices for Inventories, &c. By JOHN WHEELER, Valuer, &c. Sixth Edition, Re-written and greatly Extended by C. NORRIS, Surveyor, Valuer, &c. Royal 32mo, cloth . . . **5/0**

"A neat and concise book of reference, containing an admirable and clearly-arranged list of prices for inventories, and a very practical guide to determine the value of furniture, &c."—*Standard.*
"Contains a large quantity of varied and useful information as to the valuation for purchase, sale, or renewal of leases, annuities and reversions, and of property generally, with prices for inventories, and a guide to determine the value of interior fittings and other effects."—*Builder.*

**AUCTIONEERS: THEIR DUTIES AND LIABILITIES.**
A Manual of Instruction and Counsel for the Young Auctioneer. By ROBERT SQUIBBS, Auctioneer. Second Edition, Revised and partly Re-written. Demy 8vo, cloth . . . . . . . . . . . **12/6**

"The standard text-book on the topics of which it treats."—*Athenæum.*
"The work is one of general excellent character, and gives much information in a compendious and satisfactory form."—*Builder.*
"May be recommended as giving a great deal of information on the law relating to auctioneers, in a very readable form."—*Law Journal.*
"Auctioneers may be congratulated on having so pleasing a writer to minister to their special needs."—*Solicitors' Journal.*

**THE AGRICULTURAL VALUER'S ASSISTANT.**
A Practical Handbook on the Valuation of Landed Estates; including Example of a Detailed Report on Management and Realisation; Forms of Valuations of Tenant Right; Lists of Local Agricultural Customs; Scales of Compensation under the Agricultural Holdings Act, and a Brief Treatise on Compensation under the Lands Clauses Acts, &c. By TOM BRIGHT, Agricultural Valuer. Author of "The Agricultural Surveyor and Estate Agent's Handbook." Third Edition, Revised and further Enlarged Crown 8vo, cloth. [*Just Published.* Net **6/0**

"Full of tables and examples in connection with the valuation of tenant-right, estates, labour, contents and weights of timber, and farm produce of all kinds."—*Agricultural Gazette.*
"An eminently practical handbook, full of practical tables and data of undoubted interest and value to surveyors and auctioneers in preparing valuations of all kinds."—*Farmer.*

**POLE PLANTATIONS AND UNDERWOODS.**
A Practical Handbook on Estimating the Cost of Forming, Renovating, Improving, and Grubbing Plantations and Underwoods, their Valuation for Purposes of Transfer, Rental, Sale or Assessment. By TOM BRIGHT. Crown 8vo, cloth . . . . . . . . . . . **3/6**

"To valuers, foresters and agents it will be a welcome aid."—*North British Agriculturist.*
"Well calculated to assist the valuer in the discharge of his duties, and of undoubted interest and use both to surveyors and auctioneers in preparing valuations of all kinds."—*Kent Herald.*

## AGRICULTURAL SURVEYOR AND ESTATE AGENT'S HANDBOOK.

Of Practical Rules, Formulæ, Tables, and Data. A Comprehensive Manual for the Use of Surveyors, Agents, Landowners, and others interested in the Equipment, the Management, or the Valuation of Landed Estates. By TOM BRIGHT, Agricultural Surveyor and Valuer, Author of "The Agricultural Valuer's Assistant," &c. With Illustrations. Fcap. 8vo, Leather.
[*Just Published.* **Net 7/6**

"An exceedingly useful book, the contents of which are admirably chosen. The classes for whom the work is intended will find it convenient to have this comprehensive handbook accessible for reference."—*Live Stock Journal.*

"It is a singularly compact and well informed compendium of the facts and figures likely to be required in estate work, and is certain to prove of much service to those to whom it is addressed."—*Scotsman.*

## THE LAND VALUER'S BEST ASSISTANT.

Being Tables on a very much Improved Plan, for Calculating the Value of Estates. With Tables for reducing Scotch, Irish, and Provincial Customary Acres to Statute Measure, &c. By R. HUDSON, C.E. New Edition. Royal 32mo, leather, elastic band . . . . . . . **4/0**
"Of incalculable value to the country gentleman and professional man."—*Farmers' Journal.*

## THE LAND IMPROVER'S POCKET-BOOK.

Comprising Formulæ, Tables, and Memoranda required in any Computation relating to the Permanent Improvement of Landed Property. By JOHN EWART, Surveyor. Second Edition, Revised. Royal 32mo, oblong, leather . **4/0**
"A compendious and handy little volume."—*Spectator.*

## THE LAND VALUER'S COMPLETE POCKET-BOOK.

Being the above Two Works bound together. Leather . . . . **7/6**

## HANDBOOK OF HOUSE PROPERTY.

A Popular and Practical Guide to the Purchase, Mortgage, Tenancy, and Compulsory Sale of Houses and Land, including Dilapidations and Fixtures; with Examples of all kinds of Valuations, Information on Building and on the right use of Decorative Art. By E. L. TARBUCK, Architect and Surveyor. Sixth Edition. 12mo, cloth . . . . . . . . . **5/0**
"The advice is thoroughly practical."—*Law Journal.*
"For all who have dealings with house property, this is an indispensable guide."—*Decoration.*
"Carefully brought up to date, and much improved by the addition of a division on Fine Art. A well-written and thoughtful work."—*Land Agent's Record.*

---

# LAW AND MISCELLANEOUS.

## MODERN JOURNALISM.

A Handbook of Instruction and Counsel for the Young Journalist. By JOHN B. MACKIE, Fellow of the Institute of Journalists. Crown 8vo, cloth . **2/0**
"This invaluable guide to journalism is a work which all aspirants to a journalistic career will read with advantage."—*Journalist.*

## HANDBOOK FOR SOLICITORS AND ENGINEERS

Engaged in Promoting Private Acts of Parliament and Provisional Orders for the Authorisation of Railways, Tramways, Gas and Water Works, &c. By L. LIVINGSTONE MACASSEY, of the Middle Temple, Barrister-at-Law, M. Inst. C.E. 8vo, cloth . . . . . . . **£1 5s.**

## PATENTS for INVENTIONS, HOW to PROCURE THEM.

Compiled for the Use of Inventors, Patentees and others. By G. G. M. HARDINGHAM, Assoc. Mem. Inst. C.E., &c. Demy 8vo, cloth . . **1/6**

## CONCILIATION & ARBITRATION in LABOUR DISPUTES.

A Historical Sketch and Brief Statement of the Present Position of the Question at Home and Abroad. By J. S. JEANS, Author of "England's Supremacy," &c. Crown 8vo, 200 pp., cloth . . . . . **2/6**

## EVERY MAN'S OWN LAWYER.

A Handy-Book of the Principles of Law and Equity. With a Concise Dictionary of Legal Terms. By A BARRISTER. Thirty-seventh Edition, carefully Revised, and including New Acts of Parliament of 1899. Comprising the *London Government Act, 1899; Sale of Food and Drugs Act, 1899; Infectious Diseases Notification Act, 1899; Small Dwellings Acquisition Act, 1899; Commons Act, 1899;* besides the *Benefices Act, 1898; Marriage Act, 1898; Inebriates Acts, 1898* and *1899; Criminal Evidence Act, 1898; Vaccination Act, 1898, &c. Judicial Decisions during the year have also been duly noted.* Crown 8vo, 750 pp., strongly bound in cloth. [*Just Published.* **6/8**

\*\*\* This *Standard Work of Reference forms* A COMPLETE EPITOME OF THE LAWS OF ENGLAND, *comprising (amongst other matter)*:

THE RIGHTS AND WRONGS OF INDIVIDUALS—LANDLORD AND TENANT—VENDORS AND PURCHASERS—LEASES AND MORTGAGES—PRINCIPAL AND AGENT—PARTNERSHIP AND COMPANIES—MASTERS, SERVANTS AND WORKMEN—CONTRACTS AND AGREEMENTS—BORROWERS, LENDERS AND SURETIES—SALE AND PURCHASE OF GOODS—CHEQUES, BILLS AND NOTES—BILLS OF SALE—BANKRUPTCY—RAILWAY AND SHIPPING LAW—LIFE, FIRE, AND MARINE INSURANCE—ACCIDENT AND FIDELITY INSURANCE—CRIMINAL LAW—PARLIAMENTARY ELECTIONS—COUNTY COUNCILS—DISTRICT COUNCILS—PARISH COUNCILS—MUNICIPAL CORPORATIONS—LIBEL AND SLANDER—PUBLIC HEALTH AND NUISANCES—COPYRIGHT, PATENTS, TRADE MARKS—HUSBAND AND WIFE—DIVORCE—INFANCY—CUSTODY OF CHILDREN—TRUSTEES AND EXECUTORS—CLERGY, CHURCHWARDENS, &c.—GAME LAWS AND SPORTING—INNKEEPERS—HORSES AND DOGS—TAXES AND DEATH DUTIES—FORMS OF AGREEMENTS, WILLS, CODICILS, NOTICES, &c.

☞ *The object of this work is to enable those who consult it to help themselves to the law; and thereby to dispense, as far as possible, with professional assistance and advice. There are many wrongs and grievances which persons submit to from time to time through not knowing how or where to apply for redress; and many persons having as great a dread of a lawyer's office as of a lion's den. With this book at hand it is believed that many a SIX-AND-EIGHTPENCE may be saved; many a wrong redressed; many a right reclaimed; many a law suit avoided; and many an evil abated. The work has established itself as the standard legal adviser of all classes, and has also made a reputation for itself as a useful book of reference for lawyers residing at a distance from law libraries, who are glad to have at hand a work embodying recent decisions and enactments.*

OPINIONS OF THE PRESS.

"It is a complete code of English Law written in plain language, which all can understand. Should be in the hands of every business man, and all who wish to abolish lawyers bills."—*Weekly Times.*

"A useful and concise epitome of the law, compiled with considerable care."—*Law Magazine.*

"A complete digest of the most useful facts which constitute English law."—*Globe.*

"This excellent handbook. . . . Admirably done, admirably arranged, and admirably cheap."—*Leeds Mercury*

"A concise, cheap, and complete epitome of the English law. So plainly written that he who runs may read, and he who reads may understand."—*Figaro.*

"A dictionary of legal facts well put together. The book is a very useful one."—*Spectator.*

## THE PAWNBROKER'S, FACTOR'S, AND MERCHANT'S GUIDE TO THE LAW OF LOANS AND PLEDGES.

With the Statutes and a Digest of Cases. By H. C. FOLKARD, Barrister-at-Law. Cloth . . . . . . . . . . . **3/6**

## LABOUR CONTRACTS.

A Popular Handbook on the Law of Contracts for Works and Services. By DAVID GIBBONS. Fourth Edition, with Appendix of Statutes by T. F. UTTLEY, Solicitor. Fcap. 8vo, cloth . . . . . . . **3/6**

## SUMMARY OF THE FACTORY AND WORKSHOP ACTS

(1878-1891). For the Use of Manufacturers and Managers. By EMILE GARCKE and J. M. FELLS. (Reprinted from "FACTORY ACCOUNTS.") Crown 8vo, sewed . . . . . . . . . . **6D.**

# TABLES,
## ETC.,

FOR THE USE OF

# MATHEMATICIANS, SURVEYORS,
# ENGINEERS,

AND OTHER PRACTICAL COMPUTERS.

---

*Royal 8vo, cloth,* **21s.** *net.*

**TABLES FOR THE FORMATION OF LOGARITHMS AND ANTI-LOGARITHMS TO TWENTY-FOUR OR ANY LESS NUMBER OF PLACES,** with Explanatory Introduction and Historical Preface. By PETER GRAY.

---

*Medium 8vo, with Marginal Index,* **5s.** *net.*

**TABLE OF LOGARITHMS AND ANTI-LOGARITHMS** (Four Figures) 1 to 10,000. By MAJOR-GENERAL HANNYNGTON.

# TABLES, &c., FOR THE USE OF MATHEMATICIANS, SURVEYORS, ENGINEERS, &c.

*Super Royal 8vo, cloth,* **21s.** *net.*

## TABLE OF QUARTER-SQUARES OF ALL INTEGER NUMBERS UP TO 100,000, by which the product of Two Factors may be found by the aid of Addition and Subtraction alone. By S. L. LAUNDY.

---

*Royal 4to, cloth,* **5s.** *net.*

## A TABLE OF PRODUCTS, BY THE FACTORS 1 TO 9, OF ALL NUMBERS FROM 1 TO 100,000, by the aid of which Multiplication may be performed by inspection; with an Introduction explanatory of its use, and also of the Method of obtaining the Products of Numbers exceeding the limits of the Table. By S. L. LAUNDY.

---

*Royal 8vo, cloth,* **£2. 2s.** *net.*

## TABLES OF COMPOUND INTEREST, for each rate between ¾ and 10 per Cent. per Annum, proceeding by Intervals of One-Eighth, and from 1 Year to 100 Years.—I. Present Value of £1.—II. Present Value of £1 per Annum.—III. Amount of £1.—IV. Amount of £1 per Annum. By LIEUT.-COL. W. H. OAKES, A.I.A.

---

*Super Royal 8vo, cloth,* **21s.** *net.*

## TABLES OF THE RECIPROCALS OF NUMBERS, FROM 1 TO 100,000, with their Differences, by which the Reciprocals of Numbers may be obtained up to 10,000,000. By LIEUT.-COL. W. H. OAKES, A.I.A.

TABLES, &c., FOR THE USE OF MATHEMATICIANS, SURVEYORS, ENGINEERS, &c.

---

*Imperial 8vo, cloth,* 10s. 6d. *net.*

## TABLES FOR FINDING THE HALF-YEARLY RATE OF INTEREST, FROM 1¼ PER CENT. UPWARDS, realised on Stock or Bonds, bearing 1½, 1¾, 2, 2¼, 2½, 2¾, and 3 per Cent. Half-Yearly Interest, issued at any Premium and redeemable at Par in any number of Half-Years not exceeding 60. By LIEUT.-COL. W. H. OAKES, A.I.A.

---

*Demy 8vo, cloth,* £1. 11s. 6d. *net.*

## LOANS PAYABLE BY DRAWINGS AND DEBENTURE INTEREST TABLES. By LIEUT.-COL. W. H. OAKES, A.I.A.

---

*Royal 8vo, with Index complete. Half-calf,* £2. 2s. *net.*
*New Edition.*

## TWO TABLES OF LOGARITHMS TO NATURAL NUMBERS, and Natural Numbers to Logarithms, for all Numbers from 1 to 99,999, and all Logarithms from ·00001 to ·99999; arranged so that the Logarithm or Number required is at once obtained correctly to Five Places of Decimals, by means of a Marginal Index, and without Reference to Tables of Differences in any case. By E. ERSKINE SCOTT.

TABLES, &c., FOR THE USE OF MATHEMATICIANS, SURVEYORS, ENGINEERS, &c.

*Royal 8vo. Price* 10s. *net.*

## A SHORT TABLE OF LOGARITHMS AND ANTI-LOGARITHMS TO TEN PLACES,

in Two Parts, whereby the Logarithm of any Number to Ten Places of Decimals, and the Number corresponding to any Logarithm to Ten Places of Decimals, may be readily and correctly found, to which is added a Complete List of Constants, with Formulæ for their Application. By E. ERSKINE SCOTT.

*Demy 8vo, 76 pp. Price* 7s. 6d. *net; with Marginal Thumb Index,* 12s. 6d. *net.*

## AN IMPROVED TABLE OF FIVE-FIGURE LOGARITHMS,

arranged with a view to securing the best possible combination of accuracy and speed in use, and with special regard to avoiding unnecessary fatigue to the eyes. By E. ERSKINE SCOTT.

*Super Royal 8vo, 602 pp., cloth,* 30s. *net.*

## LOGARITHMIC TABLES TO SEVEN PLACES OF DECIMALS,

containing Logarithmic Sines and Tangents to every Second of the Circle, with Arguments in Space and Time. *Revised Edition.* With additional Preface and Examples, by Major-General Hannyngton, F.I.A., F.S.S. By ROBERT SHORTREDE, F.R.A.S., &c.

# WEALE'S SERIES

OF

# SCIENTIFIC AND TECHNICAL WORKS.

"It is not too much to say that no books have ever proved more popular with or more useful to young engineers and others than the excellent treatises comprised in WEALE'S SERIES."—*Engineer.*

## A New Classified List.

| | PAGE | | PAGE |
|---|---|---|---|
| CIVIL ENGINEERING AND SURVEYING | 2 | ARCHITECTURE AND BUILDING | 6 |
| MINING AND METALLURGY | 3 | INDUSTRIAL AND USEFUL ARTS | 9 |
| MECHANICAL ENGINEERING | 4 | AGRICULTURE, GARDENING, ETC. | 10 |
| NAVIGATION, SHIPBUILDING, ETC. | 5 | MATHEMATICS, ARITHMETIC, ETC. | 12 |

BOOKS OF REFERENCE AND MISCELLANEOUS VOLUMES . . 14

CROSBY LOCKWOOD AND SON,
7, STATIONERS' HALL COURT, LONDON, E.C.
1900.

## CIVIL ENGINEERING & SURVEYING.

**Civil Engineering.**
By HENRY LAW, M.Inst.C.E. Including a Treatise on HYDRAULIC ENGINEERING by G. R. BURNELL, M.I.C.E. Seventh Edition, revised, with LARGE ADDITIONS by D. K. CLARK, M.I.C.E. . . . **6/6**

**Pioneer Engineering:**
A Treatise on the Engineering Operations connected with the Settlement of Waste Lands in New Countries. By EDWARD DOBSON, M.INST.C.E. With numerous Plates. Second Edition . . . . . **4/6**

**Iron Bridges of Moderate Span:**
Their Construction and Erection. By HAMILTON W. PENDRED. With 40 Illustrations . . . . . . . . . . . **2/0**

**Iron and Steel Bridges and Viaducts.**
A Practical Treatise upon their Construction for the use of Engineers, Draughtsmen, and Students. By FRANCIS CAMPIN, C.E. With numerous Illustrations . . . . . . . . . . . **3/6**

**Constructional Iron and Steel Work,**
As applied to Public, Private, and Domestic Buildings. By FRANCIS CAMPIN, C.E. . . . . . . . . . . **3/6**

**Tubular and other Iron Girder Bridges.**
Describing the Britannia and Conway Tubular Bridges. By G. DRYSDALE DEMPSEY, C.E. Fourth Edition . . . . . **2/0**

**Materials and Construction:**
A Theoretical and Practical Treatise on the Strains, Designing, and Erection of Works of Construction. By FRANCIS CAMPIN, C.E. . . **3/0**

**Sanitary Work in the Smaller Towns and in Villages.**
By CHARLES SLAGG, Assoc. M.Inst.C.E. Third Edition . . **3/0**

**Roads and Streets (The Construction of).**
In Two Parts: I. THE ART OF CONSTRUCTING COMMON ROADS, by H. LAW, C.E., Revised by D. K. CLARK, C.E.; II. RECENT PRACTICE: Including Pavements of Wood, Asphalte, &c. By D. K. CLARK, C.E. **4/6**

**Gas Works (The Construction of),**
And the Manufacture and Distribution of Coal Gas. By S. HUGHES, C.E. Re-written by WILLIAM RICHARDS, C.E. Eighth Edition . . **5/6**

**Water Works**
For the Supply of Cities and Towns. With a Description of the Principal Geological Formations of England as influencing Supplies of Water. By SAMUEL HUGHES, F.G.S., C.E. Enlarged Edition . . . **4/0**

**The Power of Water,**
As applied to drive Flour Mills, and to give motion to Turbines and other Hydrostatic Engines. By JOSEPH GLYNN, F.R.S. New Edition . **2/0**

**Wells and Well-Sinking.**
By JOHN GEO. SWINDELL, A.R.I.B.A., and G. R. BURNELL, C.E. Revised Edition. With a New Appendix on the Qualities of Water. Illustrated **2/0**

**The Drainage of Lands, Towns, and Buildings.**
By G. D. DEMPSEY, C.E. Revised, with large Additions on Recent Practice, by D. K. CLARK, M.I.C.E. Third Edition . . . **4/6**

**The Blasting and Quarrying of Stone,**
For Building and other Purposes. With Remarks on the Blowing up of Bridges. By Gen. Sir J. BURGOYNE, K.C.B. . . . . **1/6**

**Foundations and Concrete Works.**
With Practical Remarks on Footings, Planking, Sand, Concrete, Béton, Pile-driving, Caissons, and Cofferdams. By E. DOBSON, M.R.I.B.A. Eighth Edition . . . . . . . . . **1/6**

WEALE'S SCIENTIFIC AND TECHNICAL SERIES. 3

**Pneumatics,**
Including Acoustics and the Phenomena of Wind Currents, for the Use of Beginners. By CHARLES TOMLINSON, F.R.S. Fourth Edition . **1/6**

**Land and Engineering Surveying.**
For Students and Practical Use. By T. BAKER, C.E. Eighteenth Edition, Revised and Extended by F. E. DIXON, A.M. Inst. C.E., Professional Associate of the Institution of Surveyors. With numerous Illustrations and two Lithographic Plates . . . . . . *Just published* **2/0**

**Mensuration and Measuring.**
For Students and Practical Use. With the Mensuration and Levelling of Land for the purposes of Modern Engineering. By T. BAKER, C.E. New Edition by E. NUGENT, C.E. . . . . . . . **1/6**

## *MINING AND METALLURGY.*

**Mineralogy,**
Rudiments of. By A. RAMSAY, F.G.S. Fourth Edition, revised and enlarged. Woodcuts and Plates . . . . . . . **3/6**

**Coal and Coal Mining,**
A Rudimentary Treatise on. By the late Sir WARINGTON W. SMYTH, F.R.S. Eighth Edition, revised and extended by T. FORSTER BROWN.
*Just published* **3/6**

**Metallurgy of Iron.**
Containing Methods of Assay, Analyses of Iron Ores, Processes of Manufacture of Iron and Steel, &c. By H. BAUERMAN, F.G.S. With numerous Illustrations. Sixth Edition, revised and enlarged . . . **5/0**

**The Mineral Surveyor and Valuer's Complete Guide.**
By W. LINTERN. Fourth Edition, with an Appendix on Magnetic and Angular Surveying . . . . . . . . . **3/6**

**Slate and Slate Quarrying:**
Scientific, Practical, and Commercial. By D. C. DAVIES, F.G.S. With numerous Illustrations and Folding Plates. Fourth Edition . . **3/0**

**A First Book of Mining and Quarrying,**
With the Sciences connected therewith, for Primary Schools and Self Instruction. By J. H. COLLINS, F.G.S. Second Edition . . . **1/6**

**Subterraneous Surveying,**
With and without the Magnetic Needle. By T. FENWICK and T. BAKER, C.E. Illustrated . . . . . . . . . . **2/6**

**Mining Tools.**
Manual of. By WILLIAM MORGANS, Lecturer on Practical Mining at the Bristol School of Mines . . . . . . . . **2/6**

**Mining Tools, Atlas**
Of Engravings to Illustrate the above, containing 235 Illustrations of Mining Tools, drawn to Scale. 4to . . . . . . . **4/6**

**Physical Geology,**
Partly based on Major-General PORTLOCK's "Rudiments of Geology." By RALPH TATE, A.L.S., &c. Woodcuts . . . . . **2/0**

**Historical Geology,**
Partly based on Major-General PORTLOCK'S "Rudiments." By RALPH TATE, A.L.S., &c. Woodcuts . . . . . . . **2/6**

**Geology, Physical and Historical.**
Consisting of "Physical Geology," which sets forth the Leading Principles of the Science; and "Historical Geology," which treats of the Mineral and Organic Conditions of the Earth at each successive epoch. By RALPH TATE, F.G.S. . . . . . . . . . . **4/6**

**Electro-Metallurgy,**
Practically Treated. By ALEXANDER WATT. Tenth Edition, enlarged and revised, including the most Recent Processes . . . **3/6**

4  WEALE'S SCIENTIFIC AND TECHNICAL SERIES.

## MECHANICAL ENGINEERING.

**The Workman's Manual of Engineering Drawing.**
By JOHN MAXTON, Instructor in Engineering Drawing, Royal Naval College, Greenwich. Seventh Edition. 300 Plates and Diagrams . **3/6**

**Fuels: Solid, Liquid, and Gaseous.**
Their Analysis and Valuation. For the Use of Chemists and Engineers. By H. J. PHILLIPS, F.C.S., formerly Analytical and Consulting Chemist to the Great Eastern Railway. Third Edition . . . . **2/0**

**Fuel, Its Combustion and Economy.**
Consisting of an Abridgment of "A Treatise on the Combustion of Coal and the Prevention of Smoke." By C. W. WILLIAMS, A.I.C.E. With Extensive Additions by D. K. CLARK, M.Inst.C.E. Fourth Edition . **3/6**

**The Boilermaker's Assistant**
In Drawing, Templating, and Calculating Boiler Work, &c. By J. COURTNEY, Practical Boilermaker. Edited by D. K. CLARK, C.E. . **2/0**

**The Boiler-Maker's Ready Reckoner,**
With Examples of Practical Geometry and Templating for the Use of Platers, Smiths, and Riveters. By JOHN COURTNEY. Edited by D. K. CLARK, M.I.C.E. Fourth Edition . . . . . . **4/0**

*\** *The last two Works in One Volume, half-bound, entitled* "THE BOILER-MAKER'S READY-RECKONER AND ASSISTANT." By J. COURTNEY and D. K. CLARK. *Price* **7/0**.

**Steam Boilers:**
Their Construction and Management. By R. ARMSTRONG, C.E. Illustrated **1/6**

**Steam and Machinery Management.**
A Guide to the Arrangement and Economical Management of Machinery. By M. POWIS BALE, M.Inst.M.E. . . . . . . **2/6**

**Steam and the Steam Engine,**
Stationary and Portable. Being an Extension of the Treatise on the Steam Engine of Mr. J. SEWELL. By D. K. CLARK, C.E. Fourth Edition **3/6**

**The Steam Engine,**
A Treatise on the Mathematical Theory of, with Rules and Examples for Practical Men. By T. BAKER, C.E. . . . . . . **1/6**

**The Steam Engine.**
By Dr. LARDNER. Illustrated . . . . . . . **1/6**

**Locomotive Engines,**
By G. D. DEMPSEY, C.E. With large Additions treating of the Modern Locomotive, by D. K. CLARK, M.Inst.C.E. . . . . **3/0**

**Locomotive Engine-Driving.**
A Practical Manual for Engineers in charge of Locomotive Engines. By MICHAEL REYNOLDS. Tenth Edition. 3s. 6d. limp; cloth boards. **4/6**

**Stationary Engine-Driving.**
A Practical Manual for Engineers in charge of Stationary Engines. By MICHAEL REYNOLDS. Sixth Edition. 3s. 6d. limp; cloth boards . **4/6**

**The Smithy and Forge.**
Including the Farrier's Art and Coach Smithing. By W. J. E. CRANE. Fourth Edition . . . . . . . . **2/6**

**Modern Workshop Practice,**
As applied to Marine, Land, and Locomotive Engines, Floating Docks, Dredging Machines, Bridges, Ship-building, &c. By J. G. WINTON. Fourth Edition, Illustrated . . . . . . **3/6**

**Mechanical Engineering.**
Comprising Metallurgy, Moulding, Casting, Forging, Tools, Workshop Machinery, Mechanical Manipulation, Manufacture of the Steam Engine, &c. By FRANCIS CAMPIN, C.E. Third Edition . . . **2/6**

**Details of Machinery.**
Comprising Instructions for the Execution of various Works in Iron in the Fitting-Shop, Foundry, and Boiler-Yard. By FRANCIS CAMPIN, C.E. **3/0**

WEALE'S SCIENTIFIC AND TECHNICAL SERIES. 5

**Elementary Engineering:**
A Manual for Young Marine Engineers and Apprentices. In the Form of Questions and Answers on Metals, Alloys, Strength of Materials, &c. By J. S. BREWER. Fourth Edition . . . . . . **1/6**

**Power in Motion:**
Horse-power Motion, Toothed-Wheel Gearing, Long and Short Driving Bands, Angular Forces, &c. By JAMES ARMOUR, C.E. Third Edition **2/0**

**Iron and Heat,**
Exhibiting the Principles concerned in the Construction of Iron Beams, Pillars, and Girders. By J. ARMOUR, C.E. . . . . . **2/6**

**Practical Mechanism,**
And Machine Tools. By T. BAKER, C.E. With Remarks on Tools and Machinery, by J. NASMYTH, C.E. . . . . . . . **2/6**

**Mechanics:**
Being a concise Exposition of the General Principles of Mechanical Science, and their Applications. By CHARLES TOMLINSON, F.R.S. . **1/6**

**Cranes (The Construction of),**
And other Machinery for Raising Heavy Bodies for the Erection of Buildings, &c. By JOSEPH GLYNN, F.R.S. . . . . . . **1/6**

---

## NAVIGATION, SHIPBUILDING, ETC.

**The Sailor's Sea Book:**
A Rudimentary Treatise on Navigation. By JAMES GREENWOOD, B.A. With numerous Woodcuts and Coloured Plates. New and enlarged Edition. By W. H. ROSSER . . . . . . **2/6**

**Practical Navigation.**
Consisting of THE SAILOR'S SEA-BOOK, by JAMES GREENWOOD and W. H. ROSSER; together with Mathematical and Nautical Tables for the Working of the Problems, by HENRY LAW, C.E., and Prof. J. R. YOUNG. **7/0**

**Navigation and Nautical Astronomy,**
In Theory and Practice. By Prof. J. R. YOUNG. New Edition. **2/6**

**Mathematical Tables,**
For Trigonometrical, Astronomical, and Nautical Calculations; to which is prefixed a Treatise on Logarithms. By H. LAW, C.E. Together with a Series of Tables for Navigation and Nautical Astronomy. By Professor J. R. YOUNG. New Edition . . . . . . . **4/0**

**Masting, Mast-Making, and Rigging of Ships.**
Also Tables of Spars, Rigging, Blocks; Chain, Wire, and Hemp Ropes, &c., relative to every class of vessels. By ROBERT KIPPING, N.A. . **2/0**

**Sails and Sail-Making.**
With Draughting, and the Centre of Effort of the Sails. By ROBERT KIPPING, N.A. . . . . . . . . . **2/6**

**Marine Engines and Steam Vessels.**
By R. MURRAY, C.F. Eighth Edition, thoroughly revised, with Additions by the Author and by GEORGE CARLISLE, C.E. . . . **4/6**

**Naval Architecture:**
An Exposition of Elementary Principles. By JAMES PEAKE . . **3/6**

**Ships for Ocean and River Service,**
Principles of the Construction of. By HAKON A. SOMMERFELDT . **1/6**

**Atlas of Engravings**
To Illustrate the above. Twelve large folding Plates. Royal 4to, cloth **7/6**

**The Forms of Ships and Boats.**
By W. BLAND. Ninth Edition, with numerous Illustrations and Models . . . . . . . . . . . **1/6**

## ARCHITECTURE AND THE BUILDING ARTS.

**Constructional Iron and Steel Work,**
As applied to Public, Private, and Domestic Buildings. By FRANCIS
CAMPIN, C.E. . . . . . . . . . . . **3/6**

**Building Estates:**
A Treatise on the Development, Sale, Purchase, and Management of Building Land. By F. MAITLAND. Third Edition . . . . . **2/0**

**The Science of Building:**
An Elementary Treatise on the Principles of Construction. By E. WYNDHAM TARN, M.A. Lond. Fourth Edition . . . . . . **3/6**

**The Art of Building:**
General Principles of Construction, Strength, and Use of Materials, Working Drawings, Specifications, &c. By EDWARD DOBSON, M.R.I.B.A. . **2/0**

**A Book on Building,**
Civil and Ecclesiastical. By Sir EDMUND BECKETT, Q.C. (Lord GRIMTHORPE). Second Edition . . . . . . . . . **4/6**

**Dwelling-Houses (The Erection of),**
Illustrated by a Perspective View, Plans, and Sections of a Pair of Villas, with Specification, Quantities, and Estimates. By S. H. BROOKS, Architect **2/6**

**Cottage Building.**
By C. BRUCE ALLEN. Eleventh Edition, with Chapter on Economic Cottages for Allotments, by E. E. ALLEN, C.E. . . . . . **2/0**

**Acoustics in Relation to Architecture and Building:**
The Laws of Sound as applied to the Arrangement of Buildings. By Professor T. ROGER SMITH, F.R.I.B.A. New Edition, Revised . . **1/6**

**The Rudiments of Practical Bricklaying.**
General Principles of Bricklaying; Arch Drawing, Cutting, and Setting; Pointing; Paving, Tiling, &c. By ADAM HAMMOND. With 68 Woodcuts **1/6**

**The Art of Practical Brick Cutting and Setting.**
By ADAM HAMMOND. With 90 Engravings . . . . . **1/6**

**Brickwork:**
A Practical Treatise, embodying the General and Higher Principles of Bricklaying, Cutting and Setting; with the Application of Geometry to Roof Tiling, &c. By F. WALKER . . . . . . . . . **1/6**

**Bricks and Tiles,**
Rudimentary Treatise on the Manufacture of; containing an Outline of the Principles of Brickmaking. By E. DOBSON, M.R.I.B.A. Additions by C. TOMLINSON, F.R.S. Illustrated . . . . . . . **3/0**

**The Practical Brick and Tile Book.**
Comprising: BRICK AND TILE MAKING, by E. DOBSON, M.INST.C.E.;
Practical BRICKLAYING, by A. HAMMOND; BRICK-CUTTING AND SETTING, by A. HAMMOND. 550 pp. with 270 Illustrations, half-bound . . **6/0**

**Carpentry and Joinery—**
THE ELEMENTARY PRINCIPLES OF CARPENTRY. Chiefly composed from the Standard Work of THOMAS TREDGOLD, C.E. With Additions, and TREATISE ON JOINERY, by E. W. TARN, M.A. Seventh Edition . . . **3/6**

**Carpentry and Joinery—Atlas**
Of 35 Plates to accompany and Illustrate the foregoing book. With Descriptive Letterpress. 4to . . . . . . . **6/0**

**A Practical Treatise on Handrailing;**
Showing New and Simple Methods. By GEO. COLLINGS. Second Edition, Revised, including a TREATISE ON STAIRBUILDING. With Plates . **2/6**

**Circular Work in Carpentry and Joinery.**
A Practical Treatise on Circular Work of Single and Double Curvature. By GEORGE COLLINGS. Third Edition . . . . . . **2/6**

**Roof Carpentry:**
Practical Lessons in the Framing of Wood Roofs. For the Use of Working Carpenters. By GEO. COLLINGS . . . . . . **2/0**

**The Construction of Roofs of Wood and Iron;**
Deduced chiefly from the Works of Robison, Tredgold, and Humber. By E. WYNDHAM TARN, M.A., Architect. Third Edition . . . **1/6**

**The Joints Made and Used by Builders.**
By WYVILL J. CHRISTY, Architect. With 160 Woodcuts . . **3/0**

**Shoring**
And its Application: A Handbook for the Use of Students. By GEORGE H. BLAGROVE. With 31 Illustrations . . . . . . **1/6**

**The Timber Importer's, Timber Merchant's, and Builder's Standard Guide.**
By R. E. GRANDY . . . . . . . . . . **2/0**

**Plumbing:**
A Text-Book to the Practice of the Art or Craft of the Plumber. With Chapters upon House Drainage and Ventilation. By WM. PATON BUCHAN. Eighth Edition, Re-written and Enlarged, with 500 Illustrations . **3/6**

**Ventilation:**
A Text Book to the Practice of the Art of Ventilating Buildings. By W. P. BUCHAN, R.P., Author of "Plumbing," &c. With 170 Illustrations **3/6**

**The Practical Plasterer:**
A Compendium of Plain and Ornamental Plaster Work. By W. KEMP **2/0**

**House Painting, Graining, Marbling, & Sign Writing.**
With a Course of Elementary Drawing, and a Collection of Useful Receipts. By ELLIS A. DAVIDSON. Seventh Edition. Coloured Plates . . **5/0**

*₊* *The above, in cloth boards, strongly bound,* **6/0**

**A Grammar of Colouring,**
Applied to Decorative Painting and the Arts. By GEORGE FIELD. New Edition, enlarged, by ELLIS A. DAVIDSON. With Coloured Plates . **3/0**

**Elementary Decoration**
As applied to Dwelling Houses, &c. By JAMES W. FACEY. Illustrated **2/0**

**Practical House Decoration.**
A Guide to the Art of Ornamental Painting, the Arrangement of Colours in Apartments, and the Principles of Decorative Design. By JAMES W. FACEY. **2/6**

*₊* *The last two Works in One handsome Vol., half-bound, entitled* "HOUSE DECORATION, ELEMENTARY AND PRACTICAL," *price* **5/0**

**Portland Cement for Users.**
By HENRY FAIJA, A.M.Inst.C.E. Third Edition, Corrected . . **2/0**

**Limes, Cements, Mortars, Concretes, Mastics, Plastering, &c.**
By G. R. BURNELL C.E. Fifteenth Edition . . . . **1/6**

## 8 WEALE'S SCIENTIFIC AND TECHNICAL SERIES.

**Masonry and Stone-Cutting.**
The Principles of Masonic Projection and their application to Construction. By EDWARD DOBSON, M.R.I.B.A. . . . . . . . **2/6**

**Arches, Piers, Buttresses, &c.:**
Experimental Essays on the Principles of Construction. By W. BLAND. **1/6**

**Quantities and Measurements,**
In Bricklayers', Masons', Plasterers', Plumbers', Painters', Paperhangers', Gilders', Smiths', Carpenters' and Joiners' Work. By A. C. BEATON **1/6**

**The Complete Measurer:**
Setting forth the Measurement of Boards, Glass, Timber and Stone. By R. HORTON. Sixth Edition . . . . . . . . **4/0**
\*\*\* *The above, strongly bound in leather, price* **5/0**.

**Light:**
An Introduction to the Science of Optics. Designed for the Use of Students of Architecture, Engineering, and other Applied Sciences. By E. WYNDHAM TARN, M.A., Author of "The Science of Building," &c. . **1/6**

**Hints to Young Architects.**
By GEORGE WIGHTWICK, Architect. Sixth Edition, revised and enlarged by G. HUSKISSON GUILLAUME, Architect . . . . **3/6**

**Architecture—Orders:**
The Orders and their Æsthetic Principles. By W. H. LEEDS. Illustrated. **1/6**

**Architecture—Styles:**
The History and Description of the Styles of Architecture of Various Countries, from the Earliest to the Present Period. By T. TALBOT BURY, F.R.I.B.A. Illustrated . . . . . . . . **2/0**
\*\*\* ORDERS AND STYLES OF ARCHITECTURE, *in One Vol.*, **3/6**.

**Architecture—Design:**
The Principles of Design in Architecture, as deducible from Nature and exemplified in the Works of the Greek and Gothic Architects. By EDW. LACY GARBETT, Architect. Illustrated . . . . . **2/6**
\*\*\* *The three preceding Works in One handsome Vol., half bound, entitled* "MODERN ARCHITECTURE," *price* **6/0**.

**Perspective for Beginners.**
Adapted to Young Students and Amateurs in Architecture, Painting, &c. By GEORGE PYNE . . . . . . . . . . **2/0**

**Architectural Modelling in Paper.**
By T. A. RICHARDSON. With Illustrations, engraved by O. JEWITT **1/6**

**Glass Staining, and the Art of Painting on Glass.**
From the German of Dr. GESSERT and EMANUEL OTTO FROMBERG. With an Appendix on THE ART OF ENAMELLING . . . . **2/6**

**Vitruvius—The Architecture of.**
In Ten Books. Translated from the Latin by JOSEPH GWILT, F.S.A., F.R.A.S. With 23 Plates . . . . . . . . **5/0**
*N.B.—This is the only Edition of* VITRUVIUS *procurable at a moderate price*

**Grecian Architecture,**
An Inquiry into the Principles of Beauty in. With an Historical View of the Rise and Progress of the Art in Greece. By the EARL OF ABERDEEN **1/0**
\*\*\* *The two preceding Works in One handsome Vol., half bound, entitled* "ANCIENT ARCHITECTURE," *price* **6/0**.

## INDUSTRIAL AND USEFUL ARTS.

**Cements, Pastes, Glues, and Gums.**
A Practical Guide to the Manufacture and Application of the various Agglutinants required for Workshop, Laboratory, or Office Use. With upwards of 900 Recipes and Formulæ. By H. C. STANDAGE . . **2/0**

**Clocks and Watches, and Bells,**
A Rudimentary Treatise on. By Sir EDMUND BECKETT, Q.C. (Lord GRIMTHORPE). Seventh Edition . . . . . . . . **4/6**

**The Goldsmith's Handbook.**
Containing full Instructions in the Art of Alloying, Melting, Reducing, Colouring, Collecting and Refining, Recovery of Waste, Solders, Enamels. &c., &c. By GEORGE E. GEE. Fifth Edition . . . . **3/0**

**The Silversmith's Handbook,**
On the same plan as the GOLDSMITH'S HANDBOOK. By GEORGE E. GEE. Third Edition . . . . . . . . . . . **3/0**
\*\* *The last two Works, in One handsome Vol., half-bound,* **7/0**.

**The Hall-Marking of Jewellery.**
Comprising an account of all the different Assay Towns of the United Kingdom; with the Stamps and Laws relating to the Standards and Hall-Marks at the various Assay Offices. By GEORGE E. GEE . . **3/0**

**French Polishing and Enamelling.**
A Practical Work of Instruction, including numerous Recipes for making Polishes, Varnishes, Glaze-Lacquers, Revivers, &c. By R. BITMEAD.
[*Just Published.* **1/6**

**Practical Organ Building.**
By W. E. DICKSON, M.A. Second Edition, Revised, with Additions **2/6**

**Coach-Building:**
A Practical Treatise. By JAMES W. BURGESS. With 57 Illustrations **2/6**

**The Brass Founder's Manual:**
Instructions for Modelling, Pattern Making, Moulding, Turning, &c. By W. GRAHAM . . . . . . . . . . **2/0**

**The Sheet-Metal Worker's Guide.**
A Practical Handbook for Tinsmiths, Coppersmiths, Zincworkers, &c., with 46 Diagrams. By W. J. E. CRANE. Third Edition, revised . . **1/6**

**Sewing Machinery:**
Its Construction, History, &c. With full Technical Directions for Adjusting, &c. By J. W. URQUHART, C.E. . . . . . . **2/0**

**Gas Fitting:**
A Practical Handbook. By JOHN BLACK. New Edition . . **2/6**

**Construction of Door Locks.**
From the Papers of A. C. HOBBS. Edited by C. TOMLINSON, F.R.S. **2/6**

**The Model Locomotive Engineer, Fireman, and Engine-Boy.**
Comprising an Historical Notice of the Pioneer Locomotive Engines and their Inventors. By MICHAEL REYNOLDS . . . . . **3/6**

**The Art of Letter Painting made Easy.**
By J. G. BADENOCH. With 12 full-page Engravings of Examples . **1/6**

**The Art of Boot and Shoemaking.**
Including Measurement, Last-fitting, Cutting-out, Closing and Making. By JOHN BEDFORD LENO. With numerous Illustrations. Fourth Edition **2/0**

**Mechanical Dentistry:**
A Practical Treatise on the Construction of the Various Kinds of Artificial Dentures. By CHARLES HUNTER. Fourth Edition . . **3/0**

**Wood Engraving:**
A Practical and Easy Introduction to the Art. By W. N. BROWN . **1/6**

**Laundry Management.**
A Handbook for Use in Private and Public Laundries. By the EDITOR of "The Laundry Journal." . . . . . . . . **2/0**

10 WEALE'S SCIENTIFIC AND TECHNICAL SERIES.

## AGRICULTURE, GARDENING, ETC.

**Draining and Embanking:**
A Practical Treatise. By Prof. JOHN SCOTT. With 68 Illustrations **1/6**

**Irrigation and Water Supply:**
A Practical Treatise on Water Meadows, Sewage Irrigation, Warping, &c.; on the Construction of Wells, Ponds, Reservoirs, &c. By Prof. JOHN SCOTT. With 34 Illustrations . . . . . . . **1/6**

**Farm Roads, Fences, and Gates:**
A Practical Treatise on the Roads, Tramways, and Waterways of the Farm; the Principles of Enclosures; and the different kinds of Fences, Gates, and Stiles. By Prof. JOHN SCOTT. With 75 Illustrations . **1/6**

**Farm Buildings:**
A Practical Treatise on the Buildings necessary for various kinds of Farms, their Arrangement and Construction, with Plans and Estimates. By Prof. JOHN SCOTT. With 105 Illustrations . . . . . . **2/0**

**Barn Implements and Machines:**
Treating of the Application of Power and Machines used in the Threshing-barn, Stockyard, Dairy, &c. By Prof. J. SCOTT. With 123 Illustrations. **2/0**

**Field Implements and Machines:**
With Principles and Details of Construction and Points of Excellence, their Management, &c. By Prof. JOHN SCOTT. With 138 Illustrations **2/0**

**Agricultural Surveying:**
A Treatise on Land Surveying, Levelling, and Setting-out; with Directions for Valuing Estates. By Prof. J. SCOTT. With 62 Illustrations . **1/6**

**Farm Engineering.**
By Professor JOHN SCOTT. Comprising the above Seven Volumes in One, 1,150 pages, and over 600 Illustrations. Half-bound . . . **12/0**

**Outlines of Farm Management.**
Treating of the General Work of the Farm; Stock; Contract Work; Labour, &c. By R. SCOTT BURN . . . . . . . **2/6**

**Outlines of Landed Estates Management.**
Treating of the Varieties of Lands, Methods of Farming, Setting-out of Farms, Roads, Fences, Gates, Drainage, &c. By R. SCOTT BURN . **2/6**
\*\*\* *The above Two Vols. in One, handsomely half-bound, price* **6/0**

**Soils, Manures, and Crops.**
(Vol. I. OUTLINES OF MODERN FARMING.) By R. SCOTT BURN . **2/0**

**Farming and Farming Economy.**
(Vol. II. OUTLINES OF MODERN FARMING.) By R. SCOTT BURN **3/0**

**Stock: Cattle, Sheep, and Horses.**
(Vol. III. OUTLINES OF MODERN FARMING.) By R. SCOTT BURN **2/6**

**Dairy, Pigs, and Poultry.**
(Vol. IV. OUTLINES OF MODERN FARMING.) By R. SCOTT BURN **2/0**

**Utilization of Sewage, Irrigation, and Reclamation of Waste Land.**
(Vol. V. OUTLINES OF MODERN FARMING.) By R. SCOTT BURN . **2/6**

**Outlines of Modern Farming.**
By R. SCOTT BURN. Consisting of the above Five Volumes in One, 1,250 pp., profusely Illustrated, half-bound . . . . . **12/0**

WEALE'S SCIENTIFIC AND TECHNICAL SERIES. 11

**Book-keeping for Farmers and Estate Owners.**
A Practical Treatise, presenting, in Three Plans, a System adapted for all classes of Farms. By J. M. WOODMAN. Third Edition, revised . **2/6**

**Ready Reckoner for the Admeasurement of Land.**
By A. ARMAN. Fourth Edition, revised and extended by C. NORRIS **2/0**

**Miller's, Corn Merchant's, and Farmer's Ready Reckoner.**
Second Edition, revised, with a Price List of Modern Flour Mill Machinery, by W. S. HUTTON, C.E. . . . . . . . . . **2/0**

**The Hay and Straw Measurer.**
New Tables for the Use of Auctioneers, Valuers, Farmers, Hay and Straw Dealers, &c. By JOHN STEELE . . . . . . . . **2/0**

**Meat Production.**
A Manual for Producers, Distributors, and Consumers of Butchers' Meat. By JOHN EWART . . . . . . . . **2/6**

**Sheep:**
The History, Structure, Economy, and Diseases of. By W. C. SPOONER, M.R.V.S. Fifth Edition, with fine Engravings . . . . **3/6**

**Market and Kitchen Gardening.**
By C. W. SHAW, late Editor of "Gardening Illustrated" . . . **3/0**

**Kitchen Gardening Made Easy.**
Showing the best means of Cultivating every known Vegetable and Herb, &c., with directions for management all the year round. By GEORGE M. F. GLENNY. Illustrated . . . . . . . . **1/6**

**Cottage Gardening:**
Or Flowers, Fruits, and Vegetables for Small Gardens. By E. HOBDAY. **1/6**

**Garden Receipts.**
Edited by CHARLES W. QUIN . . . . . . . **1/6**

**Fruit Trees,**
The Scientific and Profitable Culture of. From the French of M. DU BREUIL. Fifth Edition, carefully Revised by GEORGE GLENNY. With 187 Woodcuts . . . . . . . . . **3/6**

**The Tree Planter and Plant Propagator:**
With numerous Illustrations of Grafting, Layering, Budding, Implements, Houses, Pits, &c. By SAMUEL WOOD . . . . . **2/0**

**The Tree Pruner:**
A Practical Manual on the Pruning of Fruit Trees, Shrubs, Climbers, and Flowering Plants. With numerous Illustrations. By SAMUEL WOOD **1/6**

\*\*\* *The above Two Vols. in One, handsomely half-bound, price* **3/6**

**The Art of Grafting and Budding.**
By CHARLES BALTET. With Illustrations . . . . . **2/6**

## MATHEMATICS, ARITHMETIC, ETC.

**Descriptive Geometry,**
An Elementary Treatise on; with a Theory of Shadows and of Perspective, extracted from the French of G. MONGE. To which is added a Description of the Principles and Practice of Isometrical Projection. By J. F. HEATHER, M.A. With 14 Plates . . . . . . . . . . **2/0**

**Practical Plane Geometry:**
Giving the Simplest Modes of Constructing Figures contained in one Plane and Geometrical Construction of the Ground. By J. F. HEATHER, M.A. With 215 Woodcuts . . . . . . . . . . **2/0**

**Analytical Geometry and Conic Sections,**
A Rudimentary Treatise on. By JAMES HANN. A New Edition, re-written and enlarged by Professor J. R. YOUNG . . . . **2/0**

**Euclid (The Elements of).**
With many Additional Propositions and Explanatory Notes; to which is prefixed an Introductory Essay on Logic. By HENRY LAW, C.E. . **2/6**

*\** *Sold also separately, viz:—*
Euclid. The First Three Books. By HENRY LAW, C.E. . . . **1/6**
Euclid. Books 4, 5, 6, 11, 12. By HENRY LAW, C.E. . . **1/6**

**Plane Trigonometry,**
The Elements of. By JAMES HANN. . . . **1/6**

**Spherical Trigonometry,**
The Elements of. By JAMES HANN. Revised by CHARLES H. DOW-LING, C.E. . . . . . . . . . . **1/0**
*\** *Or with " The Elements of Plane Trigonometry," in One Volume,* **2/6**

**Differential Calculus,**
Elements of the. By W. S. B. WOOLHOUSE, F.R.A.S., &c. . . **1/6**

**Integral Calculus.**
By HOMERSHAM COX, B.A. . . . . . . **1/6**

**Algebra,**
The Elements of. By JAMES HADDON, M.A. With Appendix, containing Miscellaneous Investigations, and a Collection of Problems . . **2/0**

**A Key and Companion to the Above.**
An extensive Repository of Solved Examples and Problems in Algebra. By J. R. YOUNG . . . . . . . . . . **1/6**

**Commercial Book-keeping.**
With Commercial Phrases and Forms in English, French, Italian, and German. By JAMES HADDON, M.A. . . . . . . **1/6**

**Arithmetic,**
A Rudimentary Treatise on. With full Explanations of its Theoretical Principles, and numerous Examples for Practice. For the Use of Schools and for Self-Instruction. By J. R. YOUNG, late Professor of Mathematics in Belfast College. Thirteenth Edition . . . . . **1/6**

**A Key to the Above.**
By J. R. YOUNG . . . . . . . . . . **1/6**

**Equational Arithmetic,**
Applied to Questions of Interest, Annuities, Life Assurance, and General Commerce; with various Tables by which all Calculations may be greatly facilitated. By W. HIPSLEY . . . . . . . **1/6**

**Arithmetic,**
Rudimentary, for the Use of Schools and Self-Instruction. By JAMES HADDON, M.A. Revised by ABRAHAM ARMAN . . . . **1/6**

**A Key to the Above.**
By A. ARMAN . . . . . . . . . **1/6**

## Mathematical Instruments:
Their Construction, Adjustment, Testing, and Use concisely Explained. By J. F. HEATHER, M.A., of the Royal Military Academy, Woolwich. Fourteenth Edition, Revised, with Additions, by A. T. WALMISLEY, M.I.C.E. Original Edition, in 1 vol., Illustrated . . . . **2/0**

*⁎* *In ordering the above, be careful to say "Original Edition," or give the number in the Series (32), to distinguish it from the Enlarged Edition in 3 vols. (as follows)—*

## Drawing and Measuring Instruments.
Including—I. Instruments employed in Geometrical and Mechanical Drawing, and in the Construction, Copying, and Measurement of Maps and Plans. II. Instruments used for the purposes of Accurate Measurement, and for Arithmetical Computations. By J. F. HEATHER, M.A. . **1/6**

## Optical Instruments.
Including (more especially) Telescopes, Microscopes, and Apparatus for producing copies of Maps and Plans by Photography. By J. F. HEATHER, M.A. Illustrated . . . . . . . . . **1/6**

## Surveying and Astronomical Instruments.
Including—I. Instruments used for Determining the Geometrical Features of a portion of Ground. II. Instruments employed in Astronomical Observations. By J. F. HEATHER, M.A. Illustrated. . . . **1/6**

*⁎* *The above three volumes form an enlargement of the Author's original work, "Mathematical Instruments," price* **2/0.** *(Described at top of page.)*

## Mathematical Instruments:
Their Construction, Adjustment, Testing and Use. Comprising Drawing, Measuring, Optical, Surveying, and Astronomical Instruments. By J. F. HEATHER, M.A. Enlarged Edition, for the most part entirely re-written. The Three Parts as above, in One thick Volume. . . . . **4/6**

## The Slide Rule, and How to Use It.
Containing full, easy, and simple Instructions to perform all Business Calculations with unexampled rapidity and accuracy. By CHARLES HOARE, C.E. With a Slide Rule, in tuck of cover. Seventh Edition . . **2/6**

## Logarithms.
With Mathematical Tables for Trigonometrical, Astronomical, and Nautical Calculations. By HENRY LAW, C.E. Revised Edition . . . **3/0**

## Compound Interest and Annuities (Theory of).
With Tables of Logarithms for the more Difficult Computations of Interest, Discount, Annuities, &c., in all their Applications and Uses for Mercantile and State Purposes. By FEDOR THOMAN, Paris. Fourth Edition . **4/0**

## Mathematical Tables,
For Trigonometrical, Astronomical, and Nautical Calculations ; to which is prefixed a Treatise on Logarithms. By H. LAW, C.E. Together with a Series of Tables for Navigation and Nautical Astronomy. By Professor J. R. YOUNG. New Edition . . . . . . . . . **4/0**

## Mathematics,
As applied to the Constructive Arts. By FRANCIS CAMPIN, C.E., &c. Third Edition . . . . . . . . . **3/0**

## Astronomy.
By the late Rev. ROBERT MAIN, F.R.S. Third Edition, revised and corrected to the Present Time. By W. T. LYNN, F.R.A.S. . . . **2/0**

## Statics and Dynamics.
The Principles and Practice of. Embracing also a clear development of Hydrostatics, Hydrodynamics, and Central Forces. By T. BAKER, C.E. Fourth Edition . . . . . . . . . . **1/6**

14 WEALE'S SCIENTIFIC AND TECHNICAL SERIES.

# BOOKS OF REFERENCE AND MISCELLANEOUS VOLUMES.

**A Dictionary of Painters, and Handbook for Picture Amateurs.**
Being a Guide for Visitors to Public and Private Picture Galleries, and for Art-Students, including Glossary of Terms, Sketch of Principal Schools of Painting, &c. By PHILIPPE DARYL, B.A. . . . . . **2/6**

**Painting Popularly Explained.**
By T. J. GULLICK, Painter, and JOHN TIMBS, F.S.A. Including Fresco, Oil, Mosaic, Water Colour, Water-Glass, Tempera Encaustic, Miniature, Painting on Ivory, Vellum, Pottery, Enamel, Glass, &c. Sixth Edition **5/0**

**A Dictionary of Terms used in Architecture, Building, Engineering, Mining, Metallurgy, Archæology, the Fine Arts, &c.**
By JOHN WEALE. Sixth Edition. Edited by R. HUNT, F.R.S. . **5/0**

**Music:**
A Rudimentary and Practical Treatise. With numerous Examples. By CHARLES CHILD SPENCER . . . . . . . . **2/6**

**Pianoforte,**
The Art of Playing the. With numerous Exercises and Lessons. By CHARLES CHILD SPENCER . . . . . . . . **1/6**

**The House Manager.**
A Guide to Housekeeping, Cookery, Pickling and Preserving, Household Work, Dairy Management, Cellarage of Wines, Home-brewing and Wine-making, Gardening, &c. By AN OLD HOUSEKEEPER . . **3/6**

**Manual of Domestic Medicine.**
By R. GOODING, M.D. Intended as a Family Guide in all cases of Accident and Emergency. Third Edition, carefully revised . . **2/0**

**Management of Health.**
A Manual of Home and Personal Hygiene. By Rev. JAMES BAIRD **1/0**

**Natural Philosophy,**
For the Use of Beginners. By CHARLES TOMLINSON, F.R.S. . . **1/6**

**The Elementary Principals of Electric Lighting.**
By ALAN A. CAMPBELL SWINTON, M.INST.C.E., M.I.E.E. Fourth Edition, Revised . . . . . . . [*Just Published*] **1/6**

**The Electric Telegraph,**
Its History and Progress. By R. SABINE, C.E., F.S.A., &c. . . **3/0**

**Handbook of Field Fortification.**
By Major W. W. KNOLLYS, F.R.G.S. With 163 Woodcuts . . **3/0**

**Logic,**
Pure and Applied. By S. H EMMENS. Third Edition . . **1/6**

**Locke on the Human Understanding,**
Selections from. With Notes by S. H. EMMENS . . **1/6**

**The Compendious Calculator**
(*Intuitive Calculations*). Or Easy and Concise Methods of Performing the various Arithmetical Operations required in Commercial and Business Transactions; together with Useful Tables, &c. By DANIEL O'GORMAN. Twenty-seventh Edition, carefully revised by C. NORRIS . . **2/6**

WEALE'S SCIENTIFIC AND TECHNICAL SERIES. 15

**Measures, Weights, and Moneys of all Nations.**
With an Analysis of the Christian, Hebrew, and Mahometan Calendars.
By W. S. B. WOOLHOUSE, F.R.A.S., F.S.S. Seventh Edition . **2/6**

**Grammar of the English Tongue,**
Spoken and Written. With an Introduction to the Study of Comparative Philology. By HYDE CLARKE, D.C.L. Fifth Edition. . . . **1/6**

**Dictionary of the English Language.**
As Spoken and Written. Containing above 100,000 Words. By HYDE CLARKE, D.C.L. . . . . . . . . . . **3/6**
*Complete with the* GRAMMAR, **5/6**

**Composition and Punctuation,**
Familiarly Explained for those who have neglected the Study of Grammar.
By JUSTIN BRENAN. 18th Edition. . . . . . . **1/6**

**French Grammar.**
With Complete and Concise Rules on the Genders of French Nouns. By G. L. STRAUSS, Ph.D. . . . . . . . . **1/6**

**English-French Dictionary.**
Comprising a large number of Terms used in Engineering, Mining, &c.
By ALFRED ELWES . . . . . . . . **2/0**

**French Dictionary.**
In two Parts—I. French-English. II. English-French, complete in One Vol. . . . . . . . . . . **3/0**
\*\*\* *Or with the* GRAMMAR, **4/6**.

**French and English Phrase Book.**
Containing Introductory Lessons, with Translations, Vocabularies of Words. Collection of Phrases, and Easy Familiar Dialogues . . . . **1/6**

**German Grammar.**
Adapted for English Students, from Heyse's Theoretical and Practical Grammar, by Dr. G. L. STRAUSS . . . . . . **1/6**

**German Triglot Dictionary.**
By N. E. S. A. HAMILTON. Part I. German-French-English. Part II. English-German-French. Part III. French-German-English . . **3/0**

**German Triglot Dictionary.**
(As above). Together with German Grammar, in One Volume . **5/0**

**Italian Grammar.**
Arranged in Twenty Lessons, with Exercises. By ALFRED ELWES. **1/6**

**Italian Triglot Dictionary,**
Wherein the Genders of all the Italian and French Nouns are carefully noted down. By ALFRED ELWES. Vol. I. Italian-English-French. **2/6**

**Italian Triglot Dictionary.**
By ALFRED ELWES. Vol. II. English-French-Italian . . . **2/6**

**Italian Triglot Dictionary.**
By ALFRED ELWES. Vol. III. French-Italian-English . . **2/6**

**Italian Triglot Dictionary.**
(As above). In One Vol. . . . . . . **7/6**

**Spanish Grammar.**
In a Simple and Practical Form. With Exercises. By ALFRED ELWES **1/6**

**Spanish-English and English-Spanish Dictionary.**
Including a large number of Technical Terms used in Mining, Engineering, &c., with the proper Accents and the Gender of every Noun. By ALFRED ELWES . . . . . . . . . . **4/0**
\*\*\* *Or with the* GRAMMAR, **6/0**.

## 16   WEALE'S SCIENTIFIC AND TECHNICAL SERIES.

**Portuguese Grammar,**
In a Simple and Practical Form. With Exercises. By ALFRED ELWES   **1/6**

**Portuguese-English and English-Portuguese Dictionary.**
Including a large number of Technical Terms used in Mining, Engineering, &c., with the proper Accents and the Gender of every Noun. By ALFRED ELWES. Third Edition, revised . . . . . . . . **5/0**
    \*\*\* *Or with the* GRAMMAR, **7/0.**

**Animal Physics,**
Handbook of. By DIONYSIUS LARDNER, D.C.L. With 520 Illustrations. In One Vol. (732 pages), cloth boards . . . . . . . **7/6**
    \*\*\* *Sold also in Two Parts, as follows:—*
ANIMAL PHYSICS. By Dr. LARDNER. Part I., Chapters I.—VII.  **4/0**
ANIMAL PHYSICS. By Dr. LARDNER. Part II., Chapters VIII.—XVIII.
                                                                **3/0**

www.ingramcontent.com/pod-product-compliance
Lightning Source LLC
Chambersburg PA
CBHW020231240426
43672CB00006B/491